THE DISPOSAL OF IMPURITY

SOCIETY
OF BIBLICAL
LITERATURE

DISSERTATION SERIES

J. J. M. Roberts, Old Testament Editor
Charles Talbert, New Testament Editor

Number 101

THE DISPOSAL OF IMPURITY
Elimination Rites in the Bible
and in Hittite and Mesopotamian Literature

by
David P. Wright

David P. Wright

THE DISPOSAL OF IMPURITY
Elimination Rites in the Bible and in Hittite and Mesopotamian Literature

Scholars Press
Atlanta, Georgia

THE DISPOSAL OF IMPURITY

David P. Wright

Ph.D., 1984
University of California, Berkeley

Advisor:
Jacob Milgrom

Library of Congress Cataloging-in-Publication Data

Wright, David Pearson, 1953–
The disposal of impurity.

(Dissertation series / Society of Biblical Literature ; no. 101)
Bibliography: p.
Includes index.
1. Purity, Ritual—Biblical teaching. 2. Refuse and refuse disposal—Biblical teaching. 3. Bible. O.T.—Criticism, interpretation, etc. 4. Hittites—Rites and ceremonies. 5. Iraq—Religious life and customs. 6. Purity, Ritual—Middle East. 7. Refuse and refuse disposal—Religious aspects. I. Title. II. Series: Dissertation series (Society of Biblical Literature) ; no. 101.
BS1199.P95W75 1986 291.4'46 86-29719
ISBN 1-55540-056-6 (alk. paper)
ISBN 1-55540-057-4 (pbk. : alk. paper)

Printed in the United States of America
on acid-free paper

אני שונה
שלש מאות הלכות בבהרת עזה
ולא היה אדם ששואלני בהן
דבר מעולם . . .

Si quis sano sensu
non contemperat scripturas,
quanto subtilius intelligunt,
tanto amentior est.

To Dianne,
&
Rebekah,
Sarah,
Benjamin,
&Aharon

Contents

Preface ix
Abbreviations xiii

Introduction 1

Part One: The Disposal of Non-Human Bearers of Impurity in the Priestly Writings 13

Chapter

1. The Scapegoat 15
2. The Dispatch of Birds in the Purification of the Impurity of *Ṣāraʿat* 75
3. The Disposal of Materials Infected with *Ṣāraʿat* 87
4. The Disposal of Earthenware 93
5. The Removal of Corpses 115
6. The Disposal of *Ḥaṭṭāʾt* and Other Sacrifices 129
7. The Disposal of *Ḥaṭṭāʾt* Blood 147

Part Two: The Restriction of Human Impurities Paralleling the Disposal of Non-Human Bearers of Impurity 161

Chapter

8. The Restriction of Human Impurities and the Communicability of Impurity 163

Part Three: Conclusions 229
Chapter
9. The Place of Impurity 231
10. Conclusions 275

Appendixes
1. The Disposal of Idolatrous Impurities in the Non-Priestly Texts of the Bible 279
2. Akkadian *Kuppuru* 291

Bibliography 301

Indexes 337
Subject 337
Text 345
Word 377

Preface

This study represents, with only minor changes and additions, my dissertation completed at the University of California, Berkeley, in 1984. The bibliography has been updated with about three dozen items and some slight reformulation or added explanation appears occasionally in the text. Apart from these changes and general editorial smoothing, the text and arguments remain as they were in the original dissertation.

During and after the writing of the dissertation, sections of it in modified form were presented as papers at various professional meetings. Chapter Four was presented at the annual meeting of the Pacific Coast Section of the Society of Biblical Literature (= SBL) at the Golden Gate Baptist Theological Seminary, March, 1984. Part of Chapter Nine was presented at the annual national meeting of the SBL in Chicago, December, 1984. Part of Chapter One was presented at the annual meeting of the Rocky Mountains/Great Plains Section of the SBL at Brigham Young University, April, 1985. Chapter Six was presented at the Forty-Eighth General Meeting of the Catholic Biblical Association of America at the University of San Francisco, 1985. Chapter Two was presented at the meeting of the Rocky Mountain/Great Plains Section of the SBL at Regis College, Denver, April, 1986. And part of Chapter Eight was presented at the annual national meeting of the SBL in Atlanta, 1986.

I prepared the text of this book camera-ready for Scholars Press and by doing so quickly learned the woes that editor's of such volumes face. One particular issue that needs explanation is the manner of transliterating terms and bibliographic items from Hebrew. It seems that using a uniform system of transliteration only results in strangeness and confusion. To avoid this, but perhaps to open myself to a charge of inconsistency, I have adopted the following solution. Running text and individual words from ancient Hebrew sources (the Bible, Mishnah, Temple Scroll, etc.) are transliterated according to the guidelines in the *Society of Biblical Literature Member's Handbook* ([Chico]: Scholars, 1980). Titles of modern Hebrew books, their publishers, and Hebrew journals have been transliterated following the *Member's Handbook*, but without the inclusion of vowel diacriticals. In these cases, main Hebrew words have been capitalized (e.g., *Megillat hamMiqdaš*). With Hebrew books, I give an English translation as well as a transliteration of the title. With Hebrew articles I give only an English translation with a notation that the article is in Hebrew. When the works have a transliteration of their own for titles or publishers, or where a customary romanization exists, I have generally retained that for easy recognition (e.g., *Beth Mikra*, *Leshonenu*, Mossad Harav Kook). When article titles in Hebrew have titles with vowel points (and these are generally titles of articles in encyclopedias and dictionaries), I have transliterated with vowel diacriticals without English translation.

In citing passages of Hittite and Akkadian texts, I have tried to provide a strict transliteration rather than a grammatical transcription. Occasionally, however, I cite passages from editions of texts that are partially or wholly in transcription rather than in transliteration. This is because of the interpretive issues involved that transcription clarifies or because of dependence on these editions.

Many expressions of gratitude are in order. This work is mainly the result of the influence of Professor Jacob Milgrom of the University of California, Berkeley. His interest in the Priestly writings of the Bible has been extremely contagious. After studying with him since the Winter of 1979 in graduate seminars on portions of the books of Numbers and Leviticus and pursuing scholarly projects with him, I have been inextricably drawn into this area of study. I express here my thanks to him for his example of fine scholarship, evidenced both in the classroom and in print, and for his unfailing support as I have developed this thesis.

I would also like to thank Professors Ruggero Stefanini and Anne D. Kilmer, both of the University of California, Berkeley, for their excellent instruction in Hittite and Akkadian, respectively. I am especially indebted to them for their constructive criticism of aspects of this work.

I thank, too, Professors William J. Fulco of the Jesuit School of Theology at Berkeley and David Daube of the University of California, Berkeley, for serving on my dissertation committee and for their comments on parts of this study.

Though not involved in the critique of this work, I must acknowledge my debt to several teachers that have had significant influence on my academic perspectives: Moshe Greenberg, of the Hebrew University, Jerusalem, for his example of cautious and sound biblical scholarship; Jonas Greenfield, also of the Hebrew University, for his instruction in methods of biblical lexical study; Baruch M. Bokser, formerly of the University of California, Berkeley, now at Dropsie University, for his instruction in rabbinic literature; and Harris Lenowitz, of the University of Utah, who first introduced me to modern critical biblical scholarship.

Several people proofread all or portions of this work in its various stages or helped with its technical composition: Gerald E. Jones; Daniel C. Peterson, my colleague at Brigham Young University; and my students William J. Benecke, Eric C. Byers, Clarissa G. Cole, and Darrell L. Matthews. Danette E. Byers helped with proofreading and indexing. And my colleague Dilworth B. Parkinson was always ready to share his technical experience. To all these I give sincere thanks.

The camera-ready version of this work would not be possible without the computer facilities and staff of the Humanities Research Center at Brigham Young University. My thanks go to Kim L. Smith who spent much time getting me set up for this project, and especially to Charles D. Bush who developed the transliteration font used here and who otherwise spent many hours bringing this work into its present printed form. I also thank the College of Humanities at Brigham Young University for providing other financial support and computer facilities in 1986 and 1987.

Finally, deep gratitude is due my family—my wife, Dianne, and my children, Rebekah, Sarah, Benjamin, and Aharon—for their endurance, confidence, and support. I also thank my larger family for their encouragement, especially my brother Michael, whose gift of a computer and other assistance from the beginning made progress on this work much more rapid and complete than it would have been otherwise.

Abbreviations and Key to Texts

Abbreviations not included in this list are found in the *Society of Biblical Literature Member's Handbook* ([Chico]: Scholars Press, 1980) 83–97 or in "Instructions for Contributors" *CBQ* 46 (1984) 393–408. Full references for most of the books and articles listed below are found in the bibliography.

AA	*American Anthropologist*
AAA	*Annals of Archaeology and Anthropology*
ABD	*Anchor Bible Dictionary* (forthcoming)
ABoT	K. Balkan, ed., *Ankara Arkeoloji Müzesinde bulunan Boğazköy Tabletleri*
ʾAbot R. Nat. A/B	*ʾAbot de-Rabbi Natan* versions A and B
AHw	W. von Soden, *Akkadisches Handwörterbuch*
AJTMH	*American Journal of Tropical Medicine and Hygiene*
Allaiturahhi	Texts as edited by V. Haas and H. J. Thiel, *Die Beschwörungsrituale der Allaituraḫ(ḫ)i und verwandte Texte*
Ambazzi	*CTH* 391. Partially tr. by A. Goetze, *ANET*, 348–49
Amihatna	*CTH* 472. Ed. and tr. by R. Lebrun, "Les rituels d'Ammihatna, Tulbi et Mati contre une impureté = *CTH* 472"

AMT	R. C. Thompson, ed., *Assyrian Medical Texts*
Anniwiyani	*CTH* 393. Ed. and tr. by E. H. Sturtevant and G. Bechtel, *A Hittite Chrestomathy*, 100–26
AN.TAḪ.ŠUM^{SAR} Festival	The 16th day, *CTH* 612. Tr. by A. Goetze, *ANET*, 358–61
AOATS	AOAT,Sonderreihe
Ap-Dh	*Āpastamba-Dharmaśāstra.* Tr. by G. Bühler, *The Sacred Laws of the Aryas: Part I*
ARIVSLA	*Atti de Reale Istituto Veneto di Scienze, Lettere ed Arti*
AS	Assyriological Studies
Ashella	*CTH* 394. Tr. by J. Friedrich, "Aus dem hethitischen Schrifttum," 11–13; partially tr. by O. Gurney, *Some Aspects of Hittite Religion*, 49; H. Kümmel, "Ersatzkönig und Sündenbock," 310–11
ASKT	P. Haupt, ed., *Akkadische und Sumerische Keilschrifttexte*
ASOR	American Schools of Oriental Research
Ayatarsa	*CTH* 390. Ed. and tr. H. Kronasser, "Fünf hethitische Rituale"
Bagh. Mitt.	*Baghdader Mitteilungen*
Baud-Dh	*Baudhāyana-Dharmaśāstra.* Tr. by G. Bühler, *The Sacred Laws of the Aryas: Part II*
BBR	H. Zimmern, *Beiträge zur Kenntnis der babylonischen Religion*
BHT	Beiträge zur historischen Theologie
Birth Ritual (A, B, C, ...)	Birth ritual texts as ed. and tr. by G. Beckman, "Hittite Birth Rituals"
BN	*Biblische Notizen*

Bo	Inventory number of Boğazköy tablets
BoTU	E. Forrer, *Die Boghazkoi-Texte in Umschrift*
BRM 4	Babylonian Records in the Library of J. P. Morgan 4 (= A. T. Clay, *Epics, Hymns, Omens and Other Texts*)
Building Ritual	*CTH* 414. Ed. and tr. by B. Schwartz, "A Hittite Ritual Text"
BWL	W. G. Lambert, *Babylonian Wisdom Literature*
CHD	H. G. Güterbock and H. A. Hoffner, *The Hittite Dictionary of the Oriental Institute of the University of Chicago*
CSSH	*Comparative Studies in Society and History*
CT	*Cuneiform Texts from Babylonian Tablets in the British Museum* (1896-)
CTH	E. Laroche, *Catalogue des textes hittites*
DAWBIO	Deutsche Akademie der Wissenschaften zu Berlin, Institut für Orientforschung
DB	*Dictionnaire de la Bible*
Death Ritual	*CTH* 450 and related texts. Cited according to H. Otten, *Hethitische Totenrituale*
DES	R. C. Thompson, *The Devils and Evil Spirits of Babylonia*
DMOA	Documenta et Monumenta Oriens Antiqui
EM	*Enṣiqlopedya Miqraʾit*
ET	*Enṣiqlopedya Talmudit*
Evocatio	*CTH* 483. Ed. and tr. by L. Zuntz, "Un texto ittita di scongiuri"; tr. A. Goetze, *ANET*, 351–53
ExBib	Expositors Bible
4 R	T. G. Pinches, *A Selection from the*

	Miscellaneous Inscriptions of Assyria (The Cuneiform Inscriptions of Western Asia 4)
Gassuliyawiya	*CTH* 380. Ed. and tr. by J. Friedrich, "Aus dem hethitischen Schrifttum," 19–20; partially tr. by H. Kümmel, *Ersatzrituale für den hethitischen König*, 120–21; O. Gurney, *Some Aspects of Hittite Religion*, 55
Gaut-Dh	*Gautama-Dharmaśāstra*. Tr. by G. Bühler, *The Sacred Laws of the Aryas: Part I*
GG	*Gobhila-Gṛhyasūtra*. Tr. by H. Oldenberg, *The Grihya-Sutras, Part II*
GSAI	*Giornale della Società Asiatica Italiana*
HdO	Handbuch der Orientalistik
HMLP	A History of the Mishnaic Laws of Purity
House Purification	CTH 446. Ed. and tr. by H. Otten, "Eine Beschwörung der Unterirdischen aus Boğazköy"
HSAT	Die Heilige Schrift des Alten Testament
HT	E. A. W. Budge, *Hittite Texts in the Cuneiform Character in the British Museum*
Huwarlu	*CTH* 398. Tr. by J. Friedrich, "Aus dem hethitischen Schrifttum," 13–16; H. Kronasser, "Das hethitische Ritual KBo IV 2"
HW[1]	J. Friedrich, *Hethitisches Wörterbuch: kurzgefasste kritische Sammlung der Deutungen hethitischer Wörter*, 1st ed.
HW[2]	J. Friedrich and A. Kammenhuber, *Hethitisches Wörterbuch*, 2d ed.
IBoT	H. Bozkurt, M. Çiğ, and H. G. Güterbock, eds., *Istanbul Arkeoloji Müzelerinde bulunan Boğazköy Tabletleri*

IDBSup	*IDB*, Supplementary Volume
Instructions to Temple Officials	*CTH* 264. Ed. and tr. by E. H. Sturtevant and G. Bechtel, *A Hittite Chrestomathy*, 127–74; tr. by A. Goetze, *ANET*, 207–10
JHMAS	*Journal of the History of Medicine and Allied Sciences*
JRAI	*Journal of the Royal Anthropological Institute*
KAJ	E. Ebeling, ed., *Keilschrifttexte aus Assur juristischen Inhalts*
KAR	E. Ebeling, ed., *Keilschrifttexte aus Assur religiösen Inhalts*
KB^2	L. Koehler and W. Baumgartner, *Lexicon in Veteris Testamenti Libros*, 2d ed.
KB^3	W. Baumgartner, L. H. Koehler, B. Hartmann, and E. Y. Kutscher, *Hebräisches und aramäisches Lexikon zum Alten Testament*, 3d ed.
KBo	*Keilschrifttexte aus Boghazköi* (1916–)
KDVS	Det Kgl. Danske Videnskabernes Selskab, Historisk-filologiskeMeddelelser
KHC	Kurzer Hand-Commentar zum Alten Testament
KUB	*Keilschrifturdunden aus Boghazköi* (1921–)
Laws	Hittite Laws. Ed. and tr. by J. Friedrich, *Die hethitischen Gesetze*; tr. A. Goetze, *ANET*, 188–97
LKA	E. Ebeling, F. Kocher, and L. Rost, eds., *Literarische Keilschrifttexte aus Assur*
LSS (n.s.)	Leipziger semitische Studien (new series)
Malli	*CTH* 402. Ed. and tr. by L. Jakob-Rost, *Das*

	Ritual der Malli aus Arzawa gegen Behexung (KUB XXIV 9+)
Manu	*Manusmṛti*. Tr. by G. Bühler, *The Laws of Manu*
MAOG	*Mitteilungen der Altorientalischen Gesellschaft*
Maqlu	Ed. and tr. by G. Meier, *Die assyrische Beschwörungssammlung Maqlu*
Mastigga	*CTH* 404. Ed. and tr. by L. Rost, "Ein hethitischen Ritual gegen Familienzwist"; another version of this ritual is tr. by A. Goetze, *ANET*, 350–51
MDOG	*Mitteilungen der Deutschen Orient-Gesellschaft*
MIO	*Mitteilungen des Institut für Orientforschung*
MSS	*Münchener Studien zur Sprachwissenschaft*
MT	Masoretic Text
MTor	Maimonides, *Mišne Tora*
Mursili's Sprachlähmung	*CTH* 486. Ed. and tr. by A. Goetze and H. Pedersen, *Mursilis Sprachlähmung*
MVAG	*Mitteilungen der Vorderasiatisch-ägyptischen Gesellschaft*
OAWS	Österreichische Akademie der Wissenschaften, Philosophisch-historische Klasse, Sitzungsberichte
OECT 6	Oxford Editions of Cuneiform Texts 6 (= S. Langdon, *Babylonian Penitential Psalms*)
OTWSuid-Afrika	*Ou-Testamentiese Werkgemeenskap in Suid-Afrika*
Papanikri	*CTH* 476. Ed. and tr. by F. Sommer and H. Ehelolf, *Das hethitische Ritual des Papanikri*

	von Komana; partially ed. and tr. by G. Beckman, "Hittite Birth Rituals," 145–53
Paskuwatti	*CTH* 406. Tr. by A. Goetze, *ANET*, 349–50
PBS	*Publications of the Babylonian Section, University Museum, University of Pennsylvania*
Plague Ritual	*CTH* 424. Ed. and tr. by V. Souček, "Ein neues hethitische Ritual gegen die Pest"
Pulisa	*CTH* 407. Ed. and tr. by H. Kümmel, *Ersatzrituale für den hethitischen König*, 111–25
QS	Quaderni de semitistica
RAcc	F. Thureau-Dangin, *Rituels accadiens*
RHA	*Revue hittite et asianique*
Samuha	*CTH* 480. Ed. and tr. by R. Lebrun, *Samuha foyer religieux de l'empire hittite*, 117–43; the second half is tr. by A. Goetze, *ANET*, 346 Lebrun's line numbering is followed)
SANE	Sources and Monographs: Sources from the Ancient Near East
SB	*Śatapaṭha Brāhmaṇa*. Tr. by J. Eggeling, *Śatapatha Brâhmana*
SBE	Sacred Books of the East
Shurpu	Ed. and tr. by E. Reiner, *Šurpu: A Collection of Sumerian and Akkadian Incantations*
SKGG	Schriften der Königsberger gelehrten Gesellschaft, geisteswissenschaftliche Klasse
SMEA	*Studi Micenei ed Egeo-Anatolici*
SO	*Symbolae Osloenses*
Soldiers' Oath	*CTH* 427 E. and tr. by N. Oettinger, *Die militärischen Eide der Hethiter*, tr. by A.

	Goetze, *ANET*, 353–54
SOr	Sources orientales
StBoT	Studien zu den Boğazköy-Texten
StBoT 2	O. Carruba, *Das Beschwörungsritual für die Göttin Wisurijanza*
StBoT 3	H. Kümmel, *Ersatzrituale für den hethitischen König*
StBoT 8	H. Otten and V. Souček, *Ein althethitisches Ritual für das Königspaar*
StBoT 12	E. Neu, *Ein althethitisches Gewitterritual*
StBoT 13	H. Otten, *Ein hethitisches Festritual (KBo XIX128)*
StBoT 22	N. Oettinger, *Die militärischen Eide der Hethiter*
StBoT 25	E. Neu, *Althethitische Ritualtexte in Umschrift*
StPD	Studia Pohl: Dissertationes Scientificae de Rebus Oriens Antiqui
StPM	Studia Pohl: Series Maior
TDP	R. Labat, *Traité akkadien de diagnostics et pronostics medicaux*
Telepinu	*CTH* 324. Tr. by A. Goetze, *ANET*, 126–28
TGM	*Tropical and Geographical Medicine*
THeth	Texte der Hethiter
TS	Temple Scroll (11Q Temple)
TuL	E. Ebeling, *Tod und Leben nach der Vorstellung de Babylonier*
Tunnawi	*CTH* 409. Ed. and tr. by A. Goetze and E. H. Sturtevant, *The Hittite Ritual of Tunnawi*
Tuthaliya and Nikalmati	*CTH* 443. Ed. and tr. by G. Szabó, *Ein hethitisches Entsühnungsritual für das*

	Königspaar Tutḫaliḭa und Nikalmati
UCPNES	University of California Publications: Near Eastern Studies
UET	Ur Excavations, Texts
Uhhamuwa	*CTH* 410. Tr. by J. Friedrich, "Aus dem hethitischen Schrifttum," 10; A. Goetze, *ANET*, 347 ("Ritual Against Pestilence"); my lineation follows *HT* 1 ii 17–47
Ulippi	*CTH* 481. Ed. and tr. by H. Kronasser, *Die Umsiedlung der schwarzen Gottheit: Das hethitsches Ritual KUB XXIX 4 (des Ulippi)*
UUA	Uppsala Universitets Arsskrift
Vai-G	*Vaikhānasa-Gṛhyasūtra.* Tr. by W. Calland, *Vaikhanasasmārtasūtram*
Vas-Dh	*Vāsiṣṭha-Dharmaśāstra.* Tr. by G. Bühler, *The Sacred Laws of the Aryas: Part II*
VAT	Inventory number of tablets in the Staatliche Museen, Berlin
VBoT	A. Goetze, *Verstreute Boghazkoi-Texte*
Vis	*Viṣṇusmṛti.* Tr. by J. Jolly, *The Institutes of Vishnu*
WDWLS	William Dwight Whitney Linguistic Series
WVDOG	*Wissenschaftliche Veröffentlichungen der Deutschen Orient-Gesellschaft*

Introduction

NATURE OF THE STUDY

The present work originated in part as a response to Hayim Tawil's study of the figure Azazel in the biblical scapegoat rite, entitled "ʿAzazel the Prince of the Steepe [*sic*]: A Comparative Study" (*ZAW* 92 [1980] 43-59). In this article he argued that rites for the riddance[1] of evils in Mesopotamia represent the banishment of baneful influences to the nether world and that this same mythological conception is found in the biblical scapegoat rite. His interpretation of the data from Mesopotamia is correct, but, for various reasons that will be given in the course of this study, his conclusion about the ideas infusing the scapegoat rite is not acceptable. Nevertheless, that Tawil was able to show that disposal rites in Mesopotamia manifested a rather integrated conceptual framework suggested that a study of the total repertoire of disposal rites in a particular culture would reveal that culture's way of thinking, or an aspect of its way of thinking, about impurity and related ideas. This study contains the results of applying this approach to elimination rites in the Priestly literature of the Bible, and to a lesser extent, to those in Hittite and Mesopotamian ritual literature. The approach has been very fruitful because it has forced me to entertain and answer questions that have often gone undiscussed about purity and purification rites in the

[1]This study uses various nouns and adjectives, such as elimination, riddance, disposal, and eliminatory, to describe the rites which are the focus of this study, that have as their goal the removal of impurity or other evils from an affected object or person (or from objects or persons) and the neutralization (destruction, removal to a safe distance, etc.) of the impurity or evils that have been removed. These terms, though different, refer to the same ritual phenomenon.

Bible and in other cultures, and because it has led to a more precise view of Priestly thought regarding the proper place of impurity, purity, and holiness in the Israelite religious community.

This work is divided into three parts. The first (Chapters One through Seven) deals with the examples of the disposal of impurity in the Priestly writings. The focus there is on the dispatch, discarding, and destruction of impure nonhuman entities: the scapegoat, birds used in purification rites after recovery from *ṣāraʿat*,[2] fabrics and building materials infected with *ṣāraʿat*, impure earthenware, corpses, and the carcasses and blood of *ḥaṭṭāʾt* sacrifices. The chapters on these phenomena emphasize the method of disposal and the place where this occurs. The second part of this work (Chapter Eight) treats the restriction and exclusion of impure persons and the communicability of impurity in the Priestly literature. This supplements the information gleaned in the first part about the place where impure items are to be located and shows the relation of different kinds of impurity to the sanctuary and community. The third part (Chapter Nine) brings together the findings of the two preceding parts in order to describe and articulate the conceptual system implicit in the disposal and restriction of impurity. A "map" of cultic topography is described and drawn that displays the interrelation of the places designated holy, pure, and impure, and items or persons carrying communicable or noncommunicable impurities. The conclusion (Chapter Ten), which follows the three main parts of the study, recapitulates the major observations made throughout the work.

To analyze the different rites and phenomena just enumerated I employ a method which can be loosely termed *detailed descriptive historical exegesis.* I study each of the particular blocks of data in detail. In doing this I pay attention to the mechanics of a particular rite, the meaning of key and obscure words, the relation of one particular phenomenon to others in the Priestly writings, and the implications inherent in the text that would lead to more precise and fresh observations. Such descriptive analysis is essentially historical in nature since it attempts to determine the form, extent, and significance of rituals in the text and period in which they appear. But my historical analysis at times goes beyond the explication of isolated details. Occasionally the data lend themselves to larger historical reconstruction

---

[2]In this study I will not translate the term *ṣāraʿat*, which is often but incorrectly translated "leprosy." On this see chap. 2, n. 1.

and speculation. Though I will engage in such reconstruction from time to time, it will not be a major thrust of the work.

In the discussion of the conceptual system that emerges from an examination of the places of the disposal and restriction of impurity, I will often refer to the relationship of impurity to society as well as to the sphere of holiness. This focus on community and society does not mean this study is conducted along anthropological lines of inquiry. The concern of this work is to describe the manifest or explicit meaning of the rites—that is, how the Priestly writers might explain them and their accompanying conceptual system—rather than to describe latent or implicit meanings that the ritual symbols and their interrelation represent.[3] Nevertheless, it is hoped that this detailed analysis of the Priestly ideas of pollution will serve as a partial, yet sound, basis for future anthropological discussion of the question of purity in the Bible.

Now saying that this work seeks to describe how the Priestly writers might explain these rituals or that it attempts to determine the significance of the rituals in the period in which they appear is not to be taken as a declaration of blind confidence about the "rightness" of this (or any) attempt to understand the original significance of the system. Apart from the problem of insufficient evidence, modern historical and hermeneutical theories teach of the ultimate impossibility of discovering with certainty the structure of events and thought in history as well as original intentions and meaning behind texts we interpret. Ultimately, interpretation is done through *our* (and here, *my*) contexts and conventions and is thus a reflection of that hermeneutical situation. To say, then, that this study describes how the Priestly writers might have thought may be more a statement about this study's idiom or strategy—*how* the evidence will be discussed, rather than a description of the actual character of its results.

---

[3]R. K. Merton (*Social Theory and Social Structure* [enlarged ed.; New York: Free, 1968] 73–138) distinguishes between manifest and latent functions of social phenomena. In ritual, manifest function is that which the people performing the rite attach to it, while latent function is only obvious to the anthropological observer (see L. Mair, *An Introduction to Social Anthropology* [2d ed.; New York: Oxford University, 1972] 37). Similarly, R. Firth (*Symbols: Public and Private* [Ithaca: Cornell University, 1973] 82) discusses the explicit and implicit meanings of symbols. The explicit meaning is that which is given by those using the symbol, while the implicit meaning is the underlying sociological message of the symbol.

A note of definition is necessary here regarding what I mean by the Priestly corpus and what point of view I take toward it. I use the term "Priestly" in its broadest sense to describe the body of writing generally attributed to the source or tradition "P" by the main critical theories of the composition of the Pentateuch.[4] Of course, with this said, it is to be realized that this body is not a unity. It consists of separate sections of writing and traditions that have been woven together or juxtaposed by various editors at various times. Despite this composite nature, I conduct my analysis of the rituals in this corpus from a synchronic point of view; that is, I study them as they appear in the final form of the biblical text. This is necessary in order to reconstruct any type of underlying conceptual system and is possible because, despite obvious discrete historical levels in P, editors and authors of later periods held and perpetuated essentially the same basic ideas of earlier writers. Only when views of different periods are in conflict with one another does it become necessary to undertake a diachronic study of the development of the phenomena or ideas and to analyze the material from two or more separate synchronic points of view. Hence, in regard to the history of ideas in the Bible, my analysis tells us mostly about the ideas of the Priestly school at the end of their development when the text reached its final form.

It should be kept in mind throughout this study that the conceptual system inherent in the Priestly literature was not necessarily fully shared by the general populace of ancient Israel. For example, a belief in the existence and activity of demons seems to be suppressed in the Prieslty writings. Lay Israelites, however, may not have shared such an attitude toward the demonic. We should be careful, therefore, not to assume that the conclusions of this study regarding the Priestly conceptual system are valid for all of ancient Israel.

The limitation of this study to Priestly materials necessitates the exclusion of a detailed discussion of ultimately pertinent material from other places in the Bible. I must omit major discussion of the execution of criminals outside the community's habitation which parallels the

[4]Portions of Genesis, Exodus, Numbers, a small part of Deuteronomy, and all of Leviticus. See O. Eissfeldt, *The Old Testament: An Introduction* (New York: Harper and Row, 1965) 155–241; E. Sellin and G. Fohrer, *Introduction to the Old Testament* (Nashville: Abingdon, 1968) 101–95; R. Rendtorff, *The Old Testament: An Introduction* (Philadelphia: Fortress, 1986) 131–64.

phenomenon of disposing of impurities in this locale;[5] the Philistine disposal rite for the elimination of plague found in 1 Sam 5-6 which shows striking and historically important similarities to Hittite plague rituals (cf. Chapter One);[6] Deut 21:1-9 which contains a ritual for the transference of murder pollution from an inhabited area to an uninhabited area;[7] and the literary descriptions of disposal in Mic 7:19 where sins are cast into the sea and in Zech 5:5-11 where a container with a lead lid which holds a woman representing wickedness is carried by two winged women to Babylon.[8] Only secondary reference will be made to these in the course of this study. The only non-Priestly example of disposal discussed in detail is the disposal of idolatrous impurities in the narrative books of the Bible. This is included in Appendix One at the end of the study.

THE COMPARATIVE METHOD

A major portion of this study is devoted to a comparison of disposal rites and their underlying conceptions in the Bible to those from ancient Anatolia and Mesopotamia. In one instance I use comparative material from India. Since the manner of using comparative material in biblical study has been and is an area of controversy, a few words are in order here on the development of the use of comparison in biblical studies and the types of comparison I will use.

The field of biblical studies is a mixture of quite diverse disciplines: history, philology, religion, and anthropology, to mention a few. It

---

[5]See chap. 5, section 5.3, for a brief discussion.

[6]See chap. 9, nn. 74 and 150. Cf. J. B. Geyer, "Mice and Rites in I Samuel V–VI," *VT* 31 (1981) 293–304; L. I. Conrad, "The Biblical Tradition for the Plague of the Philistines," *JAOS* 104 (1984) 281–87.

[7]For how this relates to the present study, see my article "Deuteronomy 21:1–9 as a Rite of Elimination," *CBQ*, forthcoming. See also H. J. Elhorst, "Eine verkannte Zauberhandlung (Dtn 21 1–9)," *ZAW* 39 (1921) 58–67; R. Patai, "The ʿEgla ʿArufa or the Expiation of the Polluted Land," *JQR* 30 (1939) 59–69; A. Roifer, "The ʿEgla ʿArufa," *Tarbiz* 31 (1961) 119–43 (Hebrew); J. Milgrom, "ʿEglah ʿArufah," *EncJud* 6 (1971) 475–77; S. Loewenstamm, "*ʿEglâ ʿĂrûpâ*," *EM* 6 (1971) 77–79 (Hebrew); Z. Zevit, "The *ʿEglâ* Ritual of Deuteronomy 21:1–9," *JBL* 95 (1976) 377–90; P.-E. Dion, "Deutéronome 21,1–9: Miroir du développement légal et religieux d'Israël," *SR* 11 (1982) 13–22.

[8]See chap. 9, nn. 149 and 150.

draws on the methods of examination developed in these other disciplines, applies them to its own set of data and further develops these methods for its own purposes. Sometimes an outside discipline that first developed and contributed a particular method to biblical studies will reject it for a better method, while biblical studies, perhaps ignorant of recent advances in the outside field, holds on to the old method. Such has been, and still is to a certain extent, the situtation of biblical studies in regard to the comparative method. The type of comparison most common to biblical studies since the end of the nineteenth and through the first half of the twentieth centuries has been what I call interpretive comparison. This is where a phenomenon in one society is interpreted by means of a similar phenomenon in another. An example of this would be to say that the scapegoat in the Bible served as a substitute to suffer in the place of the Israelites because in Mesopotamian and Hittite rites a bearer of evil is often a substitute which bears the evil on behalf of another individual or group. This method of comparison derives in part from anthropologists' attempts in the nineteenth century to establish laws of cultural development or to establish regular correlations of social phenomena common to all societies. The assumption was that similar things in diverse cultures were done or came into being for the same reasons; similar phenomena had similar causes. Hence, an obscure phenomenon in one society may be interpreted by a clear one in another. Anthropology quickly saw the shortcomings of such assumptions and developed more sophisticated approaches to discussing similar phenomena in different societies.[9] But biblical studies retained certain

[9]K. E. Bock, "The Comparative Method of Anthropology," *CSSH* 8 (1965–66) 269–80; F. Eggan, "Social Anthropology and the Method of Controlled Comparison," *AA* 56 (1954) 743–63; E. E. Evans-Pritchard, *The Comparative Method in Social Anthropology* (London: Athlone, 1963); W. Goldschmidt, *Comparative Functionalism: An Essay in Anthropological Theory* (Berkeley: University of California, 1966); E. A. Hammel, "The Comparative Method in Anthropological Perspective," *CSSH* 22 (1980) 145–55; A. J. F. Köbben, "Comparativists and Non-Comparativists in Anthropology," *A Handbook of Method in Cultural Anthropology* (ed. R. Naroll and R. Cohen; New York: Columbia University, 1973) 581–96; E. R. Leach, "The Comparative Method in Anthropology," *International Encyclopedia of the Social Sciences* 1 (1968) 339–45; A. R. Radcliffe-Brown, "The Comparative Method in Social Anthropology," *JRAI* 81 (1951) 15–22; I. Schapera, "Some Comments on Comparative Method in Social Anthropology," *AA* 55

erroneous aspects of the earlier methods. Only recently has there been more attention given to formulating proper methods for comparative study.[10]

S. Talmon has offered a welcome method for those seeking to do comparative studies.[11] His proposition is simple and sound. Any feature of the Bible, be it a ritual, sociological, political, philological, or literary matter, must first be investigated and interpreted in the light of its own context. Only after this has been done may comparative study be employed. Failure to follow this procedure runs the risk of reading features and meaning of the non-Israelite society into that of the Bible. This method guides my discussions throughout this work and is applied before comparative analysis is employed.

Interpretive comparison, because it is based on unsound anthropological theory, should, theoretically, not be pursued at all. But at times it is a necessary risk. The Bible does not always tell us

---

(1953) 353–62; M. B. Singer, "Summary of Comments and Discussion," *AA* 55 (1953) 362–66; T. A. Tatje, "Problems of Concept Definition for Comparative Studies," *A Handbook of Method in Cultural Anthropology* (ed. R. Naroll and R. Cohen) 689–96. On comparison in the history of religions, see J. Z. Smith, *Map Is Not Territory: Studies in the History of Religions* (Leiden: Brill, 1978) 240–64; *Imagining Religion: From Babylon to Jonestown* (Chicago: University of Chicago, 1982) 19–35.

[10]On the comparative method in biblical studies, see H. Frankfort, *The Problem of Similarity in Ancient Near Eastern Religions* (Oxford: Clarendon, 1951); W. W. Hallo, "New Moons and Sabbaths: A Case Study in the Contrastive Approach," *HUCA* 48 (1977) 1–18; H. Ringgren, "Remarks on the Method of Comparative Mythology," *Near Eastern Studies in Honor of William Foxwell Albright* (ed. H. Goedicke: Baltimore: Johns Hopkins, 1971) 407–11; J. W. Rogerson, *Anthropology and the Old Testament* (Oxford: Basil Blackwell, 1978); S. Rummel, "Using Ancient Near Eastern Parallels in Old Testament Study," *BARev* 3/3 (1977) 3–11; S. Sandmel, "Parallelomania," *JBL* 81 (1962) 1–13; S. Talmon, "The 'Navel of the Earth' and the Comparative Method," *Scripture in History and Theology, J. Coert Rylaarsdam Jubilee Volume* (ed. A. L. Merrill and T. W. Overholt; Pittsburgh: Pickwick, 1977) 243–68; "The 'Comparative Method' in Biblical Interpretation—Principles and Problems," *VTSup* 29 (1978) 320–56; "On the Emendation of Biblical Texts on the Basis of Ugaritic Parallels," *Eretz Israel* 14 (1978) 117–24 (Hebrew; English summary p. 127*).

[11]Talmon, "Principles and Problems." See his other articles cited in the previous n. as well.

everything we wish to know about a lexical item or cultural phenomenon. In these cases of near or complete obscurity we are forced to go to other, preferably cognate, societies to determine a possible meaning for the abstruse item. In such cases, however, we should freely admit the tentative nature of the conclusions. I will make use of interpretive comparison in a major way once in this work to help explain why impure earthenware must be destroyed, since the Bible does not give any clear information about it.

Another type of comparison, methodologically more sound than interpretive comparison, is that employed in historical reconstruction.[12] The method seeks to deduce cultural connections between cultures by examining phenomenological similarities. In my view, connections between different cultures cannot be based on a few broad similarities scattered here and there, or on a few minute striking, but coincidental, similarities in a particular phenomenon. Many points of interdependence extending beyond coincidence must be sought in a broad spectrum of areas between the two cultures before connections can be convincingly displayed. Of course, the two societies being compared must be in temporal and geographical proximity so that cultural interchanges are possible. Finally, historical reconstruction is only as good as the documentation. A historical reconstruction based on only a few instances of a similar phenomenon spread out over a millennium in different cultures in the ancient world must be accorded its required amount of tentativeness. I refrain from historical reconstruction between different cultures in the present study.

The method of comparison I use most often here is contrastive comparison.[13] In contrastive comparison, essentially similar phenomena in discrete cultures are studied in detail separately and then compared. Differences between the phenomena in the two cultures are observed and questions about the nature of these differences and why they exist are asked. Answers to these questions are sought within the context of a

---

[12]This should not be confused with earlier efforts to reconstruct the prehistory of phenomena in a particular culture from supposed evolutionary models of cultural development.

[13]Cf. Hallo, "New Moons"; N. Sarna, *Understanding Genesis* (New York: Jewish Theological Seminary of America, 1966; reprint, New York: Schocken, 1970) 48. J. Neusner's remarks about the comparative method (*The Mishnaic System of Uncleanness* [SJLA 6, HMLP 22; Leiden: Brill, 1977] 10–23) are exceptionally insightful.

phenomenon's own culture. The resulting answers lead to a better assessment and understanding of the phenomena in each of the two cultures. The method is thus heuristic in nature, bringing out questions and their answers which are otherwise unapparent. This approach is methodologically sound because it does not seek to import meaning from one culture to another. Furthermore, this type of comparison can be performed on materials from cultures which are geographically and temporally far removed from one another.

I will use Hittite and Mesopotamian examples contrastively in the chapters on the scapegoat (Chapter One), the bird for purifying the impurity remaining from *ṣāraʿat* (Chapter Two), and the place of impurity (Chapter Nine). In the chapter on the disposal of earthenware (Chapter Four) I will use Hittite and Indian materials to help interpret the reason for the disposal of impure pottery in the Bible and then turn to contrastive comparison between the nonbiblical cultures and the Bible. I do not use comparative materials in the chapters on the disposal of materials infected with *ṣāraʿat* (Chapter Three), the removal of corpses (Chapter Five), the disposal of *ḥaṭṭāʾt* and other sacrifices (Chapter Six), and the disposal of *ḥaṭṭāʾt* blood (Chapter Seven) because these impurities and phenomena are unique to Israel, or because in the case of the removal of corpses the archaeological evidence is too fragmentary and unsystematized in present studies for comparison to biblical custom. I do not use comparative materials in the chapter on the restriction of impurities (Chapter Eight) because it is secondary to the main study of the disposal of impure objects.

PREVIOUS STUDIES

Literature pertaining directly to the topic of the elimination of impurities in the Bible is, except for Tawil's study mentioned at the the beginning of this introduction, virtually nonexistent. No work that I have examined has endeavored to analyze the rituals of disposal and the phenomenon of exclusion and restriction as a body or to assess what system of ideas is expressed thereby. D. Davies' structural study of sacrifice in Leviticus, which treats the conceptual system represented by the places of holiness and impurity, perhaps comes closest to the ultimate concerns of this study. But his study, focusing on sacrifice in a general way, lacks detailed analysis of all the purification rites necessary for a thoroughgoing and precise conclusion.[14] Of the rituals treated in this study, the scapegoat[15] and the *ḥaṭṭāʾt* sacrifice have received the most attention. Of note is J. Milgrom's work on the *ḥaṭṭāʾt* and its relation to the Priestly system of impurity. This has been exceptionally beneficial in the study of the scapegoat and the disposal of *ḥaṭṭāʾt* carcasses and blood.[16] Nevertheless, the substance of the works on the scapegoat and the *ḥaṭṭāʾt* has been in areas other than those of this book's interest and thus what has been said about disposal and the conceptions behind it, though often insightful, has been minimal. Consequently, these studies, plus the major monographs treating biblical purity,[17] commentaries, articles in the encyclopedias, dictionaries and handbooks, and certain works on specific subjects in the field of purity[18] all serve to a greater or lesser extent in the formation of this work, but none of them will figure prominently.

A similar state of affairs exists in the study of disposal in Hittite and Mesopotamian ritual. Again, except for Tawil's study of Mesopotamian disposal, I was left to cull the examples of this phenomenon and the observations on it from the diverse publications of ritual material. The published texts, translations, and commentaries, too numerous to

---

[14]Douglas Davies, "An Interpretation of Sacrifice in Leviticus," *ZAW* 89 (1976) 387–99.

[15]See the literature cited in chap. 1.

[16]See the bibliography under J. Milgrom.

[17]W. R. Smith, *The Religion of the Semites: The Fundamental Institutions* ([2d ed.]; London: A. and C. Black, 1894; reprint, New York: Schocken, 1972); J. Döller, *Die Reinheits- und Speisegesetze des Alten Testaments in religionsgeschichtlicher Beleuchtung* (ATAbh 7/2–3; Münster: Aschendorff, 1917); M. Douglas, *Purity and Danger: An Analysis of the Concepts of Pollution and Taboo* (London: Routledge and Kegan Paul, 1966); W. Paschen, *Rein und Unrein: Untersuchung zur biblischen Wortgeschichte* (SANT 24; München: Kösel, 1970); J. Neusner, *The Idea of Purity in Ancient Judaism* (SLJA 1; Leiden: Brill, 1973); E. Feldman, *Biblical and Post-Biblical Defilement and Mourning: Law as Theology* (New York: Yeshiva University and Ktav, 1977); I. Zatelli, *Il campo lessicale degli aggettivi di purità in Ebraico biblico* (QS 7; Firenze: Istituto di Linguistica e di Lingue Orientali, Università di Firenze, 1978). See E. Cortese, "Le recerche sulla concezione 'sacerdotale' circa puro-impuro nell'ultimo decennio," *RivB* 27 (1979) 339–57, for a summary of recent work on purity in the Bible.

[18]See the bibliography for these works.

mention in this introduction, were the major sources I drew upon in constructing my observations and conclusions about the nonbiblical phenomena. The reader may peruse the bibliography for a listing of the various works relating to Hittite and Mesopotamian ritual used in this study.

Part One

The Disposal of Non-Human Bearers of Impurity in the Priestly Writings

1

The Scapegoat

1.1 THE BIBLICAL RITE

The most familiar of all biblical disposal rites is the dispatch of the scapegoat[1] on the Day of Atonement (Lev 16). Scholars have given more attention to it than to any other disposal rite in the Bible.[2] The reason for this is its central importance on the annual day of purification and the great light it sheds, or is believed to shed, on notions of expiation and purification in the Old and New Testament traditions. In this chapter I will examine the significance of the scapegoat rite as a ritual of disposal by paying attention to the relationship of the rite to the

---

[1]I will use the term "scapegoat" to refer to the goat dispatched to the wilderness in the Day of Atonement ritual though, as we will see, the term derives from an incorrect interpretation of the term *ʿăzāʾzēl.*

[2]See, for example, S. Ahituv, "*ʿĂzāʾzēl,*" *EM* 6 (1971) 113–15 (Hebrew); "Azazel," *EncJud* 3 (1972) 999–1002; D. Ashbel, "The Goat Sent to Azazel in the Wilderness (Lev. 16:8, 10, 22)," *Beth Mikra* 27/3 (1966) 89–102 (Hebrew); M. Atidiyah, "The Goat for Azazel," *Beth Mikra* 6/11-2 (1961) 80 (Hebrew); A. Y. Brawer, "Sending the Goat to Azazel and the Bird of the Leper—Symbolic *Tašlîk,*" *Beth Mikra* 12/30 (1967) 32–33 (Hebrew); M. Delcor, "Le mythe de la chute des anges," *RHR* 190 (1976) 3–53; G. R. Driver, "Three Technical Terms in the Pentateuch," *JSS* 1 (1956) 97–105; C. L. Feinberg, "The Scapegoat of Leviticus 16," *BSac* 115 (1958) 320–33; J. G. Frazer, *The Golden Bough: A Study in Magic and Religion; Part IV, The Scapegoat* (3d ed.; London: Macmillan, 1913); *The New Golden Bough: A New Abridgement of the Classic Work by Sir James George Frazer* (ed. T. H. Gaster; New York: S. G. Phillips, 1959; reprint, New York: New American Library, 1959) 609–40; T. H. Gaster, "Azazel," *IDB* 1 (1962) 325–26; S. B. Hoenig, "The New Qumran

larger scheme of purification on the Day of Atonement, the evil or evils that the rite seeks to remove, the figure Azazel, and the meaning of dispatching the goat into the wilderness. After the study of the biblical rite itself, I will examine Hittite and Mesopotamian parallels using the method of contrastive comparison.

1.1.1 The Two-Part Day of Atonement Ritual

The scapegoat ritual is the second part of a larger two-part purification rite on the Day of Atonement. In the first part, Aaron purifies all the major areas in the Tabernacle with blood from *ḥaṭṭāʾt* sacrifices.[3] He takes blood from a *ḥaṭṭāʾt* bull brought for his and his household's benefit, goes to the adytum (the most-holy place of the Tabernacle), and sprinkles some of it once on the front of the *kappōret* and then seven times on the floor before the *kappōret* (Lev 16:14). He repeats this action with blood from a *ḥaṭṭāʾt* goat brought for the people (v 15) that was earlier in the rite designated "for *Yhwh*," as opposed to the scapegoat which was designated "for Azazel" (v 8). He next purifies the shrine (the larger room east of the most-holy place) with blood (v 16b). Lev 16 does not say how this was to be done, but it is likely that the phrase "thus shall he do for the Tent of Meeting" in v 16b refers back to the *ḥaṭṭāʾt* rite detailed in Lev 4:5–7, 16–18 which prescribes a seven-fold sprinkling of *ḥaṭṭāʾt* blood on the floor of the shrine before the veil and then an application of blood to the four horns of the incense altar. After purifying the shrine, Aaron goes out to the altar of burnt

---

Pesher on Azazel," *JQR* 56 (1965–66) 248–53; S. H. Hooke, "The Theory and Practice of Substitution," *VT* 2 (1952) 2–17; H. M. Kümmel, "Ersatzkönig und Sündenbock," *ZAW* 80 (1968) 289–318; E. Kutsch, "Sündenbock," *RGG* 6 (1962) 506–7; S. Landersdorfer. *Studien zum biblischen Versöhnungstag* (Münster: Aschendorff, 1924); "Keilinschriftliche Parallelen zum biblischen Sündenbock (Lv 16)," *BZ* 19 (1931) 20–28; B. Levine, "*Kippûrîm*," *Eretz Israel* 9 (1969) 88–95 (Hebrew); A. Louf, "Caper emissarius ut typus Redemptoris apud patres," *VD* 38 (1960) 262–77; L. Sabourin, "Le bouc émissaire, figure du Christ?" *Sciences Ecclesiastiques* 11 (1959) 45–79; H. Tawil "ʿAzazel The Prince of the Steepe [*sic*]: A Comparative Study," *ZAW* 92 (1980) 43–59. Also see the other literature cited thoughout this chapter.

[3]On the *ḥaṭṭāʾt* sacrifice generally and on its blood as a purifying agent, see chaps. 6 and 7.

offering in the court (16:18–19). He takes some blood from both the bull and goat and applies it to the horns of the altar, after which he sprinkles blood on the altar seven times. Thus the three main parts of the Tabernacle—the adytum, shrine, and outer altar[4]—beginning with the most important part and ending with a part of less importance,[5] are purified in this comprehensive annual purgation rite.

The second part of the purification rite employs the second of the two goats brought for the people which was earlier designated by lot "for Azazel" (vv 8, 10). The animal is brought forward after the sanctuary purification (v 20). Aaron places both of his hands on the animal's head and confesses over it the sins of the Israelites. By this act he puts the sins on the animal's head (v 21).[6] The goat is then sent away to the wilderness (vv 21–22).

1.1.2 The Evils or Impurities Removed

Notably the two parts of the Day of Atonement rite each remove different evils. The *ḥaṭṭāʾt* blood rites performed in the adytum, shrine, and at the outer altar efface impurity attached to these places. By sprinkling the blood in the adytum, Aaron "purges the sanctuary from the impurities of the Israelites" (*miṭṭumʾōt bĕnê yiśrāʾēl*, v 16a).

---

[4]Cf. v 20 where this is made explicit: "When he has finished purging the sanctuary, the Tent of Meeting, and the altar, . . ." For the purification in the shrine, see also Exod 30:10.

[5]For examples of rites in which a substance is applied to three places, beginning with the most prominent, see chap. 7, n. 19.

[6]This two-handed handlaying is distinct in form and meaning from the one-handed handlaying found in sacrifice (cf. Lev 1:4; 3:2, 8, 13; 4:4, 24, 29, 33). The two-handed rite identifies the scapegoat as the recipient of the ritual action (in this case, as the recipient of the sins, cf. Lev 24:14; Num 27:18, 23) while the one-handed rite in sacrifice identifies the animal as belonging to the offerer (cf. R. de Vaux, *Studies in Old Testament Sacrifice* [Cardiff: University of Wales, 1964] 28–29; see also my remarks on a hand placement gesture in Hittite ritual, below, n. 118, which has essentially the same significance as the one-handed rite in the Bible). See my article, "The Gesture of Hand Placement in the Hebrew Bible and in Hittite Literature," *JAOS* 106 (1986) 433–46 and D. P. Wright and J. Milgrom, "*Sāmak*," *TWAT* 5 (1986) 880–88. Also see J. Milgrom, "Sacrifices and Offerings, OT," *IDBSup* (1976) 765; R. Peter, "L'imposition des mains dans l'Ancien Testament," *VT* 22 (1977) 48–55.

Similarly, by applying blood to the outer altar, he purifies and sanctifies it "from the impurities of the Israelites" (*miṭṭumʾōt bĕnê yiśrāʾēl*, v 19b). That the shrine is purified from impurity is implied in v 16b: "and thus shall he do for the Tent of Meeting which dwells with them in the midst of their *impurities*" (*bĕtōk ṭumʾōtām*). The Tent being located among impure people becomes impure and, consequently, needs purification by the rite implicit in v 16b.

In contrast to these blood rites which remove *impurity* from the sanctuary, the scapegoat rite serves to eliminate the *transgressions* of the people. Aaron is to confess over the goat "all the transgressions of the Israelites" (*kol-ʿăwōnōt bĕnê yiśrāʾēl*, v 21) which the animal then carries to the wilderness (v 22; *kol-ʿăwōnōtām*).

But though there is a difference in the evils removed by the two parts of the rites, some further data in the prescriptions caution us not to completely separate the goals of the two parts. The summary phrase concerning the effect of the blood rite in the adytum, in addition to stating that impurities of the Israelites are removed, says that "their crimes including all of their sins" (*pišʿêhem lĕkol-ḥaṭṭōʾtām*, v 16aβ) are removed. The scapegoat rite lists this same evil as an object of disposal. In addition to the Israelites' transgressions, Aaron places "all their crimes including all their sins" (*kol-pišʿêhem lĕkol-ḥaṭṭōʾtām*, v 21aβ) on the head of the goat. Hence, while the two rites from one perspective eliminate different evils—impurity versus sins—from another, they work together to dispose of Israelite crimes and sins.

How can this apparently contradictory situation be explained? My tentative solution is to view the phrase (*kol*) *pišʿêhem lĕkol ḥaṭṭōʾtām* in vv 16aβ and 21aβ as an addition.[7] At an earlier stage, the rite would have distinguished clearly between the evils removed by each part of the larger rite. This clear distinction in the earlier form of the text, however, should not be taken to mean that the two parts were originally separate entities composed apart from one another and then later brought together. Though the evils are distinct, they are conceptually very intimately related. The one, impurity, is merely the effect flowing from the other, transgression. The relation of these two evils to one another is observed in the Priestly conception that the sin of an Israelite causes impurity to

---

[7]M. Löhr, *Das Ritual von Lev. 16 (Untersuchungen zum Hexateuchproblem III)* (SKGG 2/1; Berlin: Deutsche Verlagsgesellschaft für Politik und Geschichte, 1925) 3–4; K. Elliger, *Leviticus* (HAT 1/4; Tübingen: J. C. B. Mohr, 1966) 200–1, 206.

become attached to the sanctuary. This is evident from the need to bring a *ḥaṭṭāʾt* sacrifice after various sins in order to purify the sancta (Lev 4:1–5:13).[8] Moreover, certain sins are explicitly described as defiling the sanctuary. If a person does not purify from corpse contamination, that person pollutes the Lord's Tabernacle (Num 19:13, 20).[9] Sexual impurities have the potential of polluting the sanctuary if prescriptions are not properly observed (Lev 15:31). Similarly, offering children to Molech pollutes the sanctuary (20:3).[10] The relation of sin and impurity is especially patent elsewhere in the scapegoat ritual itself in the fact that the one who leads the goat away which carries sins becomes impure and must undergo ablutions (16:26). If we understand that the sanctuary acquires impurity through the unholy acts of the people, then the bipartite purification rite on the Day of Atonement makes perfect sense. The blood rite removes the impurities caused by the people's sins, and the scapegoat rite removes the sins themselves—the cause of the impurity. The two evils belong naturally together, and, consequently, the two parts of the rite belong together.[11]

The addition of the phrase (*kol*) *pišʿêhem lĕkol-ḥaṭṭōʾtām* seems to have arisen from a need to explain a feature unique to the annual rite—the purification of the adytum and the *kappōret*. The sancta purified by *ḥaṭṭāʾt* blood in rites other than the rite on the Day of Atonement are the outer altar (Lev 4:25, 30, 34), and the shrine and

---

[8]For a discussion of this idea, see J. Milgrom, "The Function of the *Ḥaṭṭāʾt* Sacrifice," *Tarbiz* 40 (1970) 1–8 (Hebrew); "Israel's Sanctuary: The Priestly 'Picture of Dorian Gray,'" *RB* 83 (1976) 390–99; "Sacrifices."

[9]Corpse contamination by itself is not a sin, only a delay of purification is. Similarly, a person who has delayed purification from a minor source of impurity needs to bring a *ḥaṭṭāʾt* sacrifice (Lev 5:2), but the contraction of the impurity itself is not a sin. See J. Milgrom, "The Graduated *Ḥaṭṭāʾt* of Lev 5:1–13," *JAOS* 103 (1983) 251–52.

[10]Note that the sinner does not need to be in the sanctuary during or after his sin to pollute it. The impurity can be caused from a distance without direct contact. See J. Milgrom, *Cult and Conscience: The Asham and the Priestly Doctrine of Repentence* (SJLA 18; Leiden: Brill, 1976) 127–28; "Israel's Sanctuary," 394; "Graduated *Ḥaṭṭāʾt*," 251.

[11]The bipartite rite on the Day of Atonement in which one animal supplies blood and another carries away impurity is similar to the *ṣāraʿat* bird rite. This similarity is further support for the original connection of the two parts of the Day of Atonement rite. See my historical reconstruction in chap. 2, section 2.1.3.

incense altar (Lev 4:5–7, 16–18). Nothing outside of Lev 16 tells about purifying the most holy place and the *kappōret*. Why the innermost part of the sanctuary requires purification is suggested in the passages about purifying the outer altar and shrine in Lev 4. These indicate that *ḥaṭṭāʾt* blood is used on these sancta in accordance with the seriousness of the sins committed. For sins by an Israelite leader or by an individual Israelite, the outer altar undergoes purification; for sins by the anointed priest or by the whole community, the shrine and incense altar must be purified. The rule underlying these prescriptions is clear: the more responsible the sinner or the more universal the sin, the more severe the pollution that penetrates the sanctuary. Consequently, a more rigorous purification is needed by bringing blood into the shrine.[12] The phrase (*kol*) *pišʿêhem lĕkol ḥaṭṭōʾtām* becomes intelligible in view of this principle. It is an explanation of the need for the blood rite in the adytum. It says that the adytum needs purification because it has been sullied by the crimes or brazen sins (*pĕšāʿîm*) of the Israelites—sins much worse than those committed by the high priest, Israelite community, or individual that have only polluted the shrine or the outer altar. The impurity caused by the crimes has penetrated to the very heart of the sanctuary (see n. 12).

The addition of the phrase in v 16aβ does not present a contradiction in regard to the evils removed by the first part of the rite. As previously noted, sins are the cause of impurity. To say, therefore, that *pĕšāʿîm* are removed when the adytum is purified only makes explicit the origin of the impurities in that locale. Accordingly, we may conclude that the addition follows the intention and spirit of the original text and complements it; it does not contradict it.

Why the phrase was also added in v 21aβ must now be explained. The most reasonable interpretation is that the editor wanted to make explicit that the crimes that polluted the adytum were being placed on the goat with all the other sins. Thus the addition in v 21 was not absolutely necessary, but was made in order to be consistent and to make the meaning unambiguous. The phrase in v 21aβ also serves to emphasize that the scapegoat carries away all of Israel's sins, not just some of them.

Lastly, the fact that the phrase has been added to both parts of the rite shows that the editor perceived the two parts to be integrally connected

---

[12]See Milgrom, "Function of the *Ḥaṭṭāʾt*"; "Israel's Sanctuary"; "Sacrifices."

with one another in purpose. This is further proof that the two parts belong together from the earliest stages of the text.

1.1.3 The Term *ʿĂzāʾzēl*

The most problematic item in the scapegoat ritual is the term *ʿăzāʾzēl* Lots are cast for the two goats brought for the people, one "for *Yhwh*" and one "for *ʿăzāʾzēl* (v 8). The latter goat is to be sent out "to *ʿăzāʾzēl* into the wilderness (vv 10, 26). What is the meaning of *ʿăzāʾzēl?* Surely the early explanation of the term as meaning "(e)scapegoat" from *ʿēz ʾôzēl* "goat that departs" or the like cannot be accepted.[13] Nor are the interpretations of the term as a place name "precipitous place" or "rugged cliff,"[14] or as an abstraction "destruction"[15] or "entire removal"[16] satisfactory. The evidence indicates, instead, that *ʿăzāʾzēl* is the name of a god or demon.[17] This is suggested first of all by the parallelism

[13]Cf. the Greek *tǭ apopompaiǭ* "for the one carrying away evil" (v 8; cf. v 10) or *ton diestalmenon eis aphesin* "the [goat] determined for dismissal" (v 26). The Latin has *caper emissarius* "dispatched goat." These translations apparently construed *ʿăzāʾzēl* to mean *ʿez ʾôzēl* "the goat that departs" or the like. Some commentators explain *ʿăzāʾzēl* by connecting it with Arabic *ʿazala* "to remove, set aside" and obtain a similar meaning. See Gaster, "Azazel," 325–26; Feinberg, "Scapegoat," 326–27.

[14]Cf. G.R. Driver, "Technical Terms," 97–98 and literature cited there.

[15]D. Z. Hoffmann, *The Book of Leviticus (Seper Wayyiqraʾ)* (2 vols.; Jerusalem: Mossad Harav Kook, 1953) 1. 304–05.

[16]BDB, 736. For discussion of the various views, see the commentaries, especially Hoffmann, *Leviticus,* 1. 304–05; also see Ashbel, "Goat," 98; Brawer, "Sending"; Delcor, "Mythe," 35–37; G. R. Driver, "Technical Terms," 97–98; Feinberg, "Scapegoat," 320–33; Gaster, "Azazel," 325–26; Hoenig, "Pesher," 248–49 and n. 3; Landersdorfer, *Studien,* 15–20; M. H. Segal, "The Religion of Israel Before Sinai," *JQR* 53 (1962) 249–51; Tawil, "ʿAzazel," 43; R. de Vaux, *Ancient Israel* (London: Darton, Longman, and Todd, 1961; reprint, 2 vols.; New York: McGraw-Hill, 1965) 2. 509; *Studies,* 97.

[17]Cf. de Vaux, *Ancient Israel,* 2. 509; Levine, "*Kippûrîm,*" 94; Tawil "ʿAzazel," 58–59; Delcor, "Mythe," 35–37; Y. Kaufmann, *The Religion of Israel from Its Beginnings to the Babylonian Exile* (Chicago: University of Chicago, 1960; reprint, New York: Schocken, 1972) 114–15; Kutsch, "Sündenbock." D. Ashbel ("Goat") thinks that Azazel is a storm god living in the wilderness to whom the goat was sent as an offering (cf. A. Y. Brawer, "Sending," 32).

between the designation "for *Yhwh*" and "for *ʿăzāʾzēl*" (v 8). As the former phrase refers to a being, so the latter should refer to a being. Secondly, the goat is sent out to the wilderness which is a place of habitation for demonic characters.[18] Thirdly, in postbiblical literature, *ʿăzāʾzēl* appears as a full fledged demonic being.[19] Lastly, though the etymology of the name is not certain, it is best explained as a metathesized form of *ʿzz-ʾl* meaning something like "fierce god" or "angry god."[20]

But though we recognize Azazel as a demon, care must be taken not to misunderstand his true character in the present rite. Caution must be exercised not to presume automatically that as a demon he functions like demons in similar rites outside biblical culture.[21] Azazel's demonic nature must be sought primarily within the framework of the Priestly literature. Significantly, this corpus says little about demonic issues. Apart from the figure of Azazel in Lev 16, the only indication that Priestly writers entertained the idea of demons is in Lev 17:7. Here the Israelites are warned not to offer their sacrifices to goat demons (*śĕʿîrîm*),

---

[18]See, below, in section 1.1.4.

[19]1 Enoch 8:1; 9:6; 10:4–8; 13:1. Cf. 54:5–6; 55:4; 69:2. For a discussion of Azazel in Enoch and the Midrash, see Tawil, "ʿAzazel," 45-47; Delcor, "Mythe," 35–40; Hoenig, "Pesher," 248–50; Landersdorfer, *Studien*, 20–25; Segal, "Religion," 250; P. L. Hanson, "Rebellion in Heaven, Azazel, and Euhemeristic Heroes in 1 Enoch 6–11," *JBL* 96 (1977) 220–25; G. Nickelsburg, "Apocalyptic and Myth in 1 Enoch 6–11," *JBL* 96 (1977) 397–401.

[20]G. A. Barton ("The Origin of the Names of Angels and Demons in the Extra-Canonical Apocalyptic Literature," *JBL* 31 [1912] 163) gives the etymology as *ʿzz–ʾl* but translates "strong one of God." B. Levine ("*kippûrîm*," 94) explains the name as *ʿzz-ʾl* meaning "God is strong, fierce." M. Delcor ("Mythe," 36) similarly understands the name as "El est fort." H. Tawil ("ʿAzazel," 57–59), after reviewing motifs of angry gods in Mesopotamia and referring to the attribution of *qšh* // *ʿzh* "fierce // overbearing" to *šʾwl* // *mwt* "Nether World // Death (personified)" in Cant 8:6, concludes that the name *ʿzz-ʾl* means "fierce god," referring to the Canaanite nether world god Mot. He compares this to the biblical name *ʿzmwt* (Azmaveth) "Mot is fierce" (e.g., 2 Sam 23:31). The form *ʿzʾzl* arose from a deliberate alteration of the name "to conceal the true demonic nature of this supernatural being." On the interpretive context for this textual change, see M. Fishbane, *Biblical Interpretation in Ancient Israel* (Oxford: Clarendon, 1985) 69-72 and n. 14 there.

[21]See the treatment of the Hittite and Mesopotamian parallels, below.

but to bring them to God at the sanctuary. Superficially this may be taken as evidence for a belief in actively functioning demons, but a second look raises questions about this assumption. The term *śĕʿîrîm* is used in this verse in a pejorative sense, subtly criticizing and undermining the supposed efficacy of sacrifice to them.[22] Consequently, we may doubt that the use of *śĕʿîrîm* is a true expression of belief in active demons.

Depreciatory use of demonic terminology is found outside of the Priestly writings and thus gives indirect support to the foregoing skepticism about *śĕʿîrîm* being real evidence of active demons in Priestly thought. The "Song of Moses" depicts Israelite faithlessness as sacrificing to "demons (*šēdîm*), no-gods—gods they did not know." (Deut 32:17). Psalm 106 says that the Israelites, after having entered the land of Canaan, sacrificed their sons and daughters to demons (*šēdîm*; v 37). These examples appear to use demonic terminology in a disparaging manner. They do not show by it a belief in real active demons or lesser gods, but use it to characterize the sins of idolatry and its negative value.[23] These demons to whom Israel sacrificed must surely be thought of as nonvital, just as elsewhere idolatrous gods are considered to be nothing more than wood, stone, and metal.[24] It is possible that, like *šēdîm* in the foregoing passages, *śĕʿîrîm* in Lev 17 should be understood as a term specially chosen to polemicize against potential Israelite idolatry. *Śĕʿîrîm* would not indicate a vital object of devotion, but would be a term of devaluation and belittlement.

The disparaging way in which *śĕʿîrîm* is used in Lev 17 and the general silence about demons in the Priestly literature lead to the surmise that there is little or no room for active demons in Priestly theology.

---

[22]D. Hillers ("Demons, Demonology," *EncJud* 5 [1971] 1523) notes the negative significance of *śĕʿîrîm* in Lev 17:7 and 2 Chr 11:15. The word in the latter passage should probably be understood as concrete idolatrous objects rather than goat demons (see S. Loewenstamm, "*Šēdîm*," *EM* [1976] 525).

[23]A. Weiser (*The Psalms: A Commentary* [OTL; Philadelphia: Westminster, 1962] 678) translates *šēdîm* simply as "idols." Note that the parallel terms *ʿăṣabbêhem* (v 36) and *ʿăṣabbê kĕnāʿan* (v 38) give a context of idolatry.

[24]Deut 4:28; 28:36, 64; 29:16; 2 Kgs 19:18; Isa 2:8, 20; 30:22; 37:19; 40:19–20; 44:9–20; 46:6–7; 48:5; Jer 10:1–15; 51:17–18; Ezek 20:32; Hos 8:6; 13:2; Hab 2:18–19; Ps 115:4–7; 135:15–17. On Israel's view of foreign gods, see Kaufmann, *Religion*, 13–17 and passim.

Consequently, Azazel should be viewed as a demon, as the etymology of the name suggests, but perhaps as an inactive one with no real role to play in the rite except to indicate the place to which the sins are dispatched.

This view of Azazel is corroborated by the fact that the scapegoat is not an offering to him.[25] This is clear not only from the prohibition, just observed, in Lev 17 against offering to anyone but *Yhwh*,[26] but also from the fact that the goat is not sacrificed to Azazel; it is merely sent to him.[27] Furthermore, the animal is not decorated to make it an attractive offering to him, as are living appeasement offerings in other ancient Near Eastern cultures.[28] Nor is the goat a substitute sent to Azazel to suffer in the place of the Israelite community.[29] The goat only serves to transport the sins of Israel away from the habitation.[30]

Finally, a hint about the impotence of Azazel in the rite may be found in the silence regarding his personality. Other than being the one to whom the goat is sent, we know nothing about him. He does not appear as an angry deity needing propitiation, nor does he appear as the custodian of evil sent to him.[31] If Azazel was considered an active

---

[25]Elliger, *Leviticus*, 212; Kümmel, "Ersatzkönig," 311; Brawer, "Sending," 33. Many commentators in the Middle Ages saw the goat as a gift to Azazel, the prince of demons. God allowed him to receive the goat for being his servant (cf. Ramban on Lev 16:8; Brawer, "Sending," 32).

[26]Priestly prohibitions on idolatry include: Lev 17:3–9; 18:21; 19:4; 20:2–5; 26:1.

[27]According to the Mishnah (*Yoma* 6:5–6), in Second Temple times the animal was put to death. This, however, was not to make it a sacrifice, but to prevent it from returning to the habitation. See the Hittite motif of prevention discussed in section 1.3.9, below.

[28]See the Hittite and Mesopotamian rites, below. In the Second Temple rite, a piece of red wool was bound on the head of the scapegoat (*m. Yoma* 4:2; 6:6). This, however, was not for decorating the animal as in nonbiblical appeasement rites.

[29]Cf. Hoffman (*Leviticus*, 1. 305): "the goat is a representation of the sinner," and S. H. Hooke ("Substitution," 8–9): "The 'primitive' features in the ritual may be defined as the selection of a goat to serve as the substitute for the corporate personality of Israel." See also C. Lattey, "Vicarious Solidarity in the Old Testament," *VT* 1 (1951) 272–74.

[30]See Kaufmann, *Religion*, 114; Gaster, "Azazel," 326; Hoenig, "Pesher," 248–49.

[31]See the Hittite Ambazzi ritual, section 1.4.4, below, and the Shurpu ritual, section 1.5.4, below.

being, one would expect him to have been more fully described as in nonbiblical rites where similar beings appear (see below).

Because of the apparent devaluation of demons in the Priestly literature, the understanding that the scapegoat is not an offering to Azazel, and the relative silence about the function of Azazel, one can suppose that Azazel was not considered an active demonic being in the present form of the rite. He has been stripped of his personality. He represents little more than the place or goal of disposal.[32] If this supposition is not completely acceptable because of its being based in part on silence, then the argument at least cautions us from going too far in the other direction and attributing to Azazel full demonic character.

1.1.4 Disposal in the Nether World?

Related to the question of whether Azazel is an active demon or not is the question of whether the dispatch of the goat and its burden of sins to the wilderness is to be viewed mythologically as the disposal of evils in the nether world. Tawil, a proponent of this view, supports it by reference to Mesopotamian texts where disposal is perceived as taking place in the nether world,[33] by reference to examples from apocryphal literature in which Azazel is placed in the underworld in the desert, and by connecting the name Azazel with the Canaanite god Mot whose domain is the nether world. Methodological caution against reading into the rite information from other cultures or from other later documents from the same culture urges us to take a careful look at the view that

---

[32]T. Gaster ("Demon, Demonology," *IDB* 1 [1962] 818) notes that "demons often survive as figures of speech (e.g., 'gremlins') long after they have ceased to be figures of belief. Accordingly, the mention of a demon's name in a scriptural text is no automatic testimony to living belief in him." He discounts the idea that Azazel is considered a real demon in the rite (821; cf. "Azazel," 326). Cf. Brawer, "Sending," 33. For Kaufmann (*Religion*, 114–15), the rite of the scapegoat is evidence of an ancient pagan rite, transmuted to fit Israelite theology. The rite was originally to expel the demon Azazel into the wilderness. (I cannot accept this particular conclusion of Kaufmann on the basis of the nonbiblical rites; see section 1.6, below.) "But the Azazel of Lev 16 is not conceived of either as among the people or as the source of danger or harm; he plays no active role at all. . . . He is merely a passive symbol of impurity—sin returns to its like."

[33]Hittite rituals show a similar conception, see section 9.4.2, below.

evils are symbolically disposed of in the nether world to see if it holds up within the context of biblical religion. To this end, I conducted a study of the terminology and passages in the Bible concerning impurity,[34] demons,[35] the nether world,[36] and the wilderness[37] in order to discover any interrelationships between the four topics. This study produced no conclusive evidence that the underworld and wilderness are to be connected in biblical thought,[38] nor did it show any connection between impurity and the nether world.

---

[34]The root *ṭmʾ*.

[35]*Deber, lîlît, māwet, mašḥît, qeṭeb, rešep, śāʿîr, śāṭān, śĕrāpîm, šĕʾôl, šēdîm.* P. Arzi, "*Lîlît,*" *EM* 4 (1962) 498–99 (Hebrew); H. Duhm, *Die bösen Geister im Alten Testament* (Tübingen: J. C. B. Mohr, 1904); Gaster, "Demons"; Hillers, "Demons"; S. Loewenstamm, "*Qeṭeb, Qōṭeb,*" *EM* 7 (1976) 109–10 (Hebrew); "*Šēdîm.*"

[36]*ʿĂaddôn, ʾereṣ, bôr, dûmâ, ḥōšek, māwet, naḥălê bĕlîyaʿal, ʿāpār, ṣalmāwet, qeber, šĕʾôl, šaḥat.* G. Beer, "Der biblische Hades," *Theologische Abhandlungen, Eine Festgabe zum 17. Mai 1902 für Heinrich Julius Holtzmann* (ed. W. Nowack, et al.; Tübingen: J. C. B. Mohr, 1902) 3–29; A. Bertholet, "Zu den babylonischen und israelitischen Unterweltsvorstellungen," *Oriental Studies Published in Commemoration of the 40th Anniversary (1883–1892) of Paul Haupt as the Director of the Oriental Seminary of the Johns Hopkins University* (ed. C. Alder and A. Ember; Baltimore: Johns Hopkins, 1926) 9–18; T. Gaster, "Dead, Abode of the," *IDB* 1 (1962) 787–88; S. Loewenstamm, "*Šĕʾôl,*" *EM* 7 (1976) 454–57 (Hebrew); N. J. Tromp, *Primitive Conceptions of Death and the Nether World in the Old Testament* (Rome: Pontifical Biblical Institute, 1969).

[37]*Ḥōreb, ḥorbâ, yĕšîmôn, midbār, ʿărābâ, ṣĕḥîḥâ, ṣiyyâ, ṣimāʾôn, śādê.* A. Haldar, *The Notion of the Desert in Sumero-Accadian and West-Semitic Religions* (UUA 3; Uppsala and Leipzig: A. B. Lundequistska and Otto Harrassowitz, 1950); J. Pedersen, *Israel: Its Life and Culture I–II* (London: Oxford University, 1926) 453–60.

[38]Tawil ("ʿAzazel," 54-55, n. 62) argues that *ʾereṣ maʾpēlĕyâ* in Jer 2:31 is a designation of the nether world and that since *midbār* is parallel to it, *midbār* has a connection with the nether world. But an underworld interpretation of these words does not suit the context well and should be rejected. Tawil also argues that in Jer 2:6 *šûḥâ* ("pit") and *ʾereṣ ṣiyyâ wĕṣalmāwet* ("land of dryness and darkness") carry the idea of the nether world and that *midbār* which is parallel to these terms should thus have chthonic meaning. Again, the context does not support this view. The terms merely refer to the arid and undesirable desert the Israelites had to traverse before coming into the fruitful land of Canaan. Similarly, the

One might attempt to reach the conclusion that disposal in the wilderness is equal to disposal in the nether world indirectly by showing that demons inhabit both the wilderness and the underworld. But this is difficult. Certainly there is some evidence that demons are inhabitants of uninhabited places—the wilderness, ruins, and the like. Besides the case of Azazel, this idea appears in Isaiah's description of the fauna dwelling among the ruins of Babylon and Edom:

> *Ṣiyyîm* will lie down there,
> And their houses will be filled with *ʾōḥîm*.
> Ostriches will dwell there,
> And *śĕʿîrîm* will dance there.
> *ʾIyyîm* will cry in its citadels,
> And *tannîm*, in the palaces of pleasure.
> (Isa 13:21–22a)

> *Qāʾat*-bird and *qippôd* will possess it.
> Owls and ravens will dwell in it.
> . . . .
> It will be a dwelling of *tannîm*,
> An abode for ostriches.
> *Ṣiyyîm* will meet *ʾiyyîm*,
> And the *śāʿîr* will call to his companion
> Even there the *lîlît* will rest,
> And find for herself a resting place.
> There the *qippôz*-snake will nest and lay eggs.
> . . . .
> Even there the *dayyôt*-birds will gather,
> One with another.
> (Isa 34:11a, 13b, 14–15)

Though the meanings of many of the terms for the ruin occupants here are not entirely clear, it is fairly certain that *śāʿîr* and *lîlît* are

---

passages given by Tromp for support of the connection of the wilderness with the nether world actually do not give the desired support upon close inspection (*Primitive Conceptions*, 131–33; besides Jer 2:6, 31, he refers to Deut 8:15; Ps 63:2; 107:40; 143:6; Job 6:18; 12:24–25). Indeed, Tromp finally admits that "the desert is never clearly and explicitly identified with the abode of the dead in the Old Testament" (p. 133). Haldar (*Notion*) also argues that the wilderness and nether world are connected but is, in my opinion, likewise unsuccessful.

demonic figures.[39] A further indication that demons inhabit uninhabited open areas might be in the warning to the Israelites not to offer sacrifices "in the open field" (*ʿal pĕnê haśśādê*, Lev 17:5) which is considered sacrificing to *śĕʿîrîm* "goat-demons" (v 7). But we must remember that doubts were raised (above) whether *śĕʿîrîm* in this passage offers clear testimony as to how the Old Testament views demons.

But if the evidence is sufficient to show that demons live in the wilderness, it is, in my opinion, insufficient to show that they inhabit the underworld. In a difficult passage from Hosea,[40] God speaks to the underworld personified: "Where, Death, are your *deber*-plagues? Where,

---

[39]The interpretation of the terms referring to animals or demons in these passages is disputed. Some understand some of the names, besides *śāʿîr* and *lîlît*, to be demonic (e.g., KB[2] [35, 801] takes *ʾiyyîm* and *ṣiyyîm* as demons [KB[3], 37, 956, leaves the interpretation open]; O. Kaiser [OTL; *Isaiah 13–39: A Commentary* (Philadelphia: Westminster, 1974) 8, 352] takes *ṣiyyîm* as demons). Others understand *śāʿîr* and *lîlît*, as well as the other terms, as animals (N. H. Snaith ["The Meaning of *Śĕʿîrîm*," *VT* 25 (1975) 115–16] takes *śāʿîr* here as nondemonic; NEB has "he-goat" and "nightjar" for the two terms respectively; see also Gaster, "Demon," 818b). The attestations of these terms are few with uninforming contexts thus making interpretation difficult. Support for the view that these terms refer to animals is found in other passages about ruin dwellers in which only animals appear (Jer 50:39; Zeph 2:14; Mal 1:3). But later tradition envisages the wilderness and ruins as the haunt of demons (cf. Bar 4:35; Tob 8:3; Matt 12:43; Luke 11:24; Rev 18:2) suggesting that this tradition may already be found in the Old Testament. See Arzi, "*Lîlît*"; H. Duhm, *Die bösen Geister*, 46–48. My reasons for viewing at least *lîlît* and *śāʿîr* as demonic are the following: (a) A demon called *lilû/lilītu*, cognate with Hebrew *lîlît*, is found in Mesopotamian literature (see *CAD* L, 190). In later Jewish literature *lîlît* appears as a major demonic figure (see T. Gaster, *The Holy and the Profane: Evolution of Jewish Folkways* [New York: W. Sloane Associates, 1955] 18–28; "Demon," 819; R. Patai, *The Hebrew Goddess* [New York: Ktav, 1967; reprint, New York: Avon, 1978] 180–225). The extent through time and cultures of these attestations indicates that *lîlît* in Isaiah is demonic. (b) Because *lîlît* is demonic in Isa 34:4 and because *śāʿîr* is demonic (though used pejoratively) in Lev 17:7, *śāʿîr* in Isa 13 and 34 is probably to be understood as a demon.

[40]See F. Andersen and D. N. Freedman, *Hosea: A New Translation with Introduction and Commentary* (AB 24; Garden City: Doubleday, 1980) 639–40, for a summary of the problems of this verse. I follow their interpretation of the syntax.

Sheol, is your *qōṭeb*-plague?" (13:14b). It is hardly clear that *deber* and *qōṭeb* are to be considered anything more than just plagues; they are not necessarily demons. This may be just a figure of speech. To be judged similarly is Jer 9:20 in which death is personified as a demon who climbs through windows and into fortresses, cutting off "infants from the streets and young men from the squares." This again is just a literary image and not a clear indication of the belief that death was a nether world demon.[41]

In summary, the Bible does not give decisive evidence of the connection of the wilderness and the nether world, of the connection of impurity with the nether world, nor of the connection of demons with the nether world. It only gives evidence of the connection of demons with the wilderness. Hence, to say that the biblical scapegoat rite is a disposal of evils in the nether world is going beyond the expressed thought of Israelite religion and must be rejected.

Why then is the goat sent out into the wilderness? Simply to remove it from the populated areas so that as a bearer of contagious impurity it can do no harm.[42] The meaning of *midbār* "wilderness" shows this to be the case. The *midbār* is arid land,[43] endowed with little vegetation except grass for pasturage.[44] Various wild animals—owls, jackals, ostriches, serpents, foxes—live in it and related places.[45] Most important, though, is the fact that the *midbār* is not inhabited by humans. Jeremiah calls it an "infertile land [literally, salty land] without inhabitant" (17:6), and Job characterizes it as a place "in which there is no man" (38:26).[46] Thus when the scapegoat is sent to the wilderness,

---

[41]Cf. S. M. Paul, "Cuneiform Light on Jer 9, 20," *Bib* 49 (1968) 373–76. The ghosts of the dead inhabit the nether world, but in Israelite religion they are not troublesome to humans nor are they the cause of evils. Hence, they do not prove to be an example of demons inhabiting the nether world (contra Beer, "Der biblische Hades," 16–20).

[42]The danger the impure scapegoat poses is reflected in the impurity contracted by the one who dispatches it (Lev 16:26). On the impurity of the scapegoat, see chap. 8, section 8.3.2.1, q.

[43]E.g., Gen 21:14–16; Exod 15:22; Num 21:5; 2 Sam 17:29; Isa 35:1, 6; 41:18; 43:19; Jer 12:10; Hosea 2:5; Ps 107:4, 33, 35.

[44]See Joel 2:22. Cf. also Jer 9:9; 23:10; Joel 1:19; Ps 65:13; 78:52; Job 24:5; 1 Chr 5:9.

[45]Deut 8:15; Isa 13:21–22; 34:11–15; 35:7; 43:19–20; Jer 2:24; 50:39; Ezek 13:4; Zeph 2:12–14; Mal 1:3; Ps 102:7; Job 24:5; 39:5–6; Lam 4:3.

[46]Cf. also Jer 22:6; 51:43.

it is sent to a place where the impurity cannot threaten human populations.

Further evidence that dispatch to the wilderness is only to remove the impure animal from human habitation is found in the term *ʾereṣ gĕzērâ* (16:22). Tawil has suggested that *ʾereṣ gĕzērâ* is "used . . . in Lev 16 as a symbolic designation of the nether world."[47] He bases this conclusion on a supposed underworld significance for some of the instances of the verb *gzr* and on a similar phrase from Akkadian, *ašru parsu* "a cut off (i.e., secluded/forbidden) place," which, he argues, can be a designation for the underworld. I cannot agree with his conclusions about *ʾereṣ gĕzērâ*. Granted that the verb *gzr* in some instances means to die or be doomed,[48] this is only a secondary semantic development from an original meaning "cut."[49] None of the examples of the root appear to carry any chthonic overtones by themselves. Consequently, it is better to interpret *ereṣ gĕzērâ* as "land of seclusion/separateness," which emphasizes the distancing of the goat and sins from the human habitation.[50]

1.1.5 Summary

To summarize this section, the purpose of the biblical scapegoat rite is to rid the community of the sins which are the cause of impurity in the sanctuary. The sins are placed on the goat and then sent to the wilderness in order to remove them from the people and from the sanctuary. The goat does not appear to be a propitiatory offering to Azazel, but only serves as a vehicle for transporting the sins. Azazel, to whom the goat is sent, is apparently not an active personality. He is simply a ritual "place holder," denoting the goal of impurity.

---

[47]Tawil, "ʿAzazel," 56.

[48]Clearly Ezek 37:11 and Lam 3:54. In Isa 53:8 and Ps 88:6, *nigzar min* means simply "to be cut off from" without any inherent chthonic significance.

[49]"Cut in two" (with direct object): 1 Kgs 3:25, 26; 2 Kgs 6:4; Ps 136:13; "cut off, separate" (with preposition *min*): Hab 3:17; 2 Chr 26:21. Isa 53:8 and Ps 88:6 are examples of this latter usage in the context of death. The verb has further development in the meaning "to decree" (Job 22:28; Esther 2:1) and "to cut off to eat" (Isa 9:19). The original meaning "to cut" is found in the nouns *gĕzārîm* "pieces" (Gen 15:17; Ps 136:13) and *magzērâ* "axe" (2 Sam 12:31). For a discussion, see M. Görg, "*Gzr*," *TWAT* 2 (1973) 1001–4 (= *TDOT* 2 [1975] 459–61).

[50]Brawer, "Sending," 33.

1.2 PARALLELS TO THE BIBLICAL SCAPEGOAT RITUAL

We now examine Hittite and Mesopotamian rites of elimination that have similarities to the biblical scapegoat rite. The purpose in studying these extrabiblical rituals is to aid in more completely determining the meaning of the biblical rite. As indicated in the introduction to this work, the method of contrastive comparison will be employed to realize this goal. To briefly reiterate, contrastive comparison focuses attention on differences between broadly similar phenomena in discrete cultures and asks questions about the nature of the differences and why the differences exist. The answers to these questions lead to a better assessment of the significance of the rites in their respective contexts.

1.3 HITTITE PARALLELS TO THE SCAPEGOAT: PURIFICATION MOTIFS

Attention first turns to parallels from Anatolia.[51] Hittite ritual material is abundant[52] and contains a vast range of responses to impure conditions. In order to better comprehend this variety, a brief survey of the various purification techniques or motifs is in order. I have formulated a list of ten purification motifs which appear in Hittite rituals. This classification is provisional, subject to expansion and reorganization as more is learned about Hittite ritual. Furthermore, it hardly need be said that the list does not necessarily represent how an ancient Hittite would view the rites. It is a somewhat artificial arrangement, structured according to modern intellectual outlook and conventions. It is formulated in order to better perceive the content of

---

[51]For a recent treatment of Hittite elimination rituals and similar Greek rites, see W. Burkert, *Structure and History in Greek Mythology and Ritual* (Berkeley: University of California, 1979) 59–77. On elimination rites in ancient North Syria and Anatolia, see B. Janowski, *Sühne als Heilsgeschehen: Studien zur Sühnetheologie der Priesterschrift und der Wurzel* KPR *im Alten Orient und im Alten Testament* (WMANT 55; Neukirchen: Neukirchener, 1982) 211–12.

[52]E. Laroche (*Catalogue des textes hittites* [Paris: Éditions Klincksieck, 1971] 69–85) lists 111 different rituals not including other numerous types of cultic texts.

the rituals. It must also be stressed that such simple rubrics do not fully bring out the complexity of the symbolism contained in Hittite ritual or that of any other culture to which they may be applied. The various motifs often occur in combinations, or a particular motif which generally accompanies a certain ritual act may be replaced by another. Such fluidity in the manifestation of these motifs is not very troublesome, if one keeps in mind that a particular symbol—and a ritual act is a symbol—does not always demand a uniform significance throughout a given culture.[53]

These motifs, apart from serving as a basis for understanding the Hittite rites themselves, will aid generally in this chapter in comparing both the Hittite and Mesopotamian rites with the biblical scapegoat rite. We will be able to ask what motifs occur in a given nonbiblical ritual and then inquire if the same motifs exist in the scapegoat rite. The presence or lack of certain motifs in the rituals will grant a more ready perception of their difference or similarity. Furthermore, using these motifs for comparison will allow us to focus on conceptual and systemic differences between the rites of the different cultures and avoid the obvious and generally insignificant differences or similarities in regard to formal content and physical objects employed in the rites.

The following is a listing and description of the ten purification motifs extracted from Hittite rituals.

1.3.1 Transfer

This motif is evident in rites where an evil of some sort is removed from the patient (i.e., the person or object suffering the evil) and transferred to another object or living being which becomes the bearer of the impurity. The bearer of impurity is usually then disposed of or banished in some way.

Transfer may be performed by waving or moving an object or animal over the patient, as we find in the Telepinu myth:

---

[53]Cf. R. Firth, *Symbols: Public and Private* (Ithaca: Cornell University, 1973) passim. Structuralist approaches stress the fact that the meaning of symbols depend on their context and thus do not always mean the same thing in a given culture (cf. J. Sturrock, *Structuralism and Since: From Levi-Strauss to Derrida* [Oxford: Oxford University, 1979] 11).

> I have waved over Telepinu this way and I have waved that way.[54] I have taken from Telepinu's body his evil. I have taken his malice. I have taken his anger. I have taken his wrath. I have taken his fury. I have taken rage.[55]

---

[54] *Wa-ar-nu-nu-un* should be understood as *wa-aḫ-nu-nu-un* "I waved," not "I burned," as written. The two words are sometimes confused in writing (see A. Goetze and H. Pedersen, *Muršilis Sprachlähmung* [KDVS 21/1; Copenhagen: Levin and Munksgaard, 1934] 28–32). That *waḫnu-* "wave" is to be understood here is also evident from the context and from the syntax (noun in dative-locative + *šer arḫa waḫnu*) which is found in other waving rituals (cf. Birth Ritual C vs. 18; Tunnawi ii 52–53; Allaiturahhi, 210: 64′–65′).

[55] *KUB* 17.10 iii 8–12 (= *ANET* 127–28). This example shows clearly that the evil is removed by the waving rite. Cf. also Allaiturahhi, 136: 41′–42′; 210: 61′–64′; Papanikri ii 55–iii 1′; Birth Ritual C vs. 9; H ii 12–14; Amihatna i 48; ii 2–3 (note after the figurine of the deity receives waving, it is purified with water); iii 40; iv 20–21; Tunn ii 4–5, 52–54 (an empty pot is waved over the patient and then broken); *KBo* 9.119 iv 11–12 (cited in V. Haas and G. Wilhelm, *Hurritische und luwische Riten aus Kizzuwatna* [AOATS 3; Kevelaer and Neukirchen: Butzon und Bercker, and Neukirchener, 1974] 44); Malli ii 48′–54′; StBoT 8 ii 30–iii 9; Mastigga, passim; Huwarlu i 62–70; ii 5–9 (this is an excellent example and will be treated in the body of the chapter, below); Death Ritual 18 vs. 16–18; Ulippi iii 19–20, 65–66; Ayatarsa i 36. An action similar to waving is holding an object over the patient (*šer ep-*; Tunnawi i 57, 60–62, 63–64; ii 8–9). Waving can serve other secondary functions besides transferring evil to the object waved. For example, in the Papanikri ritual (iv 9–10), a lamb is waved over a fire. It is clear from the ritual context in which the lamb undergoes other purification rites that the fire purifies the lamb and not the reverse as might be supposed from the other examples of waving, cited above. (In ancient Greece a fire may become impure. Thus there may some basis for viewing the fire in this Hittite rite as being impure and in need of purification. Cf. Parker, *Miasma: Pollution and Purification in Early Greek Religion* [Oxford: Clarendon, 1983] 35 and n. 10). In another example (StBoT 8 ii 44–iii 13), which I will discuss in more detail in chap. 2, section 2.3, an eagle is waved over the king and queen and then released in order to carry a message to the sun god. Here the waving rite removes the impurity from the royal pair. But the bird besides being a bearer of impurity is also a mediator requesting blessings for the couple. Finally, it is possible that in some cases the positive power of the object waved was imparted to the

Transfer may also be effected by the patient spitting his evil onto the bearer of impurity,[56] by touching an object to the body of the patient in various ways,[57] by combing the evil off the person,[58] by leaving cathartic materials near or under the patient's bed at night to absorb the evil,[59] or by passing through specially erected gates which strip evil off those who pass through.[60]

1.3.2 Detergents

The use of "detergents" for removing impurity in Hittite rites is very similar to transfer, but whereas in the case of the latter, objects or animate beings remove the impurity, in the case of detergents, liquid, paste-like, powdered, or other similar substances are used to remove it.

---

object or person over which it was waved (for similar rites with this meaning in Greek culture, see Parker, *Miasma*, 226).

For a discussion of waving, see O. Gurney, *Some Aspects of Hittite Religion* (Oxford: Oxford University for the British Academy, 1977) 54; V. Haas, *Hethitische Berggötter und hurritische Steindämonen* (Mainz: Philipp von Zabern, 1982) 175; V. Haas and H. J. Thiel, *Die Beschwörungsrituale der Allaituraḫ(ḫ)i und verwandte Texte* (AOAT 31; Kevelaer and Neukirchen: Butzon und Bercker, and Neukirchener, 1978) 45; Haas and Wilhelm, *Hurritische und luwische Riten*, 42–49.

[56]Cf. StBoT 8 i 3′–6′, 14′–17′, 36′; iv 34; Mastigga ii 26–34, 35–43; iii 14–19. The examples in the Mastigga rite speak of spitting out "curses," i.e., the evil which has affected the patients. See J. Moyer, "The Concept of Ritual Purity Among the Hittites" (PhD diss., Brandeis University, 1969) 66–67.

[57]See for example, the body part contact rites in V. Haas, "Eine hethitisches Beschwörungsmotiv aus Kizzuwatna: seine Herkunft und Wanderung," *Or* 40 (1971) 410–30, especially 413, lines 35–37, where the body parts of an animal touched to the patient "demand" the sickness from the body parts of the patient. Handlaying in the Ashella and Mursilis Sprachlähmung rituals is not for the transfer of evils, see section 1.4.2 and n. 118, below.

[58]Tunnawi ii 62–iv 5; Malli iii 36′–37′; *KUB* 12.26 ii 1–10 (cited in Haas, "Beschwörungsmotiv," 423–24; Gurney, *Aspects*, 54; and A. Goetze and E. H. Sturtevant, *The Hittite Ritual of Tunnawi* [AOS 14; New Haven: American Oriental Society, 1938] 88).

[59]Malli ii 44′–54′; iii 2′–4′; StBoT 8 ii 41–45; iv 14–34; Huwarlu i 19–21; Anniwiyani i 16–21.

[60]The ritual of Tunnawi makes it clear that passage through temporary gates is for the removal of impurity. As the patient is going through a

---

gate, the Old Woman recites to the wood of which the gate is made: "(As) the goat goes by you and you pull off of it some hair (and as) the bull goes by you pull off of it some hair, in the same way pull off of this offerer evil, impurity, sorcery, sin, divine anger, curse, the tongue of the masses, (and) a short life" (iii 35–42; for the textual problems in lines 35–36, 38, see H. Otten, "Ein Reinigungsritual im Hethitischen: ^{GIŠ}*ḫatalkišna-*," *AfO* 16 [1952–53] 70). Interestingly, Otten (69–71) has shown that the wood used for this gate (^{GIŠ}*ḫattalkišna-*) is a type of thorn bush which in other texts is characteristically described as pulling off the hair of animals. The gate was made of this kind of wood because it symbolized purification. Tunnawi (iii 46–53) also has a rite of passing through a gate of *alanza(n)-* wood. This wood must be of a nature similar to *ḫattalkišna-* wood (cf. Otten). Similar to these rites is the passage rite in the Paskuwatti ritual for sexual impotence (i 18–29) in which a gate of reeds is set up. The patient is given a mirror and a spindle, and then passes through. The officiator takes away the womanly implements and gives the patient a bow instead. The officiator declares that he has thus removed womanliness and has given manliness in return.

But though these ritual gates are clearly for the removal of impurity (see the remarks of O. Masson, "A propos d'un rituel hittite pour la lustration d'une armée: Le rite de purification par le passage entre les deux parties d'une victime," *RHR* 137 [1950] 6–8; Moyer, "The Concept of Ritual Purity," 135; cf. S. Eitrem, "A Purificatory Rite and Some Allied *Rites de Passage*," *SO* 25 [1947] 38), there may be at times another motif involved. In the Anniwiyani ritual a gate of *ḫattalkišna*-wood is erected, a dog is cut into two pieces, and half is placed on each side of the gate. The patients pass through the gate which is then destroyed by the last person going through it. They leave the area of the ritual and "nail down" the road, that is, fix the evil in its place (i 36–39; ii 9–18). Here, the gate acts like a roadblock to the evil. All pass through and then it is destroyed so the evil cannot follow. Consequently, those who perceive the gates as preventative have a basis for their view (A. Goetze, *Kulturgeschichte Kleinasiens* [2d ed.; München: C. H. Beck, 1957] 156; O. Gurney, "The Hittite Ritual of Tunnawi," *JRAS* [1941] 57; H. Kronasser, "Das hethitische Ritual KBo IV 2," *Die Sprache* 8 [1962] 106–7).

For the rite of passing between parts of animals in Hittite, Greek, and Roman ritual, as just observed in the example from the Anniwiyani ritual, see Eitrem, "Purificatory Rite"; H. M. Kümmel, *Ersatzrituale für den hethitischen König* (StBoT 3; Wiesbaden: Otto Harrassowitz, 1967) 151–52; Masson, "Rituel hittite"; Parker, *Miasma*, 225–26.

Such substances include water,[61] wine,[62] clay,[63] plants,[64] flours,[65] salt,[66] blood,[67] fire,[68] and various mixtures.[69]

The following is an example from the Allaiturahhi ritual:

> I have [ ] wiped sin(?) off of him. I have taken yellowness from him. I have wiped (it) away. I have wiped it away with flour. I have wiped it away from his body with *ḫuriya*-substance. I have taken it away from his head. Death, evil word [ ].[70]

---

[61]On water and bathing, see Tunnawi ii 61; StBoT 3, 10 vs. 26′–27′, 30′; Instructions to Temple Officials i 15–20; iii 60–65, 70–75; StBoT 8 i 14′–17′. On sprinkling water, see Mastigga ii 21–22; iii 20. For a discussion, see D. H. Engelhard, "Hittite Magical Practices: An Analysis" (PhD diss., Brandeis University, 1970) 143–47.

[62]Cf. Tunnawi ii 21.

[63]Cf. StBoT 2 vs. 7; Huwarlu i 48–52; *KUB* 17.27 ii 1–5 (= *ANET*, 347). See Engelhard, "Magical Practices," 148–53.

[64]Malli iii 33′–34′; Mastigga iv 17–20, 21–25; StBoT 2 vs. 7; Huwarlu i 44–47 (for a discussion, see O. Carruba, *Das Beschwörungsritual für die Göttin Wišurijanza* [StBoT 2; Wiesbaden: Otto Harrassowitz, 1966] 13; L. Rost, "Ein hethitischen Ritual gegen Familienzwist," *MIO* 1 [1953] 366–68).

[65]Cf. the example cited below. Also Huwarlu i 39–47, 48–54, 55–60 where dough is used.

[66]See Engelhard, "Magical Practices," 124–28, for examples.

[67]The best example of purification using blood is Ulippi iv 38–40: "They smear with blood the golden god, the wall, and the utensils of the entirely new god. The new god and the temple become clean." The latter phrase makes it clear that the blood smearing has a purgative effect. Comparable to this rite is the smearing of a new birth stool with bird blood in the Papanikri ritual (i 25–26). Since this is done just after the new stool is made, it should have a purificatory and, perhaps additionally, a consecratory effect. See Moyer, "The Concept of Ritual Purity," 31, 69; F. Sommer and H. Ehelolf, *Das hethitische Ritual des Papanikri von Komana* (Bogazköi-Studien 10; Leipzig: J. C. Hinrichs, 1924) 18.

[68]Cf. Mastigga iv 6–7; StBoT 3, 151 iv 51–56 (= Masson, "Rituel hittite," 5–6). See Moyer, "The Concept of Ritual Purity," 95–97; Goetze, *Kulturgeschichte*, 156; Engelhard, "Magical Practices," 129–35.

[69]Cf. Allaiturahhi 138 ii 13–18.

[70]Allaiturahhi 94–96 iv 9′–15′.

1.3.3 Substitution

This motif is much like transfer in that an evil is removed from a patient and put on another object or animate being. But in substitution, the evil is not just transferred for the purpose of disposal, it is transferred so that the consequences of the evil will fall on the bearer of impurity instead of the patient.[71]

An example of this motif is found in a ritual for protecting the king against portended evil. The king prays to the moon god:

> Behold, on account of which matter I have come [to] pray, hear me Moon God, my lord! [As to what you, Moon God, have] indicated by omen—if you have announced evil against me, behold, I have given [substit]utes in (my) place. Take these, [and leave me alone]![72]

After this, the scene of the ritual changes. A bull is brought forward and offered, whereupon the king says:

> [Behold], as to what you, Moon God, have indicated by omen, if you have indica[ted] some evi[l] against me [ ] you have sought to see with (your own) eyes [my] (funeral) smoke [ ] Behold, I myself have come up. To you [I have brought] these [substi]tutes. [ ] See [i]ts smoke! Let these die! But let me not die![73]

---

[71]On the difference between substitution and mere transference of evil, see Gurney, *Aspects*, 52. On substitution rites and the terminology for substitutes, see N. van Brock, "Substitution rituelle," *RHA* 65 (1959) 117–46; Gurney, *Aspects*, 52–58; M. Vieyra, "Le sorcier hittite," *Le Monde du Sorcier* (SOr 7; Paris: Editions du Seuil, 1966) 113. See also the remarks of M. Weinfeld, "Social and Cultic Institutions in the Priestly Source Against Their Ancient Near Eastern Background," *Proceedings of the Eighth World Congress of Jewish Studies: Panel Session—Bible Studies and Hebrew Language* (Jerusalem, 1983) 113-114, on the connection of Hittite substitution terminology and the Day of Atonement ritual.

[72]StBoT 3, 8 vs. 7′–11′ (= *ANET*, 355).

[73]StBoT 3, 8 vs. 13′–16′, following Kümmel's textual reconstructions (in *Ersatzrituale*).

A few lines later, a prisoner is dressed and anointed as a substitute king, and the following is said:

> Behold, this (is) the king. [I have placed] on this one the name of kingship. I have clothed this one with the roy[al clothing]. I have se[t] the royal headdress on this one. Evil omen, short years, and short days, take note of [this one]! Go after this substitute![74]

The prisoner is then released and taken back to his land.[75]

1.3.4 Entreaty and Appeasement[76]

Divinities are often called upon to remove evils afflicting a patient, to take them far away from him, and to keep them away. Such earnest appeals are generally accompanied by offerings (usually of meats, breads, and beverages) to appease the invoked deity and successfully enlist his aid. The deity thus propitiated may be the one causing the evil or it may be another requested to alter the course of affliction that another angry god has initiated. In addition to being petitioned to remove evil, the gods may be asked to grant health and well-being to the patient.

A few examples will demonstrate this motif. In the Ayatarsa ritual, the sun god of sickness is entreated to cure a child of his sickness. The ritual practitioner offers a sheep to the deity and says:

> O Sun God of sickness, behold, to you I have given an offering. The child whom I keep mentioning and whose name I speak, O Sun God of sickness, remove sickness from this child!

---

[74]StBoT 3, 10 vs. 20′–24′.

[75]On the dispatch of impurity to the enemy's land, see chap. 9, section 9.4.2, below.

[76]On this motif, see G. Furlani, "Il peccato nella religione degli Hittiti," *GSAI* 3 (1935) 134–35, 142–43. Besides occurring in rituals (see the instances, below) the ideas of entreaty and appeasement occur in prayers (cf. especially the Mursili plague prayers, *ANET*, 394–96) and in evocation rituals where gods are enticed to return with blessing for the people (see Haas and Wilhelm, *Hurritische und luwische Riten*, 143–246; *KUB* 15.34+ [= *ANET*, 351–53]; Goetze, *Kulturgeschichte*, 160; Engelhard, "Magical Practices," 105–10).

The sheep is then cut up and presented to the deity with other offerings.[77]

A specimen of entreaty and appeasement for the granting of positive virtues is found in the Hatiya ritual. Various breads are broken before the deity DMAḪ and the D*Gulšeš* divinities, and the practitioner says:

> Behold, the offerer has given an offering to you, so you, [D*Gulšeš* and DM]AḪ, [give] to the offerer life, health, vi[gor, long years, e]yesight, strength, (and) stature [fo]r the fu[ture]![78]

1.3.5 Analogy[79]

Purification by analogy is the invoking of a comparison between the impure condition of the patient and an external and essentially unrelated phenomenon whose character symbolizes analogically the desired resultant state of purity or invigoration for the patient. Though the analogical situation may only be referred to by description,[80] it is most often made concrete, either by using a phenomenon or item already present in the ritual materials or environment to which the participants

---

77Ayatarsa i 6–8. Other examples of removing evil by entreaty and appeasement are: Tunnawi iv 24–28, 29–37; Malli ii 26′–33′, 34′, 39′; iv 14–29; StBoT 8 ii 4–12; iii 10–16; iv 5–10; Tuthaliya and Nikalmati i 22–28, 29–37; ii 17–21, 22–29, 41–44; Mastigga iii 38–43, 44–48, 49–53; Ambazzi ii 2, 41–45 (see below); Papanikri i 39–47; Telepinu ii 5–9; *KUB* 17.27 ii 20–25 (= *ANET*, 347a); House Purification i 39–ii 7 and passim; Plague Ritual i 31–33; ii 3–17; Pulisa i 16–21 (see below, section 1.4.1); Ashella i 12–14, 19–23 (see below, section 1.4.2); Uhhamuwa 24–31 (see below, section 1.4.3); Gassuliyawiya Prayer ii 18–26; Anniwiyani ii 27–33.

78StBoT 2 vs. 22–25. This ritual is largely a rite of entreaty and appeasement and should be consulted in its entirety. For other examples of blessing granted by entreaty, see Tuthaliya and Nikalmati ii 36–40; Uhhamuwa iii 1–5. Mixed concepts of removing evil and granting vigor appear in Tuthaliya and Nikalmati ii 30–35; iii 28′-39′.

79See generally Goetze, *Kulturgeschichte*, 156–58. On analogy in Greek ritual, see Parker, *Miasma*, 232 and n. 152 there.

80Huwarlu i 44–46; Uhhamuwa ii 54–57.

might give their attention,[81] or, as usually is the case, by acting out the analogy.[82]

For example, in the Ambazzi ritual, the Old Woman officiant places pinecones and grain in a pan and roasts them. This mixture is extinguished while an accompanying analogical declaration is made: "As I have extinguished these, in the same way may evil also be extinguished for the offerers."[83]

In an incantation ritual involving underworld divinities, wine is poured on a roof. The act carries the words:

> As water flows down from [the roof, and] does not go [back again] to the gu[tter], so may the evil, [the impurit]y, the oath, the bloody deed, the tears, the sin, the curses, (and) the "cutting-off" of this house be poured out and not come back again.[84]

The foregoing examples have shown analogy being used to rid the patient (a human or a house) of an impure condition. Analogy can also be used to impart blessing to the patient. An excellent example is found in the Tunnawi ritual in which a patient is suffering from sexual impotency. The practitioner grabs the horn of a fertile cow and says:

> Sun God, my lord, just as this cow is fecund, and (is) in a fecund pen, and keeps filling the pen with bulls (and) cows. Indeed, in the same way may the offerer be fecund! May she likewise fill (her) house with sons, daughters, grandchildren, great-grandchildren, [ ] in successive generations.[85]

---

[81]Anniwiyani iii 42–44; Samuha ii 58–61; Telepinu ii 15–18, 19–21.

[82]Ambazzi ii 25–28; Amihatna i 30–31, 35–38; iii 9–12, 17–24; House Purification i 24–27; Huwarlu i 7–18; Mastigga i 31′–35′; ii 44–54; ii 55–iii 6; iii 54–iv 8 (cf. *CHD* L, 18); Samuha ii 36–37, 38–39; Tunnawi ii 18–20; iii 43–45; Tuthaliya and Nikalmati ii 12–16.

[83]Ambazzi ii 2–8 (the declaration is in lines 7-8); see Anniwiyani iv 1–5 for another quenching analogy.

[84]House Purification i 28–34.

[85]Tunnawi iv 7–13. Other examples of granting strength and blessing by analogy are: Building Ritual iv 9–12, 13–16, 17–21, 22–25; Huwarlu i 58–60; *KUB* 15.34 ii 25–27 (= *ANET*, 353a); Telepinu ii 23–25; Tunnawi iv 15–23; Tuthaliya and Nikalmati ii 5–7; iii 51′–52′.

To the foregoing uses of analogy to remove evil and impart vitality can be added the use of this motif in the formulations of sanctions against treaty and oath breakers.[86]

1.3.6 Concretizing[87]

The cases of transfer, detergent, and substitution are concerned with the riddance of the actual evil from the patient's person. In concretizing, abstract, intangible evils are made symbolically concrete. Certain materials that represent the evil are placed on the patient's body and then removed. This analogically expresses the desire that the evil be removed.

In the Tunnawi ritual, for example, the patient is dressed in black clothing. The Old Woman rips off the patient's black shirt, takes off his black footwear, takes away some black wool stuffed in his ears and says:

> Behold, I am taking away from him blackness and yellowness arising from a word of uncleanness, on account of which word of uncleanness he became black and yellow. I am taking sin away.[88]

The evil is represented by the black clothing which is then removed to symbolize purification.

Another common method of concretizing the riddance of evil is placing threads, often colored, on the patient and then removing them and disposing of them in some way. Two paragraphs from the Malli ritual which contains a series[89] of thread manipulations illustrate this:

> The Old Woman pla[ces a thread] on the man's knees. The [Old Wo]man [places] it upon his head. She sa[ys the following]: "Whoever keeps b[inding] him and [be]witching him, now, I am [tak]ing the [sorcery from

---

[86]See the Soldiers' Oath throughout and *KUB* 13.3 ii 29–iii 2 (= *ANET*, 207a; J. Friedrich, "Reinheitsvorschriften für den hethitischen König," *MAOG* 4 [1928–29] 47, 49): Suppiluliuma and Kurtiwaza treaty, *ANET*, 206. Cf. Goetze, *Kulturgeschichte*, 155.

[87]Vieyra ("Sorcier," 119) suggested this motif.

[88]Tunnawi ii 46–49. following K. K. Riemschneider, "Hethitisch 'gelb/grün,'" *MIO* 5 (1957) 144–45. For another example of clothing removal, see Mastigga iv 7.

[89]Malli i 31′–ii 16′.

> him] and [am giving] it back to [its] master." [She winds] the [th]read around the figures.
>
> ---
>
> [Nex]t [she makes a thread] of red wool [in the same way and says: "Whoever has made] him blood red, [now, I am] tak[ing from him blood]redness [and] I am giv[ing it back to] i[ts master. She] winds the th[read around the figure]s.[90]

In these paragraphs the threads represent evil. In the first, the thread is used to signify the binding influence of the evil. The thread is removed, signifying the loosening of the spell, and put back on figurines representing the sorcerer who caused the affliction.[91] In the second paragraph, the evil is represented by a red thread. Similarly, in ensuing paragraphs of this ritual, black, yellow, and blue threads are employed in the same way. The colors represent the unnatural and mortifying evils that afflict the patient. They are removed and put on the figures, thus indicating the purification of the patient.[92]

1.3.7 Annulment[93]

This motif is exhibited in ritual actions which represent a reversal or cancellation of the impurity. This motif was present in the examples from the Malli ritual, cited in the previous section on concretizing, in

---

[90] i 31–36, 37–40.

[91] On binding and loosing as a representation of evil and purification, see V. Haas, "Die Unterwelts- und Jenseitsvorstellungen im hethitischen Kleinasien," *Or* 45 (1976) 204–5 and Haas and Thiel, *Beschwörungs-rituale*, 40–46.

[92] For a discussion of thread manipulation, see Goetze, *Kultur-geschichte*, 156; Riemschneider, "Hethitisch 'gelb/grün,'" 141–47; L. Jakob-Rost, *Das Ritual der Malli aus Arzawa gegen Behexung (KUB XXXIV 9+)* (THeth 2; Heidelberg: Carl Winter, 1972) 86–87. Other examples of thread manipulation are Ambazzi ii 15–20; Anniwiyani i 10–25; Huwarlu i 27–32, 33–37; StBoT 8 iv 14–22; Tunnawi ii 28–40 and see the texts discussed, below. Though one may argue that threads are used as objects of transfer which absorb the evil from the patient (cf. Engelhard, "Magical Practices," 138–40), the fact that they are colored or "bound" on the patient indicates that they represent the evil rather than absorb it.

[93] This category is taken from Vieyra, "Sorcier," 118.

which evil was put back on the sorcerer who caused it. Annulment is also seen in the onion analogy in the Samuha ritual. The practitioner is given an onion and says:

> If before a god someone [keeps sa]ying the following: "Behold, just as an onion is wrapped up with layers, one [not] able to separ[ate] from the other, let evil, oath, curse, and uncleanness be wrapped up like an onion around the temple!" Now, behold, I have peeled away this onion (and) have retained this one scanty stalk. In this way may evil word, oa[th, cu]rse, and uncleanness be peeled away from [befor]e the god! Let the god and offerer be clean from th[at ma]tter![94]

Here, the supposition is that someone has used the analogy of an onion to bring impurity on the temple. The practitioner therefore reverses the curse by peeling the layers off the onion. The remaining bare stem represents the purified temple.[95]

1.3.8 Disposal

This motif is manifested when evils or materials considered to be infected with evil or symbolizing evil are finally discarded. Since this particular motif is the subject of this larger study, no examples are necessary here. I mention this motif here separately only to give a more complete list of the various motifs appearing in Hittite rituals.

1.3.9 Prevention

This motif is evident in acts that seek to keep an evil from returning after it has been dispelled or to prevent it from having any effect in the first place.

In the Huwarlu ritual, a model dog is made and given the following commission:

---

[94]Samuha rs. 36–41.

[95]See also the next ritual action in the Samuha ritual (rs. 42–47), where it is supposed that the one who has brought evil on the god twisted a cord to the left. The evil is annulled by twisting the cord to the right. Cf. *KUB* 17.27 ii 28–41 (= *ANET*, 347); Engelhard, "Magical Practices," 136–40.

> You are the small dog of the table of the king and queen. As during the day you do not let another man into the house, (so) let no baneful word in during this night![96]

Somewhat differently in the Malli ritual, cathartic materials loaded with evil are buried and secured in the ground with pegs to prevent the escape of the impurity:

> She (i.e., the Old Woman) throws all this on the figures. The Old Woman takes up five breads, one jug of beer, peg(s), (and) *karšani*-plant. She goes outside. In the area she digs the ground (and) places the ritual materials therein. She scatters mud on top (and) smooths (it) over. She hammers the pegs. She says the following: "Whoever has bewitched this (person), now, I have taken his bewitching back (and) I have placed it down in the earth. I have fixed it. Let the bewitching (and) evil dreams be fixed! Let it not come back up! Let the Dark Earth (i.e., the nether world) keep it![97]

In this example we have a hint of an additional feature of the prevention motif: asking the gods to keep the evil away from the patient. In the ensuing portion of this ritual, this sort of request is explicitly made, accompanied by appeasement offerings.[98] Such requests are frequent when impurities are being discarded.[99]

The idea of disposing of evil so that it cannot return is also found in discarding impurities in the *ukturi-* dumping place or in sealing impure bathing water in a pot.[100]

---

[96]Huwarlu i 23–26; cf. ii 13–23.

[97]Malli ii 16′–25′. On nailing down evils with pegs, see Ambazzi iv 28–32; Riemschneider, "Hethitisch 'gelb/grün,'" 146 (citing *VBoT* 3 iii 9–16); E. H. Sturtevant and G. Bechtel, *A Hittite Chrestomathy* (WDWLS; Philadelphia: Linguistic Society of America and the University of Pennsylvania, 1935) 121 (citing *KUB* 12.44 iii 2–9); and also Engelhard, "Magical Practices," 115–17; Goetze, *Kulturgeschichte*, 159. Compare also Birth Ritual H ii 4′–8′ where pegs are fixed outside a room, perhaps as an apotropaic device (see the note of G. Beckman, "Hittite Birth Rituals" [PhD diss., Yale University, 1977] 121–22).

[98]Malli ii 26′–33′, 34′–39′.

[99]Cf. Ambazzi iv 28–32; House Purification iii 1–12.

[100]See chap. 9, section 9.4.2, below.

1.3.10 Invigoration

One last motif which we have seen already in some of the examples in the discussion on analogy, entreaty and appeasement is that of invigoration. This is when, after the evil has been removed, rites and prayers are performed to bring health and well-being to the patient.[101]

1.4 HITTITE PARALLELS: THE TEXTS

We are now ready to examine a few Hittite rituals of disposal and compare them with the biblical scapegoat rite. I will treat each ritual passage separately, giving a translation followed by a discussion.

1.4.1 The Ritual of Pulisa

i
1. [Th]us (says) Pulisa [if the king]
2. smites the [la]nd of an enemy an[d from the border of the land of the enemy]
3. he marches [away of the land of the enemy]
4. [ei]ther some [male]god [or a female god among(?)]
5. the people a plague occur[s]

---

6. When he [marches a]way from the border of the land of the enemy,
7. they take one prisoner and one woman of the land. [On which road] the ki[ng]
8. came from the land of the enemy, to that road the king m[oves].
9. All the leaders move down to him. One prisoner
10. and one woman they bring forth to him. He removes the clothes from himself.
11. They put them on the man. But on the woman
12. [they p]ut clothes of a woman. The king speaks

---

[101]See the examples in sections 1.3.4 and 1.3.5. Also cf. Goetze, *Kulturgeschichte*, 155–56. To this category belongs the Glückwunschformel (see A. Kammenhuber, "Hethitisch *innarauu̯atar*, $^{(LÚ)}$KALA-*tar* und Verwandtes," *MSS* 3 [1958] 33–36; also Carruba, *Beschwörungsritual*, 18; G. Szabó, *Ein hethitisches Entsühnungsritual für das Königspaar Tutḫalii̯a und Nikalmati* [THeth 1; Heidelberg: Carl Winter, 1971] 66, 87, n. 7).

13. thus to the man—bu[t] if it is [not] convenient to the king, then he sen[ds] another person. That one
14. takes care of the rite. That one [spe]aks [to the] man thus: "If
15. some male god of the enemy land has caused this plague, b[ehol]d, to him
16. I have given the decorated man as a substitute man. At his head this o[ne is gr]eat,
17. at the heart this one is great, at the member this o[ne is gre]at.
18. You, male god, be appeased with t[his de]corated man.
19. But to the king, the [leaders], the ar[my, and the]
20. land of Hatti, tur[n yourself fa]ithfully. [ ] But
21. let this prisoner b[ear] the plague and carry (it) ba[ck into the land of the enemy."]

---

22. And [t]o the woman he speak[s l]ikewise regarding the fema[le go]d.

---

23. Afterward, [they drive up] one bull and one e[we] of the la[nd] of the enemy.
24. Him, his ears, earrin[gs(?)]
25. red wool, green wool, bla[ck] wool, [white wool] from the king's
26. mouth he dra[ws] forth. [He speaks the following:]
27. "In regard to the king becoming blood [red, green,]
28. [d]ark, and white]
29. [th]is back to the land of the en[emy]
30. and [to the king] himself, the leaders, the ar[my], the [ho]rse[s]
31. [do not] pay attention, (but) take note of it for the land of the enemy." [ ]
32. [ ] takes. It on emmer [ ]
33. [The bull with e]arrings
34. He spe[aks] thus: "The god of the en[emy who caused this plague]
35. if he is a male god, to you I have gi[ven] the deco[rated],
36. [ear]ringed approved(??) [bull]. You, male god,
37. be appeased. Let [th]is bull carry [this plague]
38. back into the land of the enemy. [To the king, the]

king'[s sons],
39. the leaders, the army, and the la[nd of Hatti turn yourself faithfully."]

---

40. Afterwards, the deco[rated] ewe [ ]
41. he speaks likewise, regarding the female god [ ]

42–43. Then th[ey se]nd forth the decorated bull [and the ewe to the prisoner] and the woman.
(The rest is broken.)

The goal of this ritual is to banish a plague, caused by an angry deity, that breaks out among the Hittite army as it is returning from battle waged in an enemy's land.[102] To achieve this purpose, two humans, a male and female captive from the foreign country (line 7), and a bull and ewe, also from the foreign land (line 23), are selected as substitutes and bearers of the plague.

Various motifs of purification appear interwoven throughout this ritual. Attention is first directed to those manifested in the case of the male prisoner. The first thing to note is that the prisoner is offered as a gift of appeasement to the angry deity. He is clothed with the king's attire (lines 10–11), after which the king (or his representative, lines 13–14) seeks to entice the god to accept the man as a gift and be reconciled. He does this by indicating to the god that the man is "decorated" (line 16) and that he is a possessor of superb physical qualities (lines 16–17).[103] This positive description is capped with the request that the deity be appeased with the prisoner (line 18).

But the prisoner is more than a gift to the god. By putting on the king's clothes he becomes a substitute for the king. This is made explicit in the prayer where he is called a "substitute man" (LÚ *PU-ḪI-*

---

[102]For an example of real plague occurring after contact with an enemy, see the "Plague Prayers of Mursilis," paragraph 4 (= *ANET*, 395).

[103]On the commendation or praise of the substitute to the god, see Kümmel, *Ersatzrituale*, 120–21. We will see, below, the praising of rams to a god in the Ashella ritual (lines 20–21). In the Gassuliyawiya Prayer (vs. 10–14), a substitute is praised before the afflicting divinity: "For you, this is my substitute. I have sent her to you decorated. (In comparison) to me, she is good, she is pure, she is brilliant, she is white, she is furnished with everything. Now god, my lord, look on this one." Also compare the Huwarlu ritual, ii 9–10, below.

ŠU; line 16). Of course, he is not only a substitute for the king, but for the whole of the army afflicted by the plague and, more generally, the people of the land, as indicated by the request that the god establish peaceful relations with the king, the army, its leaders, and the land of Hatti (lines 19–20).

The woman is treated in much the same way as the man (note the clothing difference in lines 11–12), and so we, like the ritual's author, Pulisa, need not say much about her except to note that her rite is performed with regard to a female deity (line 22). It appears that rather than taking an oracle to determine if a male or female deity was responsible (cf. line 4), as was possible when the source of evil was unknown,[104] the performers of the rite would use both a man and a woman to cover all possibilities.

In the last part of the ritual (lines 22–41), a bull and ewe (note again the sexual congruence corresponding to the male and female divinities; cf. lines 40–41) are prepared to serve the same functions as the humans. The instructions given apply directly to the bull, but it is clear from lines 40–41 that the ewe was treated similarly. A notable difference in this part of the ritual is the appearance of the motif of concretization. Various colored threads are pulled from the mouth of the king and placed on the bull (lines 25–26).[105] The prayer which follows this placement of the threads shows that they represent the evil that has been affecting the king (lines 27–31). By being concretized, the evil can be symbolically transferred from the king to the animal, leaving the king unaffected. But, as is possible and expected with ritual symbols, the colored threads have multiple meanings and therefore signify more than just evil. They are also a decorative device to make the animal more attractive to the deity. These, together with the earrings (cf. lines 24, 33), make the animal acceptable as a propitiatory offering (lines 35–37).[105a]

---

[104]Cf. Mursilis Sprachlähmung (vs. 9–11) where the cause for Mursili's affliction is determined by oracle.

[105]The text does not expressly say that the wools are placed on the animal. However, this is to be understood from the context of other similar rites (cf. Gurney, *Aspects*, 48; Kümmel, *Ersatzrituale*, 120).

[105a]W. W. Fowler (cited apud V. Turner, "Sacrifice as Quintessential Process: Prophylaxis or Abandonment," *HR* 16 [1977] 203) says the decorating of an animal in Roman sacrifice was to "mark it off from the other animals as holy."

At the end of the rite, after all the preparations and prayers are completed, the animals and people are sent away to the enemy land (lines 20–21, 37–38, 42–43). This means that they are not simply substitutes to suffer the evil in the place of the army, but are also transporters of evil which carry it away to an innocuous locale.

The biblical scapegoat rite, though having a general scheme like that of the Pulisa rite, significantly contrasts with it. One of the main differences in the biblical rite is the lack of the appeasement motif. In Lev 16 as it is presently constituted, there is no angry deity to appease. It is true that the goat is sent to Azazel. But that is all we know about Azazel; he figures only as the goal to which the goat is sent. He otherwise has no part to play in the rite and concomitant theology. The Hittite rite, on the other hand, is wholly devoted to the appeasement of an angry deity mentioned repeatedly as an active agent throughout the ritual. The contrast between the treatment of the deity in the Pulisa rite to that of Azazel in the Bible—and I cannot stress this difference enough—underscores the impression that Azazel is not to be thought of as a demon receiving an appeasement offering, but merely as a signifier of the destination of impurity.

The lack of the appeasement motif in the scapegoat rite is also observed in the treatment of the dispatched goat. It is not decorated, sacrificed, or otherwise made appealing as a gift of appeasement to Azazel. It is simply sent away as a carrier of evil.

This leads to another significant contrast. In the Pulisa rite, the persons and animals are substitutes. They become the object of the god's wrath and plague. In the Bible's rite, the goat is just a transporter of impurity. There is no indication that the goat suffers in the place of the people when their sins are placed on it.

Both rites are essentially similar in that the impurity is removed from the community and sent away from it to the open country or to the enemy land. The difference in the specific place of disposal is determined partly by each society's concept of the proper place of evil and partly by the geographical setting of the rites. As for the Bible, communicable impurity is generally disposed of outside the habitation.[106] Thus the open country is sufficiently remote for disposal, yet sufficiently close for the convenience of those performing the ritual. In Hittite ritual, the enemy land is often designated as a place of disposal. In this particular rite, it is chosen because the evil originates from it, and the army,

---

[106]See chap. 9.

according to the context, is still close enough to the foreign land to make disposal there possible.[107]

Finally, deserving of mention is the difference between the evils removed in the two rites. In the Bible, Israel's *sins* are placed on the animal, whereas in the Pulisa rite, a deity-caused *plague* is dispatched.[108] The difference is not terribly significant since elimination rites may treat any one of a number of evils. But the difference is important since it brings to our attention the fact that the evil in the scapegoat rite is not a demonically active force attacking Israel.[109]

1.4.2 The Ritual of Ashella

1. Thus (says) Ashella, the man of Hapalla:
2. If in the land or in the army a plague occurs (variant: if the year is bad/inimical and i[n] the army [a plague occurs]),
3. I perform this ritual:

---

4. I take this (variant: I do the following): When day becomes night,
5. all whoever are the leaders of the army, each
6. one prepares a ram. If the ram(s) are white
7. or black it does not matter. A cord
8. of white wool, red wool, (and) green wool I wind together. He weaves them (into) one(?).
9. I bring together one *erimmatu*-bead and one ring of iron and lead (variant: one ring of chalcedony).
10. I bind them on the necks and horns of the rams.
11. They bind them (i.e., the rams) before the tents at night.
12. They say the following at that time: "Whatever god is moving about,
13. whatever god has caused this plague, for you, behold, these rams
14. I have tied up. Be herewith appeased!"

---

[107]See chap. 9, section 9.4.2.

[108]On the similarity and difference of mere pollution versus the anger of a deity in Greek religion, see Parker, *Miasma*, 8–10.

[109]For non-Priestly examples of disposal in a foreign land, see chap. 9, n. 150.

15. At morning, I drive them to the open country. With each ram
16. they take a jug of beer, one thick bread, (and) one cup of milk(?). Before the tent of the king
17. he has a decorated woman sit. He places with the woman one *ḫuppar*-vessel of beer and three thick breads.

---

18. Then, the leaders of the army place their hands on the rams.
19. Thereupon, they say the following: "Whatever god has caused this plague,
20. now, behold, the rams are standing; they are very fat in liver,
21. heart, and member.
22. Let the flesh of humans be hateful to him. Moreover,
23. be appeased with these rams." The leaders of the army show reverence
24. to the rams, and the king shows reverence to the decorated woman.
25. Then they bring the rams and the woman, the bread, and the beer out through the army.
26. They drive them to the open country. They go and make them run inside the border of the enemy
27. (so that) they do not arrive at any place of ours.
28. Thereupon in this way they say: "Behold, whatever evil of this army
29. was among men, cattle, sheep, horses, mules,
30. and donkeys, now, behold,
31. these rams and woman have taken it out from the camp.
32. Whoever finds them, may that land receive this evil plague."

The Ashella ritual manifests the same general concerns as the Pulisa ritual, but with some interesting variation. The evil in the two is the same: a plague caused by an angry deity in the army or, as Ashella adds, in the land in general (line 2). An unspecified number of rams (one for each leader of the army, lines 4–6) and a woman (line 17), all probably spoils from the enemy land like the substitutes in the Pulisa rite, are selected to be carriers of the evil.

The Ashella rite contains the same purification motifs as does the Pulisa rite. First to be observed is the concretizing of evil in the placement of colored wools, an *erimmatu*-bead, and a ring of iron and lead on the rams (lines 8–10). This placement surely signifies the transfer of evil to the animals though there is no explicit act of removing the wools and other objects from the patient symbolizing the transfer as in the Pulisa rite. But if the motif of transfer is not clearly evident in the placement of the wools, it is certainly to be found in the bringing of the rams and woman through the army (lines 25–26).[110] This is similar to the Roman ritual of *lustratio* in which a bearer of impurity is led or carried about an area or among people from which it will take the evil.[111] By passing through the army, the rams and woman receive the evil and are then disposed of.[112]

The disposal of the impurity here is much the same as that in the Pulisa rite, but prescribed in a little more detail. The rams and woman are driven to the open country (lines 15, 26) and then further on to the enemy land (line 26). The final release of the evil carriers is

---

[110]Cf. G. Furlani, *La religione degli Hittiti* (Storia delle religioni 13; Bologna: N. Zanichelli, 1936) 219, n. 125.

[111]See Boehm, "Lustratio," *Paulys Real-Encyclopädie der classischen Altertumswissenschaft* 13 (1926) 2029–39; Parker, *Miasma*, 225–26. Cf. Servius on Vergil's Aeneid, ii 75, cited in J. Harrison, *Prolegomena to the Study of Greek Religion* (2d ed.; Cambridge: Cambridge University, 1908; reprint, London: Merlin, 1962) 107–8. A specially prepared person is "led about through the whole city to the accompaniment of curses, in order that upon him may fall all the ills of the whole city, and thus he is cast headlong down."

[112]Another Hittite ritual contains an excellent example of *lustratio*:

> He/she brings a goat and *šurašura*-bird through the city. From which gate they take people out to execute (them), from it you take out these (animals). In which place people die, to that place you bring them. They burn the goat and bury the *šurašura*-bird. He/she says: "as this goat and *šurašura*-bird has gone down under the earth, so may this sickness, blood, oath, and the tongue of the many go down under the earth."

(*KUB* 30.34 iv 19–29; partially cited in Engelhard, "Magical Practices," 161; H. Otten, *Hethitische Totenrituale* (DAWBIO 37; Berlin: Akademie, 1958] 9.)

accompanied by a prayer stating that they have taken away the evil (lines 28–31). The last line adds the hope that the plague become active in the enemy land.

One motif present in the Ashella rite not found in Pulisa is that of prevention. The carriers are not just sent to the enemy land, but are taken there in such a way that they will not be able to return to the land of Hatti (line 27). Though a sure way of preventing their return would be to put them to death, it appears that they were only led to a place where foreigners would find and keep them (line 32).[113]

In addition to the motifs of concretizing, transfer, disposal, and prevention, the motifs of appeasement and substitution appear. Appeasement is indicated by the decoration of the rams with wools and the necklace made of *erimmatu*-beads and a metal ring (lines 7–10), and the decoration of the woman (lines 16–17).[114] This idea is further seen in leaving the rams over night with a prayer to the plague causing deity that he be appeased with the rams (lines 12–14). The request for appeasement occurs again in a later prayer where the superb physical qualities of the rams are pointed out to the god (lines 19–23). The rams and woman are also provided with beer, bread, and milk which are certainly to be understood as appeasement offerings to the god (lines 16–17, 25).

Substitution is visible in the prayer that accompanies the handlaying rite (lines 18–23). The leaders ask the god to be satisfied with the rams instead of their human flesh. Here is expressed the idea that plague is the god's feasting on human victims. The god is therefore offered a more pleasing object on which to feast so that the humans may be left alone.

As we turn to a comparison with the scapegoat rite, much of what was said in the comparison of the Pulisa and scapegoat rites applies here. The feature of an angry deity who needs appeasement stands again in stark contrast to the shadowy figure of Azazel in the Bible. This is a further indication that Azazel is not to be considered a being who needs to be propitiated. The lack of the idea of appeasement in the Bible is

---

[113]Cf. 1 Sam 6:10–16.

[114]Haas (*Berggötter*, 173–74) suggests that the *erimmatu*-bead and metal ring form a type of amulet which prevents the evil from spreading. R. Stefanini (private communication), more correctly, believes that they are representations of the evil (private communication).

also evident in the plain, unadorned scapegoat. It is not decorated nor is it provided with offerings of appeasement, such as breads or wine.

Another significant difference in the scapegoat and Ashella rite is the meaning of the handlaying act (lines 18–23). As we noted in the discussion of the scapegoat, the handlaying together with the confession of the sins serves to transfer the sins to the head of the animal. Some investigators, perhaps influenced by the meaning of handlaying in Lev 16, assume that the handlaying in the Ashella rite similarly transfers the evil to the rams.[115] The context, however, does not bear this out. The rite is accompanied by a prayer (lines 18–23) asking the god to be appeased with the high quality rams and to leave the humans alone. There is no mention of the transference of evil, as one finds, for example, in the Ambazzi ritual,[116] when cathartic materials are removed from a patient and placed on a "scapemouse" or in the biblical scapegoat handlaying act. The context of the gesture in the Ashella rite indicates that it signifies the *designation* of the animals as the leaders' gifts of appeasement to the angry deity.[117] This conclusion is further supported by the phenomenon of handlaying in Hittite ritual generally. It is the means of identifying offering materials or other objects as ritually belonging to the one who performs the handlaying.[118]

---

[115]Furlani, *Religione*, 203–4, 219 and n. 125.

[116]Ambazzi ii 37–39; see below.

[117]A. M. Rodriguez ("Substitution in the Hebrew Cultus and in Cultic Related Texts" [PhD diss., Andrews University, 1980] 216) recognizes this meaning for the rite, but he erroneously adds that it also signifies substitution. The general scheme of handlaying in Hittite ritual prevents us assigning this latter meaning to the act. See the next note.

[118]In Hittite handlaying, an offerer places one hand on an object or at a distance from it. The gesture is usually found with offering materials, usually prepared foods such as bread, wine, cheese, and livers. Much less frequently live animals receive handlaying as in the Ashella rite. In examples where the ritual description continues with the distribution of the offerings, another cultic functionary, not the one who performed the handlaying, makes the distribution. This division of duties indicates that handlaying serves to ritually identify the offering material as coming from the handlayer, even though the handlayer does not make the offering personally. Thus the handlayer receives the ritual credit as if he or she performed the entire offering. An example of handlaying which verifies this meaning of the rite is found outside the scheme of offerings in a purification ritual where a patient shoots an arrow signifying the dispatch of evil. The text reads: "The offerer, if a male, . . .[ ] he shoots (the

One last difference between the scapegoat and the Ashella rites is the lack of the motif of prevention in the former. In later Judaism, the animal was killed to prevent its return, but in the early Priestly ritual it seems concern about the animal's return was minimal.[119] Hittite literature too does not always show a concern to complete the disposal rite by doing something to prevent the return of a living bearer of impurity. In the Pulisa ritual, for example, nothing is said about preventing the return of the substitutes.

1.4.3 The Ritual of Uhhamuwa

ii 17. Thus (says) Uhhamuwa, the man of Arzawa: If in the land

---

arrow) by himself. But if a female, she places her hand on the bow and the ^{LÚ}AZU shoots (the arrow)" (*KUB* 29.8 ii 8–11; cf. the comments of H. Hoffner, "Symbols for Masculinity and Femininity: Their Use in Ancient Near Eastern Sympathetic Magic Rituals," *JBL* 85 [1966] 331, n. 27 and Engelhard, "Magical Practices," 40). Notably, the terminology describing the handlaying here is exactly the same as found with other handlaying rites: *nu-uš-ša-an A-NA* ^{GIŠ}BAN *QA-TAM da-a-i*. Since the woman does not shoot the arrow herself, she places her hand over it so that when the ^{LÚ}AZU performs it, it is as though she did it. (This reminds one of the gesture of King Joash and Elisha in 2 Kgs 13:15–17.)

One problematic example of handlaying is Mursili's performance of the gesture in the rite to remove the evil causing a speech defect of some sort (Mursilis Sprachlähmung). It was determined by oracle that he should send a substitute bull (GUD *puḫugari*) and other items to the temple at Kumanni as part of his repentance. The bull was decorated and Mursili placed his hand on it (vs. 15–16). The bull was sent to Kumanni and there burned (vs. 11–12; rs. 36–37). Though it may be tempting to view the handlaying here as a transfer of the evil to the bull (cf. E. Neu, *Ein althethitisches Gewitterritual* [StBoT 12; Wiesbaden: Otto Harrassowitz, 1970] 47; M. Vieyra, "Rites de purification hittites," *RHR* 119 [1939] 136), it actually has the same meaning as other handlaying examples. Since Mursili is not going to Kumanni and will not officiate in the rite personally, he places his hand on the bull to show that notwithstanding his absence, it is still his offering and he is to be given credit by the god for offering the animal. For a detailed study, see Wright, "Hand Placement"; Wright and Milgrom, "*Sāmaḵ*." On biblical handlaying, see n. 6, above.

[119]See n. 27, above.

18. they keep dying, and if some god of
19. the enemy has caused it, I perform the following:

---

20. They drive up one ram. Blue wool, red wool, green wool,
21. black wool, and white wool they twine together. They
22. make it as a wool crown. They put it on the head of the ram. The ram
23. they drive forth to the road of the enemy.
24. They say the following to him: "Whatever god
25. of the enemy has caused this plague, behold, this
26. crowned ram to you, O god,
27. we have driven up for peaceful relations. As the herd is strong
28. and is peaceful toward this ram,
29. so may you, whatever god who has caused this plague,
30. be likewise peaceful toward Hatti land.
31. Turn faithfully toward Hatti land."
32. The crowned ram
33. they drive away into the enemy land.

As in the Pulisa and Ashella rituals, the removal of a plague caused by an angry deity is the object of the Uhhamuwa ritual. The plague here, however, is said to be occurring only in the land, not in the army (lines 17–19). Still, the angry god is an enemy god, and the disposal of the plague will occur in the enemy land (lines 23, 32–33).

Motifs found in this rite in addition to disposal are the concretizing of evil by using colored threads (lines 20–21), the transfer of the evil to the animal in the form of threads (lines 21–22), the offering of the ram as a decorated appeasement gift (lines 21–22, 26), and the use of the animal as a substitute which is implicit in the similarity of the rite to the Pulisa and Ashella rites and in the words: "this crowned ram to you, O god, we have driven up for peaceful relations" (lines 25–27).

A new feature in this ritual is the appearance of the idea of invigoration in the form of a positive analogy (lines 27–31). The ram, which is being used as a carrier of the impurity, an appeasement gift, and a substitute, is now being used as the subject of an analogy. It is hoped that as the ram is the recipient of peaceful behavior from the herd, so Hatti land will be the recipient of peaceful behavior from the angry god. A hint of invigoration has already been encountered in the Pulisa ritual when the god was requested to act faithfully toward the Hittites (cf. there, lines 19–20, 38–39).

The Uhhamuwa ritual contrasts with the biblical ritual in the same ways as the Pulisa and Ashella rites do. This rite is essentially an appeasement and disposal rite while the scapegoat is only a disposal rite.

1.4.4 The Ritual of Ambazzi[120]

ii 34. She wraps a little tin on the bowstring.
35. She puts it on the right hand (and) feet of the offerers.

---

36. Then she takes it away
37. and puts it on a mouse (saying): "I have
38. taken away from you evil and I have put it on
39. the mouse. Let this mouse take it to the high mountains,
40. the deep valleys (and) the distant ways."

---

41. She lets the mouse go (saying): "Alawaimi,
42. drive this (mouse) forth, and I will give to you a goat to eat."
(Offerings to Alawaimi and other gods follow.)

This segment of the larger Ambazzi ritual which is performed to rid the patients of "evil sickness"[121] and "evil tension"[122] is significantly different from the foregoing Hittite plague rituals and more conceptually similar to the biblical scapegoat rite because it lacks the idea of substitution[123] and appeasement of an evil-causing deity by means of the dispatched animal. It is merely a rite of transfer and disposal as is the biblical rite.

---

[120] This section of the Ambazzi ritual is paralleled by i 34–44 and iii 38–47.

[121] *Idalu inan*, cf. ii 29; iii 33; iv 10′.

[122] *Idalu ḫuitteššar*, cf. i 19; ii 20; iii 25.

[123] Though Alawaimi may be an evil-causing deity (cf. ii 2–5), I cannot agree with Engelhard ("Magical Practices," 171) that the mouse is a substitute punished in place of the patients. The mouse is merely a carrier of evil.

The transfer of the evil is thoroughly lucid. A bowstring wrapped with tin thus concretizing the evil[124] is placed on the patients and is then removed and placed on a mouse (lines 34–37). The officiator accompanies this action with a declaration to the patients that the evil has been transferred to the mouse (lines 37–39). The mouse, charged with the task of disposing of the evil by taking it to remote places (lines 39–40), is let loose (line 41).

To this point, the conceptual outline of this rite and the biblical rite has been much the same. But the Ambazzi ritual adds a motif. The practitioner entreats the divinity Alawaimi to help in removing the evil-laden mouse. A goat is offered to the god to ensure his aid.[125] It is possible that in a pre-Priestly form of the scapegoat rite Azazel functioned as the custodian of the evil like Alawaimi. But, just as the silence of the present biblical text does not provide evidence that Azazel is a god or demon in need of propitiation, there is likewise no evidence that Azazel is now to be considered the custodian of the evil. Again we see that in comparison to the divinities in the Hittite texts, Azazel remains a very opaque figure.

1.4.5 The Ritual of Huwarlu

ii
5. . . . They take a small live dog.
6. They wa[ve] it over the king and queen
7. and they wave it inside the palace. The Ol[d Woman thus]
8. speaks: "Whatever [magical]
9. word is in the king and queen, in his(!) body, and in the palace, behold,
10. (his) member (is) great, his heart (is) great. He, the 'ass,' will bear (it).

---

[124]In the preceding paragraphs (ii 15–23), a cord and a bowstring are strung on the patient to symbolize the "evil tension" afflicting them. The bowstring and tin here are also to be understood as representing the evil.

[125]In section iii 38–47 the god is told to "take" the mouse rather than to "drive" it away. Certainly it makes no sense to think that the mouse is for appeasement. The word "take" here should be understood as "take away," and not "take for yourself."

11. He has overcome it. Let him take away the evil, the ma[gical word].
12. Wherever the gods have designated it,
13. there let him carry it." When they
14. take away the small live dog, . . .

This section of the Huwarlu ritual, as well as the rest of the ritual, is devoted to the elimination of "magical word" (*kallar uttar*[126]) from the royal pair and the palace. It appears to be a rite of transfer, not of substitution, and thus is essentially similar to the Ambazzi passage just examined.

A live dog is chosen as the bearer of impurity. The transfer is effected by waving the dog over the couple (line 6). It is also waved inside the palace (line 7), similar to the *lustratio*-type rite in the Ashella ritual where the rams and woman are brought through the army. An incantation is recited, exorcising the evil (lines 8–13). In this speech, the dog is praised, as were the bearers of impurity in the Pulisa (lines 16–17, 35–36), Ashella (lines 20–21), and Uhhamuwa (lines 25–26) rituals. But, whereas in these other rituals the praise of the bearer was for the purpose of proving to the deity that the animal or person was an acceptable appeasement offering, in the Huwarlu rite, the praise is not directed to an angry god and thus serves only as a means of magically increasing the dog's capability as a bearer of evil. Note particularly the metaphor in line 10 where the dog is called an ass. Such aggrandizement enables the dog to more effectively remove the evil.[127] Once the evil has been transferred to the dog, the animal is taken away, but there is no indication of where it is taken. We only know that it was dispatched "wherever the gods have designated it" (line 12). Other items used in this ritual are thrown away (lines 30–31; not cited here), apparently in the open country (line 28). In the Tunnawi ritual[128] a pig and dog are burned after having been "held over" a patient. In the Mastigga ritual[129] a dog is killed and buried after patients have spit into its mouth, thereby

---

[126]See Kronasser, "Das hethitische Ritual," 100–01.

[127]Earlier in the ritual (i 62–70) various cathartic materials are identified with the "Staff men of the Weather God" (*ŠA* ^{D}IM LÚ^{MEŠ} ^{GIŠ}GIDRI), apparently to enhance their purgative ability. See also i 14.

[128]i 60–64; iii 17–20.

[129]iii 14–16.

transferring the evil. We can assume that some similar method of disposal was carried out with the dog in the Huwarlu ritual.

This Hittite rite seems to be the most similar to the scapegoat rite in regard to the purification motifs it bears. In both rites, a live animal receives the impurity and transports it away. But apart from the general motifs that form the basis of this comparison, there are significant differences. One is the incantation expressing the ability of the dog to bear the evil (lines 8–13). The scapegoat rite lacks any similar expressions. Why? Priestly legislation generally rejects oral accompaniments to its purification rites. We do not find any prescriptions for recitations or prayers to accompany ritual acts. Only actions are prescribed.[129a] Incantations like the one in the Huwarlu ritual would be theologically unthinkable in the Priestly material since they attribute the effectiveness of the rite to the cathartic instruments rather than to God. The sins are not removed because the scapegoat has the power by itself to receive them and bear them away. They are removed because of the divine power and supervision accompanying the performance of the ceremony.

1.5 MESOPOTAMIAN PARALLELS TO THE SCAPEGOAT

The Mesopotamian corpus of ritual material, like the Hittite corpus, yields many examples of the elimination of evils by transfer and disposal which relate conceptually to the biblical scapegoat rite.[130] In such rites the demonic ill of an affected patient or building is transferred to another object which is then disposed of in an appropriate place.[131] In this section I will examine a few key texts which contain the central motifs of transfer and disposal at the same time noting some of the other motifs that occur.[132]

[129a]See J. Milgrom, "Magic, Monotheism and the Sin of Moses," *The Quest for the Kingdom of God: Studies in Honor of George E. Mendenhall* (ed. H. B. Huffmon, et al.; Winona Lake: Eisenbrauns, 1983) 251–65.

[130]There are many rites of this type. Kümmel in his study on elimination rites in Mesopotamia, Anatolia, and the Bible ("Ersatzkönig," 313) discounted the prevalence of elimination rites in Mesopotamia. Our study shows that elimination rites were as common in Mesopotamia as in Anatolia.

[131]See chap. 9, section 9.4.1.

[132]A few other examples of transfer rites worth mentioning include:

(a) The rituals for treatment of a *lamaštu* attack (D. W. Myhrman, "Die Labartu-Texte: Babylonische Beschwörungsformeln nebst Zauberverfahren gegen die Dämonin Labartu," *ZA* 16 [1902] 194: 34–38; cf. 192: 20–25; 160: 23–27) prescribe that one should make a figurine of the demon and place it at the head of a patient for three days. This contact or proximity is probably to transfer the demonic infection to the model (cf. B. Meissner, *Babylonien und Assyrien* [2 vols.; Heidelberg: Carl Winter, 1925] 2. 223). At the end of the third day, the figurine is taken out, cut up (*maḫāṣu*) with a knife, and buried in a corner of the wall. A protective flour circle is then apparently drawn around the burial place. The one performing the rite leaves without looking back. A variation of this is where a model of the *lamaštu* and an ass are made, provisioned with various foods and then, after three days, the items are taken out to the steppe (Myhrman, "Labartu-Texte," 164–66: iv 3–11). On the *lamaštu* in art, see chap. 9, n. 75.

(b) In a namburbi rite to avert the evil of a creaking beam (Caplice, "Namburbi Texts in the British Museum, V," *Or* 40 [1971] 133), dust from the beam is put on a live fish. Due to damage in the text, it is not clear what is done with the fish, but since it is to be caught alive and in view of incantations elsewhere that make reference to fish carrying evil to the *apsû* (see chap. 2, section 2.2), it seems likely that the fish was put back into the river alive, as a "scapefish," to carry away the evil.

(c) In another ritual (*CT* 17.32: 1–20 = *DES* 2. 108), a figure of the patient is made and water is passed over it (*šubūʾu*; on this action, see n. 136, below). It is not clear if the object of this action, LÚ *šú-a-tú*, refers to the man or to his figurine. I take it as the latter since the water is gathered up in a vessel which would be more feasible with the smaller figure. The water, having flowed off his body with the accompanying statement, "may *namtaru* flow from his body like water," is put into a pot and then poured out in the plaza (*rebītu*). Then follows this wish: "Let the plaza carry the affliction which lessened his strength, let the spittle be poured out like water, let sorcery which is mixed with spittle return behind!"

(d) One text, often brought into the discussion of the biblical scapegoat rite (see Ahituv, "*ʿĂzāʾzēl*," 114; Tawil, "ʿAzazel," 54; M. Weinfeld, "The Teaching of Julius Wellhausen: A New Estimation After a Century Since the Appearance of his Book *Prolegomena to the History of Ancient Israel*," *Shenaton* 4 [1980] 85 [Hebrew]; "Social and Cultic Institutions," 113), should be mentioned here. In this ritual (*KAR* 33 = *TuL* 73–76), a patient has a sickness which does not allow him to eat or drink. A goat is tied up at the head of his bed. A stick with twined wools, a cup of water, and an almond branch are obtained. The next morning the goat and other objects are taken to the wilderness (*mu-da-bi-*

1.5.1 The Fifth Day of the *Akītu* Festival[133]

One of the most widely known disposal rites from Mesopotamia is that occurring on the fifth day of the *akītu* festival for the purification of the Ezida cella of the god Nabu in Marduk's larger temple, Esagila.[134]

---

ri). The stick and cup are left in one place, while the almond branch and goat are placed in another place. The goat is slaughtered. The legs are put in the skin, the head is cut off, and the flesh is cooked. Bronze bowls with honey and oil in them are brought. The skin is put around the almond branch. The front legs are tied with snares. A hole is dug in which the honey and oil are placed. A foreleg (uzu*da-ra-*ʾ) is cut off and put in the hole. The almond branch is placed in the hole, and on top of it, the other foreleg. From here the text is broken and obscure. We can only understand fully the last lines which say that the patient has been healed. This rite does not seem to exhibit transfer and elimination. Rather, the goat is a substitute for the man. The slaughter and cooking of the animal, plus the deposit of honey, oil, and flesh parts into the hole are to be considered an offering, not a disposal of an impure scapegoat. Ahituv has suggested that this is an offering taken and given to a demon in the wilderness. More specifically, I think it is either an offering given to a god to aid the patient in his quest for healing or, better, an offering given to the demon (*ilu raṣmu*, cf. vs. 1; rs. 10) who is affecting him as a substitute for himself. In this way it would be much like the Hittite plague rituals which manifest the motif of substitution. But this understanding is complicated by the patient's eating of the meat which should be for the angry god ([U]ZU.MEŠ *an-nu-u* KÚ, rs. 7; the text is broken here and thus the activity is not entirely clear). It seems somewhat strange for a patient to eat the meat intended to placate a deity. Further, it is not clear how the wilderness locale is to be viewed here. It may have no significance in this particular rite as a place where evil is disposed. With all these obscurities and complications, the text cannot really be effectively compared to the biblical rite.

133A copy, transliteration and translation of this ritual is published in F. Thureau-Dangin, *Rituels accadiens* (Paris: Ernest Levoux, 1921) 127–54. An English translation appears in *ANET*, 331–34. For a recent treatment of the *akītu* festival in general, see J. A. Black, "The New Year Ceremonies in Ancient Babylon: 'Taking Bel by the Hand' and a Cultic Picnic," *Religion* 11 (1981) 39–59. A recent comparison of this section of the ritual with the Day of Atonement ritual is in M. Weinfeld, "Social and Cultic Institutions," 111-13.

134In lines 345–47, the *mašmaššu*, the "exorcist" (see *CAD*, *AHw*, s.v.; cf. J. Renger, "Untersuchungen zum Priestertum in der altbabylonischen

After purifying the larger temple by use of a copper bell,[135] censer, and torch,[136] the *mašmaššu*

346–47. enters the Ezida, the cella of Nabu.
347–48. He purifies the temple[137] [ ] with censer and torch and *egubbû*-vessel
348–49. He sprinkles water from the Tigris and Euphrates cisterns.
350. He anoints the doors of the entire chamber with cedar oil.[138]
351. In the middle of the court of the cella, he places a silver censer.

Zeit, 2. Teil," *ZA* 59 [1969] 223–30), enters the Ezida, which is defined as the cella of Nabu (*pa-pa-ḫi* ᵈ*Nabu*). The rest of the rite that we are concerned with occurs in this cella (cf. lines 348, 350, 351, 356). Ezida is usually to be understood as the name of Nabu's temple in Borsippa, but such an interpretation does not fit here. S. A. Pallis (*The Babylonian Akîtu Festival* [KDVS, 12/1; Copenhagen: Bianco Lunos, 1926] 87) shows correctly that the Ezida here is a smaller chapel within the Esagila structure.

[135]NÍG.KALA.GA.URUDU (line 342); *RAcc* "timbale," *ANET* "kettle-drum." *CAD* H, 34, translates the relevant line: "the *mašmaššu* . . . will make the copperbell(?) (an unidentified percussion instrument) sound forth shrilly." The exorcistic use of this bell may be compared to the *lilissu* drum which was used in purification rites (see F. Thureau-Dangin, "Un Acte de Donation de Marduk-Zâkir-Šumi," *RA* 16 [1919] 145 for a Mesopotamian illustration of this drum on a clay tablet; cf. A. L. Oppenheim and E. Reiner, *Ancient Mesopotamia: Portrait of a Dead Civilization* [rev. ed.; Chicago: University of Chicago, 1977] 178–79; *CAD*, under *lilissu*). See the bronze bell in *ANEP*, picture 665, which has an exorcistic scene on it. "The bell was probably used to drive out the evil spirits by sound" (description, p. 329).

[136]NÍG.NA = *nignakku* "censer"; GI.IZI.LÁ = *gizillû* "torch of reed for cultic purposes" (*CAD* G, 113). Both the *nignakku* and the *gizillû* are often found in tandem as in the present ritual. They are often accompanied by the verb *šubū'u* which designates the act of moving the censer and torch alongside of something or someone, or inside a room, in order to purify them (*CAD* B, 181–82). See the segment from the *asakkī marṣūti* ritual, below, line 86.

[137]This is still Nabu's cella; see n. 134.

[138]Ì.GIŠ.ERIN is cedar oil, not cedar resin (so *ANET*); see *CAD* E, 227.

352. On top he mixes perfumes and cypress.
353. He summons the slaughterer.[139] He decapitates a ram.
354. The *mašmaššu* wipes the temple with the carcass of the ram.
355. He recites the incantations for exorcising the temple.
356. He purifies the whole cella including its surrounding areas and then takes down the censer.
357. The *mašmaššu* takes up the carcass of that ram
358. and goes to the river. He sets his face westward and
359. throws the carcass of that ram into the river.
360. He goes to the open country.[140] The slaughterer does the same with the ram's head.
361–62. The *mašmaššu* and the slaughterer go out to the open country. As long as Nabu is in Babylon, they shall not enter Babylon.
363. From the fifth day to the twelfth day they dwell in the open country

This rite is simply for the transfer and disposal of evils affecting Nabu's cella; it contains no motif of substitution as often appears in Hittite and other Mesopotamian rituals. The carcass of the ram is used to wipe away evils present in the room (line 354). It thereby becomes saturated with impurity and must be disposed of properly by casting it into the river (line 359).[141] Because the rite only manifests the ideas of transfer and disposal, it is conceptually similar to the scapegoat rite.

Another notable similarity between the two rites is the pollution incurred by the officiants. In the *akītu* rite, the *mašmaššu* and the slaughterer cannot return to the sanctuary complex but must remain in the open country until the end of the festival (lines 360–363). This implies that they have suffered pollution from the rite. This perception

---

[139]Read GÍR.LÁ as *ṭābiḫu* (*AHw*, 1376).

[140]EDIN = *ṣēru* "steppe, open country." See chap. 9, section 9.4.1, below.

[141]The rite is similar to the disposal of the *ḥaṭṭā't* remnants (Lev 16:27). The body of the *ḥaṭṭā't* animal is impure after the blood application in various parts of the Tabernacle; hence, the animal must be discarded. However, instead of casting it into a river, it is burned in a pure place outside the camp (cf. Lev 4:11). See chap. 6.

is underscored by the stipulation that the *šešgallu*[142] is not to observe the exorcising of the temple lest he become impure. Only after the rite is completed can the *šešgallu* resume his work in the temple.[143] In the scapegoat rite, the one who led the goat out to the wilderness and the one who burned the *ḥaṭṭāʾt* carcasses are impure and need to bathe before reentering the camp (Lev 16: 26, 28).

Another similarity between the two rites is that both are used once a year in connection with cleansing a sanctuary. Yet, beyond this broad similarity, the two rites are in striking contrast. The scapegoat rite is the climax (or one of the climaxes) of the ceremonies on the Day of Atonement, carrying away all of the nation's sins. The Babylonian rite, however, is relatively minor, being concerned with only one of many cellae in the larger temple, and that of a visiting god, Nabu. The purification of Nabu's cella is by no means one of the great climaxes of the *akītu* festival, such as the procession to the *akītu* house, the ritual battle, or the arrival of Nabu for the festival. This cleansing rite, together with setting up the "Golden Heaven" in the cella and arranging various offerings,[144] are all preparatory acts done prior to Nabu's arrival from Borsippa. Consequently, it is inappropriate to consider this rite an annual temple cleansing rite on the same order as the Day of Atonement in the Bible.

1.5.2 A Ritual from the *Utukkī Lemnūti* Series[145]

A ritual segment from the *utukkī lemnūti* series shows a disposal rite similar to the New Year festival rite, but for the benefit of a person rather than a building. Ea instructs his son, Marduk, how to purify the patient who is beset by demons:

> 115–16. At evening, bring a *mašḫultuppû*-goat to the man's body, son of his god.
>
> 117–18. Bind his head with the headband of the *mašḫultuppû*-goat.

---

[142]Do not read *urigallu*; see *AHw*, 1220a.

[143]Lines 364–68, not cited here.

[144]Lines 369–70, not cited here.

[145]Edited and translated by O. Gurney, "Babylonian Prophylactic Figures and their Rituals," *AAA* 22 (1935) 86–89.

119. Whether it is an evil *utukku*-demon, an evil *alû*-demon, an evil *eṭimmu*-demon, an evil *gallû*-demon, an evil god, an evil *rābiṣu*-demon,
120. a *lamaštu*-demon, a *labaṣu*-demon, an *aḫḫāzu*-demon,
121. an *utukku*-demon which overcomes a man, an *eṭemmu*-demon which has seized a man,
122. an evil one, one who has an evil face, an evil mouth, an evil tongue,
123. headache, toothache, chest pain or intestinal disease—
124–25. by means of this incantation let them be torn away from his head!
126–27. May Ishum, the great messenger and exalted overseer of the gods, stand at his head! May he not cease (to stand at his head)!
128–29. Let your pure and exalted mouth say: "Arise from the body of the restless man!
130–31. Let everything evil arise and go out to the place of Ereshkigal!"[146]
132–33. Carry away the skin of the *mašḫultuppû*-goat from the body of the restless man.
134–35. [Throw it] into the square, in the wide street.
136–37. Let everything evil ret[urn] to the earth! (See n. 146.)

This ritual, like the foregoing rite for the cleansing of Nabu's cella and the scapegoat ritual, contains only the motif of transfer and disposal. Substitution is not present. A goatskin[147] is placed on or near the patient (lines 115–16, 132–33). After an incantation calling on Ishum to help in the removal of the evil (lines 126–31)—an example of entreaty—the text speaks of removing the goat skin and throwing it into the street (lines 132–35).[148] This symbolizes the return of the evil to the underworld (lines 136–37). The goat's headband placed on the patient (lines 117–18) serves to absorb the evil or, like the colored wools in Hittite rites, to concretize the evil. The expression in lines

---

[146]The place of Ereshkigal is the nether world. The term "earth" (KI = *erṣitu*) indicates the underworld also.

[147]Lines 115–16 do not say that only the skin is placed by the patient, but lines 132–33 seem to indicate this was the case since only a goatskin is removed from him.

[148]On disposal in the street, see chap. 9, section 9.4.1.

124–25 ("by means of this incantation let them be torn away from his head!") implies that when this was said, the headband was removed from the patient's head, symbolizing the removal of the evil.[149]

An important contrast with the biblical scapegoat evident in this rite is the nature of the evils removed. Here the evil is demonic afflictions as the long list of demons in lines 119–23 indicates. In the scapegoat rite, only the people's sins which affect the sanctuary are removed. There is no concern about exorcising demons. Another contrast is found in the idea of discarding evils in the underworld (lines 130–31, 136–37). The biblical rite does not carry this idea as we determined earlier.

1.5.3 A Ritual from the *Asakkī Marṣūti* Series[150]

68–69. He cannot sleep, he ca[nnot] rest.
70–71. He has caused his god concern.[151]
72. Marduk noticed. "Whatever I know.[152] Go my son!
73–74. Take a white goat of Dumuzi.
75–76. Lay it near the sick person.
77–78. Remove its heart.
79–80. Place it in the hand of that man.
81. Recite the incantation of Eridu.
82–85. Wipe that man with the goat whose heart you removed and with bread and dough.[153]
86. Pass censer and torch alongside of him.[154]

149For a similar action, but with an unclean type of headgear which is thrown into the *rebītu*, see *CT* 17.26: 73–79 (= *DES* 2. 94–96). In another ritual, a *tigillû* ("Koloquinte") and goathair are tied to a patient's head (*CT* 17.19–20: 36–51 = *DES* 2. 67–68). These items are to take away headache. The disposal of them is not specified. Cf. also *TuL* 68 vs. 13–14.

150*CT* 17.10–11: 68–87 (= *DES* 2. 32–35).

151Cf. *CAD* A/2, 423a.

152The phrases "Marduk noticed. 'Whatever I know.'" are abbreviations of a larger dialogue between Ea and Marduk often found in ritual instructions. A full form is observed in Shurpu vii 37–50 (note especially 37, 51, 53, where the phrases in this line of the *asakkī marṣūti* rite occur).

153The verb *kuppuru* can take two accusatives, one of the object wiped and one of the material used for wiping (see appendix 2 on *kuppuru*). See the translation in *CAD* A/1, 239a.

154See n. 136.

87. Dump (the materials[?]) out in the street.
88–89. Draw a flour circle (around) that man."

This ritual segment from the *asakkī marṣūti* series is again an example of transfer and disposal. Ea instructs Marduk to take a goat and place it near a person suffering from demonic affliction who is now restless and cannot sleep (lines 68–69). The heart is removed and placed in the patient's hand (lines 77–80). After an incantation, the goat and some bread and dough are used to wipe the man (lines 82–85). A censer and torch are then passed over the patient (line 86). Finally the wiping materials, censer, and torch are apparently thrown into the street (line 87).[155] This rite is similar to the one in the *utukkī lemnūti* series. Thus the contrasts with the biblical rite are much the same and do not need discussion.

1.5.4 A Ritual from the Shurpu Series

A most intriguing example of transfer and disposal is found in the Shurpu series. Ea instructs Marduk how to relieve a person suffering from demonic sickness. He says:

vii 53. [Go my son, Mar]duk!
54–55. Take seven loaves of bread made of pure *tappinni*-flour.
56. String (them) on a bronze (skewer).
57. Set a carnelian bead (on it).
58–59. Wipe the man (with it), son of his god, whom the curse has seized.
60–61. Cast his spit upon the wiping material.
62. Cast the incantation of Eridu (upon it).
63. Take (it) out to the open country, the pure place.

---

[155]It is not absolutely clear that the wiping materials are placed in the street since no object is explicitly mentioned (line 87: SILA.ŠÈ U.ME.NI.DUB.DUB.BU "you shall dump in the street"). The syntactic unit immediately preceding mentions the censer and torch. Hence, it might be thought that these items alone are put in the street. However, due to the fact that in other rites, wiping materials and other objects of transfer may be thrown into the street (see chap. 9, section 9.4.1), I am persuaded that in addition to the censer and torch, the kid, bread and dough were also placed in the street.

64. Place (it) at the base of an *ašāgu*-bush.[156]
65–66. Remove from his body [the disease? that be]set him.
67–68. Deliver his curse [to the] Lady of the Open Country and Plain.[157]
69–70. May Ninkilim, lord of animals, transfer his serious illness to the vermin of the ground!

The transfer of evil is effected by wiping the patient with loaves of bread (lines 58–59). The patient also spits on the breads to further transfer his affliction (lines 60–61).[158] The materials are taken far from the patient to the open country and put in the custody of gods in charge of this area and the animals there (lines 67–70). Though an animal is not used here as the vehicle of transfer, the rite is extraordinarily similar to the biblical rite since, like the scapegoat, the impurity laden material is disposed of in the wilderness. Even more striking is the mention of deities of the steppe and animals to which the impurity is delivered. The phrase "deliver his curse [to the] Lady of the Open Country and Plain" (lines 67–68) is amazingly similar to the biblical requirement of sending the goat to Azazel in the wilderness (Lev 16:10). Yet it is in this very similarity that the greatest contrast is found. The desert deities in Shurpu are very prominent and active. Ninkilim is called upon to act in transferring the evil to the vermin (line 69–70). The ensuing portion of the ritual calls upon other deities to revive, purify, and bless the patient.[159] In contrast, Azazel does not act; he has no personality. The name refers more to a locale than a supernatural figure.

1.5.5 A Namburbi Ritual for the Evil of a Dog[160]

Vs.10–11. A namburbi ritual for the evil of a dog which howls and moans in a man's house

---

[156]Compare the burial of figurines at the base of an *ašāgu*-bush in Castellino, "Rituals and Prayers Against 'Appearing Ghosts,'" *Or* 24 (1955) 260, line 24.

[157] d*Bēlit* EDIN *u ba-ma-a-ti.* In Maqlu (iv 25) the patient's affection by sorcery is described in part as being delivered over to this personality.

[158]Cf. the Hittite examples in n. 56, above.

[159]Lines 71–85.

[160]Caplice, "Namburbi Texts in the British Museum, II," *Or* 36 (1967) 1–8; E. Ebeling, "Beiträge zur Kenntnis den Beschwörungsserie Namburbi [Part 9]," *RA* 50 (1956) 90–94.

12. [o]r spatters its urine on a man. You recite (the incantation) three times.
13. The evil of that dog will not come near the man and his house.

---

14. Its ritual: You make a dog of clay.
15. You place cedar wood on its neck. You sprinkle oil on its head.
16–17. You put goathair on it. You place horsehair for its tail. You set up a reed altar at the river bank before Shamash.
18. You arrange twelve loaves of emmer. You pile up dates and fine flour.
19. You set out *mirsu*-confection, honey, and ghee.
20–21. You set up a *pīḫu*-jug. You fill two *kukkubu*-containers with fine beer and set (them) out. You set out a censer of juniper wood.
22. You libate fine beer. You make the man kneel.
23. He lifts up that figurine and says the following:

---

24. Incantation: Shamash, king of heaven and earth, judge of areas above and below,
25. luminary of the gods, governor of mankind,
26. the one who gives judgement on the great gods—
27. I turn to you; I seek you. Among the gods command that I live!
28. Let the gods who are with you command my prosperity!
29–30. On account of this dog who has urinated on me I am afraid,
31. disturbed, and worried.
32. Avert the evil of this dog from me
33. so that I may proclaim your glory.

---

34. [Wh]en he has recited this before Shamash,
35. you say the following over that figurine:

---

36. I have given you [as] my [ ]; I have given you as my substitute.
37. [I have stripped off all the evil] of my body onto you.

Rs. 1. I have stripped off, I have strip[ped off] all the evil of my flesh onto you.

2. I have stripped off all the evil of my bodily figure onto you.
3. [I have st]ripped off all the evil before and behind me onto you.

---

4. When you have recited this, you leave the presence of Shamash and
5. go [off] before the ri[ver]. You recite the following:

---

6. Incantation: You, River, are the creator of everything.
7. I, so-and-so, the son of so-and-so, whose god is so-and-so, whose goddess is so-and-so—
8. that d[og] has spattered his urine on me.
9. I am afraid and disturbed.
10. [Just as] this figurine will not return to its place,
11. (so) may its evil not come near! [May it not ap]proach! May it not draw near!
12. May it not appear to [m]e! May the evil of that dog be far from my body
13. so that I may da[ily bl]ess you;
14. so that those who s[ee m]e may forever proclaim your [glor]y.
15. Incantation: Car[ry] that dog to the depths.
16. Do n[ot re]lease it! Take it down to your depths.
17. Remov[e] the evi[l] of the dog from my body!
18. Give me happiness and health!

---

19. When you have recited this three times,
20. you throw that dog (i.e., the figurine) into the river. Tha[t m]an
21. shall not look behind him. He enters a tavern and [its] e[vil will be undone].

The purpose of namburbi rites in general is to avert portended evil.[161] In this particular ritual some indefinite calamity is signaled by a dog howling in a person's house (lines vs. 10–11) or by a dog urinating on a

---

[161]Caplice, "Namburbi Texts in the British Museum, I," *Or* 34 (1965) 105; *The Akkadian Namburbi Texts: An Introduction* (SANE 1/1; Malibu: Undena, 1974) 7–9.

person (lines vs. 12, 29–30; rs. 8). A rite containing the motifs of transfer and substitution is prescribed to cancel the omen and avert or annul the coming evil. The ritual officiator makes a clay dog (lines vs. 14–17). The patient kneels, lifts the figurine up before Shamash (line vs. 23) to whom various offerings have been given (lines vs. 17–22), and recites an incantation to the god requesting the god's aid in freeing him of the evil (lines vs. 24–33). The officiator then recites an incantation directed to the model, apparently on behalf of the patient, stating that the evil has been stripped off the patient and put on the model (lines vs. 36–rs. 3). This is not just a transfer of evil to the dog, but it also makes the model a substitute for the patient (line vs. 36). The model now becomes the target of the impending evil, releasing the patient from danger.

The last part of the rite concerns the disposal of the model dog. The officiator and patient go to the river (lines rs. 4–5). The officiator, again on behalf of the patient, recites two incantations to the river requesting its aid in disposing of the evil (lines rs. 6–14, 15–18). An analogy is used in lines rs. 10–11 expressing the hope that the evil will remain far from the patient. The motif of prevention is found in the latter incantation which requests the river to take the model dog to its depths and not release it. The final act in the rite is casting the figurine into the river (lines rs. 19–20). This disposal in the river reminds us of the disposal of the ram carcass used to cleanse Nabu's cella in the *akītu* festival.

The use of a model dog indicates another motif present in the rite—that of concretizing. The model by its form represents the dog and the evil that it portended. It gives the evil concrete reality so that it might be easily discarded.

This rite significantly differs from the scapegoat rite because it has a number of motifs foreign to the latter: substitution, entreaty and appeasement, analogy, concretization, annulment, and prevention. Though the general schemes of the rites are similar, they are conceptually far apart.

1.6 CONCLUSION

We now can summarize the results of this chapter. There is a definite conceptual gulf between the Hittite and Mesopotamian rites referred to here and the biblical scapegoat rite. This is mainly visible in the lack of the ideas of substitution and appeasement in the latter. Azazel does not appear to be an angry deity who needs to be appeased nor a desert demon who is the custodian of evil. The goat, moreover, is not an offering of appeasement, nor is it a substitute to suffer Azazel's anger or some other evil in the place of the Israelites. The animal merely receives the community's sins and bears them to a harmless locale.

Of course, not all of the nonbiblical rites carry the motifs of substitution and appeasement (cf. the Huwarlu and *akītu* rituals), but they are still distinct from the biblical rite in other respects. One of the main impressions obtained from a study of elimination rites in Hittite and Mesopotamian religion is that they are used quite frequently. In contrast, the Priestly regulations, and even the Bible at large, seem to limit the use of such rites. Furthermore, in the nonbiblical cultures, the rites are employed for diverse purposes and occasions, sometimes for purifying sanctuaries, but usually for relieving the impure maladies of individuals and objects. We do not observe any overlying systematization in their intent and use. But the Priestly rites of elimination have been systematized with a common cultic orientation. The high frequency and unsystematized character of the nonbiblical rites is probably due, in part, to the conception of evil and impurity among the people who employ them. Mankind and its concerns are perceived as being frequently beset by many types of evils: plague caused by angry deities, witchcraft, sorcery, sickness, demons who cause evils, and the like. Such frequency and multiplicity of affections demand frequent and variously applied rites. Conversely, the Priestly rules limit the frequency and types of rites because this corpus' conception of evils is limited. The object of purification rites is always ritual impurity except for sins in the scapegoat rite. We never find the wrath of angry deities, demonic attack, witchcraft, sorcery, and sickness as objects of purification in P.

Another important contrast is that the Bible does not view the dismissal of the scapegoat to the wilderness as a disposal of evil in the nether world as some of the nonbiblical rites have exhibited. Sending the goat to the wilderness is only to remove the impurity from the sanctuary and habitation so that they might become and remain clean.

Finally, a few words of speculation about what the scapegoat rite might have been like before incorporation into Priestly legislation. That there was a preexistence to this rite is indicated by the figure Azazel. It makes little sense to suppose that a depersonalized demon with little functional purpose as a demon was cast in a rite that originated with the Priestly legislators. We would expect that P would have constructed the rite without such a figure. Azazel as presented by the text can only be part of the baggage of a rite already in existence which was taken over by the Priestly writers and reformulated to accord with Priestly conceptions. The reformulation left the personality depersonalized. What was Azazel like in the earlier non-Priestly form of the rite? We can only speculate broadly from the similar nonbiblical rites. He could have been an angry deity (as the etymology ʿzz-ʾl "fierce god" implies) causing havoc among people. If so, then the goat could have been an appeasement offering. As in the Hittite plague rituals, the evil would have been placed on the appeasement goat and sent away to angry Azazel. If not an angry deity, Azazel could have been a custodian of the evil like the divinities in the Ambazzi and Shurpu rituals. In this case, the goat would have been only a transporter of evil, not an offering, but perhaps accompanied by offerings such as breads and wine, for appeasement or payment. The impossibility of getting significantly beyond the present form and meaning of the rite is obvious. It quickly becomes a construction of suppositions. Nevertheless, the possibility of an earlier form such as I have suggested shows how radically Priestly legislation has altered the rite.

2

The Dispatch of Birds in the Purification of the Impurity of *Ṣāraʿat*

2.1 INTRODUCTION: THE BIBLICAL RITE

Conceptually similar to the disposal of impurity by means of the scapegoat are the rites using live birds to carry away the residual impurity of *ṣāraʿat*[1] from a person healed from this condition or a

[1]I use the transliteration *ṣāraʿat* for the human skin disease or nonhuman fungal growth discussed in Lev 13–14 and elsewhere in the Bible for want of a satisfactory translation. It is common knowledge now that biblical *ṣāraʿat* is not modern leprosy (Hansen's disease) and that the translation "leprosy" is misleading (see D. P. Wright and R. N. Jones, "Leprosy," *ABD*, forthcoming). Other translations such as "scale disease" or "skin disease" do not adequately describe *ṣāraʿat* in reference to humans on the one hand, and building materials and fabrics on the other. On *ṣāraʿat*, see M. W. Dols, "Leprosy in Medieval Arabic Medicine," *JHMAS* 36 (1979) 314–33; "The Leper in Medieval Islamic Society," *Speculum* 58 (1983) 891–916; K. P. C. A. Gramberg, "Leprosy and the Bible," *TGM* 11 (1959) 127–39; E. V. Hulse, "The Nature of Biblical 'Leprosy' and the Use of Alternative Medical Terms in Modern Translations of the Bible," *PEQ* 107 (1975) 87–105; F. C. Lendrum, "The Name 'Leprosy,'" *AJTMH* 1 (1952) 999–1008; J. J. Pilch, "Biblical Leprosy and Body Symbolism," *BTB* 11 (1981) 108–113; J. Tas, "On Leprosy in the Bible," *Actes du septieme Congrés International d'Histoire des Sciences* (ed. F. S. Bodenheimer; Paris: Academie Internationale d'Histoire des Sciences and Hermann, 1953) 583–87. On *ṣāraʿat* in houses and fabrics, see chap. 3.

renovated house (Lev 14:2–7, 48–53).[2] In this chapter I will discuss the meaning of these disposal rites which use birds and their relationship to the Day of Atonement purification ritual. I will then examine rites using birds as bearers of impurity in Mesopotamian and Hittite texts to help assess the relation of the biblical bird rites to the larger conceptual framework of the biblical cult.

2.1.1 The Purification of a Healed Person and Renovated House

When a priest confirms that a person who had *ṣāraʿat* has recovered from the condition, he orders that two ritually clean birds, cedar wood, scarlet stuff, and hyssop be brought for the person's purification (Lev 14:2–4). The priest has one of the birds slaughtered into an earthenware vessel[3] containing fresh water (v 5). He next takes the other bird, the cedar wood, the scarlet stuff, and hyssop and dips these in the blood-water mixture, sprinkles the liquid on the person seven times (vv 6–7), and then dispatches the bird into the open country (*ʿal pĕnê haśśādê;* v 7b).[4]

The purification of a house once infected with *ṣāraʿat* is much like that of the healed person. At the end of an implicit seven day waiting period,[5] after the renovation of the house which consists of removing

---

[2]Cf. A. Bertholet, *Leviticus* (KHC; Tübingen: J. C. B. Mohr, 1901) 46; A. Y. Brawer, "Sending the Goat to Azazel and the Bird of the Leper—Symbolic *Tašlîk*," *Beth Mikra* 12/30 (1967) 32–33 (Hebrew); D. Davies, "An Interpretation of Sacrifice in Leviticus," *ZAW* 89 (1976) 397; H. M. Kümmel, "Ersatzkönig und Sündenbock," *ZAW* 80 (1968) 311; B. Levine, *In the Presence of the Lord* (SJLA 5; Leiden: Brill, 1974) 88; J. Milgrom, "The Paradox of the Red Cow (Num. XIX)," *VT* 31 (1981) 70.

[3]On the reason for the earthenware vessel, see chap. 4, n. 14.

[4]*M. Neg.* 14:1 and *Tem.* 7:4 say that the slaughtered bird was buried. Note that the dispatched bird, like the scapegoat on the Day of Atonement, does not need to be killed (cf. D. Hoffmann, *Leviticus [Seper Wayyiqrāʾ]* [2 vols.; Jerusalem: Mossad Harav Kook, 1953] 1. 275; A. B. Ehrlich, *Randglossen zur hebräischen Bibel* [7 vols.; Leipzig: J. C. Hinrichs, 1908–14] 2. 47).

[5]The flow of the prescription in vv 37–53 should be understood in the following way. When a householder suspects *ṣāraʿat*, a priest is summoned. If the priest finds greenish or reddish spots on the wall, he closes up the house for seven days (vv 37–38). On the seventh day the priest returns for another examination. If the plague has spread, he orders

infected stones and all of the plaster in the house and then replacing them (vv 39–42), a priest comes to inspect the house (v 48). If the plague has not spread, he pronounces the house clean (v 48) and obtains the same materials for a purification rite as used in the person's purification rite (v 49). He prepares a blood-water mixture as in the rite for the healed person; dips the live bird, wood, scarlet stuff, and hyssop in the liquid; and sprinkles it seven times on the house (vv 50–51). Lastly, he sends the bird away toward the open country outside the city (*ʾel-miḥûṣ lāʿîr ʾel-pĕnê haśśādê*; vv 52–53).

2.1.2 The Meaning of the Bird Rites

The basic meaning of these rites is, with little reservation, clear.[6] Blood, a common ritual detergent in Priestly ritual, obtained from the

---

the infected stones to be removed, the inside of the house to be scraped, and new stones and a new coating of plaster to be installed (vv 39–42). After this renovation, there is another implicit waiting period (no doubt seven days long) after which the priest returns. (Compare the requirement to inspect an infected garment after seven days after having made an attempt to wash the plague out in Lev 13:54–58.) Vv 43–45 deal with the case in which the plague reappears during this waiting period. They should be translated:

> If the plague returns and breaks out in the house after the stones have been removed, after the house has been scraped, and after replastering, when the priest comes, he shall inspect (it). If the plague has spread in the house, it is malignant *ṣāraʿat* in the house. It is unclean. The house shall be torn down—its stones, its timber, and the house's plaster—and shall be taken outside the city to an unclean place.

The rules about the treatment of a *ṣāraʿat* infected house are concluded with a statement about the communicability of the impurity of an infected house in vv 46–47. Vv 48–53 continue the prescription about the priest's inspection after the house has been renovated. If the plague has not reappeared or spread, then the purification rite with birds is performed. On understanding the prescription this way, see *m. Neg.* 12:7; 13:1; Hoffmann, *Leviticus*, 1. 285.

[6]It is not our purpose to examine the significance of the cedar wood, scarlet stuff, and hyssop, whose meaning is difficult to ascertain.

slaughtered bird is used to remove *ṣāraʿat* impurity from the healed person or the renovated house.[7] As the blood-water mixture is sprinkled on the object of purification, the impurity is transferred to the live bird. The mechanics of this transfer of impurity is very much like that which occurs in the *ḥaṭṭāʾt* sacrifice ritual. When *ḥaṭṭāʾt* blood contacts a sanctum, such as the burnt offering altar, the incense altar, or the *kappōret*, the impurity of the sanctum infects the blood and by extension, the carcass of the animal.[8] The transfer of impurity to the live bird in the ritual for purification from *ṣāraʿat* impurity leaves the person or the house pure. This is indicated by the summary statements following the release of the birds ("thus he purifies him" *wĕṭihărô*, v 7b; "thus he purifies the house" *wĕḥiṭṭēʾ ʾet-habbayit*, v 52; see n. 7). The dispatch of the bird into the open country completes the purification of the person or the house by removing the impurity from the environment of the formerly plagued person or house and from the community generally. The intent to distance the evil from the community is spelled out clearly in the version of the rite for the house when it says that the priest is to send the bird "*outside of the city* to the open country" (v 53).

2.1.3 The Bird Rites and the Day of Atonement

These bird rites have a striking similarity to the two-part purification rite on the Day of Atonement. This leads to the supposition that the bird rites and Day of Atonement ritual may have a common background and origin. Both use slaughtered and live animals, a slaughtered one for

---

T. Frymer-Kensky ("Pollution, Purification, and Purgation in Biblical Israel," *The Word of the Lord Shall Go Forth: Essays in Honor of David Noel Freedman in Celebration of his Sixtieth Birthday* [ed. C. Meyers and M. O'Connor, ASOR Special Volume Series 1; Philadelphia and Winona Lake: ASOR and Eisenbrauns, 1983] 400) has offered an alternative meaning of the bird release rite: "the symbolism focuses on the living bird who has been in contact with death (dipped in the blood of the killed bird) and is then set free; so too the leper has been set free from his brush with death." This interpretation is possible, but it does not take into consideration the use of the bird's blood as a "detergent" and it can only very abstractly apply to the case of the renovated house.

[7]The bird rite does not remove all of the impurity from the healed person as is evident from the other purification rites he must undergo. The house, on the other hand, only needs the bird rite for its purification.

[8]See chap. 6 for a fuller discussion of the *ḥaṭṭāʾt* sacrifice.

supplying blood as a detergent and a live one for carrying away evil.[9] But there are also important differences in the two rites which must first be detailed before we can assess the possible historical and developmental relationship of the two.

First, in the Day of Atonement rite, two animals—a bull for the high priest and his household, and a goat for the people—supply the blood for purifying the sanctuary (Lev 16:3, 5, 11–19), while only one animal—a goat from the people—is used for disposing of the sins (vv 20–22). In contrast, only one animal supplies the blood and one carries away the impurity in the bird rites.

Secondly, in the Day of Atonement rite, the two goats from the people are called a *ḥaṭṭāʾt* sacrifice (16:5) and the slaughtered goat is performed as a *ḥaṭṭāʾt* (vv 15–19). In the *ṣāraʿat* bird rite, the birds are not treated as a *ḥaṭṭāʾt* at all.[10]

A third difference in the two rites is the relationship of the purification with the blood to the dispatch of the live animal. In the bird rites the purification and dispatch are intimately connected; the blood removes the impurity, transferring it to the live bird which then carries it away. In the Day of Atonement rite, however, the blood and scapegoat remove two different evils—impurity and sins, respectively.[11] Remembering the observation made in the previous chapter that these two evils are different sides of the same coin—that sins are the cause of impurity in the sanctuary—mitigates somewhat the divergence between the bird rites and the Day of Atonement rites. Nevertheless, the reference to different impurities in the Day of Atonement rite, though ultimately conceptually connected, loosens the connection of these two parts of the rite.

These similarities and differences suggest that a historical development has possibly taken place in which originally similar rites

---

[9]The two animals are conceptually one, cf. Y. Tas, "*Ṣāraʿat*," *EM* 6 (1971) 775 (Hebrew).

[10]On the rite's connection to the *ḥaṭṭāʾt* scheme see Y. Kaufmann, *The History of Israelite Belief: From Ancient Times Until the End of the Second Temple (Toledot haʾEmuna hayYiśreʾelit Mime Qedem ʿad Sop Bayit Šeni)* (4 vols; Jerusalem and Tel-Aviv: Bialik Institute and Dvir, 1937-38) 1. 569. We should caution against calling the slaughter of the bird a sacrifice (contra Douglas Davies, "Interpretation," 396–97) since it is not performed with reference to God and its blood is not used at or in connection with the sanctuary.

[11]See chap. 1, section 1.1.2.

have become quite different from one another. I propose the following tentative and admittedly speculative historical reconstruction of the development. Originally, the bipartite sanctuary cleansing rite was very similar to the bird rites. Two goats were used, one to provide blood to cleanse a building or sanctuary of impurity and another to carry away this impurity. The rite was, in time, assimilated to Israelite temple practice and theology. As a result, the animals were labeled a *ḥaṭṭāʾt* and one was performed as such. The requirement that one goat supply cleansing blood was expanded to a requirement for two animals, a bull for the priests in addition to the goat for the people. Moreover, a distinction was made in the evils removed by the different parts of the rite. The dispatched goat was no longer the bearer of sanctuary impurities, but became the bearer of the cause of those impurities, the people's sins.

In contrast to this supposed adaptation of a two-goat purification rite to the *ḥaṭṭāʾt* system featured in the Day of Atonement ceremony, the *ṣāraʿat* bird rites were never adapted to the *ḥaṭṭāʾt* sacrificial scheme.[12] Because they were not totally assimilated to Priestly theology, their value to the historian is that they provide examples of very ancient rites which retain much of their pre-Israelite character.[13] Yet we must be cautious not to assume that there has not been any assimilation to Priestly theology. An examination of nonbiblical rites similar to the biblical bird rites and the contrasts between them will show that, in fact, the bird rites are very much adapted to the Priestly system of thought.

2.2 SIMILAR RITES FROM MESOPOTAMIA

Our attention now turns to rites from Mesopotamia and Anatolia that have similarities to the bird release rites for persons and houses recovered from *ṣāraʿat* in the Bible. Mesopotamian literature displays two uses of birds as bearers of evil. With the first, birds are actually released; with the second, the dispatch of an evil-carrying bird occurs only as a literary figure expressing the desire that the evil be entirely removed from the

---

[12]Cf. the Red Cow rite of Num 19 which has been adapted to the *ḥaṭṭāʾt* system while retaining certain abnormalities within that system. See Milgrom, "Paradox," 67–72.

[13]On the pristine character of the rite, see Milgrom, "Paradox," 69–70.

sphere of the patient.

The first use is found in namburbi rituals whose goal is to remove evil portended by a bird.[14] In one example,[15] after various rites of purifying the patient and propitiating gods, the patient requests by incantation that the evil be taken far away from him. This recital is followed by the release of a male bird "to the east, before [Shamash]."[16] This represents the dismissal of evil from the patient. Similarly, in another ritual,[17] a male and female partridge are obtained. The patient raises them with his hands and recites an incantation before Shamash which includes a request that the evil be distanced from the patient.[18] Upon completion of the rite, the male bird is released to the east, before the sun god.[19]

The second use, in which the released-bird motif is only mentioned but not acted out, is found in many types of rituals. For example, in the "*Lipšur* Litanies," we find the request: "May a bird take my sin up to the sky; may a fish take my sin down to the abyss!"[20] In another namburbi ritual, which does not deal with the evil of a bird, it is hoped: "Like a bird of heaven may (the evil) fly away!"[21] Finally, in a ritual to get rid of "headache" an incantation says: "May headache fly like a dove to the nest, like a raven to the [ ] of heaven, like a bird to the wide place!"[22]

---

[14]There is a namburbi rite in *OECT* 6, 25 rs. 7–11 which uses birds, but it is not clear if they are released as in the following examples.

[15]R. Caplice, "Namburbi Texts in the British Museum, II," *Or* 36 (1967) 34–38.

[16]Line rs. 6′.

[17]R. Caplice, "Namburbi Texts in the British Museum, III," *Or* 36 (1967) 273–78.

[18]Cf. line vs. 11′: "May the evil of this bird cross over [the mountain]."

[19]Lines rs. 28′–29′.

[20]E. Reiner, "*Lipšur* Litanies," *JNES* 15 (1956) 140–41: 22′; also see 142: 37′, with *māmītu* instead of *arnu.* Reiner (p. 148) gives another example from 4 R 59, 2, rs. 12–16: "May I cast off the evil which is upon me! Let a bird carry it to the sky! Let a fish take away my anguish! Let the river carry it off!" Also E. E. Knudsen, "An Incantation Tablet from Nimrud," *Iraq* 21 (1959) 57–60: rs. 38–41: "let him eat and a bird will take his *namtaru* up to heaven [ ] let him eat and a fish will carry his *asakku* down to the *apsû.*"

[21]Caplice, "Namburbi Texts in the British Museum, V," *Or* 40 (1974) 140: 4′: MUŠEN.AN.GIN₇ ḪA.BA.DAL

[22]*CT* 17.22: 140–44 (= *DES* 2. 76): *mu-ru-uṣ qaq-qa-di* [*ki-ma su*]-*um-*

2.3 SIMILAR RITES FROM ANATOLIA

Several Hittite rituals also contain the release of a bird to remove evils. In a rite performed for the benefit of the royal pair,[23] an eagle and model clay soldiers are waved over the king and queen.[24] After other actions, the eagle is let loose.[25] The meaning of the release is not immediately clear since it is accompanied by a request to the eagle that he go to the sun god and weather god and declare to them the wish that the royal family be blessed with eternal life such as the gods have.[26] This request suggests that the bird is used as a messenger to the gods, carrying a prayer to heaven, rather than as a means of disposing of the evil from the royal pair.[27] It appears, however, that there is a mixture of two functions in this rite. The bird is truly a messenger, but it also carries away the evil. The full context makes this clear. At the beginning of the rite, the bird is waved over the couple. Waving is regularly used for transferring evil from the patient to the object waved.[28] That the bird receives the evil of the pair is further supported by the activity performed with the clay soldiers. They are waved over the couple just like the bird, but unlike the bird, they are disposed of by burial.[29] An incantation accompanying this declares: "O Sun God and Weather God, behold, I have buried for the king, queen, and their children in Hatti their sickness, blood, evil, and fright. Let not this come back up!"[30] Thus

---

ma-ti ana ap-ti ki-ma a-ri-bi [*ana*] AN-e *ki-ma iṣ-ṣu-ri áš-ri rap-ši lit-tap-ra-âš* (cf. the translation of the last phrase in *CAD* I, 211b).

[23]StBoT 8 ii 44–iii 13.

[24]ii 45–46, 51.

[25]iii 3.

[26]iii 6–7: "As the Sun God and Weather God are eternal, so may the king and queen be eternal" (cf. iii 1–2).

[27]See V. Haas, "Die Unterwelts- und Jenseitsvorstellungen im hethitischen Kleinasien," *Or* 45 (1976) 200; D. H. Engelhard, "Hittite Magical Practices" (PhD diss., Brandeis University, 1970) 156–57. On mediation of prayer by a god to another god on behalf of a petitioner, see *KUB* 21.27 iv 26–46 (= *ANET*, 394); *KUB* 6.45+ ii 34–36 (= *ANET*, 398); *KUB* 30.10 vs. 2–5 (= *ANET*, 400). Cf. A. Archi, "Il culto del focolare presso gli Ittiti," *SMEA* 16 (1975) 86.

[28]On waving, see chap. 1, n. 55.

[29]StBoT 8 iii 8.

[30]iii 10–13.

the bird should be viewed as carrying away the evil, like the clay soldiers, while at the same time carrying a request for blessing heavenward.[31]

In another ritual, birds and a goat are used to dispatch evil:

> Let there not be any anger at all! Let there not be any wrath at all! You shall wave in the house [bird(?)]s and a goat. He shall strike them on the four corners. You shall drive them out. You shall release the eagle and hawk. You shall pour water back into the water gutter.[32]

It is difficult to determine what the damaged sign is that I rendered "[bird(?)]s." At any rate, it appears that the eagle and hawk are used in a waving rite and then are dispatched to carry away the evil.[33]

2.4 CONTRASTIVE ANALYSIS

By now employing the method of contrastive comparison, we can determine the uniqueness of the biblical bird rite and better estimate its position within the scope of Priestly ritual. This comparison will show that, though the biblical rite has not been assimilated to the *ḥaṭṭāʾt* system, it has been otherwise adapted to or interpreted by the Priestly

---

[31]These two concepts—purification and bestowal of blessing or invigoration—are complementary as we have already seen in the treatment of motifs in Hittite purification rituals in the previous chapter (see chap. 1, section 1.3.10). In the Bible, the two motifs are found when certain objects are purified and consecrated, i.e., set apart and empowered to perform their particular functions. See Milgrom, "Two Kinds of *Ḥaṭṭāʾt*," *VT* 26 (1976) 333–37.

[32]*KUB* 30.34 iv (9) *nu kar-tim-mi-ya-az li-e ku-it-ki nu ša-a-wa-ar* (10) *li-e ku-it-ki nu-uš-kán* É-*ri an-da wa-aḫ-nu-ši* (11) [MUŠE]N(?)$^{ḪI.A}$ MÁŠ.GAL-*an-na nu-uš-kán* 4 *ḫal-ḫal-du-ma-ri wa-al-aḫ-zi* (12) *nu-uš-kán pa-ra-a u-un-na-at-ti nu ḫa-a-ra-an* (13) [*k*]*al-li-kal-li-in-na ar-ḫa tar-na-at-ta* (14) *nu wa-a-tar* EGIR-*pa* ^{GIŠ}PISÁN *la-aḫ-ḫu-ut-ti*.

[33]Other examples of Hittite bird release rituals are: *KUB* 30.33 iv 5–9; 30.35 iv 2–4; 41.11 i 12 (= H. Hoffner, "Incest, Sodomy, and Bestiality in the Ancient Near East," *Orient and Occident: Essays Presented to Cyrus H. Gordon on the Occasion of his Sixty-fifth Birthday* [ed. H. Hoffner; AOAT 22; Kevelaer and Neukirchen: Butzon und Bercker, and Neukirchener, 1973] 87); StBoT 8 iv 36–37. Cf. *VBoT* 24 i 27 (= Anniwiyani).

system of thought.

First we note that the evils removed by the biblical rite and the nonbiblical rites are different. In the Akkadian namburbi rituals, the dispatch of a bird represented the dispatch of the evil portended by a bird. The impurity is not transferred to the bird, but rather, the bird by its bodily form represents the evil. This use of a bird to represent or concretize the portended evil is like the use of a dog figurine to represent evil portended by a dog which we studied in the previous chapter.[34] Apart from the namburbi rites in which birds are actually released, Akkadian incantations using the bird release motif mention various types of evils such as "sin" (*arnu*), "curse" (*māmītu*), "headache" (*diʾu*), and "fate demon" (*namtaru*). The Hittite rituals speak of "sickness" (*irma-*), "tongues" (*lala-*), "impurity" (*papratar*), "bloody deed" (*ešḫar*), "evil" (*idalu-*), "frightful thing" (*ḫatuga-*), "anger" (*kartimmiyatt-*), and "wrath" (*šawar*).[35] These evils contrast with the evil removed by the biblical bird rite: the residual impurity of *ṣāraʿat*.[36] One might suppose that as the Mesopotamian rites remove "headache" and as the Hittite rites remove "sickness," so the biblical rite may remove the disease of *ṣāraʿat*.[37] It is clear, however, that this is not the case; the biblical rite is not a healing rite. The rite is only performed after the person has recovered and after the house has been cleansed of *ṣāraʿat* and renovated. Again, if it is

---

[34]See chap. 1, section 1.5.5.

[35]*Irma-* (StBoT 8 i 12′; iii 11; iv 2); *lala-* (i 11′; ii 11); *papratar* (ii 11; iii 20; iv 2); *ešḫar* (iii 11, 19); *idalu-* (iii 11; iv 2); *ḫatuga-* (iii 12, 19; iv 2). See also the sicknesses listed in StBoT 8, 40 iv 5′. *KUB* 30.34 iv 9 has *kartimmiyatt-* and *šawar*. *KUB* 30.33 iv 9 lists *lingai-* "curse/oath" and *pa-ga-u-wa-aš* EME-*aš* "tongue of the many."

[36]Cf. Milgrom, "Paradox," 69–70, n. 21; S. R. Driver and H. A. White, *The Book of Leviticus* (New York: Dodd, Mead, and Co., 1898) 77; J. Michman, "Leprosy," *EncJud* 11 (1972) 34.

[37]Ehrlich (*Randglossen*, 2. 47) says that on the bird "die letzten Ueberreste der Krankheit übertragen wurden" and G. Wenham (*The Book of Leviticus* [NICOT; Grand Rapids: W. B. Eerdmans, 1979] 209) says that "the bird carried away the polluting skin disease." As we will see, these judgements are not correct. In contrast to the Priestly purification rite, Naaman's immersing in the Jordan seven times was for the removal of the disease itself (2 Kgs 5:10, 13–14). In ancient Greece, there were rites whose purpose was to remove skin diseases (R. Parker, *Miasma: Pollution and Purification in Early Greek Religion* [Oxford: Clarendon, 1983] 212, 216).

assumed that *ṣāraʿat* in many cases might have been considered a punishment for some sin,[38] one might suppose that as the Mesopotamian and Hittite rites can remove sin, so the biblical rite seeks to remove the sin which caused the *ṣāraʿat*. But, if there is no reason to believe that the rite removes the disease, there is even less reason to believe that the rite removes the sins which caused the disease. What this contrast between the biblical and nonbiblical rites in regard to the evils removed suggests is that the biblical rite limits itself to a very small segment of a whole spectrum of possible evils. This limitation is almost certainly a result of the influence of the Priestly system which, except for the sins of the Israelites placed on the scapegoat, only perceives cultic impurity, not moral impurity (= sins) or disease, to be the object of purification in its purgation rituals.[39]

Another contrast appears in the motif of distancing evil from the patient. All the rites, both biblical and nonbiblical, seek to remove the evil far from the patient. In the nonbiblical rites, the evil is wished on its way to the mountains,[40] the sky, the abyss, and, surprisingly similar to the biblical rite, to the "wide place" (*ašri rapši*) which the *CAD* renders "desert."[41] But the biblical rite has a broader purpose in sending the evil far away. An indication of this is in the house purification rite in which the bird is sent "outside the city to the open country." This

---

[38]Cf. the cases of Miriam (Num 12:10–15), Gehazi (2 Kgs 5:27) and Uzziah (2 Kgs 15:5; 2 Chr 26:20–21) who were punished with *ṣāraʿat*. Also note the curse on the house of Joab (2 Sam 3:29) and the reverse example of Naaman who was cured because of obedience (2 Kgs 5). See J. Döller, *Die Reinheits- und Speisegesetze des Alten Testaments in religionsgeschichtlicher Beleuchtung* (ATAbh 7/2–3; Münster: Aschendorff, 1917) 79; J. Milgrom, *Cult and Conscience: The Asham and the Priestly Doctrine of Repentance* (SJLA 18; Leiden: Brill, 1976) 80–82. For later rabbinic observations on the connection of sin and *ṣāraʿat*, see L. Rabbinowitz, "Leprosy: In the Second Temple and Talmud; in the Aggadah," *EncJud* 11 (1972) 37–39; J. Neusner, *The Idea of Purity in Ancient Judaism* (SJLA 1; Leiden: Brill, 1973) 17, 24, 80–85, 90–91, 98–100, 117.

[39]See chap. 1, section 1.6, above. Of course sins cause impurity (see section 1.1.2), but these sins are not the object of purification. Only the impurity arising from them is.

[40]See n. 18, above.

[41]*CAD* I, 211b. *AHw* (957a) describes it as "Steppe, Gelände," etc., connected with *ṣēru rapšu* and *ugārē rapšūti*.

phrase expresses the desire to remove the evil not only from the individual, but from the habitation, in order to keep the community pure and the sanctuary and its sancta holy.[42] The nonbiblical rites do not have this broad goal. This feature again shows adaptation of the rite to the Priestly system of purification.

2.5 CONCLUSION

To conclude, the biblical bird dispatch rites for removing the residual impurity of *ṣāraʿat* are examples of rites that have not been fully reinterpreted by and adapted to the Priestly system. The bird rites simply use a pair of birds, one to provide blood as a detergent for removing impurity, the other to carry away the impurity. There is no multiplication of animals required for the rite and there is no bifurcation in purpose for the two birds. Both serve together to remove the impurity of *ṣāraʿat* from the object of purification. Only in a few areas do we find clear adaptation to the Priestly system of purification, that is, in the limitation of purification to the residual ritual impurity of *ṣāraʿat* and in the dispatch of the evil away from the community and sanctuary.[43]

---

[42]See chap. 1, section 1.6 and chap. 9.

[43]A variation of the disposal of impurity by birds is found in Zech 5:5–11. Here, a container containing a woman symbolizing evil is transported to Babylon by two winged women. See chap. 9, n. 150.

3

The Disposal of Materials Infected with *Ṣāraᶜat*

3.1 INTRODUCTION

We turn our attention away from the dispatch of birds to remove the residual impurity of *ṣāraᶜat* and move to an examination of the disposal of items incurably infected with *ṣāraᶜat.* Here we discover two methods for eliminating objects plagued with this impurity. Infected building materials are dumped in an impure place outside the habitation; infected fabrics are burned.

3.2 INFECTED BUILDING MATERIALS

First, building materials infected with *ṣāraᶜat.* After treating the symptoms and diagnosis of *ṣāraᶜat* in humans and in fabrics, and after detailing the mode of purifying persons once they have recovered from the condition, the Bible treats the diagnosis of *ṣāraᶜat* in houses and how to purify them when the infection has been removed (Lev 14:34–53).[1]

---

[1]The pericope about *ṣāraᶜat* infected houses is placed, or misplaced as it may seem (cf. S. R. Driver and H. A. White, *The Book of Leviticus* [New York: Dodd, Mead, and Co., 1898] 76–78), at the end of the discussion of the diagnosis of and purification from other types of *ṣāraᶜat.* This location, however, is not illogical when we consider that the passage deals with the *ṣāraᶜat* law as it applies to habitations under settled conditions (note the terminology "house" and "city" instead of "tent" and "camp") as opposed to the regulations about *ṣāraᶜat* in humans and fabrics which are applicable already in the wilderness setting (cf. D. Hoffmann,

Our present concern lies not in the purification of the house (vv 48–53; see the previous chapter), but in what is done with irreclaimably infected building materials (vv 34–45). When a householder first suspects *ṣāraʿat,* he summons a priest to come and diagnose the affection. The house is cleared of its contents before the examination so that they do not become contaminated. The priest enters and looks to see if the plague consists of greenish or reddish spots[2] which appear to be deep in the wall.[3] If such symptoms appear, the house is shut up[4] for seven days, after which the priest again inspects the spots. If they have spread, the infected stones are removed and dumped outside the city in an unclean

---

The Book of Leviticus [Seper Wayyiqra'] [2 vols; Jerusalem: Mosad Harav Kook, 1953] 1. 281; G. Wenham, *The Book of Leviticus* [NICOT; Grand Rapids: W. B. Eerdmans, 1979] 211–12).

[2]The meaning of *šĕqaʿărûrōt* is obscure. It is a plural noun most likely derived from the Šafʿel conjugation from the root *qʿr,* meaning "recessions, depressions" (cf. *GKC* § 55i; BDB, 891; KB[2], 1009; A. Bertholet, *Leviticus* [KHC; Tübingen: J. C. B. Mohr, 1901] 48; A. Dillmann, *Die Bücher Exodus und Leviticus* [3d ed.; Leipzig: S. Hirzel, 1897] 566; K. Elliger, *Leviticus* [HAT 14/1; Tübingen: J. C. B. Mohr, 1966] 190, n. 61; N. H. Snaith, *Leviticus and Numbers* [London: Thomas Nelson, 1967] 105). Arabic *qaʿara* means "be deep, hollowed out." *Tg. Onq.* has *paḥătān* "depressions." For other interpretations, unacceptable in my view, see J. L. Kraemer, "*Šeqaʿărūrōt*: A Proposed Solution for an Unexplained Hapax," *JNES* 25 (1966) 125–29 and M. Görg, "'Ausschlag' an Häusern: zu einem problematischen Lexem in Lev 14,37," *BN* 14 (1981) 20–25.

[3]The color of the affection indicates that it is a type of mold or mildew and not a deterioration by the formation of salt peter (cf. Bertholet, *Leviticus,* 48; S. R. Driver and H. A. White, *Leviticus,* 76–78; K. Elliger, *Leviticus,* 189; R. K. Harrison, "Leprosy," *IDB* 3 [1962] 113; E. V. Hulse, "The Nature of Biblical 'Leprosy' and the Use of Alternative Medical Terms in Modern Translations of the Bible," *PEQ* 107 [1975] 94; Snaith, *Leviticus,* 104; Wenham, *Leviticus,* 211; D. P. Wright and R. N. Jones, "Leprosy," *ABD* (forthcoming).

[4]The "shutting up" does not appear to be a literal closure of the structure since there remains the possibility that people might enter (vv 46–47). Cf. A. B. Ehrlich, *The Bible According to Its Plain Meaning (Miqra' Kipešuto)* (3 vols.; Berlin 1899–1901; reprint, New York: Ktav, 1969) 1. 227; *Randglossen zur hebräischen Bibel* (7 vols.; Leipzig: J. C. Hinrichs, 1908–14) 2. 50.

place (v 40). The wall plaster is also scraped off and discarded in the same place (v 41). New stones are then installed and the inside of the house is replastered. Presumably at this point a seven day waiting period passes after which the priest comes and inspects the house. If it is free of *ṣāraʿat,* then it is purified using the rite prescribed in vv 48–53.[5] If, however, the plague reappeared during the seven day waiting period after the renovation,[6] then the house cannot be purified, but is irretrievably unclean and must be demolished (v 44).[7] All the building materials—stones, lumber, and plaster—must be taken to the unclean place outside the city (v 45).

The reason for discarding the infected materials outside the city is due to the communicable impurity they carry. The communicability of the impurity is evident in the necessity to clear the plagued house before the priest's inspection (v 36) and in the fact that those who enter a quarantined house contract impurity (vv 46–47).[8] The unclean building materials are removed from the human habitation so that the people and the objects around them will not become polluted. It is very likely that a dump (or dumps) for *ṣāraʿat*-infected materials, if these laws were ever practiced, would be a precisely defined locale, known and recognized by all, so that it would be avoided and so that people would not use the discarded materials in other building projects.[9]

The dump for infected materials is designated an impure place. This characterization contrasts with that of the place for the disposal of sacrificial refuse located outside the camp which is called a pure place.[10] The reason for the distinction in pure and impure dumps is clearly due to the nature of the materials discarded. Sacrificial refuse must be treated in accordance with its holy nature by being thrown away in a pure place, while *ṣāraʿat*-infected materials, having no connection with the cult, do not require such care.

---

[5]See chap. 2, n. 5, on this understanding of the law in vv 37–53.

[6]There is a difficulty in knowing what the text means by spreading in v 44. Contextually, it must refer to the recurrence of the plague after the renovation (see Hoffmann, *Leviticus,* 1. 285).

[7]On the meaning of *ṭāmēʾ hûʾ,* see chap. 4, n. 13.

[8]See chap. 8, section 8.3.2.1, i, on the impurity of an infected house.

[9]Cf. Ibn Ezra on Lev 14:40. Only certain places outside the city are impure, not the whole area. See chap. 9, n. 35.

[10]See chap. 8, section 8.3.2.1, i.

3.3 INFECTED FABRICS

The method of disposing of *ṣāraʿat*-infected fabrics (Lev 13:47–59) is different than that of infected building materials. If a greenish or reddish spot[11] appears on a piece of wool or linen, on the warp or woof of the linen and wool, on a piece of leather, or on anything made of leather, it is to be shown to the priest. He inspects it and quarantines it for seven days, after which he reexamines it to see if the spot has spread. If it has, the article is unclean and must be totally burned (v 52). If the spot has not spread, the article is to be washed and quarantined for another seven days. If after this washing and second quarantine period[12] the priest sees that the spot has not changed color, even though it has not spread, the article is unclean and must be burned (v 55). If, however, after the washing and second isolation period (see n. 12) the spot has faded, the discolored portion is ripped out of the article and is burned (v 56).[13] The remaining portion of the aritcle is now free of the plague and is therefore clean.[14] Nonetheless, if the plague recurs in the leftover portion, it must be entirely burned (v 57). If the spot completely disappears from the article after the washing and second quarantine period, the item is washed again and is clean (v 58).[15]

Though the manner of disposing of *ṣāraʿat*-infected fabrics is different than that of infected building materials, the reason is the same. The

---

[11]Again, the affection is a fungus (cf. S. R. Driver and H. A. White, *Leviticus*, 76–78; Elliger, *Leviticus*, 185; Harrison, "Leprosy," 113; Hulse, "Nature," 94; J. Michman, "Leprosy," *EncJud* 11 (1972) 34; Snaith, *Leviticus*, 97; Wright and Jones, "Leprosy."

[12]Vv 55 and 56 only say "after it is washed," not mentioning the quarantine period, but it is contextually clear that the inspection occurs after both the washing and quarantine period. The seven day period is not mentioned in these verses because the washing is the more important of the two acts.

[13]Burning the torn out part is not mentioned, but clear from the general intent of the regulation (Elliger, *Leviticus*, 186).

[14]The fact that it is clean is implied in that nothing is said about anything being done to the remaining portion after tearing out the stained part. See the next note.

[15]There is some difficulty in understanding the relation of the cases presented in vv 56–58. It might be thought that v 58 deals with the portion that remains after the stained part has been torn out, and that this

infected article transmits impurity[16] and must be removed to preclude any chance of contamination.

It is not said where the infected fabrics are to be burned. Though not conclusive, the silence of the text in this matter may indicate that any fire would suffice, whether in or outside the camp.[17]

The choice of burning instead of dumping outside the camp is certainly in part due to the organic, and hence, combustible nature of the infected cloth and leather as opposed to stones and plaster from a house.

Finally we may note that burning is a common method of disposal in the Bible. The impure carcasses of the priestly-sanctuary *ḥaṭṭāʾt* are burned as well as leftover portions from edible sacrifices.[18] In the narrative books there are examples of burning idolatrous impurities.[19]

---

remaining portion needs washing (cf. Elliger, *Leviticus*, 186). Interpreting vv 56–58 as dealing with the same piece of fabric, however, presents extreme difficulties. If the stained part has been removed, what sense does it make to state the condition "if the plague disappears" (v 58)? Certainly it has already been removed by ripping it out. And if one argues that some stain remains in the torn portion, how long is one to wait to see if the stain disappears? The text is actually speaking of two distinct cases. In vv 56–57, if after the washing and quarantine a faded stain remains, it is torn out. It is clean unless it recurs. Another case is presented in v 58. If after the washing and quarantine the spot is found to have completely disappeared, the article is washed again and is clean (cf. Rashi on 13:58; Hoffmann, *Leviticus*, 1. 271; Bertholet, *Leviticus*, 48). Washing is not required for the rent remnant of vv 56–57.

[16]See chap. 8, section 8.3.2.1, n, on the impurity of *ṣāraʿat*-infected fabrics.

[17]A similar question comes up regarding the place where sacrificial remnants are burned. See chap. 6, section 6.6.4. Of course to say that infected fabrics may be burned in any fire does not mean that they are burned in fires that pertain to the cult, such as at the ash dump.

[18]See chap. 6.

[19]See appendix 1. To be considered in the general scheme of disposal by fire is execution of criminals by burning (Gen 38:24; Lev 20:14; 21:9). Compare particularly the case of Achan and company who were first stoned and then burned (Josh 7:25).

4

The Disposal of Earthenware

4.1 INTRODUCTION

Scattered throughout the Priestly regulations in the Old Testament are prescriptions for the purification of utensils and objects made of various materials. One rule among these stands out as unique: contaminated earthenware vessels cannot be purified, but must be destroyed by breaking. Questions immediately arise regarding this requirement. Why must impure pottery be destroyed? Because earthenware, due to its porous nature, would retain impurity despite efforts to extricate it by washing or other methods? If this be the reason, why are not other porous materials like wood, leather, and cloth similarly discarded when they become impure? This chapter argues that porosity is indeed the reason why impure earthenware needs to be discarded and finds that the Bible does not require other porous materials to be discarded because of economic reasons; a common Israelite could not afford to discard wood, leather, and cloth objects. The course of the chapter will be to look first at the Priestly prescriptions in detail and then study similar Hittite and Indian practices to help understand better, through interpretive comparison (see the Introduction), the reason for the disposal of earthenware in the Bible. Finally contrastive comparison will be employed to help determine why the Bible does not require the disposal of other porous objects and materials.

4.2 THE BIBLICAL PASSAGES

There are five passages in the Old Testament which make direct or indirect reference to the disposal of impure earthenware vessels.

(a) The most extensive of these is Lev 11:32–35 which delineates the treatment of utensils which have become impure by a dead *šereṣ*. Vv 32–33 read:

> Anything upon which one of them falls when dead shall be unclean—any utensil[1] of wood, a garment, a leather item, or sacking; any utensil which one may use. It shall be immersed[2] in water and remain unclean until the evening, then it will be clean. But as for any earthenware vessel into which one of them falls, all its contents shall be unclean and you shall break it.

V 35 gives further details about other clay objects so contaminated: "an oven or stove shall be broken up."

This passage opens with the general stipulation that anything can be made unclean by a *šereṣ* carcass (v 32aα). This presumably would include all types of utensils, even metal ones.[3] The law, however, ignores the many possiblities and instead focuses only upon utensils made of organic materials: wood, cloth, leather, and sacking. These articles are of any shape and size as indicated by the inclusion of "a garment, a leather item, or sacking."[4] Consequently, the preposition *ʿal* "upon" (not *ʾel tôk* as in

---

[1]Hebrew *kĕlî* denotes not only a vessel; it may be used of weapons (Gen 27:3; Judg 18:11, 16–17), implements or tools in general (Num 35:16, 18, 22), ornaments (Isa 61:10; Ezek 16:17), clothing (Deut 22:5), and musical instruments (Amos 6:5; 1 Chr 15:16; see the lexicons). Therefore, *kĕlî ʿēṣ* has a much broader meaning than just a wooden bowl or tray.

[2]*Bammayim yûbāʾ* means to immerse in water (a synonym of *hʿbyr bmym*, Num 31:23; cf. Rashi on Lev 11:32; and see Ezek 47:3, 4). Cf. Jer 13:1; Ezek 27:26.

[3]See n. 69, below.

[4]The Mishnah appears to view these verses as referring only to utensils that form receptacles. It states that flat utensils made of wood, leather, bone, and glass do not become impure (*m. Kelim* 2:1; 15:1; 27:1; 30:1; there are exceptions to this since, in reality, some flat items do become impure, cf. *m. Kelim* 15:2–4; see J. Neusner, *Kelim Chapters Twelve through Thirty* [SJLA 6, HMLP 2; Leiden: Brill, 1974] 49). When vessels made of such materials are broken or destroyed so they no longer function as receptacles, they are no longer susceptible to uncleanness (*m. Kelim* 16:1–4; 17:1–3; in 20:1, sacks and bags that are damaged to the extent that they cannot hold things are not susceptible to uncleanness as

v 33) is used when describing the disposition of the falling *šereṣ*. These items may be purified by immersion in water.

The passage continues with a contrasting regulation. Contaminated earthenware vessels, clay ovens, and stoves cannot be purified; they must be destroyed. Since earthenware vessels (*kĕlê ḥereś*[5]) which by nature have a receptacle[6] are the subject of v 33, and not utensils of other shapes as in the previous verse, the preposition *ʿel tôk* is used. In the case of both organic and earthenware utensils, the Bible conceives of the *šereṣ* falling down onto or into the object and resting upon it.

In sum, this passage, the most detailed we have about the treatment of impure objects and vessels, allows for the purification of all articles polluted by a *šereṣ* carcass except earthenware objects.

(b) More tersely formulated than Lev 11:32–35 is the rule about the condition of articles touched by a *zāb*, a male with an abnormal genital discharge: "the earthenware vessel which he touches shall be broken, but any wooden utensil shall be rinsed with water" (Lev 15:12). As in Lev 11, an article made of an organic material—wood—may be purified, while one made of earthenware must be destroyed.

(c) The rule about disposing of impure pottery is also found regarding the pots in which the *ḥaṭṭāʾt* sacrifice is cooked: "An earthenware vessel in which it is cooked shall be broken, but if it was cooked in a bronze vessel, it shall be scoured and rinsed with water" (Lev 6:21).[7] The

---

vessels, but they are susceptible to *midrās* uncleanness, cf. Maimonides on *m. Kelim* 2:1 and Neusner, *Kelim Chapters Twelve through Thirty*, 51). Similar principles are found with clay vessels. Flat earthenware is not susceptible (2:3). When they cannot function as receptacles, they are no longer susceptible (3:1–8).

[5]*Kĕlî ḥereś* is the regular term for an earthenware vessel, cf. Lev 14:5, 50; Num 5:17; Jer 32:14. See J. Kelso, *The Ceramic Vocabulary of the Old Testament* (*BASOR* Supp. Studies, 5–6; New Haven: American Society of Oriental Research, 1948) 21; "Pottery," *IDB* 3 (1962) 849.

[6]Flat earthenware objects are apparently a rare exception. Kelso ("Pottery," 851) notes that "the thin plate such as we use today was a difficult ceramic form to manufacture, and it was little used until NT times." See the various pottery types in R. Amiran, P. Beck and U. Zevulun, *Ancient Pottery of the Holy Land from its Beginnings in the Neolithic Period to the Iron Age* (New Brunswick: Rutgers University, 1970) where the flattest ware is still bowl shaped.

[7]K. Elliger (*Leviticus* [HAT 1/4; Tübingen: J. C. B. Mohr, 1966] 98) says this rule was to encourage the use of metal pots. However, in view

vessels have presumably become contaminated by the *ḥaṭṭāʾt* meat; therefore, the rules concerning purification of vessels govern them.[8]

(d) A passage implicitly reflecting the regulation is Num 31:19–24. Israelite soldiers returning from war against Midian are to remain outside the camp for seven days and purify themselves, their captives, and items of cloth, leather, sacking, wood, and metals from corpse contamination. Noticeably absent in the list of materials to be purified are earthen vessels. This lack is to be explained by the principle evidenced in the foregoing examples. Corpse-contaminated pottery cannot be purified and therefore must be discarded.

(e) Num 19:15 qualifies the foregoing conclusion that corpse contamination pollutes earthenware vessels. It states that every vessel without a fastened cover in a tent where a corpse lies becomes impure. Conversely, by implication, every vessel with a fastened cover does not become impure, or at least not to as great an extent. The significance of this prescription lies in the fact that it refers exclusively to earthenware vessels.[9] Three considerations bear this out. First, *kōl kĕlî* most

---

of the desirability to use disposable earthenware in rituals dealing with impurity (see n. 14) this cannot be the intent of the verse.

[8]On the impurity of the *ḥaṭṭaʾt* sacrifice, see chap. 6, section 6.2. The rabbinic interpretation of Lev 6:21 does not view the pots as impure. Instead, the pots are washed or broken for fear that the bits of meat remaining in them might become *nôtār* "remnant (of sacrificial meat)." This interpretation is derived from prescriptions about remnants of other sacrifices (Exod 12:10; 29:34; Lev 7:15, 17–18; 8:32; 19:6; 22:30; Num 9:12). Because the possibility of *nôtār* exists with all cooked sacrifices, this rule applies to all sacrifices (cf. *m. Zebaḥ.* 11:7; *t. Zebaḥ.* 10:11; Rashi on Lev 6:21; D. Hoffmann, *The Book of Leviticus (Seper Wayyiqraʾ)* [2 vols.; Jerusalem: Mossad Harav Kook, 1953] 1. 167–68).

Another interpretation of the passage views the washing and breaking of the vessels as a means of desanctification. V 20a stipulates that anything which touches the *ḥaṭṭāʾt* flesh becomes holy. Thus the vessels used for cooking the flesh become holy and need desanctification. This desanctification would also apply to the *minḥâ* and *ʾāšām* offerings which also make things holy (Lev 7:11; on this verse and the *yiqdāš* clause in general, see J. Milgrom, "Sancta Contagion and Altar/City Asylum," *VTSupp* 32 [1981] 278–310).

I reject these latter two interpretations since they attempt to expand the rule in Lev 6:21 to other sacrifices besides the *ḥaṭṭāʾt*.

[9]The Targumim explain *kĕlî* as "earthenware vessel." So also the rabbinic commentaries.

naturally refers to earthenware since clay is the usual material for vessels.[10] Secondly, there is clear archaeological evidence that clay pots and lids could be formed with special loops and handles through which a string is passed in order to tie down the lid.[11] This corresponds with the datum of a tightly fastened lid in Num 19:15. Thirdly, the diagnoses of uncleanness in vv 14–16 show that earthenware is intended in v 15. V 14 says that "everyone that comes into the tent and every (person or object) that is in the tent becomes unclean for seven days."[12] Similarly, v 16 says that anyone touching a corpse or related item "becomes unclean for seven days." V 15, however, differs by simply stating that an open vessel "is unclean" (*ṭāmēʾ hûʾ*). No time period is given. This appears to mean that the vessels here are indefinitely and irrecoverably unclean.[13] Such a rule, according to what has been observed, fits only with earthenware vessels.

With v 15 understood this way, the passage legislates that open earthenware vessels unclean from corpse contamination must be broken, while other vessels, including closed earthenware, only become unclean for seven days (v 14). These latter vessels would be purified by being sprinkled with the water of purgation (v 18). The reason for this

---

[10]See n. 70.

[11]See the discussion and pictures in E. Neufeld, "Hygiene Conditions in Ancient Israel (Iron Age)," *BA* 34 (1971) 56–59. Milgrom informed me of this feature of clay vessels and how it applies to this verse.

[12]*Śipre Num* (126; H. S. Horovitz, *The Sifre on Numbers and Sifre Zutta (Sipreʾ ʿal Seper Bammidbar weSipreʾ Zuttaʾ)* [Leipzig: Gustav Fock, 1917; reprint, Jerusalem: Wahrmann, 1966] 162–63) understands *wĕkol ʾăšer bāʾōhel* as referring to objects as well as persons (cf. *Tg. Ps.-J.*, Ibn Ezra, Ramban). That this phrase refers both to persons and things is deduced from v 18 where *kēlîm* and the persons in the tent need to be sprinkled. Note that v 18 basically repeats the cases in vv 14, 16.

[13]Or as *Sipre Num* says: "What does scripture mean by *ṭāmēʾ*? *ṭāmēʾ lĕʿôlām*" (126; Horovitz, *Sifre*, 163: 12). The declaration *ṭāmēʾ hûʾ* is found with other indefinite or irreversable impurities (cf. Elliger, *Leviticus*, 193): various forms of *ṣāraʿat* (Lev 13:11, 15, 36, 44, 46); those with severe irregular sexual flows (Lev 15:2, 25); various unclean animals (Lev 11:4, 5, 6, 7, 8, 26, 27, 28, 35, 38). Especially to be noted is the use of this phrase with fabrics or a house infected with *ṣāraʿat* which, after being declared unclean, can only be destroyed (Lev 13:51, 55; 14: 44). Similarly, the imperfect *yiṭmāʾ* without any modifying phraseology can be used to indicate indefinite impurities (Lev 15: 4, 9, 20).

exception to the general rule that all impure earthenware must be broken may lie in the manner in which the vessel contracts impurity. With the *šereṣ* carcass and the *zāb* the impurity makes actual contact with the vessel, whereas in Num 19:15 the impurity is conveyed by "tenting," i.e., by being in the same enclosure with the corpse (cf. Lev 14:36, 46-47) without any direct contact. Since the vessel was not directly contacted, it acquires a slightly lesser degree of impurity which does not require breakage. If so, we may further assume that actual physical contact of the corpse with the closed earthenware vessel would bring a severer impurity requiring the vessel to be broken.

In the foregoing examples, the text does not state any general principle to the effect that all earthenware made impure by any impurity needs to be broken. Only instances with specific impurities are given. Still, such a general principle may be deduced. The impurities encountered represent all of the major classes of Priestly impurity: death related, disease related, sexual, and cultic. It is therefore safe to assume that other communicable impurities can pollute earthenware vessels and that, as a result, they must be broken, while nonearthenware articles may be purified by washing and other means.[14]

---

[14]This postulate can help elucidate other passages dealing with earthenware vessels. In purifying a person who has recovered from *ṣāraʿat* (see chap. 3) the blood of a bird is mixed with water in a clay vessel (Lev 14:5, 50) which is then sprinkled on the person. An earthen pot is apparently used so that after having become unclean from the rite, it may simply be discarded.

Similarly, the water of bitterness used for the ordeal of the suspected adulteress is to be mixed in an earthen vessel (Num 5:17). Again, this type of container was apparently prescribed so that it could be discarded after having become infected with the impurity of the curse from the words rubbed off in the water (v 23).

Though it is not stated, an earthen vessel would probably be used to mix the water of purgation for cleansing from corpse contamination (Num 19:17; only *kĕlî*, undefined, is mentioned, but *Tg. Ps.-J.* has *māʾn dĕpĕḥar* "earthen vessel"; yet *m. Para* 5:5 and *Sipre Num* 128 say that any type of vessel may be used to mix the water). It, like people who handle the *mê niddâ* (Num 19:21), would become impure and consequently be disposed of.

Finally, complementary to the disposal of contaminated earthenware is the desire to use new vessels in certain rituals. Elisha, when he heals the waters, requests that a *ṣĕlōḥît ḥădāšâ* "new dish" with salt be brought for the rite (2 Kgs 2:20; see J. Gray, *I and II Kings: A Commentary* [OTL 2d

We now turn to the pressing question why earthenware must be discarded. Generally it has been supposed that it is due to the porosity of pottery.[15] The impurity penetrates the walls of the vessel and thus becomes inextricable.[16] Since there is no way to remove the pollution, the vessel must be discarded. This explanation is quite sensible, but a question arises which throws it into doubt. If pottery must be disposed of because of its porousness, should not wood, leather, and cloth items likewise be discarded? Surely other materials, especially wood, are porous and would retain the physical impurity. This objection can best be answered after digressing for a few moments to study the treatment of impure vessels in Hittite and Indian literatures.

4.3 HITTITE USAGE

In order to discuss custom surrounding vessels in Hittite literature, the meaning of the sumerogram GIR_4 as used in Hittite texts must first be established.

---

ed.; Philadelphia: Westminster, 1970] 478–79 for other examples of using new items in ritual acts). The Mishnah prescribes that the purification rite for a person who has recovered from *ṣāraʿat* be done with a new earthen vessel (*m. Neg.* 14:1; cf. *b. Soṭa* 15b). Some MSS of the Mishnah state, and some Sages argue, that a new earthen cup is to be obtained for the *sôṭâ* rite (cf. *m. Soṭa* 2:2; *b. Soṭa* 15b; *y. Soṭa* 2:2 [17d]; *Sipre Num* 10 [Horovitz, *Sifre*, 16: 6]). Certain Indian rituals prescribe that items used should be new to help the rite succeed (cf. J. Gonda, *Vedic Ritual: The Non-Solemn Rites* [HdO 2.4/1; Leiden: Brill, 1980] 48–50, 133, 170).

[15]See J. Döller, *Die Reinheits- und Speisegesetze des Alten Testaments in religionsgeschichtlicher Beleuchtung* (ATAbh 7/2–3; Münster: Aschendorff, 1917) 62, and the commentaries.

[16]The porosity of earthenware is well known. It is used to advantage when water is allowed to soak through to the outside and evaporate, thus cooling the contents (Kelso, *Ceramic Vocabulary*, 14, and see the article "Pottery," *Encyclopedia Britannica* 14 [1975] 895). Potsherds saturated with impure liquids could contaminate ovens since the liquids in the shards would eventually exude (*m. Kelim* 9:5). The porosity of pots can be checked by glazes, or before these were used or to avoid expense, by bitumen (cf. R. J. Forbes, *Studies in Ancient Technology* [vol. 1; Leiden: Brill, 1955] 86–90).

4.3.1 Excursus: Hittite GIR$_4$

Hittite GIR$_4$ is usually attested in connection with vessels or articles of some sort[17] and appears to indicate material out of which the items are made: *UNŪT/UNŪTE*$^{\text{MEŠ/ḪI.A}}$ GIR$_4$ "implement(s) of GIR$_4$,"[18] GAL GIR$_4$ "cup of GIR$_4$,"[19] DUG GIR$_4$ "vessel of GIR$_4$,"[20] *tapišana*-GIR$_4$ "a *tapišana*-vessel of GIR$_4$,"[21] and various animal models of GIR$_4$.[22] That GIR$_4$ represents a material is further evident in terminology paralleling that used with GIR$_4$ to describe objects of other materials.[23] The material that GIR$_4$ represents and the manner in which it signifies it are the problems to be solved in this excursus.

---

[17]In the Akkadian status constructus or in the periphrastic genitive construction with Akkadian *ŠA*. See the examples that follow.

[18]*UNŪT* GIR$_4$ (Bo 2072 ii 33–34; noted in H. Otten, *Hethitische Totenrituale* [DAWBIO 37; Berlin: Akademie, 1958] 125); *Ú-NU-TE*$^{\text{[ḪI.]A}}$ [G]IR$_4$(?) (Bo 4951+ rs. 17; *KBo* 17.68 and VAT 6212; ed. by G. Beckman, "Hittite Birth Rituals," [PhD diss., Yale University, 1977] 155); *Ú-NU-UT* GIR$_4$ (*KBo* 15.9 iv 13 [= StBoT 3, 66]); *Ú-NU-UT* GIR$_4$ (*KBo* 17.65+ vs. 24 [ed. Beckman, "Birth Rituals," 164]); [*Ú-N*]*U-TE*$^{\text{(M)EŠ}}$ GIR$_4$ (*KBo* 17.65+ rs. 28 [Beckman, "Birth Rituals," 168]); *Ú-NU-UT* GIR$_4$ (*KUB* 7.33 vs. 15); *Ú-NU-UT* GIR$_4$ (Tunnawi i 20); ⸢*Ú*⸣*-NU-TE*^{MEŠ} GIR$_4$ (*KUB* 13.4 iii 64); *ŠA* GIR$_4$ *Ú-NU-UT-TE*^{MEŠ} (*KUB* 41.1 iii 3; variant to Malli ii 63′).

[19]Death Ritual, 20 ii 3; 22 iv 3; 32 i 29; 46 iv 26; 72 ii 3; 74 ii 14, 22; 76 iii 39; 82 i 8′; *KBo* 2.4 ii 7, 8, 9, 33; 15.9 ii 21 (variant to 15.2 rs. 27; ed. StBoT 3, 62–63); *KBo* 17.65+ vs. 11 (ed. Beckman, "Birth Rituals," 163); *KUB* 11.9 iv 23 (?) (cf. *BoTU* ii 24); Mastigga iii 49.

Often variants are found where GAL GIR$_4$ simply occurs as GAL, e.g., *KBo* 15.9 ii 21′ has GAL GIR$_4$ which is a variant to GAL in *KBo* 15.2 rs. 21 (= StBoT 3, 62 plus n. 76 there); Mastigga iii 49 has a variant GAL (Bo 6342 x+8; see L. Rost, "Ein hethitischen Ritual gegen Familienzwist," *MIO* 1 [1953] 362 and n. 158). Within the same text we find this variation, cf. Death Ritual 76 iii 39 GAL GIR$_4$ while line 32 has merely GAL.

[20]Death Ritual 32 vs. 19. In line 29 it is called GAL GIR$_4$.

[21]*KUB* 2.13 i 43, 46. On *tapišana*-, see H. T. Bossert, "Untersuchung hieroglyphenhethitischer Wörter," *MIO* 2 (1954) 272–73.

[22]7 ANŠE.KUR.RA GIR$_4$ 7 GUD GIR$_4$ 7 MUŠEN GIR$_4$ "seven horses of GIR$_4$, seven bulls of GIR$_4$, seven birds of GIR$_4$" (Papanikri ii 38).

[23]*UNŪT* GIR$_4$ *UNŪT* AD.KID "implement(s) of GIR$_4$ and implement(s) of reed work" (Bo 2072 ii 33–34 [cited in Otten, *Totenrituale*, 125]); [*Ú*-

The search for the meaning of the material indicated by GIR$_4$ began with F. Sommer and H. Ehelolf who correctly identified the Hittite sign with the Mesopotamian sign GIR$_4$. They erred, however, in determining its precise meaning when they supposed that, since the Akkadian *kīru* (= GIR$_4$) was an oven for melting down bitumen, Hittite GIR$_4$ meant "asphalt."[24]

The meaning was more correctly assessed by H. T. Bossert.[25] He noted that GIR$_4$ never means asphalt in Mesopotamian cuneiform, only oven or kiln. He argued further that the *kīru* was not only used for melting down bitumen, but was also used as a kiln for baking clay ware. He concluded that in Hittite texts, cups, implements, models, etc. of GIR$_4$ should be understood according to this latter use of the *kīru* as "Gegenstände des Brennofens," i.e., "gebrannte Tonwaren." Thus GIR$_4$ would describe the material of which the articles are made (baked clay) by reference to the method of manufacture (firing in a GIR$_4$, "kiln"), rather than by describing the material directly.[26]

N]*U-TE*$^{(M)EŠ}$ GIR$_4$ *Ú-NU-TE*$^{(M)EŠ}$ GIŠ-*ya* "implements of GIR$_4$ and implements of wood" (Beckman, "Birth Rituals," 168 rs. 28); *Ú-NU-*[*TE*]^{MEŠ} *IṢ-ṢI Ú-NU-TE*^{MEŠ} GIR$_4$ "implements of wood (and) implements of GIR$_4$" (*KUB* 13.4 iii 64).

[24]F. Sommer and H. Ehelolf, *Das hethitische Ritual des Papanikri von Komana* (Bogazköi-Studien 10; Leipzig: J. C. Hinrichs, 1924) 56, followed provisionally by *HW*[1], 274. On *kīru*, see *CAD* K, 415–16. GIR$_4$ never means asphalt in Mesopotamia. Forbes' idea (*Studies*, 20–21) that GIR$_4$ was a "special kind of bitumen" is based upon the incorrect definition given by P. A. Deimel (*Šumerisches Lexikon* [4 vols.; Rome: Pontifical Biblical Institute, 1928–33] item #430: 2). Deimel's attestations of "asphalt" for GIR$_4$ are from Boghazkoi.

[25]Bossert, "Untersuchung," 270–72.

[26]Cf. *HW*[1], 1. Erganzungsheft, 26, which gives GIR$_4$ "Brennofen" following Bossert.

H. Otten (*Totenrituale*, 125) attempted to add further support to Bossert's proposition by noting the apparent interchange of *UNŪT*/*UNŪTE*^{MEŠ} GIR$_4$ ("implement[s] of GIR$_4$") with *UNŪT*/*UNŪTE*^{MEŠ} ^{LÚ}DUG.QA.BUR ("implement[s] of [i.e., made by] the potter"; H. Hoffner, "An English-Hittite Glossary," *RHA* 25/80 [1967] 62, n. 123, reads ^{LÚ}DUG.QA.BUR as ^{LÚ}BAḪÁR). In some texts there are series of implements where *UNŪT* GIR$_4$ occurs while in other texts there are series where *UNŪT* ^{LÚ}DUG.QA.BUR occurs. The terms appear to occur exclusively of one another suggesting that the two terms are synonymous.

B. Rosenkranz, picking up on the meaning of GIR4 as suggested by Bossert, gave examples of GIR4 occurring alone without any accompanying noun (such as GAL, *UNŪT*, DUG, etc.) in the meaning of "oven" or "kiln."[27] The clearest example[28] is in a ritual for the divinities DMAḪ and D*Gulšeš*.[29] The text prescribes that the Old Woman is to set up (?)[30] 3 GIR4ḪI.A[31] toward the sun god. After other ritual acts, the GIR4ḪI.A are thrown over, broken up, and put (?)[32] into a fire. The terminology 3 GIR4ḪI.A indicates that GIR4 is here a concrete object and not a material. It is highly probable that GIR4 in this passage is an oven made of clay[33] which is portable.[34]

Four additional arguments can now be given in support of the contention that objects of GIR4 are objects made of fired clay:

(1) That GIR4 is not bitumen is suggested by a passage from the Tunnawi ritual in which a list of items required for the rite is found. Among these items are 6 *Ú-NU-UT* GIR4 TUR-*TIM* GE6 "six small black vessels of GIR4."[35] The implication of the use of the adjective

---

Unfortunately, the interchange is not between variants of the same text, but between discrete texts. Therefore, Otten's evidence is not conclusive.

[27]B. Rosenkranz, "Ein neues hethitisches Ritual für DLAMA KUŠ*kuršaš*," *Or* 33 (1964) 248–49.

[28]Rosenkranz claims there is an example of GIR4 occuring alone in the text which he edits ("Ein neues hethitisches Ritual," 239; *KBo* 12.96 i 21). However, the remains of the sign before GIR4 in the copy of the text appears to be part of an UD sign which suggests the restoration [*Ú-NU-U*]*T* GIR4. Thus this text cannot be used as an example of GIR4 occurring alone.

[29]*KUB* 17.27 ii 25–37 (= *ANET*, 347).

[30]Line 25, *an-da ḫar-pa-a-iz-zi*, is unclear. *HW*1, 59a, tentatively connects it with *ḫarp*- "absondern; . . . gesondert hinstellen."

[31]Literally, "three GIR4 objects."

[32]At the end of line 36 the text breaks off and the verb cannot be read.

[33]The ovens here are "completely broken" (*arḫa duwarnai-*). Similarly, another type of oven, the IM.ŠU.NÍG.NIGÍN.NA, and other items, are "completely broken" (*arḫa duwarnai-*) in StBoT 22 iii 36–38. Breaking up is found with other clay objects, e.g., smashing a pot in Tunnawi ii 53. Such breaking seems to fit best with portable clay ovens rather than objects of asphalt. On *duwarnai-*, see n. 43, below.

[34]On portable ovens and stoves in Mesopotamia, see A. Salonen, "Die Öfen der alten Mesopotamier," *Bagh. Mitt.* 3 (1964) 102, 110.

[35]Tunnawi i 20.

GE$_6$ "black" is that items of GIR$_4$ are not necessarily or characteristically black, otherwise the adjective would not be needed. Since bitumen is characteristically black,[36] such a material is excluded here. Moreover, in the same list of articles others made of clay are also modified by GE$_6$.[37] This leads us away from the meaning "bitumen" for GIR$_4$.

(2) A. Goetze has argued that some texts reveal that GIR$_4$ is a combustible material and therefore cannot be fired clay, yet he left the question open whether we should return to the definition "bitumen."[38] His main proof came from a damaged text whose lacunae he filled in by logical conjecture.[39] His interpretation of GIR$_4$ rested largely on this restoration. Fortunately, we now have a more complete text due to additional joins.[40] The new state of the text shows that the implements of GIR$_4$ were in fact not burned at all. Thus Goetze's argument is, in the main, negated.

Another example which for him showed the combustibility of GIR$_4$ is the ritual for the divinities ^{D}MAḪ and ^{D}*Gulšeš* (mentioned above) used by Rosenkranz to show that GIR$_4$ was an "oven" or "kiln." Rosenkranz doubts that the text shows that GIR$_4$ was burned. Though the ritual prescribes placing (?) the broken pieces of the GIR$_4$ objects in a fire, it does not say that they are consumed by burning.[41] Placing broken pieces of clay in a fire may be understood as a sort of "symbolic" disposal.[42] With these corrections of Goetze's earlier observations there seems to be no evidence that objects of GIR$_4$ were combustible.

(3) Articles of GIR$_4$ are items which can be shattered and broken. Cups of GIR$_4$ (GAL GIR$_4$) are ritually waved and broken (*duwarnai-* /*walḫ-*) on the ground in rituals for the dead.[43] This action of breaking

---

[36]Cf. *CAD* I, 311a, which cites a text referring to a "man whose body was as black as bitumen."

[37]i 20–21, ^{DUG}*paḫḫunali*, ^{DUG}UTÚL GAL, ^{DUG}*KUKUB*, etc.

[38]Goetze, "[Review of *KBo* 9]," *JCS* 14 (1960) 116, on *KBo* 9.126.

[39]*ABoT* 25 iii 24–25.

[40]*KBo* 17.65+ rs. 28–29 (cited below; edited by Beckman, "Birth Rituals," 168).

[41]Rosenkranz, "Ein neues hethitisches Ritual," 249.

[42]See the burning of a clay figure in the Akkadian ritual Maqlu ii 125–134.

[43]Death Ritual 46 iv 26; 76 iii 39. On *arḫa duwarnai-* and clay objects, see n. 33, above. *Duwarnai-* indicates fracturing and shattering. It is used of breaking the pegs of a birth stool (Papanikri i 4, 45; iv 40)

suits the brittle nature of baked clay more than the rubbery nature of bitumen.[44]

(4) The most decisive datum for the interpretation of GIR$_4$ as baked clay comes from the Malli ritual. In ii 63′, the main text has *ŠA* IM *Ú-NU-UT-TE*$^{\text{(M)EŠ}}$ "implements of clay." A variant has *ŠA* GIR$_4$ *Ú-NU-UT-TE*$^{\text{(M)EŠ}}$ "implements of GIR$_4$."[45] This variant virtually provides a definition of the material signified by GIR$_4$—that is, clay, or more precisely, fired clay.

To summarize this excursus, Hittite GIR$_4$ in absolute use means "oven" or "kiln." Since, however, it most often occurs in a genitive relation with various nouns, it refers more to the material of which the objects are made by referring to an aspect of their production. The material signified when GIR$_4$ occurs in this construction is fired clay.

4.3.2 Hittite Usage (Continued)

Now that the meaning of GIR$_4$ has been ascertained, we can proceed to examine some Hittite texts that address the notion of the purity of vessels and implements used in ritual contexts. As in the Bible, the Hittite texts distinguish between vessels which can be purified and those which cannot and must be discarded.

The first text to examine is a passage from the Instructions to Temple Officials.[46] Amid admonitions to kitchen officials about the state of purity that must prevail in their work is a command about what to do should a pig or dog approach the holy implements and the punishment that will follow if the cooks are lax in this matter:

---

and in the Laws of breaking a hand or foot (§§ 11, 12) or the horn of an ox (§ 74). The iterative form is used of breaking various pots (Mastigga iii 32–33, 35; cf. iv 12–13) and of breaking animal bones (*KUB* 13.4 iv 28).

[44]Pliny (*Naturalis Historia* vii 5) says: "The bitumen, which is elastic and 'lazy,' cannot be torn to pieces. It sticks to everything with which it comes into contact" (cited in Forbes, *Studies*, 1. 55).

[45]*KUB* 41.1 iii 3; L. Jakob-Rost, *Das Ritual der Malli aus Arzawa gegen Behexung (KUB XXIV 9+)* (THeth 2; Heidelberg: Carl Winter, 1972) 40, n. 37.

[46]J. Moyer ("The Concept of Ritual Purity Among the Hittites" [PhD diss., Brandeis University, 1969] 106) noted the similarity of the Temple Officials text to the biblical material.

> If the implements of wood and implements of fired clay which you hold—if a pig or a dog ever approach (them), but the kitchen official does not throw them away (and) he gives to the god to eat from an unclean (implement), then to him the gods will give excrement and urine to eat and drink.[47]

Here implements of wood and fired clay (GIR$_4$) must be thrown away when they have become polluted.[48] To be compared with this text is

---

[47](64) *ma-a-an Ú-NU-*[*TE*]^{MEŠ} *IṢ-ṢI* ⸢*Ú*⸣*-NU-TE*^{MEŠ} GIR$_4$ *ku-e ḫar-te-ni* (65) *na-aš-ta ma-a-an* ŠAḪ*-aš* UR.GI$_7$*-aš ku-wa-pi-ik-ki an-da ša-a-li-qa* (66) EN UTÚL*-ma-at ar-ḫa* UL *pí-eš-še-ya-zi nu a-pa-a-aš* DINGIR^{MEŠ}*-aš pa-ap-ra-an-da-za* (67) *a-da-an-na pa-a-i a-pí-e-da-ni-ma* DINGIR^{MEŠ}*-eš za-ak-kar :du-u-ur* (68) *a-da-an-na a-ku-wa-an-na pí-an-zi* (*KUB* 13.4 iii 64–68).

[48]The verb *anda šaliq-* "draw near" (also "offend; violate"; *HW*^{1}, 179–80) does not indicate how the articles are polluted. Pigs and dogs appear to be considered naturally unclean in Hittite texts; consequently, if these animals simply touched the holy foods they would pollute them. Elsewhere in the Instructions to the Temple Officials we read: "For you let the place of broken bread be swept and sprinkled! Let not a pig or dog cross the threshold!" (cf. iii 59–60). The pig and dog were also particularly fit as offerings to chthonic deities (see Beckman, "Birth Rituals," 379, n. 75; D. H. Engelhard, "Hittite Magical Practices: An Analysis" [PhD diss., Brandeis University, 1970] 165–70; H. M. Kümmel, *Ersatzrituale für den hethitischen König* [StBoT 3; Wiesbaden: Otto Harrassowitz, 1967] 152; Moyer, "The Concept of Ritual Purity," 95–96). It is not clear if the impurity of the pig and dog is manifested in the laws according to which bestiality with these animals brings the death penalty while bestiality with a horse or mule is not an offense (§§ 199–200), since bestiality with a bovine or sheep, presumably clean animals, is a capital offense (§§ 187–88; see H. Hoffner, "Incest, Sodomy, and Bestiality in the Ancient Near East," *Orient and Occident: Essays Presented to Cyrus H. Gordon on the Occasion of his Sixty-fifth Birthday* [ed. H. Hoffner, AOAT 22; Kevelaer and Neukirchen: Butzon und Bercker, and Neukirchener, 1973] 82–84). In Indian religion, "if implements are licked by dogs etc. wooden ones are to be burnt, earthenware is to be thrown into the water, metal ones are to be cleansed with ashes" (Gonda, *Vedic Ritual*, 171). The impurity of dogs and pigs in Hittite culture and of dogs in Indian culture is in significant contrast to the impurity of animals in the Bible. In the nonbiblical cultures, the animals may pollute while alive. In the Bible, animals can only pollute when dead (see Lev 11). On the impurity of the pig and dog in Hittite culture, see also J. C. Moyer,

another which deals with inquiries concerning the reason for divine anger. One paragraph treats cultic pollution by a dog:

> Since a dog approached the table and consumed the daily bread, they "consume" the table.[49]

Goetze interprets the "consuming" of the table as "they will discard the table."[50] R. Stefanini suggests that it should be interpreted as meaning "destroy."[51] If this is correct, this is another example of pollution of an item, perhaps made of reed,[52] which cannot be purified.

A final example from a birth ritual shows clearly a distinction between certain utensils which may be purified and reused and others that cannot. In the preparations listed for the birth, it says:

> [Implemen]t(s) of wood and implement(s) of fired clay, the stool, and the beds—each one new, empty [they tak]e, whereas implement(s) of bronze, they burn therein. [They (i.e., the implements of bronze) may be taken again. They take a]ll these. Nothing remains.[53]

On the reverse of the tablet, in an apparently different version of the rite, the same passage occurs with slight variation:

"Hittite and Israelite Cultic Practices: A Selected Comparison," *Scripture in Context II: More Essays on the Comparative Method* (ed. W. Hallo, et al.; Winona Lake: Eisenbrauns, 1983) 29–33. On the pig in Mesopotamia, see, for example, *BWL*, 215 iii 5–16.

49UR.GI$_7$-*ša-an ku-it* ^{GIŠ}BANŠUR-*i ša-li-ik-ta nu* NINDA.KUR$_4$.RA *U*$_4$-*MI ka-ri-pa-aš* ^{GIŠ}BANŠUR *ka-ri-pa-an-zi* (*KUB* 5.7 vs. 34).

50*ANET*, 497. *HW*^{1}, 99, refers to our passage under *karap-* "fressen, verzehren."

51Private communication. He noted that *karap-* is used of gods "consuming" or destroying people.

52For examples of reed or wicker wood tables, cf. Evocatio i 19; Papanikri ii 31.

53(24) [*Ú-NU-U*(*T* GIŠ-*ya Ú-NU-UT* GIR$_4$-*ya* ^{GIŠ}*ḫa-a*)]*š-ša-al-li* ^{GIŠ}NÁ$^{\text{ḪI.A}}$-*ya ḫu-u-ma-an* GIBIL-*TIM* (25) [(*da-an-na-ra-an-da*) (*d*)*a-an-z*]*i Ú-NU-UT* ZABAR-*ma ku-e na-aš-ta an-da wa-ar-nu-wa-an-zi* (26) [*na-at* EGIR-*pa da-aš-ki-it-ta-ri nu*(?) *ḫu-u-m*(*a-an-da-pát*)] *da-aš-kán-zi* NU.GÁL *ku-it-ki ut-tar* (*KBo* 17.65 vs. 24–26; Beckman, "Birth Rituals," 164).

> [Imple]ments of fired clay and implements of wood—each one empty—[they] ta[ke], where[as implements of br]onze they burn there[in]. They may be taken again. [all these] th[ey take.] Nothing re[mains].[54]

Here only implements of wood and fired clay (GIR$_4$) which are new can be used. This corresponds to the passage in the Instructions to Temple Officials where clay and wood items are discarded when impure. The birth ritual shows, moreover, that bronze implements can be reused after they have been purified by "burning therein" (*anda warnu-*).[55]

To summarize to this point, both the Priestly and Hittite literatures make a distinction between articles which may be reused and those which may not. In Hittite literature, both wood and earthenware items are discarded, while in the Bible, only earthenware is. The birth ritual stating that bronze utensils may be reused when they are purified by burning is paralleled by Num 31:19–24 according to which corpse-contaminated metal articles are to be purified by fire. Unfortunately the Hittite texts give hardly a clue why earthenware and wood must be thrown away. The only hint is found in the nature of these substances. Both are porous and would tend to retain the impurity. It is likely that this was the reason for disposal.

4.4 INDIAN USAGE

The Vedic *smṛti* literature contains much information about *patraśuddhi* "cleansing of vessels." In contrast to the sparse number of passages that discuss a limited number of vessel types in the Priestly and Hittite literatures, the Hindu law books show an interest in vessels made of all sorts of material (gold, silver, copper, iron, lead, zinc, shell, ivory, bone, horn, wood, stone, earthenware, etc.), the various types of impurities which may affect them, and how to get rid of those

---

[54](28) [*Ú-N*]*U-TE*^(M)EŠ GIR$_4$ *Ú-NU-TE*^(M)EŠ GIŠ-*ya ḫu-u-ma-an da-a*[*n-n*]*a-ra-an-da-an* (29) *da-a*[*š-kán-zi Ú-NU-UT* ZABA]R-*m*[*a ku-e na-aš-ta a*]*n-da wa-ar-nu-an-zi na-at* EGIR-*pa da-aš-ki-i*[*t*]*-ta-ri* (30) [*nu ḫu-u-ma-an-da-pát da-aš-ká*]*n-z*[*i* NU.G]ÁL *ku-it-ki ut-tar* (Beckman, "Birth Rituals," 168 rs. 28–30).

[55]I agree with Beckman ("Birth Rituals," 198) that the purpose of this burning is for purification.

impurities. We can by no means be exhaustive in our discussion of the many and often divergent stipulations regarding the purification of pots in India; nevertheless, a few examples will yield a general picture of the concerns.

The best example for present purposes comes from the *Visnusmṛti:*

> What has been defiled by the impure excretions of the body, by spirits,[56] or by intoxicating drinks, is impure in the highest degree. All vessels made of iron (or of other metals or of composition metals such as bell-metal and the like), which are impure in the highest degree, become pure by exposure to the fire. Things made of gems or stones or water-shells, (such as conch-shells or mother-of-pearl, become pure) by digging them into the earth for seven days. Things made of horns (of rhinoceroses or other animals), or of teeth (of elephants or other animals), or of bone (of tortoises or other animals, become pure) by planing them. Vessels made of wood or earthenware must be thrown away.[57]

There are important similarities and contrasts here to the biblical and Hittite passages. First, earthenware and wooden vessels that bear serious impurities[58] cannot be purified for reuse. Many texts state this rule.[59]

---

[56]"Spirits," the inebriating kind, *surābhirmadyairvā* "by spiritous liquors or intoxicating drinks."

[57]*Vis* 23:1–5 (the translation is J. Jolly's, *The Institutes of Vishnu* [SBE 7; Oxford: Clarendon, 1880] 97–98).

[58]There is a distinction between greater and lesser impurities. The former may be excreta, urine, semen, blood, fat, marrow, liquor, and other intoxicants, while the latter may be dogs, swine, cats, their urine, ear-wax, nail clippings, phlegm, discharges from the eyes, and perspiration (P. V. Kane, *History of Dharmasastra (Ancient and Mediaeval Religious and Civil Law)* [vol. 4; 2d ed.; Poona: Bhandarkar Oriental Research Institute, 1973] 316). Also among lesser impurities are the touch of an impure person and food remnants. *Baud-Dh* I 6 13:26–28 states that wooden vessels polluted by these latter impurities may be cleansed by scraping or planing. See also G. Jha, *Manu-Smṛti* (vol. 3; Calcutta: University of Calcutta, 1929) 415.

[59]*Baud-Dh* I 6 13:28 (G. Bühler, *The Sacred Laws of the Aryas: Part II* [SBE 14; Oxford: Clarendon, 1882] 189): "(wooden vessels) defiled by

The principle behind the disposal of these items is that "(objects) that have been defiled very much may be thrown away."[60] Thus not only earthenware and wooden items may be discarded, but other items also such as cloth.[61] For a vessel to be pure, all physical signs of the impurity must be removed.[62] For example, the *Devalasmṛti* says: "When there is defilement, the removal of the stain, the grease, and the smell, by means of earth, water, cowdung, and such things constitutes purification."[63] Such impurities may be removed from metal vessels by methods such as scraping, scouring, and washing, and from items of

---

urine, ordure, blood, semen, and the like (very impure substances shall be) thrown away." *Vas-Dh* 3:58–59 (Bühler, *Aryas: Part II*, 241) says: ". . . an earthen pot (is purified) by another burning. But an earthenware vessel which has been defiled by spiritous liquor, urine, ordure, phlegm, pus, tears, or blood cannot be purified even by another burning." *Samvarta* (cited in Jha, *Manu-Smṛti*, 415): "When a house has been defiled by the presence of a dead body in it, all earthen vessels and cooked food should be thrown away" (cf. Num 19:15–18). If one moves into a new house when a birth or death has occurred (defiling occasions, see Kane, *History*, 269–75) he can only proceed with the rites of the new house after "having thrown away the old earthen vessels and having taken new ones" (*Vai-G* 3:16; cf. Gonda, *Vedic Ritual*, 170–71). Cf. *Baud-Dh* I 5 8:49; I 6 13:32; *Manu* V 123; *SB* 12 5 2:14; Jha, *Manu-Smṛti*, 413; Kane, *History*, 322. In some cases, it is prescribed that one is not to eat out of an earthenware vessel (*GG* III 2 60; *Ap-Dh* I 5 17:9–10; Gonda, *Vedic Ritual*, 276–77).

[60]*Gaut-Dh* I 34.

[61]*Vis* 23:6 (Jolly, *Institutes*, 98): "Of a garment, which has been defiled in the highest degree, let him cut off that part which, having been washed, is changed in colour." Compare this to the treatment of *ṣāraʿat* infected cloth in the Bible (Lev 13:47–59).

[62]*Baud-Dh* I 5 8:48 (Bühler, *Aryas: Part II*, 169): "(Objects) which have been defiled by urine, ordure, blood, semen, or a dead body, (but) are agreeable to the eye and the nose, shall be rubbed seven times with one of the substances mentioned above" (i.e., cowdung, earth, ashes; I 5 8:32). *Manu* V 126 (G. Bühler, *The Laws of Manu* [SBE 25; Oxford: Clarendon, 1886]): "As long as the (foul) smell does not leave an (object) defiled by impure substances, and the stain caused by them (does not disappear), so long must earth and water be applied in cleansing (inanimate) things." For other similar statements, see Jha, *Manu-Smṛti*, 405, 418–420; Kane, *History*, 314; *Manu* V 112; *Vas-Dh* 3:48.

[63]Cited in Jha, *Manu-Smṛti*, 419.

bone, ivory, etc., by planing.[64] However, porous items such as clay and wood cannot be purified so that all traces of impurity disappear; consequently, they can only be disposed of. Porosity, then, is the reason for the disposal of such items.

The Vedic literature, however, does not require that clay and wood vessels be disposed of in the case of lesser impurities. For example: "Wooden vessels which have been touched by impure men (shall be) scraped, and those which are defiled by stains of remnants (shall be) planed"[65] and "earthenware vessels that have been touched by impure persons (must be) exposed to (the flame of) a fire of *kuśa*-grass. Those defiled by stains of remnants (of food must be) exposed to another burning."[66] Obviously, allowing an earthenware vessel to be purified after an impure person has touched it is the opposite of the Priestly rule that such a pot must be broken.

Finally, there is a similarity in the *Visnusmṛti* passage with the Bible and Hittite texts in that metal items may be purified by putting them in or holding them over fire. The *śuddhi-prakāśa* reflects how this fire purification was practiced in medieval India. Vessels made of gold, silver, conches, shells, bones, precious stones, bell metal, brass, tin, lead

> that are polluted for a long time owing to being used by sudras[67] or owing to contact with leavings of food should first be scoured with salts (ashes) and water three times and should then be cast into fire so long as it can be borne (without the vessels being broken, melted or burnt up) and then they become pure.[68]

---

[64]Metals, gems, stones, etc., are often scoured, usually with detergents like cowdung, earth, ashes (*Ap-Dh* I 5 17:11; *Baud-Dh* I 5 8:32; *Gaut-Dh* 1: 29; *Manu* V 111; *Vas-Dh* 3:49–50; on the use of ashes, see Gonda, *Vedic Ritual*, 137–38). Acids may be used to remove impurity from metals (*Baud-Dh* I 5 8:33; *Manu* V 114). Mere water may be used (*Gaut-Dh* 1: 29; *Manu* V 112; *Vas-Dh* 3:49). Wood (in cases of lesser impurity), ivory, and bone are planed or scraped (*Ap-Dh* I 5 17:12; *Baud-Dh* I 5 8:35; I 6 13:26–27; *Gaut-Dh* 1: 29, 31; *Vas-Dh* 3:49, 51; *Vai-G* 10: 3).

[65]*Baud-Dh* I 6 13:26–27.

[66]*Baud-Dh* I 6 14:1–2 (Bühler, *Aryas: Part II*, 190).

[67]A *śūdra* is one who belongs to the lowest of the four original *varnas* ("classes"). See A. L. Basham, *The Wonder That Was India* (London: Sigwick and Jackson, 1956; reprint, New York: Grove, 1959) 137–46.

[68]Cited in Kane, *History*, 326. Another example of fire purification: "Of objects, jewels and ornaments made of gold or silver are purified by

4.5 THE RATIONALE FOR EARTHENWARE DISPOSAL

We now return to the question of why impure earthenware must be discarded in the Bible. Biblical scholars who understood such vessels as being irretrievably impure due to porosity are supported by the similar phenomena in Indian and Hittite texts. Clearly Indian religion understands porosity to be the reason for the disposal of certain items and this seems to be the case in Hittite religion, too. But granting that porosity is the reason for pottery disposal in the Bible, how do we explain the lack of disposal of wooden and other porous items? Viewed against the comparative backdrop of the Hittite and Indian literatures, it appears that the Bible has deliberately made an exception in the case of wood and other porous items. As we have already observed, the passages in the Old Testament that explicitly state the regulation do not list every possible type of material. They only list a small number of cases: wood versus earthenware (Lev 15:12); wood, cloth, leather, sacking versus earthenware (Lev 11:32–33); bronze versus earthenware (Lev 6:21). Leaving aside Lev 6:21 which by its context referring to cooking vessels excludes organic materials, the other passages contrast porous organic articles with porous earthenware vessels.[69] These biblical prescriptions seem to be answering implicitly the query: "What is one to do with porous materials when they become impure? Must they be thrown away?" Such questions are not at all out of place in cultures that concern themselves with the purity of utensils, as our examination of Hittite and Indian usage has shown. The Bible gives its answer by

---

water or by holding them over the fire" (*Vai-G* 10:3; W. Caland, *Vaikhanasasmārtasūtram* [Bibliotheca Indica 251; Calcutta: Asiatic Society of Bengal, 1929] 216). See also Kane, *History,* 326–27; *Ap-Dh* I 5 17:10; *Gaut-Dh* 1: 29; *Manu* V 123; *Vas-Dh* 3:49, 59.

[69]I cannot accept L. Finkelstein's argument (*The Pharisees: The Sociological Background of Their Faith* [3d ed., 2 vols.; Philadelphia: Jewish Publication Society of America, 1962] 1. 129) that metal utensils were excluded because they were not used in the houses of the Israelites. That Lev 6:21 and Num 31:19–24 speak about the purification of metal utensils shows that purity of these items was a concern to Priestly legislators. I believe that metal items do not receive much attention because they do not constitute a marginal case. Since they are not porous, no question arises about whether they should be purified or discarded.

referring to the borderline cases: all porous articles may be purified and reused except for earthenware. Only one exception is made in the case of a clay pot with a fastened lid in a tent where a corpse is. It may be reused after being sprinkled by the water of purgation.

The reason for such a distinction between the treatment of various porous materials which have become impure appears to be economic. Clay was an almost inexhaustible resource and hence inexpensive. It was the most prevalent material from which vessels could be fabricated.[70] In contrast, wood, leather, and cloth were less ubiquitous and more expensive to obtain and manufacture. For these reasons, the Bible allows these materials to be reused after purification. The only exception is the burning of cloth or leather items when *ṣāraʿat* cannot be removed from them (Lev 13:47–59; see Chapter Three). Generally speaking, however, only earthenware needed to be disposed of because of its inexpensiveness.

Accomodation of ritual demands due to economic considerations is not foreign to the Priestly writings. Sacrifices are brought according to one's economic ability: an *ʿōlâ* may be a bull, sheep or goat, or bird (Lev 1); the graduated *ḥaṭṭāʾt* may be a female sheep or goat, two birds, or a flour offering (Lev 5:1–13); a parturient brings a lamb and a bird, or just two birds (Lev 12:6–8); a person purifying from *ṣāraʿat* brings two male lambs and a ewe, or one male lamb and two birds (Lev 14:10–11, 21–22).

To conclude, the Bible shows leniency in stipulating that only earthenware vessels need be disposed of when impure. And even here, closed earthenware vessels in a tent with a corpse do not contract

---

[70]Elliger, *Leviticus*, 153; Kelso, *Ceramic Vocabulary*, 14; "Pottery," 848, 853. The Mishnah (*Neg*. 12.5) shows the relative cheapness of clay vessels in discussing the items which the Bible intended when it prescribed the evacuation of a *ṣāraʿat*-infected house (Lev 14:36):

> Rabbi Meir said: "What of his property does it render unclean (if it stayed in the *ṣāraʿat*-infected house)? If you say his wooden articles, his clothing, and his metal articles, he may immerse these and they are clean. What does the Torah (really) have in mind? His earthenware vessels, his jar, and his jug. If thus the Torah has consideration for his insignificant (*bāzûy*) property, how much more for that property precious to him."

impurity severe enough to require their disposal. Other porous items such as wood, leather, and cloth, which might be considered liable to disposal because of porosity require only purification in water. This leniency contrasts with that in Indian literature. There, articles of both clay and wood are disposed of when contaminated by a severe impurity, but in the case of lesser impurities, both wood and earthenware items may be purified by scraping, planing, heating, and washing.

5

The Removal of Corpses

5.1 INTRODUCTION

Another example of the disposal of impure objects is the removal of corpses from the habitation and their burial. This chapter will examine this phenomenon in the Priestly writings and augment the sparse data in that source with an investigation of removal and burial practices from other parts of the Bible and from rabbinic literature and the Temple Scroll. In connection with the study of the biblical material, we will look at archaeological evidence of burial practices of First Temple times to see if it accords with the conceptions expressed by the Priestly and other writings.

5.2 THE PRIESTLY WRITINGS

The Priestly writings have only one brief passage reflecting the need to remove corpses from the area of human habitation. After the death of Aaron's sons, Nadab and Abihu who brought "strange fire" before God, Moses summons Mishael and Elzaphan to come and remove the bodies from the sanctuary and take them *outside the camp* (Lev 10:4–5).

In light of the levitical scheme of impurity, the reason for this elimination is obvious. The corpse is the most powerful impurity, being the only source that can pollute persons and objects for seven days.[1] If other less powerful impurities are excluded, restricted, or disposed of, such as a corpse-contaminated person, people with abnormal sexual discharges, persons with *ṣāraʿat*,[2] materials with *ṣāraʿat*,[3] etc.,

---

[1]See chap. 8, section 8.3.2.1, f, on corpse contamination.

[2]See chap. 8, sections 8.3.1.1–3.

[3]See chap. 3.

surely the "father of the fathers of uncleanness,"[4] the corpse, must be removed from the human dwelling place.

5.3 NON-PRIESTLY BIBLICAL TEXTS

The concern to ban corpses from settlements is alluded to in certain extra-Priestly texts that deal with burial. A burial place for common people was located in the Kidron Valley, outside Jerusalem, in First Temple times (2 Kgs 23:6).[5] Some tombs occupied hillsides or cliffs which suggests that they were located outside the city (Josh 24:33; 2 Kgs 23:16; Isa 22:16).[6] The story about the revival of the corpse which came into contact with Elisha's bones implies that the tomb of the prophet was outside the habitation since the most natural place for spotting an invading Moabite band would be in the open country outside the town (2 Kgs 13:20–21). Samson was buried in his family grave, between Zorah and Eshtaol, indicating that the tomb was not in the bounds of any particular town (Judg 16:31).

These examples hint at a custom of burying outside habitations. Unfortunately, the reports concerning burial are often laconic and leave out information about the exact location of interment. And indeed, there are some reports which locate burial inside the habitation area, thus presenting a conflict with the supposed ideal. These will be discussed momentarily. But we should first observe that the execution of criminals outside the habitation provides additional reason to suppose that the proper place of corpses was outside the habitation.[7] This custom is found scattered throughout the Pentateuch and other narrative books. Dinah, convicted of harlotry, was taken out, meaning out of the town, to be burned (Gen 38:24–25). The half-Israelite who blasphemed God's name was taken outside the camp and stoned (Lev 24:14, 23). The wood-gathering Sabbath breaker was taken out of the camp and stoned (Num 15:35–36). In Deuteronomy, an apostate is brought

---

[4]This is the later rabbinic designation of the corpse which signifies the potency of its impurity (cf. Rashi on *b. Pesaḥ.* 14b, 17a).

[5]On the disposal of other impurities in the Kidron Valley, see below in this chapter and appendix 1.

[6]N. Avigad ("The Epitaph of A Royal Steward from Siloam Village," *IEJ* 3 [1953] 150–52), following Y. Yadin, speculates that the "Royal Steward's" tomb found in the Silwan necropolis in the Kidron Valley may be that of Shebna (Isa 22:15–16).

[7]Cf. M. Greenberg, "Crimes and Punishments," *IDB* 1 (1962) 741b.

outside the gate of the city to be stoned (17:5); a rebellious son is taken out the gate of the city, judged, and then stoned (21:19, 21); and adulterers are brought outside the gate and stoned (22:24). Naboth was taken outside the city and stoned (1 Kgs 21:13). Less obvious, but probably in line with the preceding examples is the execution of Achan. Joshua and the Israelites take him, his family, and his property to the Valley of Achor where Achan and his family were stoned and their bodies and the property were burned (Josh 7:24–25). This means that the culprits were removed from Israel's war camp for the execution.[8] In view of the aversion towards corpses, it is highly reasonable to suppose that execution took place outside of the places of residence partly in order to avoid contamination from the dead body.

The ideal of removing corpses from human dwelling places, however, is not unanimously reflected in biblical burial customs. Apart from some texts which are too vague to use as decisive evidence that bodies may have been buried inside towns and even in houses,[9] the accounts of

---

[8]Another more oblique example is the execution of the Saulides on a mountain, presumably outside the town (2 Sam 21:9). Also see Acts 7:58; Heb 13:12. There is an exception to the requirement of performing executions outside the dwelling place in Deut 22:21. A daughter who turned out not to be a virgin when given in marriage is stoned at the door of her father's house. This exception may be made in order to stigmatize the father for misrepresenting his daughter as a virgin in the marriage deal. Should the son-in-law accuse the daughter of not being a virgin, it is up to the father to produce proof that she is. If the father can produce such evidence, then the son-in-law is punished. However, if the father cannot produce proof, the implication is that he has contracted the marriage in bad faith and hence is subject to a sort of punishment. (J. Milgrom privately related the general outline of this interpretation.)

[9]Several passages say that persons were buried in a particular town (cf. Num 20:1; Deut 10:6; Josh 24:30; Judg 2:9; 10:2, 5; 12:7, 10, 12, 15; 1 Sam 25:1; 28:3; 2 Sam 2:32; 21:14; 1 Kgs 16:6, 28; 22:37; 2 Kgs 10:35; 13:9; 14:16). These reports, however, are of a general nature and may only indicate the town near which, not in which, the persons were buried. 1 Sam 25:1 (cf. 28:3) states that Samuel was buried *bĕbêtô bārāmâ*. Some interpret this as meaning he was literally buried in his house in the city Ramah (cf. Hertzberg, *I and II Samuel: A Commentary* [OTL; Philadelphia: Westminster, 1964] 198–99; *RSV*; *NEB*). However, *bĕbêtô* is certainly intended in a more general sense of "place, home(town)" (cf. *NJPS*; *JB*). The same observation applies to the case of Joab who was buried *bĕbêtô* in the open country (1 Kgs 2:34).

the burial of Judah's kings in the books of Kings and Chronicles clearly show that the majority, if not all of the monarchs, were buried inside the confines of the City of David.[10] Almost as a cliché, the books of Kings report that thirteen kings—David, Solomon, Rehoboam, Abijam (Abijah), Asa, Jehoshaphat, Joram, Ahaziah, Joash, Amaziah, Azariah (Uzziah), Jotham, and Ahaz—were buried in the City of David.[11] The Chronicles essentially repeat the statements found in Kings in the cases of Solomon, Rehoboam, Abijam (Abijah), Asa, Jehoshaphat, Amaziah, and Jotham, and add that the priest Jehoiada was also buried in the City of David in the royal tombs.[12] The burial places of David and Ahaziah are not mentioned. Chronicles differs from Kings in the location of the burials of the remaining four rulers, perhaps because of variant traditions, but more likely because the Chronicler perceived that they were undeserving of burial with the other kings since they had various moral or physical defects.[13] Joram and Joash were buried in the City of

---

[10]See G. Barkai, "On the Location of the Tombs of the Latter Kings of the Davidic Dynasty," *Between Hermon and Sinai (Ben Ḥermon leSinay)* (ed. M. Broshi; Jerusalem: Yedidi, 1977) 75–92 (Hebrew); S. Krauss, "Moriah-Ariel: The Sepulchres of the Davidic Dynasty," *PEQ* (1947) 102–11; L. Y. Rahmani, "Ancient Jerusalem's Funerary Customs and Tombs [Parts 1-4]," *BA* 44 (1981) 171–77, 229–35; 45 (1982) 43–53, 109–19; J. Simons, *Jerusalem in the Old Testament: Researches and Theories* (Leiden: Brill, 1952) 194–225; E. J. Smit, "Death- and Burial Formulas in Kings and Chronicles Relating to the Kings of Judah," *OTW Suid-Afrika* 9 (1966) 173–77; P. L.-H. Vincent and P. A. M. Steve, *Jerusalem de l'Ancien Testament* (Paris: J. Gabalda, 1954) 313–331; R. Weill, *La Cité de David, compte rendu des fouilles executées à Jerusalem, sur le site de las ville primitive* (Paris: P. Geuthner, 1920) 157–83; S. Yeivin, "The Sepulchres of the Kings of the House of David," *JNES* 7 (1948) 30–45.

[11]In respective order: 1 Kgs 2:10; 11:43; 14:31; 15:8; 15:24; 22:51; 2 Kgs 8:24; 9:28; 12:22; 14:20; 15:7; 15:38; 16:20.

[12]Respectively, 2 Chr 9:31; 12:16; 13:23; 16:14 (the Chronicler has more detail than Kings); 21:1; 25:28 (instead of "City of David" Chronicles has "City of Judah," but no apparent difference is intended, cf. J. M. Myers, *II Chronicles* [AB 13; Garden City: Doubleday, 1965] 144); 27:9; 24:16.

[13]S. Yeivin ("Sepulchres," 32) says that the differences in Chronicles are correct historically. It is difficult, however, to ignore the probability, given the tendentious nature of the Chronicler in other places, that the author is stigmatizing these kings who had various flaws (cf. Simons,

David, but not with the other kings of Judah.[14] Ahaz was buried in Jerusalem, but he, too, was not interred with the other kings.[15] Less clear is Uzziah's burial "in the burial field pertaining to the kings." It is not clear whether this was in the city or not.[16] In sum, though Chronicles has some variants to Kings, all of its reports on the burials of kings through Jotham, except in the unclear case of Uzziah, locate the burials within city confines.

Turning to post-Jothamic royal burials, we discover an interesting change of custom, though it does not affect the general picture that kings were buried in the city. We no longer hear of burial in the City of David as with the previous kings of Judah which indicates that for some reason, perhaps overcrowding in the original burial area, burials of later kings were located elsewhere.[17] Though Kings does not mention the place of Hezekiah's interment (cf. 2 Kgs 20:21),[18] Chronicles places it in the "upper part of the tombs of the sons of David" (2 Chr 32:33). The exact location of this tomb in relation to the others is unclear, but seems to be in proximity to the graves of earlier kings. Manasseh was buried in "the garden of his house, in the garden of Uzza" (2 Kgs 21:18; cf. 2 Chr 33:20). Similarly, Amon was buried "in his tomb in the Garden of Uzza" (2 Kgs 21:26). Josiah was brought home from Megiddo and buried in "his tomb" (2 Kgs 23:30). Chronicles differs saying that Josiah was buried "in the tombs of his fathers" (2 Chr 35:24). Though the location of the burial of these last four kings has changed from the earlier kings, it appears that they, too, were buried within the bounds of the city.[19]

Jerusalem, 205; E. L. Curtis and A. A. Madsen, *A Critical and Exegetical Commentary on the Books of Chronicles* [ICC; New York: Charles Scribner's Sons, 1910] 418, 439, 462; W. Rudolph, *Chronikbücher* [HAT 1/21; Tübingen: J. C. B. Mohr, 1955] 269, 279–80, 293).

[14]2 Chr 21:20; 24:25.

[15]2 Chr 28:27.

[16]2 Chr 26:23. It is clear that Chronicles is taking exception to 2 Kgs 15:7 which allowed Uzziah burial with the kings. Since he had *ṣāraʿat*, his interment should not be among the others. He is therefore buried apart from the others in "the field of burial belonging to the kings."

[17]On this change in custom, see Krauss, "Moriah-Ariel," 103–6; Simons, *Jerusalem*, 206–9; Yeivin, "Sepulchres," 33–35.

[18]However, compare the Greek which in several manuscripts adds that he was buried in the City of David.

[19]Cf. Simons, *Jerusalem*, 207; Yeivin, "Sepulchres," 34.

5.4 ARCHAEOLOGICAL EVIDENCE AND BURIAL

Why could the burial of kings take place within Jerusalem's boundaries? Was it because aversion to corpse contamination did not exist then?[20] Such an interpretation though superficially tempting, is not correct. Archaeological evidence from Jerusalem of the First Temple period indicates that this aversion did play a major role in determining where other, nonroyal tombs were located.[21]

Earlier in this chapter reference was made to 2 Kgs 23:6 which mentioned that burial places of the general populace were located in the Kidron Valley. Tombs, apparently dating to the First Temple period, have been identified in the Kidron Valley area, located in the north section of the modern village of Silwan.[22]

B. Mazar, when excavating immediately west of the western wall of the Temple Mount in 1969–70, found empty tombs dating to First Temple times dug in the eastern face of the western hill. The scenario painted by the original excavators and expanded by M. Broshi, who connected the datum of the tombs with the section of Jerusalem's wall

---

[20]Weill (*La Cité*, 35–40) argues that purity laws came into force under Hezekiah and thus the kings from Hezekiah were buried outside of the city in accordance with the new law. This interpretation has been correctly refuted by Simons, *Jerusalem*, 207.

[21]See L. Y. Rahmani, "Funerary Customs," in particular *BA* 44 (1981) 233–34. Several researchers express (or imply) the idea that aversion to corpse contamination determined the location of tombs, cf. M. Broshi, "The Expansion of Jerusalem in the Reigns of Hezekiah and Manasseh," *IEJ* 24 (1974) 21; J. Licht, "*Qeber, Qĕbûrâ*," *EM* 7 (1976) 4; J. Milgrom, "Santification," *IDBSup* (1976) 783a; W. L. Reed, "Burial," *IDB* 1 (1962) 475b.

[22]See N. Avigad, "Epitaph"; "The Second Tomb-Inscription of the Royal Steward," *IEJ* 5 (1955) 163–66; D. Ussishkin, "On the Shorter Inscription from the 'Tomb of the Royal Steward,'" *BASOR* 196 (1969) 16–22; "The Necropolis from the Time of the Kingdom of Judah at Silwan, Jerusalem," *BA* 33 (1970) 34–46; "A Monolithic Tomb Recently Discovered in Silwan Village," *Qadmoniot* 3 (1970) 25–27 (Hebrew); "The Rock Called Peristereon," *IEJ* 24 (1974) 70–72. S. Loffreda ("Typological Sequence of Iron Age Rock-Cut Tombs in Palestine," *Liber Annuus* 18 [1968] 259; "The Late Chronology of Some Tombs of the Selwan Necropolis, Jerusalem," *Liber Annuus* 23 [1973] 7–36) doubts the antiquity of some of these tombs.

found on the western hill by N. Avigad, is that before the expansion of Jerusalem to the western hill, burials took place on the eastern face of the western hill which was then outside the city. As the city was expanded under Hezekiah and Manasseh, the tombs were emptied so that the corpses would not remain inside the city.[23]

R. Amiran recognized that certain tombs west of the Jaffa Gate near Mamilla Street were to be dated to the First Temple period. Writing before Avigad excavated the portion of the First Temple wall on the western hill, she theorized that the city had expanded to the western hill as evidenced by the location of the tombs which would have been near but outside the city wall.[24]

South of the tombs described by Amiran, a tomb has been excavated near the Sultan's Pool which is dated to the First Temple period.[25]

Other tombs have been excavated and examined which lie north of the city, north of the Damascus Gate, and have been dated to the First Temple period.[26] A. Mazar connects the burial caves examined in this area, as did Amiran, with the expansion of the city to the western hill.

The location of these tombs from the monarchic period outside the city on the east, north, and west, and the very likely possibility that the

---

[23]N. Avigad, "Excavations in the Jewish Quarter of the Old City of Jerusalem, 1970 (Second Preliminary Report)," *IEJ* 20 (1970) 129–140; M. Avi-Yonah, "The Newly Found Wall of Jerusalem and its Topographical Significance," *IEJ* 21 (1971) 168–69; M. Broshi, "Expansion"; "La population de l'ancienne Jerusalem," *RB* 82 (1975) 8–9; B. Mazar, *The Excavations in the Old City of Jerusalem Near the Temple Mount: Preliminary Report of the Second and Third Seasons, 1969–1970* (Jerusalem: Israel Exploration Society, 1971) 24–34; J. Milgrom, "Sanctification," 783a.

[24]R. Amiran, "Two Tombs in Jerusalem from the Period of the Kings of Judah," *Judah and Jerusalem (Yehuda wiYrušalayim)* (Jerusalem: Israel Exploration Society, 1957) 65–72 and 8 plates.

[25]D. Davies and A. Kloner, "A Burial Cave from the End of the First Temple Period on the Slope of Mt. Zion," *Qadmoniot* 11 (1978) 16–19 (Hebrew).

[26]G. Barkai and A. Kloner, "Burial Caves North of the Damascus Gate," *IEJ* 26 (1976) 55–57; G. Barkai, A. Mazar, and A. Koner, "The Northern Burial Area of Jerusalem in the Days of the First Temple," *Qadmoniot* 8 (1975) 71–76 (Hebrew); A. Mazar, "Iron Age Burial Caves North of the Damascus Gate, Jerusalem," *IEJ* 26 (1976) 1–8.

caves B. Mazar found west of the western wall were emptied in this early period as the city expanded, show that the place for burial at this time was outside the habitation. Consequently, the answer to the question why the kings were buried in the city must be other than that there was no aversion to the impurity of corpses in the dwelling place. The most reasonable explanation is that the exception was due to honor that kings should receive. They were to be given a certain amount of reverence when dead. Granting them a choice burial spot within the city was an expression of respect. Moreover, it is possible that this custom of burying kings in the city had non-Israelite roots as suggested by S. Yeivin who noted similar royal burial customs for neighboring peoples of the same era.[27] Thus there were two customs: burial of kings and perhaps other nobles, as indicated by the case of Jehoiada, inside the city which was politically motivated, and the burial of others outside the city which was religiously motivated.[28] These two practices would certainly have been in a state of tension.[29]

5.5 EZEKIEL 43:7–9

A passage from Ezekiel reveals this tension and prescribes a correction to it. God describes to Ezekiel the ideal state of holiness and purity of the temple and its environs that should obtain in the future age of peace (43:7–9):

> [The Lord] said to me: "Mortal, (see)[30] the place of my throne and the place of the soles of my feet where I will dwell among the Israelites forever. The house of

---

[27]See Yeivin, "Sepulchres," 36–38.

[28]In the classical period of Greece, a similar bifurcation of burial customs is found. Burial was generally outside the habitation, but the founders of the community could be buried inside the town in the agora (see R. Parker, *Miasma: Pollution and Purification in Early Greek Religion* [Oxford: Clarendon, 1983] 42).

[29]On this conflict of ideal and practice, see Rahmani, "Funerary Customs, Part One," 172–73.

[30]On the textual problem, see W. Zimmerli, *Ezechiel* (BKAT 13/1, 2; Neukirchen: Neukirchener, 1969) 1072. I follow the suggestion of *GKC* (§§ 117i, m) in construing a verb of some sort with the nominal phrase with *ʾet*.

> Israel shall no longer pollute my holy name, both they and their kings, by their whoredom and by the corpses of their kings in their death,[31] when they set their threshold by my threshold, and their doorpost near my doorpost and (only) a wall exists between me and them; (thus) they pollute my holy name by their abominations that they do. I will consume them in my anger. Now, let them remove far away their whoredom and the corpses of their kings from me so that I may dwell among them forever.

This passage seems to indicate that before the time of this revelation to Ezekiel the temple area had suffered impurity or profanation because the dead bodies of the kings were interred near it. Hence, they were to be removed in the future. The main obstacle to this interpretation is the meaning of the word *pĕgārîm* "corpses" in the phrase *pigrê malkêhem* "corpses of their kings," which must now be examined.

D. Neiman has suggested that Ugaritic *pgr* should be understood as "stele" and that the word in Ezekiel should be similarly interpreted.[32] This suggestion has been followed by many.[33] More recently, however, J. Ebach has shown that Ugaritic *pgr* does not mean "stele" but rather "offering."[34] Thus, according to Ebach, *pgr* in Ezekiel has nothing to do with royal memorial stelae, but warns against the performance of an idolatrous sacrificial practice. He derives support from the context which talks of "whoredom," that is, idolatry, and from the occurrence of *pgr* in Gen 15:11 and Jer 31:40 which he says means "offering."

I must, however, reject Ebach's solution since it is not really borne out by the use of *pgr* in the Old Testament. When the instances of the word are carefully examined, we find that it never means "offering." It is

---

[31]*Bāmôtām* is syntactically difficult. Some manuscripts and versions have *bĕmôtām* "in their death" which fits the context better (cf. Zimmerli, *Ezechiel*, 1072).

[32]D. Neiman, "*Pgr:* A Canaanite Cult-Object in the Old Testament," *JBL* 67 (1948) 55–60.

[33]Cf. Zimmerli, *Ezechiel*, 1082–83 and those whom he cites there.

[34]J. Ebach, "*Pgr* = (Toten-)Opfer? Ein Vorschlag zum Verständnis von Ez. 43, 7. 9," *UF* 3 (1971) 365–68. Ebach's solution is accepted by M. Dietrich, O. Loretz, and J. Sanmartin, "*Pgr* im Ugaritischen: zur ugaritischen Lexicographie IX," *UF* 5 (1973) 289–91.

usually used of dead human bodies, generally in a negative context.[35] Once it is used of idols in a secondary sense.[36] In the one case where it is clearly used of animals (Gen 15:11), it is doubtful that the animals are to be considered offerings.[37] That there are birds of prey descending on the *pĕgārîm* shows that the word is better understood as "carcasses" not "offerings." The instance in Jer 31:40 probably refers to human corpses. If, however, it does refer to animals, it would signify animal carcasses which are disposed of after sacrifice and would not be a term for sacrifice.[38] Thus *pgr* in the Old Testament means simply "dead body" of a man or animal. With this understanding of the word in its biblical context, the construction *pigrê malkêhem* in Ezekiel 43 can only mean the "corpses of their kings."

With the proper meaning of *pgr* in place, one is compelled to connect the divine admonition in Ezekiel 43 with the burial practices of Judah's kings.[39] The kings had been buried uncomfortably close to the temple, if not in their own palace areas as may have been the case with Manasseh and Amon, at least within the walls of the holy city Jerusalem. God tells Ezekiel that such a custom must cease since it

---

[35]Lev 26:30; Num 14:29, 32, 33; 1 Sam 17:46; 2 Kgs 19:35 (= Isa 37:36); Isa 14:19; 34:3; 66:24; Jer 33:5; 41:9; Ezek 6:5; Amos 8:3; Nah 3:3; 2 Chr 20:24.

[36]Lev 26:30.

[37]See N. Sarna, *Understanding Genesis* (New York: Jewish Theological Seminary of America, 1966; reprint, New York: Schocken, 1970) 126. He notes that "there is no altar, no mention of blood, no suggestion of consumption by the heavenly fire or by Abraham."

[38]See appendix 1, n. 21.

[39]Those who connect Ezek 43:7–9 with the burial of kings include: G. A. Cooke, *A Critical and Exegetical Commentary on the Book of Ezekiel* (ICC; Edinburgh: T. and T. Clark, 1936) 464; M. Greenberg, "The Design and Themes of Ezekiel's Program of Restoration," *Interpretation* 38 (1984) 192; Kimhi (on Ezek 43:7–9); Kraus, "Moriah-Ariel," 106–8; B. Mazar, *Excavations*, 30; "Excavations Near the Temple Mount," *Qadmoniot* 5 (1972) 89 (Hebrew); Rahmani, "Funerary Customs, Part One," 173; Rashi (on Ezek 43:7–9); Reed, "Burial," 475b; Simons, *Jerusalem*, 207, n. 1. Within this group there is a range of views regarding the place of the kings' burial indicated by Ezekiel. For example, Krauss believes that Ezekiel shows that the kings were buried in the temple court itself, while Rahmani believes the intent is more general referring to burial in the city.

compromises the purity and holiness of the Deity's abode. The royal privileges of the kings of Judah must bow to the more important concerns of purity in the temple and Jerusalem.[40]

5.6 EARLY RABBINIC WRITINGS AND THE TEMPLE SCROLL

The idealism expressed by Ezekiel did not succeed to reality. Though a burial inscription dating to the latter part of the Second Temple period has been found stating that the bones of king Uzziah had been relocated,[41] later Jewish tradition acknowledged and preserved the right of the kings to remain buried in Jerusalem, requiring only that other graves that interfered with human dwellings or activities, whether in Jerusalem or elsewhere, be disinterred and transplanted in innocuous locales, though not necessarily outside the habitation. An example of this tradition comes from the Tosefta:

> A grave which a city surrounded, whether on four sides, on three sides, or on two sides, one opposite the other—if it (i.e., the grave) is more than fifty cubits (from the city) on one side and fifty cubits on the other side, they do not empty it out (i.e., the grave). If it is less than this, all graves are emptied out except for the grave of a king and the grave of a prophet. Rabbi Akiba says: "Even the grave of a king and the grave of a prophet are emptied out." They replied to

---

[40]Rahmani, "Funerary Customs, Part One," 173.

[41]W. F. Albright, "The Discovery of an Aramaic Inscription Relating to King Uzziah," *BASOR* 44 (1931) 8–10; Y. N. Epstein, "On the Inscription of Uzziah," *Tarbiz* 2 (1931) 293–94 (Hebrew); E. L. Sukenik, "The Inscription of Uzziah, King of Judah," *Tarbiz* 2 (1931) 288–92 (Hebrew); "Funerary Tablet of Uzziah, King of Judah," *PEQ* 63 (1931) 217–21; "[Additional Note on] The Funerary Tablet of Uzziah," *PEQ* 64 (1932) 106–7. The inscription which reads, "The bones of Uzziah, King of Judah, were brought here, not to be opened," dates to between 130 BC and 70 AD (Albright). The location of its discovery is not known. It is not clear why the bones were moved, or if, in fact, the bones moved were really Uzziah's. For various assessments, see G. A. Barrois, "Tombs of the Kings," *IDB* 4 (1962) 669a; A. Guttman, "Jerusalem in Tannaitic Law," *HUCA* 40–41 (1969–70) 260, n. 15; B. Mazar, *Excavations*, 30; E. Shatran, "*Qeber, Qĕbûrâ*," *EM* 7 (1976) 20; Simons, *Jerusalem*, 206–7; Yeivin, "Sepulchres," 31–32.

> him: "Were not the graves of the House of David and the grave of Huldah the prophetess in Jerusalem, and nobody ever touched them?" He said to them: "Is that proof? They (i.e., the graves) had an underground cavity and it would conduct the impurity to the Kidron Valley."[42]

The first part of this citation indicates that graves are to be located at least fifty cubits from the area of actual habitation. If graves are found closer than this, they are to be disinterred and relocated. A similar sentiment is found in the Mishnah: "carcasses, graves, and a tannery are to be distanced fifty cubits from the city."[43] Elsewhere we learn that corpses may be taken about the street of a walled city as part of a funeral ceremony, but once they have been taken outside the walls, they may not be brought back in.[43a] Furthermore, burial is not to take place in levitic cities.[44]

The concern of the people of this era to separate corpses from their habitations is found in Josephus' account of the settling of Tiberias. Herod the Tetrarch built the city on a graveyard. Anticipating the resistance he would encounter from the people because of the impurity, he had to resort to force or to granting compensatory inducements in order to populate the city.[45]

The second part of the Tosefta passage, cited above, deals with the problem of the burial of the kings and prophets in Jerusalem. The anonymous sages implicitly opine that the burial of the kings and

---

[42]*T. B. Bat.* 1:11 (cf. J. Neusner's translation, *The Tosefta: Neziqin—The Order of Damages* [New York: Ktav, 1981] 149). For other similar statements, cf. *t. Neg.* 6:2; *y. Nazir* 9:3 (57d); *ʾAbot R. Nat. A* 35:2; *ʾAbot R. Nat. B* 39; *Semaḥot* 14; Maimonides, *MTor*, ʿAboda, Bet habBeḥira 7:13. See also Guttmann, "Jerusalem"; Krauss, "Moriah-Ariel," 109–10; Simons, *Jerusalem*, 209 and n. 2; Yeivin, "Sepulchres," 39.

[43]*M. B. Bat.* 2:9. Though the distancing of these items from the habitation is partly due to their bad smell (cf. H. Albeck, *The Six Orders of the Mishnah (Šisa Sidre Mišna)* [6 vols.; Jerusalem and Tel-Aviv: Bialik Institute and Dvir, 1957–59] 4. 123), the impure nature of corpses and carcasses is also a factor.

[43a]*M. Kelim* 1:7.

[44]*Y. ʿErub.* 5:3 (22d). Maimonides, *MTor*, ʿAboda, Bet habBeḥira 7:13, says that burial may take place in the town if the population agrees to it.

[45]*Ant.* 18.2.3 §§ 36–38. On the impurity and treatment of graves in general, see *m. Ohol.* 16–18.

prophets in the city was because of their high position. Akiba retorts that no exception can be made because of position. Purity and burial laws apply to all. To justify the burial of the leaders in the city, he cleverly corrects the anomaly, bringing it into harmony with rabbinic purity regulations, by noting there is a passage way through which the impurity may escape to the Kidron thus preventing contamination of persons and things that are in a position over the grave.[46]

In sum, these examples from early rabbinic literature reveal the desire to remove corpses altogether from habitations or at least, if burial was in the general confines of the dwelling area, to locate the tombs at a distance where they could do no harm.[47]

The picture of burial in rabbinic sources contrasts with the ideal presented in the Temple Scroll. There we read (48:11–14):

> Do not do like the nations do. They bury their dead in any place; they even bury inside their houses. Instead, you shall set apart places inside your land in which you shall bury your dead. For every four cities you shall appoint one place in which to bury.

The Scroll indicates that burial places are to be limited to one per four cities. The places are certainly located outside the bounds of the cities, though this is not said. The Scroll engages explicitly in a polemic against pagan practices of burying in houses,[48] but implicitly there may also be criticism of Jewish ideas about burial similar to those that would be manifested in the later rabbinic literature which, in the Scroll's view, almost amount to allowing burial "in any place."[49] The rigor of the Scroll in regard to burial is part of the overall strictness it exhibits in regard to questions of the restriction of impurity.[50]

---

[46]See the *Magen Abraham* and *Minḥat Bikkurim* on *t. B. Bat.* 1:7 (Zuckermandel ed. 1:11).

[47]See Y. Yadin's discussion of the rabbinic material (*The Temple Scroll [Megillat hamMiqdaš]* [3 vols.; Jerusalem: Israel Exploration Society, 1977] 1. 249–51).

[48]Cf. *m. Nid.* 7:4; *t. Nid.* 6:15.

[49]Yadin (*Temple Scroll,* 1. 250) recognized the polemical nature of the passage.

[50]See chap. 8, n. 33.

5.7 CONCLUSION

To summarize, we have observed that Priestly tradition requires the removal of corpses from the area of human habitation. Though the evidence is minimal, it seems reasonable to suppose, in view of the general Priestly attitude toward impurity, that the writers of this corpus would have prohibited all burial within the habitation. Ezekiel, a conservative voice of Priestly tradition, gives evidence of this when he requires the burial of the kings to take place far from the sanctuary. The ideal of removing corpses entirely from the habitation is reflected in non-Priestly writings in examples of burial outside of towns and in the general requirement that executions be performed outside the city or camp. But there are exceptions to this rule, particularly in allowing the Judahite monarchs to be buried inside Jerusalem. Yet even with this anomaly, archaeological evidence from First Temple Jerusalem shows that the tendency in other cases of interment was to bury outside the city precincts. It would be of great interest to carefully examine the multitude of archaeological reports for all Israelite cities in both the First and Second Temple periods to ascertain to what extent burial took place outside the habitation and to correlate this data with the laws and attitudes regarding corpse contamination. Such a survey, however, is a work in itself.[51] Still, from the present, necessarily abridged study, it is clear that the fear of pollution from corpses was a factor influencing the place of burial in both pre- and postexilic times.

---

[51]The recent comprehensive dissertation of J. R. Abercrombie ("Palestinian Burial Practices from 1200 to 600 B.C.E." [PhD diss., University of Pennsylvania, 1979]) is a valuable summary of preexilic burial practices. It does not help us, however, with our particular question of the location of burials in relation to the habitation.

6

The Disposal of *Ḥaṭṭā*ʾ*t* and Other Sacrifices

6.1 INTRODUCTION

Attention centers now on the phenomenon of the disposal of various sacrificial portions by incineration.[1] There are three varieties of sacrificial disposal: (a) the burning of the carcasses of *ḥaṭṭāʾt* sacrifices whose blood is used in the Tabernacle enclosure or which belong to the priests, (b) the burning of the portions of edible sacrifices which remain beyond the time allotted for consumption, and (c) the burning of sacrificial portions which have become impure. The main concern in this chapter is the disposal of the *ḥaṭṭāʾt* sacrifice since it is an example of the disposal of something impure. The other aspects of sacrificial disposal are examined in order to gain as complete a picture of the phenomenon as possible.

6.2 IMPURITY OF THE *ḤAṬṬĀʾT* SACRIFICE

The impure character of the *ḥaṭṭāʾt* is born out by the manner in which its blood is used.[2] The blood is always applied to a Tabernacle

[1]The verb *śrp* is used to describe the burning of these sacrificial portions. It is never used of burning offering portions on the altar for which the verb *hqṭyr* is used. *Śrp* therefore indicates elimination or disposal by burning when used of sacrfices (D. Hoffmann, *The Book of Leviticus [Seper Wayyiqraʾ]* [2 vols.; Jerusalem: Mossad Harav Kook, 1953] 1. 95; J. Milgrom, "Sacrifices and Offerings, OT," *IDBSup* [1976] 766).

[2]See J. Milgrom, "The Function of the *Ḥaṭṭāʾt* Sacrifice," *Tarbiz* 40 (1970) 1–8 (Hebrew); "Israel's Sanctuary: The Priestly 'Picture of Dorian Gray,'" *RB* 83 (1976) 390–99; "The Paradox of the Red Cow (Num. XIX),"

sanctum, such as the outer[3] or inner[4] altars, the *kappōret*,[5] the adytum,[5] or shrine[6]—never to a human[7]—with the purpose of purging the object of impurities that have become attached to it.[8] The blood becomes impure because of its use in stripping away these impurities. Since the blood is used *pars pro toto* for the entire animal, the carcass by extension becomes likewise infected with these impurities[9]

The impurity of the *ḥaṭṭāʾt* carcass and its blood is further indicated in various rules surrounding the sacrifice. The one who burns the *ḥaṭṭāʾt* on the Day of Atonement becomes unclean and must launder and bathe (Lev 16:27–28).[10] Vessels in which the edible *ḥaṭṭāʾt* is cooked need scouring and rinsing if made of copper, or breakage if earthenware. This

---

VT 31 (1981) 62–72; "Sacrifices"; "Two Kinds of *Ḥaṭṭāʾt*," *VT* 29 (1976) 333–37.

[3]Exod 29:12; Lev 4:25, 30, 34; 5:9; 8:15; 9:9; 16:18–19. Cf. Ezek 43:20.

[4]Exod 30:10; Lev 4:7, 18.

[5]Lev 16:14, 15. On this rite, see chap. 1, section 1.1.1 and J. Milgrom and D. P. Wright, "*Nazāh*," *TWAT* 5 (1985) 324.

[6]Lev 4:6, 17. See Milgrom and Wright, "*Nazāh*," 324. In addition to these objects, *ḥaṭṭāʾt* blood is applied to the doorposts of the temple and inner court in Ezek 45:19.

[7]Cf. Milgrom "Function," 1–4; "Israel's Sanctuary," 390–91; "*Kipper ʿal/bĕʿad*," *Leshonenu* 35 (1971) 16–17 (Hebrew); "Sacrifices," 766b. *Kippûr* "purgation" (see the next note) is not done to persons (i.e., on their bodies), only on their behalf.

[8]On the Day of Atonement, it is said that the blood rites purify the adytum of the impurities and sins of the Israelites (Lev 16:16a). The daubing of blood on the horns of the outer altar purifies it from Israelite impurities (16:18–19; see chap. 1, section 1.1.2, above). That the *ḥaṭṭāʾt* sacrifice purifies is indicated by its name which means "purification (offering)" (cf. Milgrom, "Function," 1–2; "Sin Offering or Purification Offering?," *VT* 21 [1971] 237–39; see also B. Levine, *In the Presence of the Lord* [Leiden: Brill, 1974] 101–2 and n. 123; J. Milgrom and D. P. Wright, "*Niddāh*," *TWAT* 5 [1984] 250–53). See also Exod 29:36; Lev 8:15; Ezek 43:20, 22, 23; 45:18 where the *ḥaṭṭāʾt* is described as purifying (*ḥiṭṭēʾ*) various sancta. The verb *kipper* when used of the *ḥaṭṭāʾt* means simply "to purge" (Milgrom, "Israel's Sanctuary," 391).

[9]Milgrom, "Paradox," 63–64; "Sacrifices," 767a; "Two Kinds," 336–37. Cf. Levine, *Presence*, 103.

[10]The one who dispatches the scapegoat suffers a similar impurity (16:26).

rule is found only with the *ḥaṭṭā't* sacrifice and therefore seems to be based on and reflect its impure nature (Lev 6:21).[11] *Ḥaṭṭā't* blood spattered on a garment needs to be washed out (6:20). Again, this rule is found only with the *ḥaṭṭā't* and consequently seems to be due to the impure nature of the blood.[12] Finally, all who participate—the priest, the burner, and the one who gathers the ashes—in the preparation of the ashes from the Red Cow, a type of *ḥaṭṭā't* (Num 19:9),[13] become unclean (Num 19:7, 8, 10).[14] The one who uses the Red Cow ashes for purifying another from corpse contamination also becomes impure (19:21).[15] All these examples display the paradox inherent in the *ḥaṭṭā't* sacrifice.[16] Its purpose is to purify objects from impurity, but having done so, it is capable of polluting other objects and persons. As a consequence, the remnants must be handled carefully and must be disposed of to prevent reinfection.

6.3 TWO KINDS OF *ḤAṬṬĀ'T*

Though, generally speaking, *ḥaṭṭā't* sacrifices are repositories of uncleanness, there is a distinction between two sorts of *ḥaṭṭā't* sacrifices. This distinction influences how the impurity of the offering is to be viewed.[17] One type is that whose blood has been used for purification

---

[11]See chap. 4, section 4.2 and n. 8 there.

[12]See chap. 8, section 8.3.2.1, r, on the *ḥaṭṭā't* sacrifice.

[13]On the relationship of the Red Cow rite to other *ḥaṭṭā't* rites, see Milgrom, "Paradox." The Red Cow rite is highly anomalous in comparison to other *ḥaṭṭā't* rites, but there are a few notable similarities, one being the impurity it causes. See D. P. Wright, "Red Heifer," *ADB*, forthcoming.

[14]See chap. 8, section 8.3.2.1, p, on the Red Cow.

[15]See chap. 8, section 8.3.2.1, o, on the impurity of the water of purgation.

[16]See Milgrom, "Paradox."

[17]See Milgrom, "Two Kinds," and the literature he cites throughout. I cannot accept (with Milgrom) Levine's solution (*Presence*, 101–8) that the two types of *ḥaṭṭā't* were originally two distinct sacrificial types, one being a gift of the people for expiation given to the priests and the other an offering made by the priesthood in order to protect the purity of the sanctuary. I proceed from the assumption that both types were originally alike, only differing in the sancta they purified. Later a concession was introduced allowing the priests to eat the *ḥaṭṭā't* whose blood was not used in the sanctuary (see below).

rites inside the sanctuary building (Lev 4:2–12, 13–21; 6:23; 10:18; 16:27) or which is brought by the priests for their own benefit (Exod 29:14; Lev 8:17; 9:8–11). The carcass of this animal is discarded by burning (see below). The other type is that whose blood is used only at the outer altar (Lev 4:22–35). Instead of disposing of its meat as in the case of the sanctuary-priestly *ḥaṭṭāʾt*, it is given to the priests to eat (6:18–22; 10:16–18). That priests may eat this latter type of *ḥaṭṭāʾt* indicates that it has a lesser impurity than the burned *ḥaṭṭāʾt*. One should not, however, go as far to say that since it was used at the outer altar to purge lesser sins the animal carcass of this particular type did not contract impurity and was for this reason given to the priests to eat.[18] The fact that the meat appears to pollute vessels in which it is cooked (6:21) and the blood appears to pollute clothing (v 20) shows that the edible portions are impure. The solution to the inconsistency of allowing the pure and holy priests to eat impure offerings is simply to view it as a concession. Other similar concessions are found in Priestly legislation, such as not requiring a priest to bathe after performing a *ḥaṭṭāʾt* of whatever type.[19]

6.4 IS EATING THE *ḤAṬṬĀʾT* DISPOSAL?

Since we are dealing with the disposal of the *ḥaṭṭāʾt*, I caution against an interpretation connected with the edible *ḥaṭṭāʾt:* that the priests' eating of this sacrifice is a form of disposal that parallels the burning of the sanctuary-priestly *ḥaṭṭāʾt*.[20] The supposed proof for this view is Lev 10:17, where the last half of the verse is taken to mean: "and he gave it (i.e., the *ḥaṭṭāʾt*) to you (i.e., the priests) to bear the iniquity of the congregation, to do expiation for them before the Lord." But J. Milgrom, following A. Ehrlich, has given another interpretation of this

---

[18]Milgrom, "Two Kinds," 336.

[19]The Mishnah solves the problem of the impurity of the *ḥaṭṭāʾt* by saying that the carcass does not pollute until it has left the temple precincts (*m. Zebaḥ.* 12:6; *Yoma* 6:7). Thus any *ḥaṭṭāʾt* still in the court, which includes the eaten *ḥaṭṭāʾt*, does not pollute.

[20]Y. Kaufmann, *The History of Israelite Belief: From Ancient Times Until the End of the Second Temple (Toledot haʾEmuna hayYiśreʾelit Mime Qedem ʿad Sop Bayit Šeni)* (4 vols.; Jerusalem and Tel-Aviv: Bialik Institute and Dvir, 1937–56) 1. 568–59; N. H. Snaith, *Leviticus and Numbers* (London: Thomas Nelson, 1967) 80.

verse: "and he has given it to you for bearing the responsibility of the community by performing purgation rites on their behalf before the Lord."[21] The meat given to the priests according to this understanding of the verse is only a reward or wage for their service. They do not eat in order to "bear away" or dispose of the impurity of sin that exists in the meat. We can conjecture that had the concession to eat not been given to the priests, the carcass would have been burned like the sanctuary-priestly *ḥaṭṭā't*.[22]

---

[21]A. B. Ehrlich, *Randglossen zur hebräischen Bibel* (7 vols.; Leipzig: J. C. Hinrichs, 1908–14) 2. 37; Milgrom, "Two Kinds," 333–34; "Sacrifices," 766a.

[22]Milgrom informs me that he is not as sure about this interpretation as he once was and that he is in fact leaning in the opposite direction. Eating the *ḥaṭṭā't* may actually be a means of disposal. Moses' anger at Aaron's sons in Lev 10:17–18 is difficult to explain if the *ḥaṭṭā't* was merely a prebend given to the priests. This passage indicates that there is a *requirement* to eat the sacrifice and that this consumption has expiatory significance. There is some evidence in other cultures that cathartic materials could be consumed for disposal. For example, in E. E. Knudsen, "An Incantation Tablet from Nimrud," *Iraq* 21 (1959) 57–60 rs. 27–41, various types of flour are mixed into a dough (*qēm šiguši,* called the *ikkib eṭimmē* "the forbidden thing of ghosts"; *qēm kibti,* called the *ikkib* DINGIR.MEŠ "the forbidden thing of gods"; and *qēm innini*). The person is wiped (see appendix 2) with it: *a-me-lu* DUMU DINGIR-*šú kup-pir-ma.* Then, the patient eats the wiping material. It appears these materials not only cleansed the outside of the patient, but also his inside. The accompanying phrases state: "let him eat and it will remove his illness [ ] let him eat and it will tear out his illness."

But there is also some nonbiblical evidence that cathartic sacrifices may be given to officiants merely as prebends, with no intention of disposal. In the Mastigga ritual (iii 38–42; cf. the parallel version in *ANET,* 351, ii 47–53) a sheep is brought forward and designated as a *nakušši.* This term, according to O. Gurney (*Some Aspects of Hittite Religion* [Oxford: Oxford University for the British Academy, 1977] 52), means "a carrier of evil" and would thus indicate that the sheep serves a cathartic purpose. Moreover, the sheep, when offered to the sun god, is described as having a "mouth and tongue." This indicates that the animal is laden with evils or represents them since angry words spoken with the "mouth and tongue" are the object of purification in this ritual (cf. i 2–4: "If a father and son, or a husband and wife, or a brother and sister quarrel, when I bring them together, I perform the following"; i 8–10 [in

6.5 DISPOSAL OF THE SANCTUARY-PRIESTLY *ḤAṬṬĀʾT*

In regard to the disposal of the sanctuary-priestly *ḥaṭṭāʾt*, the Bible prescribes that the skin, meat, head, legs, entrails, and excrement are to be taken outside the camp to the ash dump (*šepek haddešen*) and there be burned (Exod 29:14; Lev 4:11–12, 21; 6:23; 8:17; 9:11; 16:27). The ash dump is not just for the disposal of *ḥaṭṭāʾt* carcasses, but serves as a general disposal place for various unusable cultic refuse items. As the name ash dump indicates, it was the place where ashes from the burnt offering altar were discarded (Lev 6:4).[23] Furthermore, the *murʾâ* (crop?) and *nôṣâ* (plumage) of the *ʿōlâ* bird were thrown in the ash place (*mĕqôm haddešen*) near the altar (1:16; cf. 6:3) and then taken out to the ash dump with the ashes (6:4). Perhaps other sacrificial remnants were disposed of in the ash dump (see below).

The ash dump, being a place of disposal, is properly located outside the camp so that cultic impurities, such as the *ḥaṭṭāʾt* carcass, will not contaminate the community. But as was seen in Chapter Three, this dump contrasts with other extracamp disposal sites, such as that for building materials infected with *ṣāraʿat* which is termed an "impure place" (Lev 14:40, 41, 45), by being characterized as a "pure place." The reason why the ash dump must be a pure place is obvious. The items discarded there, even though they are refuse, and even though *ḥaṭṭāʾt* carcasses are impure, are still holy and must therefore be treated in a manner commensurate with that status.

---

the version found in *ANET*, 350b]: "Whatever thou spokest with [thy] mouth [and] tongue, . . . Let it be cut out of your body these days!" [Goetze's translation]). This evil-carrying or evil-respresenting sheep, after the presentation to the sun god, is given to the Old Woman who is officiating. Nothing else is said about what is done with it. It therefore appears to be just a prebend given to her in partial exchange for her performance of the rite.

On the inedibility of cathartic sacrifices in ancient Greece, see R. Parker, *Miasma: Pollution and Purification in Early Greek Religion* (Oxford: Clarendon, 1983) 283 and n. 11.

[23]Cf. Exod 27:3; Num 4:13. See the article "*Diššûn Mizbēaḥ haḤiṣôn*," in the *Enṣiqlopedya Talmudit* 8 (1957) 3–12. For the disposal of ashes from the inner altar and ashes and old oil from the menorah discussed in rabbinic sources, see the articles "*Diššûn hamMĕnôrâ*," *ET* 8 (1957) 1–3 and "*Diššûn Mizbēaḥ hapPĕnîmî*," *ET* 8 (1957) 12–16.

Ezekiel follows Priestly regulation when he requires *ḥaṭṭā᾿t* carcasses to be burned in the *mipqād* (43:21). It is not clear where this place is. All that is known is that it lies outside the entire temple complex (*miḥûṣ lammiqdāš*).[24] It may be connected in some way with the *mipqād* gate of Neh 3:31.[25]

As a parallel to the disposal of *ḥaṭṭā᾿t* carcasses outside the camp, we may refer to the rite of the Red Cow. As noted, above, the Cow while being burned and the resulting ashes cause impurity.[26] For this reason the entire rite is performed outside the camp (Num 19:3) and the ashes are stored outside the camp in a pure place (v 9).[27]

6.6 DISPOSAL OF OTHER SACRIFICES

To complement the discussion of *ḥaṭṭā᾿t* disposal and to discover further reasons for it, it is necessary to investigate the disposal of sacrificial portions that were leftover after the eating period has been completed and the disposal of those portions which have become impure.

6.6.1 Legislative Strata and the *Pesaḥ, Tôdâ, Millu᾿îm* and *Šĕlāmîm*

Priestly prescriptions about the disposal of leftover *pesaḥ, tôdâ, šĕlāmîm* and *millu᾿îm* offerings appear to reflect a two-stage development. The terminology used in describing the eating and disposal of these offerings suggests this perception. The prescriptions concerning the *pesaḥ* and *tôdâ* say that the meat is *not to be leftover to the following morning,* while those concerning the *šĕlāmîm* and *millu᾿îm* say that the uneaten portion that *remains until morning must be*

---

[24]*Miqdāš* in Ezekiel usually means the entire temple complex, including the courts. Cf. 44:1, 7, 9, 11.

[25]Cf. W. Eichrodt, *Ezekiel: A Commentary* (OTL; Philadelphia: Westminster, 1970) 554; Milgrom, "Two Kinds," 335; W. Zimmerli, *Ezechiel* (BKAT 13/1, 2; Neukirchen: Neukirchener, 1969) 1103.

[26]See chap. 8, section 8.3.2.1, p.

[27]The Temple Scroll (16:10–14) perhaps indicates that the *ḥaṭṭā᾿t* sacrifice is burned in a place separate from other cultic refuse when it says that it is to be burned "in a place set apart (*mûbdāl*) for *ḥaṭṭā᾿t* sacrifices."

burned.[28] The two expressions, not leaving over versus burning the remnant, occur exclusively of one another. The rules about the *pesaḥ* (except in one case, see below) and *tôdâ* which prohibit leaving the sacrifices over until morning say nothing of burning the remnant on the next day, and the rules about the *šĕlāmîm* and *millu'îm* which allow burning on the next day, or the third day in the case of the *šĕlāmîm*, do not prohibit leaving part of the sacrifice over until morning.

One exception to this is Exod 12:10 dealing with the *pesaḥ* which contains both phrases: "you shall not leave any of it until morning; you shall burn the part of it remaining until morning with fire." The latter phrase seems to be a secondary accretion for three reasons. (1) The phraseology used with the various sacrifices sorts itself out neatly

---

[28]The phrases are copied here in full for comparison:

Pesaḥ:

wĕlōʾ tôtîrû mimmennû ʿad bōqer (Exod 12:10a)
wĕhannôtār mimmennû ʿad bōqer bāʾēš tiśrōpû (Exod 12:10b; this may be a later addition, see below)
lōʾ yašʾîrû mimmennû ʿad bōqer (Num 9:12)
wĕlōʾ yālîn labbōqer zebaḥ ḥag happāsaḥ (JE, Exod 34:25; cf. JE Exod 23:18: *wĕlōʾ yālîn ḥēleb ḥaggî ʿad bōqer*)
wĕlōʾ yālîn min habbāśār ʾăšer tizbaḥ bāʿereb bayyôm hāriʾšôn labbōqer (Deut 16:4)

Tôdâ:

lōʾ yannîaḥ mimmennû ʿad bōqer (Lev 7:15)
lōʾ tôtîrû mimmennû ʿad bōqer (Lev 22:30)

Šĕlāmîm:

wĕhannôtār mibbĕśar hazzābaḥ bayyôm haššĕlîšî bāʾēš yiśśārēp (Lev 7:17)
wĕhannôtār ʿad yôm haššĕlîšî bāʾēš yiśśārēp (Lev 19:6)

Milluʾîm:

wĕʾim yiwwātēr mibbĕśar hammilluʾîm umin halleḥem ʿad habbōqer wĕśāraptā ʾet hannôtār bāʾēš (Exod 29:34)
wĕhannôtār babbāśār uballāḥem bāʾēš tiśrōpû (Lev 8:32)

between two groups of sacrifices (*pesaḥ* and *tôdâ* vis-à-vis the *millu᾽îm* and *šĕlāmîm*).[29] (2) Other instances of the passover rule do not contain the latter burning requirement (see note 28). (3) Exod 12:10 with both parts presents a contradiction: the second part presupposes a remnant which is prohibited in the first part. That the prohibition of not leaving sacrificial meat over to the next day is strict, and not one that could somehow be harmonized with the requirement of burning the leftover material the next day, is indicated by three passages. (a) Exod 12:4 instructs the Israelites to proportion the passover meat so that there will not be more for each person than what he or she can eat, implying that all was to be eaten at the night festival. (b) The story and regulations about eating the manna use the same language as the passover and *tôdâ* regulations: "no one shall leave any of it over until morning" (Exod 16:19, 20, 24). One was only to gather as much manna as needed on a particular day (vv 16–18). Only on the sixth day may extra manna be gathered so that it may be leftover for the Sabbath. (c) The same language is also found in the rule to pay laborers on the day of their work: "the pay of a hired person shall not remain with you until morning" (Lev 19:13).

The foregoing evidence can be interpreted as reflecting two stages in the development of the Priestly rules. That is, the legislation was more strict at an early stage in regard to the eating of the *pesaḥ* and *tôdâ*. These sacrifices were to be entirely eaten before morning. In contrast, the meat of the *millu᾽îm* which was only consumed on the day it was offered, could be left until morning when it was to be burned.[30] Similarly, the *šĕlāmîm*, which was eaten on the first and second days, could be kept over until the third day when the remaining meat was burned.

---

[29]A. B. Ehrlich (*The Bible According to Its Plain Meaning (Miqra᾽ kiPešuṭo)* [3 vols.; Berlin, 1899–1901; reprint, New York: Ktav, 1969] 1. 218; *Randglossen*, 2. 23–24) to a certain extent recognized the distinction in language between the various sacrifices.

[30]I am admittedly uncomfortable with the inconsistency between the rules for the *pesaḥ* and *tôdâ* vis-à-vis the *millu᾽îm* at the early stage. The former offerings could only be consumed on the first day. But why can the *millu᾽îm*, being quasi most-holy (see chap. 9, nn. 1 and 5), be leftover to the next day, while the others mentioned here, lesser holy offerings, could not? An equal or greater stricture should apply to the *millu᾽îm!* A possible solution is to assume that the prescriptions about the *millu᾽îm* have been written in accordance with the later view, perhaps

At a later stage, Priestly legislation became more lenient in regard to the *pesaḥ* and *tôdâ*. This is evidenced in the case of the *pesaḥ* where the phrase "you shall burn the part of it remaining until morning with fire" has been added in Exod 12:10. At this later level the phrase "you shall not leave any of it over until morning" out of logical necessity changed its significance to mean none of it should be leftover until morning *for the purpose of eating it.* That is, it may be leftover for the purpose of disposing of it. With the meaning of the phrase changed, the same relaxation presumably would have occurred in connection with the remnants of the *tôdâ*, though its prescription has not been textually modified as in the case of the *pesaḥ*. This historical development is summarily shown in fig. 6.1.

TYPE	EARLIER STAGE	LATER STAGE
pesaḥ	eat before morning	eat 1 day, burn 2nd
tôdâ	eat before morning	eat 1 day, burn 2nd
milluʾîm	eat 1 day, burn 2nd	eat 1 day, burn 2nd
šĕlāmîm	eat 2 days, burn 3rd	eat 2 days, burn 3rd

Fig 6.1: Development of Sacrificial Eating Prescriptions

---

to avoid another inconsistency in requiring the five priestly initiates to do the near impossible: to consume an entire ram before morning. But this explanation fails if we make the assumption (which seems logical) that the prescriptions requiring consumption before morning allow burning of the remnant before morning if the meat could not be eaten. A better solution is to explain the laxity of the rule with the *milluʾîm* being due to the fact that the priestly initiates would remain at the sanctuary (cf. Lev 8:35). They would be there the next day to dispose of the remnant properly. Conversely, in the case of the *tôdâ*, the participants would possibly be leaving at the end of the first day or early the next morning to return home. Hence it was necessary to consume it or burn it before the coming of the new day. In the case of the *pesaḥ*, the leftover meat was consumed or destroyed before the next day because it was to be eaten in haste (*bĕhippāzôn;* Exod 12:11).

6.6.2 The *Ḥaṭṭā'ṯ*, *'Āšām* and *Minḥâ*

The rules about the eating periods and disposal of the remnants of other sacrifices must be indirectly deduced.[31] The edible *ḥaṭṭā'ṯ* can only be eaten on the first day after which the remnant is disposed of by burning. This is intimated in Lev 10:16–20 where Aaron and his sons burn the *ḥaṭṭā'ṯ* that they should have eaten on the day it was offered. Further, it may be argued that if the *tôdâ* and *pesaḥ*, lesser holy offerings, must be consumed in one day and the remnant burned the next, the same rule at least should apply to the most holy offerings which include the *ḥaṭṭā'ṯ*.[32] Lastly, rabbinic tradition and Josephus held that the *ḥaṭṭā'ṯ* was eaten in one day.[33]

The *'āšām* is certainly also to be burned after an eating period of one day since it is most holy and described as being "like the *ḥaṭṭā'ṯ*" (Lev 7:7).[34] Josephus also gives one day as the eating period.[35]

Finally, the *minḥâ*, a most holy offering, was probably eaten on the first day and the remnant was burned by or on the second. Evidence comes from the requirement that breads accompanying the *millu'îm* were to be eaten in one day and the leftovers to be burned on the next (Exod 29:34; Lev 8:32). Rabbinic tradition, moreover, limits eating to the first day (*m. Zebaḥ.* 6:1).

---

[31]Because of the lack of evidence, I refrain from fitting the other offerings into the historical recontruction that I presented for the *pesaḥ*, *tôdâ*, *šělāmîm*, and *millu'îm* offerings.

[32]Hoffmann, *Leviticus*, 1. 175; J. Milgrom, *Cult and Conscience: The Asham and the Priestly Doctrine of Repentance* (SJLA 18; Leiden: Brill, 1976) 41, n. 154.

[33]*M. Zebaḥ.* 5:3; Josephus, *Ant.* 3.9.3–4 §§ 230–35.

[34]The statement that the *'āšām* is like the *ḥaṭṭā'ṯ* (Lev 7:7) appears to be contextually connected with the prescriptions about eating (cf. vv 6–7) which would include related rules about the period of eating and the disposal of the leftovers. See 6:10b where the *minḥâ* is described as being like the *ḥaṭṭā'ṯ* and *'āšām*. Here the comparison regards eating as vv 10a, 11 and the lack of comparison to the *'ōlâ*, which is not eaten, show (cf. Hoffmann, *Leviticus*, 1. 160–61; Milgrom, *Cult*, 15, n. 48).

[35]*Ant.* 3.9.3–4 §§ 230–35.

6.6.3 Reason for the Disposal of Other Sacrifices

The question that now surfaces is why must these leftover portions be burned? Is it because they have in some way become impure? As we have seen, the main reason for burning the sanctuary-priestly *ḥaṭṭāʾt* carcass was because of its impurity. We also learn from the prescriptions about the *šĕlāmîm*—and it is clear that this would apply to other types of offerings—that if the meat becomes impure by coming in contact with anything unclean, it is to be burned (Lev 7:19). Because burning is the method of disposing of impure offerings, some have concluded that the leftover portions of edible sacrifices are burned because of some sort of impurity or defect in the meat.[36] Specifically, they argue that the portions have begun to decompose and are thus in a way unclean. Though the rules for disposal are influenced to some degree by the fact that the meat does spoil, there are inconsistencies in viewing spoilage as the reason for disposal. The *minḥâ*, explicitly the bread accompanying the *milluʾîm*, is to be disposed of after one day, but it cannot be said that it has begun to spoil.[37] Moreover, the spoilage theory cannot explain why some offerings can be eaten only on one day while others can be eaten for two days. Spoilage, if it was a consideration in the disposal of the remnants of edible sacrifices, has been overshadowed by another conceptual factor.

6.6.3.1 The Word *Piggûl*

To discover this conceptual factor, I turn to an examination of the word *piggûl* which is found in connection with the leftover portions of

---

[36]E.g., Philo, *De Specialibus Legibus* 1.40 §§ 220–23; Maimonides, *More Nebukim,* 3:46; A. Bertholet, *Leviticus* (KHC 3; Tübingen: J. C. B. Mohr, 1901) 22; A. Dillmann, *Die Bücher Exodus und Leviticus* (3d ed.; Leipzig: S. Hirzel, 1897) 491; W. R. Smith, *The Religion of the Semites: The Fundamental Institutions* ([2d ed.]; London: A. and C. Black, 1894; reprint, New York: Schocken, 1972) 387; G. Wenham, *The Book of Leviticus* (NICOT; Grand Rapids: W. B. Eerdmans, 1979) 124–25. Bertholet and Smith suggest the limit of one day with the offerings of higher sanctity was to protect them by disposing of them before they could begin to badly decompose.

[37]Hoffmann, *Leviticus,* 1. 175.

the *šĕlāmîm* (Lev 7:18; 19:7).[38] The word occurs only four times in the Bible and, consequently, derivation of a contextual definition is difficult. To be sure, some interpreters understand it to mean "stench, rottenness," and thus obtain support for the idea of disposal due to spoilage.[39] A careful examination of the word in its contexts will yield a different meaning which will in turn lead to the reason for the disposal of the remnants of edible sacrifices.

In the case of the *šĕlāmîm* offerings, there is a caveat that if the meat is eaten on the third day, the offering will not be accepted (Lev 7:18; 19:7), it will be a *piggûl*. Note first that *piggûl* is morphologically a Piʿel nominal formation (hence my inclusion of the indefinite article).[40] Though a noun may be construed adjectivally in translation, we should

---

[38]The word has recently been treated by M. Görg ("*Piggul* und *pilaegaeš*—Experimente zur Etymologie," *BN* 10 [1979] 7–11). He proposes a dual etymology for the word from Akkadian *bugurru* "an edible organ of a sacrificial animal" (*CAD* B, 307a) and Egyptian *pꜣ-grg* "the falsehood." By the combination of the meanings of these near homonyms, biblical Hebrew came to possess a word which meant an abominable portion of sacrificial meat. Besides phonological difficulties in connecting *piggûl* with these foreign words, this theory is based upon too much historical speculation to be convincing. Görg admits that it is quite speculative. On the word, see also B. Levine, "*Piggûl*," *EM* 6 (1971) 435–36.

[39]Cf. Wenham, *Leviticus*, 124–25; *NEB* "tainted"; *JB* "defiled flesh." See the discussion of views in Gorg, "*Piggul*," 7–9. This interpretation is supported somewhat by the fact that in prescriptive passages the word only occurs with the *šĕlāmîm*, the only offering allowed two days for consumption and, hence, the one which would become the most spoiled. But as will be shown, below, this interpretation ignores the fact that *piggûl* is due to eating on the third day, not to the meat being around three days.

The reason why *piggûl* only occurs with the *šĕlāmîm* probably lies in the place where it was eaten. The *tôdâ*, which is eaten in one day, was likely eaten at the sanctuary where it would be supervised by the priests. They would prevent misuse of the offering. Also, according to the historical reconstruction charted above, the *tôdâ* was consumed or destroyed before the morning. For these two reasons then, eating the *tôdâ* outside its period for consumption which would cause it to become a *piggûl* is precluded. On the other hand, that the *šĕlāmîm* can become a *piggûl* implies that it was eaten outside the sanctuary without any priestly supervision.

[40]*GKC* § 84i; P. Jouon, *Grammaire de l'Hebreu biblique* (Rome: Institut Biblique Pontifical, 1947) § 88 Ic.

not ignore the fact that *piggûl* is a noun. An examination of the syntax in which the word occurs is additionally instructive. Lev 7:18 says: "If some of the flesh of his *zebaḥ šĕlāmîm* is eaten on the third day, it will not be accepted. It will not be reckoned to the one who offers it. It will be a *piggûl*'[41] (the subject of the verb *yihyê* is the offering). Significantly, the sacrifice is a *piggûl* only if the offering is eaten on the third day; it is not a precondition of the meat (e.g., rottenness) before the wrongful consumption. If there is no eating, there is no *piggûl.* This interpretation is confirmed by 19:7: "If it is eaten on the third day, it is a *piggûl;* it will not be accepted."

At this point in the argument, since *piggûl* occurs in the environment of statements about the offering not being accepted, a meaning like "invalid sacrifice" or "unaccepted offering" is suggested for the word. Still the meaning can be made more precise by examining the other occurrences of the word. Ezekiel is instructed to act out the wretched conditions to which the Israelites will be subjected by cooking his food on human dung (Ezek 4:12). He responds in startled protest that he has never before partaken of anything unclean, including *bĕśar piggûl* "*piggûl* meat" (v 14). The context of impurity suggests that *piggûl* means "impurity" or the like. A similar context is found in Isa 65:4 where it says faithless Israelites spend time among tombs and eat swine's flesh and broth[42] of *piggûlîm.* The same semantic field "impurity" is suggested by this example. By combining the ideas of disqualification and impurity, I propose that *piggûl* in Leviticus and the prophets means a "desecrated, profaned sacrifice."

The notion of desecration is found elsewhere in the stipulations about the eating and disposal of the sacrificial remnants and lends important support to the foregoing interpretation of *piggûl.* One who eats of the *šĕlāmîm* on the third day "shall bear his penalty because he has profaned (*ḥillēl*) a holy offering of the Lord; that person shall be cut off from his people" (Lev 19:8). This is tantamount to defining *piggûl* as "desecration" or "desecrated offering" since in v 7 eating on the third day is called *piggûl.* Similarly, one must not eat the *milluʾîm* after the first day "because it is holy" (Exod 29:34), implying that eating would cause

---

[41]On this interpretation of the syntax, see Ehrlich, *Randglossen,* 2. 24.

[42]Read *mĕraq* "broth" with the Masora and some other versions (see *BHS*).

profanation. In Lev 7:18 it is most reasonable to understand *piggûl* as "desecrated offering" and translate: "If some of the flesh of his *zebaḥ šĕlāmîm* is eaten on the third day, it will not be accepted. It will not be reckoned to the one who offers it. It will be a desecrated offering (*piggûl*). The person who eats of it shall bear his penalty."

This assessment of *piggûl* has led us to what appears to be the foremost reason why offering remnants were disposed of: *to prevent their profanation.* The reason for one day versus two day eating is a reflection of and due to the sanctity of the offerings. The most holy and the more important lesser holy offerings were to be eaten in one day. The least holy offering, the *šĕlāmîm*, was given a two day consumption period.[43]

The disposal of offering remnants to prevent profanation is highlighted by the disposal of other holy materials. Earlier in this chapter it was seen that ashes from the burnt offering altar were taken outside the camp to the ash dump (Lev 6:3–4). Though the ashes are refuse, they are still holy. Disposal in the pure cultic refuse place removes them from the chance of profanation. Similarly, the hair of a nazirite who has properly fulfilled his vow is burned in the fire which cooks his *šĕlāmîm* offering (Num 6:18).[44] The reason is the same. When making the vow the nazirite sanctified his head (Num 6:5, 9, 11) and his hair thereby became holy.[45] When he shaves it, he prevents desecration of it by destroying it in fire.[46]

---

[43]Cf. Bertholet, *Leviticus,* 22; K. Elliger, *Leviticus* (HAT 1/4; Tübingen: J. C. B. Mohr, 1966) 100.

[44]The "fire under the *zebaḥ haššĕlāmîm*" in Num 6:18 is the fire under the pot in which the *šĕlāmîm* is cooked. Some have thought this is the fire on the altar in which *šĕlāmîm* fat portions were burned (G. B. Gray, *A Critical and Exegetical Commentary on Numbers* [ICC; Edinburgh: T. and T. Clark, 1903] 68; M. Noth, *Numbers: A Commentary* [OTL; Philadelphia: Westminster, 1968] 56–57). The phrase "fire under the *zebaḥ haššĕlāmîm,*" however, is a very odd way to refer to the altar fire. If the altar fire was intended, we would expect a more obvious description. Furthermore, the context of v 19 is cooking and thus indicates that the fire in v 18 pertains to cooking. Nothing is said in the entire passage of burning the *šĕlāmîm* fat portions on the altar. Cf. the tradition preserved in *Tg. Onq.* and *Tg. Ps.-J.* on Num 6:18 and *m. Nazir* 6:8; *Mid.* 2:5.

[45]Cf. Milgrom, *Cult,* 66–67 and n. 240; "Sanctification," *IDBSup* (1976) 783a.

[46]Rabbinic tradition says that the hair of a nazirite who accidently became unclean (Num 6:9–12) is to be buried (*m. Tem.* 7:4).

6.6.4 The Place of the Disposal of Other Sacrifices

Before concluding the present discussion, it is proper to inquire about the place where sacrificial remnants and portions made impure were burned. The Bible gives no real clue about this. It is possible that these portions were to be burned at the ash dump where the sanctuary-priestly *ḥaṭṭāʾt*, altar ashes, and *ʿōlâ* bird parts were discarded.[47] There is reason to suppose, however, that these portions could be burned in any available fire suitable to the context of the particular type of sacrifice; i.e., most holy offerings could be disposed of in any nonsacrificial fire in the sanctuary court area and lesser holy offerings could be disposed of in any fire in or outside the sanctuary area. First, the very lack of a prescription about where they are to be incinerated is a hint that freedom prevailed in the matter. Secondly, since the lesser holy offerings could be theoretically eaten anywhere that is pure, such as in the priests' or laypersons' homes, it appears that the destruction would be a private concern not connected with the sanctuary ash dump.[48] Thirdly, the burning of the nazirite's hair in the fire under the cooking pot for the *šĕlāmîm* shows that holy items may be burned in places other than the ash dump. Finally, rabbinic tradition, perhaps reflecting Second Temple custom, requires these portions to be burned in places other than the ash dump.[49]

To the examples of the disposal of holy items, we can add the rule in JE that the firstborn of an ass must have its neck broken (Exod 13:13; 34:20). This reflects the idea, present in the cases we are discussing, that an irredeemable or unusable sanctum must be destroyed. In P, the impure firstborn may be redeemed or sold (Lev 27:27; Num 18:15; on the difference in these rules, see S. R. Driver, *A Critical and Exegetical Commentary on Deuteronomy* [3d ed., ICC; Edinburgh: T. and T. Clark, 1901] 185–87; J. Milgrom, "First-born," *IDBSup* [1976] 338). According to Lev 27:29, the human under *ḥērem* is to be put to death.

[47]Milgrom (private communication) believes that impure sacrificial portions would not be burned at the ash dump because of their impurity. To me, that they may be burned at the ash dump is still a possibility because they are a sanctum.

[48]On the place of eating sacrifices, see chap. 9, section 9.2.2.1

[49]The Gemara says there were three places for burning: one in the court where disqualified portions of the most holy sacrifices, fat parts of lesser holy offerings, and some sanctuary *ḥaṭṭāʾt* sacrifices were burned; the second outside the court but on the Temple Mount where other disqualified

6.7 CONCLUSION

The reasons for and the places of incinerating sacrifices or portions of them are not uniform. The sanctuary-priestly *ḥaṭṭā't* is burned outside the camp in the ash dump in order to remove contagious impurity from the holy and profane spheres. Study of the disposal of sacrificial remnants has granted an additional perspective of why the *ḥaṭṭā't* carcass is burned: it is a sanctum which has no further use and so, to prevent possible desecration, it is destroyed. Sacrificial portions that have become impure are disposed of partly because their impurity is contagious to other holy offerings, but since the impurity is not communicable to the profane sphere,[50] the main reason must be that the portions are now unusable and are destroyed to prevent further desecration.[51] Leftover portions of edible sacrifices are to be burned to

---

sanctuary *ḥaṭṭā't* sacrifices were burned; and the third, the ash dump outside the city (*b. Zebaḥ.* 104b; Maimonides, *MTor,* ʿAboda, Maʿaśe haqQorbanot 7:3–4). On the burning places inside and outside the court, cf. *m. Šeqal.* 8:6, 7; *Zebaḥ.* 12:5 (cf. *t. Zebaḥ.* 11:18). Lay persons may burn leftovers of the *pesaḥ* or a small portion of it which has become impure at home (*m. Pesaḥ.* 7:8). Less holy offerings taken out of Jerusalem become invalid and are to be burned where the person is if he is too far from the burning place on the Temple Mount (*m. Pesaḥ.* 3:8). Otherwise, lesser holy offerings could or should be burned at the burning place on the Temple Mount (cf. *m. Zebaḥ.* 8:4, 5; *Ker.* 6:1; *Mid.* 3:3; *t. Zebaḥ.* 7:6; *Tem.* 4:16). On burning of sacrifices in general, see Maimonides, *MTor,* ʿAboda Pesule hamMuqdašin, chap. 19.

[50]The impurity that offering meat would contract is logically a minor type, not communicable to the profane sphere. The only communicable impurity it could contract would be corpse contamination (other communicable impurities do not apply). This latter impurity would be rare in connection with offerings. See chap. 9.

[51]No sanctions are described for one who eats impure sacrificial meat such as *kārēt* for one who eats a sacrifice while he or she is impure (Lev 7:20–21). The Mishnah stipulates that one who eats unclean sacrificial meat is to be punished with lashes (*Mak.* 3:2; cf. *t. Zebaḥ.* 5:12). Elsewhere, the Mishnah says the one who eats impure sacrificial meat is not liable to *kārēt* nor to bringing a sacrifice (*Zebaḥ.* 13:2; see H. Albeck, *The Six Orders of the Mishnah [Šiša Sidre Mišna]* [6 vols.; Jerusalem and Tel-Aviv: Bialik Institute and Dvir, 1957–59] 5. 48 on *Zebaḥ.* 13:2 ; see also Maimonides' Mishnah commentary on this passage).

avoid profanation, not because they have become impure due to spoilage. Remnants of edible portions and impure sacrificial portions may be disposed of anywhere in contrast to the sanctuary-priestly *ḥaṭṭāʾt* which must be burned in the cultic ash dump.

7

The Disposal of *Ḥaṭṭāʾt* Blood

7.1 INTRODUCTION

Related to the disposal of sanctuary-priestly *ḥaṭṭāʾt* carcasses is the disposal of blood from *ḥaṭṭāʾt* sacrifices. Since the blood is an impure substance, this offers another example of how impurities were to be eliminated according to Priestly legislation. *Ḥaṭṭāʾt* blood leftover after it has been ritually placed or sprinkled on sancta is discarded by pouring it out at the base of the outer altar. The disposal is described by the verbs *šāpak*[1] and *yāṣaq*,[2] both meaning "pour out," and, in the case of a *ḥaṭṭāʾt* bird, by the verb *māṣâ* "squeeze out."[3] Pouring out the *ḥaṭṭāʾt* blood is not part of the *ḥaṭṭāʾt* ritual proper and therefore does not seem to have any particular ritual or theological significance other than just being a means for disposing of an impure sanctum.[4] This disposal contrasts with other blood manipulations found with the *ḥaṭṭāʾt*, *ʿōlâ*,

---

[1]Exod 29:12; Lev 4:7, 18, 25, 30, 34.

[2]Lev 8:15; 9:9.

[3]Lev 5:9.

[4]It is not clear if Lev 8:15, which ends in the phrase *wayĕqaddĕšēhû lĕkappēr ʿālāw* "(thus) he shall sanctify it by performing expiation on it" after describing the slaughtering, placement of blood on the altar horns, and pouring out blood at the base of the altar, is proof that the pouring out of blood at the base has a sanctifying or expiatory effect. Note that another summarizing statement *wayĕḥaṭṭēʾ ʾet-hammizbēaḥ* "(thus) he purifies the altar" occurs between the statements about the placement of blood on the horns and the pouring of the blood at the altar base. This separation of blood manipulations by a summarizing statement may suggest that the last phrase of the verse does not refer to the pouring out at the base, but only to the placement of blood on the horns.

and *šĕlāmîm* that are more ritually or theologically significant. In the *ḥaṭṭāʾt* rituals, depending on the type of *ḥaṭṭāʾt* being performed,[5] the blood may be applied (*nātan*) to the horns of the incense and burnt offering altars and may be sprinkled (*hizzâ*) in the shrine and adytum.[6] These various blood applications purge the sancta of impurity and constitute the central ritual act of the *ḥaṭṭāʾt* sacrifice. In *ʿōlâ, ʾāšām,* and *šĕlāmîm* sacrifices, the blood is dashed (*zāraq*) on the four sides of the altar.[7] The blood dashing appears to dedicate the animal as an offering to the Lord. For the *ʿōlâ* and *ʾāšām* this blood application may have expiatory effect as well.[8] In the present chapter, I will ignore these latter blood rites that have extensive or primary ritual significance and focus on the reasons for and the method of disposing of *ḥaṭṭāʾt* blood. We will have recourse to extra-Priestly and postbiblical examples in order to determine how Priestly writings may have intended the blood to be discarded.

In the rabbinic view, the disposal of blood did not have ritual significance. Not disposing of it did not impair the expiatory effect of the sacrifice (*m. Zebaḥ* 5:1–2; Maimonides, *MTor,* ʿAboda, Maʿaśe haqQorbanot 19:4). If J. Milgrom's revised interpretation of the eating of the *ḥaṭṭāʾt* is accepted (that it is a form of disposal and expiation; see chap. 6, n. 22), then by analogy the disposal of *ḥaṭṭāʾt* blood and the burning of *ḥaṭṭāʾt* carcasses may have ritual significance; i.e., these acts have an expiatory function which completes that which was begun by applying blood to the altar horns. See below, section 7.3.1, on *ḥaṭṭāʾt* blood disposal having an expiatory significance in Ezekiel's system.

[5]See chap. 6, section 6.3.

[6]See chap. 6, section 6.2.

[7]Exod 29:16, 20; Lev 1:5, 11; 3:2, 8, 13; 7:2, 14; 8:19, 24; 9:12, 18; 17:6; Num 18:17; cf. 2 Kgs 16:13, 15; Ezek 43:18; 2 Chr 29:22; 30:16; 35:11. The application of the blood of the *ʿōlâ*-bird to the altar is described with the root *mṣh* "squeeze out" (Lev 1:15). Deut 12:27 uses *špk* of the application of blood from *šĕlāmîm* offerings to the altar. In the context, this verb is obviously used to parallel the pouring out (*špk*) of the blood of profanely slaughtered animals on the ground (vv 16, 24; 15:23).

[8]See Lev 1:4 for the expiatory nature of the *ʿōlâ* and the context of Lev chaps. 5 and 7 for that of the *ʾāšām* (see also J. Milgrom, *Cult and Conscience: the Asham and the Priestly Doctrine of Repentance* [SJLA 18; Leiden: Brill, 1976] passim). For a good summary, see J. Milgrom, "Sacrifices and Offerings, OT," *IDBSupp* (1976) 768–69.

7.2 REASONS FOR THE DISPOSAL OF *ḤAṬṬĀʾT* BLOOD

The reasons for the disposal of *ḥaṭṭāʾt* blood can be given without much discussion, since they are already evident from the study of the disposal of *ḥaṭṭāʾt* carcasses (Chapter Six). First, the blood of the *ḥaṭṭāʾt* is impure as is the carcass of the sacrifice. For example, the blood can pollute clothing (Lev 6:20). Consequently, the blood is thrown away to prevent any possible contamination of persons or objects.[9] Second, since the blood is an unusable portion of a sacrifice, it, like the remnants of offerings in general, must be discarded to prevent profanation and sacrilege.

7.3 THE METHOD OF THE DISPOSAL OF *ḤAṬṬĀʾT* BLOOD

The manner of disposal is not immediately evident. Specifically, our question in this chapter is how was the *ḥaṭṭāʾt* blood to be discarded at the Tabernacle altar according to the Priestly view? The passages that speak about *ḥaṭṭāʾt* blood disposal mention pouring the blood out at the base of the altar, but beyond this there is no specific information about how this is to be done, particularly from an architectural point of view. A reasonable solution to the question may be obtained by examining the design and purposes of the drainage systems of Ezekiel's altar and that of Second Temple times, and then by reexamining the construction of the portable Tabernacle altar.

7.3.1 Blood Disposal at Ezekiel's Altar

The interpretation of the data given in Ezek 43:13–17 regarding the structure of the altar in the court of Ezekiel's temple is not free of obscurity. The altar consists of four levels: (a) On the top is the upper hearth stage (*haharʾēl* or *hāʾărîʾēl*,[10] vv 15, 16). It is four cubits high,

---

[9]See chap. 6, section 6.2.

[10]The significance of *haharʾēl/hāʾărîʾēl* in this passage is unclear. Nevertheless, it is obvious that it is the name of the top block of the altar set on top of the larger *ʿăzārâ*, its height being four cubits and its width and length each twelve cubits. Altar horns (not animal horns, cf. N. H. Tur-Sinai, "*ʾĂrîʾēl*," *EM* 1 [1954] 558–60) are on its four corners. Many have attempted to explain the term etymologically, but no proposal carries convincing weight (cf. S. Feigin, "The Meaning of Ariel," *JBL* 39

surmounted by four horns on the corners which are probably one cubit high.[11] This stage is twelve cubits square. (b) Below this is the intermediate stage, called the "larger stage" (*hāʿăzārâ*[12] *haggĕdôlâ*, v 14) or simply the "stage" (*hāʿăzārâ*, v 17; cf. v 20; 45:19). It is four cubits high and fourteen cubits square. (c) Below the "larger stage" is the next level, called the "smaller" or "lower stage" (*hāʿăzārâ haqqĕtannâ, hāʿăzārâ hattaḥtônâ*, v 14). This is two cubits high and sixteen cubits square. (d) Supporting these three levels is the base. This part of the altar, which is of particular concern to us, has been subject to various reconstructions

---

[1920] 131–37; W. F. Albright, "The Babylonian Temple-Tower and the Altar of Burnt-Offering," *JBL* 39 [1920] 137–42; *Archaeology and the Religion of Israel* [5th ed.; Baltimore: Johns Hopkins, 1968; reprint, Garden City: Doubleday, 1968] 146–47; H. G. May, "Ephod and Ariel," *AJSL* 56 [1939] 44–69; N. H. Tur-Sinai "ʾAriel," *Leshonenu* 14 [1946] 1–6 [Hebrew]; L. H. Vincent, "L'autel des holocaustes et le caractere du Temple d'Ézéchiel," *Analecta Bollandiana* 67 [1940] 10–11; S. Segert, "Die Sprache der moabitischen Königsinschrift," *ArOr* 29 [1961] 240; R. de Vaux, *Ancient Israel* [London: Darton, Longman, and Todd, 1961; reprint, 2 vols., New York: McGraw-Hill, 1965] 2. 412; K. Galling, "Altar," *IDB* 1 [1962] 98; C. R. North, "Ariel," *IDB* 1 [1962] 218; H. Donner and W. Röllig, *Kanaanäische und aramäische Inschriften* [3d ed., 3 vols.; Wiesbaden: Otto Harrassowitz, 1971–76] 2. 50–51, 175; see also the commentaries and lexicons). I doubt whether knowledge of the etymology would give us architectural information that would help describe this stage better. It seems to carry theological rather than architectual overtones (the form *haharʾēl* is certainly to be understood as "the mountain of God").

[11]The Greek says they are one cubit high (v 15). This proportion is attested by the horns on the altar found at Beer-Sheba (see the picture in the *IDBSupp* [1976] 94) and on small, horned incense altars (cf. *EncJud* 2 [1972], 766). I cannot agree with the *NJPS* and J. de Groot (*Die Altäre des salomonischen Tempelhofes: eine archäologische Untersuchung* [Stuttgart: Kohlhammer, 1924] 46) that they were four cubits high. *ʾArbaʿ* at the end of v 15 in the MT appears to refer to the number of horns, not their height.

[12]*ʿĂzārâ*, also used of the temple court in 2 Chr 4:9; 6:13, must be defined by context as "stage, platform." Albright ("Temple-Tower," 140, n. 5) and Vincent ("L'autel," 10) connect it with the root *ʿḏr* "to help, support" hence "terrace, terrace-platform" or "étage."

depending on the interpretation of the obscure terms *ḥêq* or *ḥêq hā᾽āreṣ*[13] (vv 13, 14, 17) and *gab*[14] (v 13). It is preferable to interpret *ḥêq* as meaning "channel, gutter" as indicated by 1 Kgs 22:35 which says that blood from Ahab's mortal wound ran down into the *ḥêq* "hollow" of his chariot. Thus the term can refer to a gutter surrounding the altar. It is

---

[13]Albright's connection of *ḥêq hā᾽āreṣ* with Akkadian *irat irṣitim* and *irat kigalli* meaning "foundation" ("Temple-Tower," 139–40; *Archaeology*, 146–47) has been followed by several researchers (Vincent, "L'autel," 9–10; G. Fohrer and K. Galling, *Ezechiel* [HAT 13; Tübingen: J. C. B. Mohr, 1955] 238; de Vaux, *Ancient Israel*, 412; Galling, "Altar," 98; Y. Yadin, "The First Temple," *The Book of Jerusalem [Seper Yerušalayim]* [ed. M. Avi-Yonah, vol. 1; Jerusalem and Tel-Aviv: Bialik Institute and Dvir, 1956] 184; "Temple: First Temple: Structure," *EncJud* 15 [1972] 949). But some of these later writers also want *ḥêq* to have a meaning "cavity, recess," thus describing a gutter at the altar base. It does not seem that one can accept the Babylonian etymology and at the same time essentially ignore it and interpret *ḥêq* as "depression, recess." *Ḥêq* must be either a foundation or a depression, not both (Zimmerli, [*Ezechiel* (BKAT 13/1, 2; Neukirchen: Neukirchener, 1969) 1029] rightly rejects such a "Kompromiss"). I follow those who understand *ḥêq* as "depression, cavity," hence, "gutter" as indicated by 1 Kgs 22:35 (cf. de Groot, *Altäre*, 46; K. Elliger, *Leviticus* [HAT 1/4; Tübingen: J. C. B. Mohr, 1966] 69; M. Haran, "*Mizbēaḥ*," *EM* 4 [1952] 774; see in particular Zimmerli, *Ezechiel*, 1092; G. André, "*Ḥêq*," *TWAT* 2 [1977] 912–15 [= *TDOT* 4 (1980) 356–58]). *Ḥêq hā᾽āreṣ* does not have any Babylonian connections. The similarity to *irat irṣitim* is merely coincidental. *Ḥêq hā᾽āreṣ* simply means "the gutter on the ground." The word *hā᾽āreṣ* distinguishes it from a gutter which is on the edge of the larger stage (v 17, see below). The very fact that *ḥêq* is used of the upper gutter shows that *ḥêq* in *ḥêq hā᾽āreṣ* cannot be connected with the Babylonian *irat irṣitim*.

[14]There is a temptation for some to emend this word to *gobah* "height" following the Greek (cf. *BHS* and commentaries), but this is not necessary. *Gab* basically signifies a gibbous protuberance or eminence and elsewhere refers to an idolatrous (?) structure, a "base, eminence" (Ezek 16:24, 31, 39; parallel to a structure called a *rāmâ*); to a person's back (Ps 129:3; Ezek 10:12; cf. Dan 7:6); to the protruding boss of a shield (Job 15:26; and perhaps also Job 13:12 in a more extended sense of "defenses"); to eyebrows (Lev 14:9); and to wheel rims (1 Kgs 7:33; Ezek 1:18). The word in Ezek 43:13 then refers to the substructure of the altar as described in the first part of v 13 (cf. Haran, "*Mizbēaḥ*," 774; Vincent, "L'autel," 12–13; de Groot, *Altäre*, 45; Zimmerli, *Ezechiel*, 1090, 1092–93).

one cubit deep and one cubit wide.[15] That it is set in the ground appears to be indicated by the terminology *ḥêq hāʾāreṣ* "ground gutter" (v 14). As we will see later, this term is used in distinction to another *ḥêq* that is not on the ground (cf. v 17). On the outer edge of the *ḥêq* is a "boundary" (*gĕbûl*) one span high (v 13). Measured from the outer edge, the area covered by the *ḥêq* and its interior would be eighteen cubits in length and width. Within the bounds of the *ḥêq*, subtracting the cubit width of the *ḥêq* all around, there would remain a section sixteen by sixteen cubits, rising one cubit above the bottom of the *ḥêq*. This raised portion is called the *gab*, that is, the "mound" or "platform" of the altar (v 13; see n. 14).

One last architectural detail needs to be explained—the *ḥêq* and *gĕbûl* in v 17. Some interpreters have understood the *ḥêq* and *gĕbûl* here to be the same as those at the base of the altar described in v 13.[16] They usually add a description of the width and length of the "lower stage" after v 17a which they assume is missing. Thus vv 16–17 with this addition would describe the *hāʾăriʾēl/haharʾēl*, the two *ʿăzārôt*, and the foundation gutter in descending order. However, a literal reading of the verse shows that the *ḥêq* and *gĕbûl* described pertain to the larger stage and not the foundation. Four considerations make this clear. First, feminine pronouns are used in v 17b (*ʾôtāh, lāh*) which clearly refer back to *ʿăzārâ* in v 17a. Second, the dimensions of the foundation's *ḥêq* and *gĕbûl* have already been described in v 13. In such an economic presentation of details about the altar, it would seem highly redundant to give the dimensions of the base gutter a second time. Third, if v 17b is taken to refer to the base of the altar, then there is a conspicuous lack of describing the dimensions of the lower stage, as many commentators have noticed. However, if v 17b refers to a gutter on the upper stage ledge, then the lack of the description of the lower stage is not necessarily felt. Fourth, *ḥêq hāʾāreṣ* should be shorn of any Babylonian

---

[15]The phrase *wĕḥêq hāʾammâ* in v 13, literally, "the *ḥêq* of the cubit" is unintelligible. I therefore redivide the words and read, like the Vulgate and Syriac, *wĕḥêqōh ʾammâ* "and its *ḥêq*, (one) cubit (deep)" (cf. *BHS*; K. Galling, "Altar," 98; Haran, "*Mizbēaḥ*," 774; Zimmerli, *Ezechiel*, 1090).

[16]Cf. *BHS*; Fohrer and Galling, *Ezechiel*, 238; P. Heinisch, *Das Buch Ezechiel* (HSAT 8; Bonn: Peter Hanstein, 1923) 207, 238; Vincent, "L'autel," pl. 1; W. Eichrodt, *Ezekiel: A Commentary* (OTL; Philadelphia: Westminster, 1970) 553; Galling, "Altar," 98; Zimmerli, *Ezechiel*, 1090, 1094.

origin and meaning. It merely means "gutter of the ground" and thus implicitly indicates that there is another gutter which is not on the ground. Thus I concur with those who say that there is a cubit wide gutter bordered by a half cubit high wall on its outside edge on the ledge of the upper stage.[17] I draw the altar as shown in fig. 7.1.

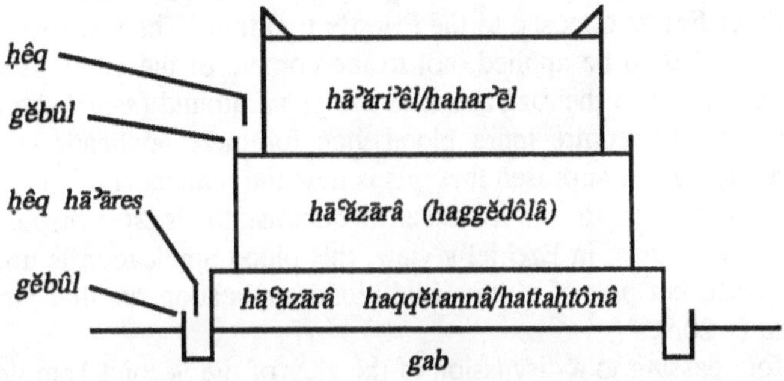

Fig. 7.1: Ezekiel's Altar

The gutters on the ledge of the *'ăzārâ* and at the base of the altar are certainly for the drainage of sacrificial blood, though this is not explicitly said.[18] The structure of the Second Temple altar will corroborate this assumption (see below). Circumstantial evidence in Ezekiel also supports this. Later in chap. 43, the rites for dedicating the altar are described. In these rites, *ḥaṭṭā't* blood is to be applied to the horns of the altar, to the corners of the *'ăzārâ* (i.e., the *'ăzārâ gĕdôlâ*), and on the border around the bottom of the altar (v 20).[19] This verse and 45:19 where *ḥaṭṭā't* blood is applied to the corners of the *'ăzārâ* (again,

---

[17]Haran, "*Mizbēaḥ*," 774–75; Milgrom, "Altar," *EncJud* 2 (1972) 763; cf. David Kimhi on v 17. De Groot (*Altäre*, 47–49) puts the *ḥêq* and *gĕbûl* in v 17 on the upper stage, but puts the *gĕbûl* on the inside of the *ḥêq*.

[18]Cf. Zimmerli, *Ezechiel*, 1090, 1092.

[19]It is not clear which *gĕbûl* is meant in v 20. The one at the base appears to be intended because it seems that this application of blood seeks to purge the whole altar by application of the blood to three distinct parts of the altar. Other passages support this. In 45:19, *ḥaṭṭā't* blood is applied to the temple doorposts, the corners of the upper stage, and the doorposts of the gate of the inner court. Thus the temple is

the upper stage) suggest that the upper *ḥêq* serves to drain away blood that drips down from the altar horns and that is applied to the corners of the *ʿăzārâ*. The *ḥêq* at the base would drain away blood that is poured there or that might be thrown (*zrq*, cf. 43:18) on the lower sides of the altar.

Note that v 20 may reflect a slightly different understanding of the *ḥaṭṭāʾt* sacrifice as opposed to the Priestly tradition. The verse says that *ḥaṭṭāʾt* blood is to be applied, not to the corners of the *gĕbûl* as when blood is applied to the *ʿăzārâ*, but to the *gĕbûl* around (*sābîb*) the altar. This act would require more blood than for mere application to the corners. It may be surmised that this is how the remainder of the *ḥaṭṭāʾt* blood is used up. If so, it stands in contrast to Priestly disposal of *ḥaṭṭāʾt* blood, since, in Ezekiel's view, this blood application is not just for disposal, but part of a three-fold blood application rite that purifies the altar (v 20b).[20]

Before passing to a discussion of the altar of the Second Temple, we should note the possible historical connection of Ezekiel's altar with the altar at Jerusalem. Several researchers are of the opinion that Ezekiel's altar is not a pure invention, but is most likely based on the structure of the altar at the Jerusalem temple before the exile.[21] Consequently, the drainage system depicted in Ezekiel, in its general scheme if not in its

---

totally purged by application to three selected locations beginning at the temple itself moving outwards. (On the application of blood to the doorposts, see J. Milgrom, "*Mĕzûzâ*," *TWAT* 3 [1984] 801–04.) This same scheme is found in the application of blood from the ram of ordination to the ears, thumbs, and big toes of Aaron and his sons when they are consecrated (Exod 29:19–20; Lev 8:22–24) and the application of *ʾāšām* blood and oil to the ear, thumb, and big toe of one recovered from *ṣāraʿat* (Lev 14:14, 17, 25, 28). From these examples, one might expect that in Ezek 43:20 the blood is applied to three separate locations, from top to bottom: altar horns, upper *ʿăzārâ* corners, and the *gĕbûl* at the base.

[20]This may be a special use only intended for the dedicatory rites of the altar. In 45:19, the blood is applied to only one part of the altar and lastly to the doorposts of the inner court. There was certainly blood leftover from this rite. It was probably to be disposed of by pouring out at the base of the altar, as prescribed in Priestly texts, without any ritual significance.

[21]Haran ("*Mizbēaḥ*," 774–75) says it reflects Ahaz's altar. Albright thinks it reflects the altar Solomon built (*Archaeology*, 219, n. 81; cf. de Groot, *Altäre*, 44; Yadin, "The First Temple," 176, 184; "Temple: First

details, may be a reflection of earlier altar construction. A drainage system is expected, for example, with Ahaz's altar since blood is thrown on the side of it (2 Kgs 16:13, 15).[22]

7.3.2 Blood Disposal at the Altar of the Second Temple

The Mishnah and Tosefta describe the burnt-offering altar and its base in Second Temple times and how *ḥaṭṭā'ṭ* and other sacrificial blood was discarded. Though these documents do not perfectly reflect temple architecture and practice prior to its destruction at 70 C. E., it does not seem gratuitous to assume that they are historically accurate in these details to some extent.

According to these sources, there were two holes in the altar's base at the southwest corner.[23] The extra blood from *ḥaṭṭā'ṭ* sacrifices whose blood was used in the temple building was poured out at the western base of the altar.[24] That of *ḥaṭṭā'ṭ* sacrifices used only on the outer altar was poured out on the southern base.[25] The blood of these sacrifices would drain through the holes, pass into a water channel[26] that flowed through the court, and be carried out to the Kidron Valley. The blood was then sold to gardeners as fertilizer.[27] This water channel served other purposes besides the disposal of *ḥaṭṭā'ṭ* blood. Any sacrificial blood that

---

Temple," 949). Zimmerli (*Ezechiel*, 1095–96) offers a more cautious assessment of the evidence. Also see Elliger, "Die grossen Tempelsakristeien im Verfassungsentwurf des Ezechiel (42, 1ff.)," *Geschichte und Altes Testament* (ed. W. F. Albright; Tübingen: J. C. B. Mohr) 81, n. 3.

[22]See also 2 Chr 29:22; 30:16; 35:11.

[23]*M. Mid.* 3:2; *Yoma* 5:6; Maimonides, *MTor*, ʿAboda, Bet habBeḥira 2:11. See also M. Avi-Yonah, "The Second Temple," *The Book of Jerusalem (Seper Yerušalayim)* (ed. M. Avi-Yonah, vol. 1; Jerusalem and Tel-Aviv: Bialik Institute and Dvir, 1956) 407; F. J. Hollis, *The Archaeology of Herod's Temple* (London: J. M. Dent, 1934) 215–16, 306–08.

[24]*M. Zebaḥ.* 5:1–2; *Yoma* 5:6.

[25]*M. Zebaḥ.* 5:3; *Yoma* 5:6.

[26]Called the *'ammâ* or *'ammat hammayim.*

[27]*M. Yoma* 5:6; *Meʿil.* 3:3; *Mid.* 3:2; *t. Zebaḥ.* 6:9; Maimonides, *MTor*, ʿAboda, Meʿila 2:11. According to some, the law of sacrilege still applied to the blood in the Kidron which meant that people could not benefit from it unless it was desanctified by purchasing it.

had become invalid was poured out into the gutter.[28] Moreover, it is the opinion of Rabbi Judah that a *ḥaṭṭā't* bird which could not be eaten should be thrown into the gutter. It would then be carried by the water out to the Kidron.[29] Finally, ashes that fell from the silver censer near the outer altar when transferring hot coals to the gold censer for use on the incense altar were swept into the water channel.[30] The channel thus served as a general sewer for sacrificial refuse. The Kidron was an ideal place for disposal of impure materials since it was a place of burial and the place where kings dumped idolatrous impurities.[31]

7.3.3 Blood Disposal in the Temple Scroll

In connection with the drainage system for sacrificial blood in the Second Temple, we must note a corresponding architectural feature in the description of the "laver building" (*bêt hakkiyôr*) in the Temple Scroll.[32] The laver building, located on the southeast of the temple building, contained the laver at which the priests washed.[33] Around this a channel was constructed near the wall of the building.[34] Water taken from the laver for washing would drain into this channel.[35] The channel led from

---

[28]*M. Zebaḥ.* 8:7, 8, 9, 11; *t. Zebaḥ.* 8:16–24; *m. Ker.* 6:1; Maimonides, *MTor*, ʿAboda, Pesule hamMuqdašin 2:11, 13, 21, 23.

[29]*M. Tem.* 7:6, and see the further explanation of *t. Tem.* 4:16. The opinion from which Judah diverges is that the bird must be burned. The Tosefta explains that to throw it in the gutter is equivalent to burying it.

[30]*M. Tamid* 5:5. The reason for the spillage of ashes is that the silver censer held four *kabs* while the gold censer only held three (cf. *Yoma* 4:4).

[31]See appendix 1 and *t. B. Bat.* 1:11 cited in chap. 5, section 5.6.

[32]TS 31:10–33:7.

[33]Cf. Exod 30:19–21; 40:30–32; 2 Chr 4:6.

[34]TS 32:12–15.

[35]Washing was not done in the laver. Water was taken from it and washing was performed around it. This is suggested by the structure of the laver at the Jerusalem temple which was fitted with twelve spigots from which the priests washed (*m. Yoma* 3:10; see H. Albeck, *The Six Orders of the Mishnah [Šiša Sidre Mišna]* [6 vols.; Jerusalem and Tel-Aviv: Bialik Institute and Dvir, 1957–59] 2. 231–32 on this passage and p. 467; *b. Yoma* 37a; *b. Zebaḥ.* 21a; *y. Yoma* 3:8 [41a]; Maimonides, *MTor*, ʿAboda, Bet habBeḥira 3:18; Bi'at hamMiqdaš 5:10; Avi-Yonah, "Second Temple," 407). The basis for this custom is found in Exod 30:19 and 40:31 which say the priests are to wash "from" the laver, not "in" it.

the laver building to an underground cavity where the water dispersed and was absorbed into the ground. This particular drainage system was devised so that no one would touch the water "because some blood from the *ʿôlâ* sacrifice is mixed with it (i.e., the water)."[36] That is to say, the priests, after performing the *ʿôlâ* washed themselves with water from the laver thus mixing the sacrificial blood on them with the water. There appears to be a polemic inherent in the Scroll's prescription about the disposal of water mixed with sacrificial blood against the practice at Jerusalem which is later reflected in the Mishnah and Tosefta.[37] In these writings we learn that, according to some, *ḥaṭṭā'ṭ* blood did not retain its sanctity when it flowed out to the Kidron, or, according to others, it retained its sanctity but could be desanctified by purchase.[38] In any case, people were allowed to use it for fertilizer. The Temple Scroll will have none of this. For it, *ʿôlâ* blood, and by extension, all sacrificial blood including that of the *ḥaṭṭā'ṭ*, retains its sanctity after the rites are completed and must therefore be disposed of so that no one has the opportunity to handle it in an impure or sacrilegious way.

7.3.4 The Blood Drainage System with the Altar of the Priestly Tabernacle

From the descriptions of disposal gutters of Ezekiel's altar and that of the Second Temple period, we would expect to find a similar type of structure with the Tabernacle altar to allow for the disposal of surplus blood. However, the descriptions of the altar in Exod 27:1–8 and 38:1–7 give no hint of how the base was constructed, if it had one at all. M. Haran is of the opinion that since the Priestly texts talk of pouring *ḥaṭṭā'ṭ* blood out at the base of the altar, there must have been one. Consequently, he pictures the Tabernacle as consisting of two levels, the base and the upper level, the latter of which is depicted in Exodus.[39] In my view, Exodus has completely described the altar. No foundation is detailed because it did not have one. The terminology about pouring *ḥaṭṭā'ṭ* blood at the foundation of the altar is idiomatic, probably deriving

---

[36]TS 32:15.

[37]See Y. Yadin, *The Temple Scroll (Megillat hamMiqdaš)* (3 vols.; Jerusalem: Israel Exploration Society, 1977) 1. 173; J. Milgrom, "The Temple Scroll," *BA* 41 (1978) 116.

[38]See n. 27, above.

[39]Haran, "*Mizbēaḥ*," 771–72.

from usage in connection with a fixed altar that had an actual foundation. But if the Tabernacle altar did not have a constructed foundation with a gutter into which the blood was poured, how was the blood disposed of?

A hint of what was done with surplus blood in the case of the Tabernacle altar is found in the description of Elijah's altar when he confronted the priests of Baal on Mt. Carmel (1 Kgs 18:30–35). He built an altar of twelve stones around which he dug a trench. He had twelve jugs of water poured over the *ʿōlâ* pieces and the wood that were on the altar. The water ran down and filled the trench at the base. It is likely that the trench around Elijah's altar was not an *ad hoc* invention, but a reflection of a structural feature of temporary altars at which liquids, such as blood, wine, and water were used as offerings. The trenches would control the flow of the liquids and prevent the ground from becoming muddied around the altar. The trench could be dug to allow the liquids to flow away from the altar, but it is likely that before this could occur the liquids would soak into the ground in the trench.[40]

I propose that the Priestly legislation implicitly understood the Tabernacle altar to have an excavated trench around it, like that around Elijah's altar, into which surplus *ḥaṭṭāʾt* blood was poured and into which blood that was thrown on the altar could drain. This type of make-

---

[40]There are a few archaeological examples which show drainage systems in connection with altars or sacrificial installations. Unfortunately, much of what can be said about these installations and their use amounts to guesswork.

At the Arad sanctuary, the altar in the northwest corner of the courtyard has plastered channels on its top surface surrounding a flint slab. N. Gadegaard ("On the So-Called Burnt Offering Altar in the Old Testament," *PEQ* 110 [1978] 38–39) has argued that the top of this altar could not have been used for burnt offerings, as Y. Aharoni and R. Amiran claim ("Tel Arad," *RB* 72 [1965] 559), since normal flint could not stand the temperatures without breaking. The slab and the channels suggest this altar was merely a place for slaughtering. The channels provided a means of draining the blood and perhaps other sacrificial liquids from the altar (for a picture of the altar, see Aharoni and Amiran, pl. 29a; *ANEP* # 873; *EncJud* 2 [1972] 767; on the altar see J. Ouellette, "Temple of Solomon," *IDBSup* [1976] 872–73; Z. Herzog, M. Aharoni, A. F. Rainey, S. Moshkovitz, "The Israelite Fortress of Arad," *BASOR* 254 [1984] 11 [a picture is also published here]). Y. Aharoni ("Arad," *EM* 6 [1972] 380) compares the channels on the Arad altar to the *ḥêq* on Ezekiel's altar.

shift "foundation" fits well with the portable nature of the altar. The altar needed to be as light as possible and thus its design is limited to the hearth. When the Tabernacle was set up and the altar was in place, a trench would be dug around it.

Before leaving this subject, we can compare the disposal of *ḥaṭṭāʾt* blood at the Tabernacle altar with the disposal of blood from animals that are not offered as offerings, but that are profanely slaughtered or killed for food. In the Priestly literature, when one hunts game, be it bird or beast, he is to pour out (*špk*) the blood on the ground and cover it with earth (Lev 17:13). Deuteronomy, in allowing nonsacrificial slaughter, stipulates that the blood of slaughtered animals cannot be eaten, but must be poured out (*špk*) on the ground like water (Deut 12:16, 24; 15:23). In both the disposal of *ḥaṭṭāʾt* blood at the Tabernacle altar and the disposal of nonsacrificial blood at home or at the hunting grounds, the blood is discarded by pouring it out on the ground.

R. A. S. Macalister (*The Excavation of Gezer, 1902–1905 and 1907–1909* [3 vols.; London: J. Murray for the Committee of the Palestine Exploration Fund, 1912] 2. 378–81; vol. 3 pl. 27; cf. de Vaux, *Ancient Israel,* 2. 407) notes that at Gezer, there is an "orifice" with a "channel, that opens into the roof of cave 17 IV" (2. 378; see vol. 3, pl. 1, for the location). In his view, the orifice is a channel "whereby blood and other fluid offerings were passed to divinities supposed to dwell in the cave" (2. 378–79). If this orifice is truly to be connected with sacrifice, it may be merely a channel to dispose of sacrificial liquids rather than to make chthonic offerings. Cf. the Temple Scroll which has underground disposal of water mixed with sacrificial blood (see section 7.3.3., above).

Part Two

The Restriction of Human Impurities Paralleling the Disposal of Non-Human Bearers of Impurity

8

The Restriction of Human Impurities and the Communicability of Impurity

8.1 INTRODUCTION

Priestly legislation contains several prohibitions against or cautions concerning impure persons and things coming in contact with two different spheres: that of the holy and that of the profane (i.e., the nonholy or common). These prohibitions and cautions when viewed together as a system indicate that whether an impurity is restricted from both the holy and profane or just from the profane is contingent upon the *strength* of the particular impurity. Specifically, only communicable impurities, those which can pollute the profane sphere, are excluded from or restricted in this sphere, while noncommunicable impurities, those which cannot affect other nonholy persons and objects, are not excluded from or restricted in this sphere. These lesser impurities, like all impurities, are only restricted from the holy sphere. Certainly this thesis is, *a priori*, sensible and thus one might wonder about the need to prove it valid. While this chapter will indeed show its validity, the goal here is more to show *how* it is valid, that is, to show through a detailed study the way in which this idea is reflected by or applies to the various impurities in P. To do this, I will first treat the prohibitions and warnings about impure persons contacting the holy and profane spheres. Though the focus of this chapter is how impurities relate to the profane, the initial discussion regarding the restriction of human impurities from the sacred will help in understanding that the ultimate concern of restricting impurity from the profane is to protect the sacred. The study of the relation of impurity to the sacred and profane will lead to an examination of the extent to which impurities, both human and nonhuman, can engender impurity in other nonholy persons or objects—in other words, the "chain" or "generations" of impurity caused by various major impurities. The results of this examination will then be correlated with the data concerning the restriction of impure humans and objects along with the data concerning the disposal of impure objects studied in the previous chapters to show the correctness of the assumption just described.

8.2 THE RESTRICTION OF HUMAN IMPURITIES FROM THE SACRED

There are several passages in P which exhibit the concern of restricting impure persons from sacred matters. The discussion of the *zebaḥ šĕlāmîm* sacrifice in Lev 7 contains a brief treatment of the state of purity that should surround the sacrifice. The sacrificial meat is not to come in contact with anything or anyone impure.[1] V 19a says that sacrificial meat which has contacted impurity is to be burned and not eaten. Vv 19b–21 go on to give a warning about those who would eat the sacrifice in impurity. The meat can only be eaten by pure people (v 19b). Persons with a major or self-generated impurity (e.g., *ṣāraʿat*, menstruation, etc.) are liable to the *kārēt*[2] ("cutting-off") penalty if they eat the sacrifice (v 20). Also those with even minor secondary impurities that eat the sacrifice are liable to this penalty (v 21).[3]

---

[1]*Bĕkol ṭāmēʾ* in Lev 7:19 means anything or anyone unclean. Since the *zebaḥ šĕlāmîm*, a lesser holy offering, could be eaten outside the temple area in the homes of the offerers (see chap. 9, section 9.2.2.1), there was always danger of the sacrificial meat coming in contact with impure cooking or eating utensils.

[2]"Cutting off" (*kārēt*) is a divine punishment of childlessness. See D. J. Wold, "The Meaning of the Biblical Penalty *Kareth*" (PhD diss., University of California, Berkeley, 1978); "The *Kareth* Penalty in P: Rationale and Cases," *Society of Biblical Literature 1979 Seminar Papers* (vol. 1; Missoula: Scholars, 1979) 1–45.

[3]Vv 20 and 21 appear to talk of two separate aspects of impurity. The two verses are constructed parallel to one another; note that both end with

Corresponding to the foregoing rules about the *šĕlāmîm* are those given to the priests concerning how they should treat holy offerings. If a priest misuses[4] them by contacting them in a condition of uncleanness, he suffers *kārēt* just as one who pollutes the *zebaḥ šĕlāmîm* (Lev 22:3). The rules list specific impurities which a priest may suffer that debar him from eating the holy offerings: *ṣāraʿat*, an abnormal sexual flux, contamination from corpse-contaminated persons or objects, seminal emission, pollution from touching a *šereṣ* carcass, or a human derived impurity (vv 4–6). Thus the whole range of possible impurities, from the most serious to the least serious, is represented. The offerings may not be eaten until the priest has become clean according to the prescriptions that apply to the respective impurities (cf. vv 4, 6–7). Elsewhere the purity necessary for the priests and their households to eat the holy offerings is reiterated (Num 18:11, 13).[5]

---

the *kārēt* penalty. V 21 is clearer. It talks of a person touching the impurity of other persons (*beṭumʾat ʾādām*), an impure animal (*bibhēmâ ṭĕmēʾâ*) or any impure "abomination" (*bĕkol-šeqeṣ ṭāmēʾ*; on this see n. 63, below). The impurity resulting from such contact is minor, as will be brought out later. V 20, in contrast, seems to talk about another type of impurity, not that which is acquired from another source as in v 21, but one that is self-generated, like a seminal emission, menstruation, *ṣāraʿat*, and so forth. Note the phrasing "and his impurity is on him" (*wĕṭumʾātô ʿālāw*).

[4] *Yiqrab. . . ʾel* (in 22:3) does not mean merely to approach, but indicates here illicit use of the holy offerings or deliberately handling them in an unclean state. See J. Milgrom, *Studies in Levitical Terminology, I: The Encroacher and the Levite; the Term* ʿAbodah (UCPNES 14; Berkeley: University of California, 1970) n. 140 and passim.

[5] Lev 21:16–23 stipulate that priests having certain bodily defects cannot participate in performing offerings and other ritual acts. This restriction is not because the defects have rendered them impure. Such priests are still pure as seen in the fact that they may eat the most holy and holy offerings (v 22). And though they are restricted from altar and other service, they may still enter the sanctuary area as is evident from their being permitted to eat the most holy offerings which are to be consumed in a holy place, meaning within the Tabernacle precincts (see chap. 9, section 9.2.1). Interestingly, the Temple Scroll develops the prohibitions of this biblical passage in two ways when it states that blind

Another example of a prohibition against contacting holy offerings while in a state of impurity is found in Num 9:6–13. This prescribes that persons impure from corpse contamination are not to partake of the passover sacrifice, but must defer the celebration until a month later.

The preceding pericopae spoke of restricting impure persons from the offerings that are eaten.[6] From these rules one would expect that impure persons would also be restricted from the sanctuary area. This restriction is explicitly evidenced in the case of the parturient. The woman has three stages of purification: (a) the initial period following birth which is as severe as menstrual impurity, lasting seven days in the case of a male child and fourteen days in the case of a female (Lev 12:2, 5); (b) a period of lighter impurity, lasting 33 or 66 days in the case of a male or female child, respectively (vv 4, 5); and (c) the last stage when sacrifices are offered and full purity is achieved (vv 6–8). During the second stage, she

---

persons (which is a catch-all term for all bodily defects; cf. Y. Yadin, *The Temple Scroll [Megillat hamMiqdaš]* [3 vols.; Jerusalem: Israel Exploration Society, 1977] 1. 224–25; J. Milgrom, "Studies in the Temple Scroll," *JBL* 97 [1978] 514, n. 42) "shall not come to it (i.e., the temple city) all their days" (45:12–13). First, it expands the law that in the Bible only refers to priests to all of the Israelites (cf. Yadin, *Temple Scroll*, 1. 224–25; Milgrom, "The Temple Scroll," *BA* 41 [1978] 117). Second, the defects are considered impure as is clear from the stated reason for their banishment: "so that they will not defile (*yṭmʾw*) the city in which I dwell" (45:13).

[6]Outside of the Priestly writings there are several examples of restriction of impure persons from sacrificial materials. For example: (a) Deut 12:15, 22; 15:22 allow nonsacrificial meat to be eaten by those impure which implies that only the pure may eat sacrificial meat. (b) In Deut 26:14, an Israelite confesses that he has not eaten of the tithe while in a state of mourning (*bĕʿōnî*; this noun is somewhat obscure, usually connected with *ʾāwen* "trouble, misfortune" in a transferred sense to mean "mourning," cf. S. R. Driver, *A Critical and Exegetical Commentary on Deuteronomy* [3d ed., ICC; Edinburgh: T. and T. Clark, 1901] 291; BDB 20a; cf. F. Andersen and D. N. Freedman, *Hosea, A New Translation with Introduction and Commentary* [AB 24; Garden City: Doubleday, 1980] 526), perhaps implying that he is in a state of corpse contamination, and that he has not cleared any of it out "as an unclean person." (c) In 1 Sam 16:5, purification (*qdš*) precedes a sacrificial feast. (d) 1 Sam 20:26 says that David did not attend a sacrificial meal because he was supposedly impure.

suffers only minor impurity (though of long duration) which cannot contaminate other people. Nonetheless, at this time the woman must not make any contact with the sancta nor go to the sanctuary (v 4).[7]

Another example of restriction of impurities from that which is holy is the prohibition that a nazirite, whose head and hair are holy (cf. Num 6:5, 9, 11), not defile himself by corpse contamination (vv 6–12).[8] Similarly, priests are restricted in varying degrees from contacting the dead (Lev 21:1–4, 10–12; cf. Ezek 44:25–27).

In sum, an impure person (and implicitly an impure object) with even the most minor impurity, is a threat to holy matters and must be restricted from them. Should one contact holy items while impure, the attainment of cultic goals would be obstructed. For example, polluted *šĕlāmîm* meat could not be eaten, but only be disposed of by burning. To prevent desecration of holy things, all impure persons are kept out of the sanctuary precincts. Moreover, when lesser holy offerings are taken from the sanctuary to be consumed in the homes of the priests and people, they are to be eaten in a pure place (Lev 10:14),[9] which means a place where no unclean persons or objects are that could contaminate the offerings. One who partakes of or misuses the offerings while in an impure state is subject to the severe punishment of *kārēt*.

8.3 THE RESTRICTION OF HUMAN IMPURITIES FROM THE PROFANE

In this section, I will examine the types of impure persons that were excluded or restricted in some way from the profane sphere as well as the sacred sphere. It will become clear from a study of these examples and a

---

[7]Ezek 44:26–27 implies that a corpse-contaminated priest is barred from the sanctuary until he is purified. According to 2 Chr 23:19, King Jehoiada stationed gatekeepers to prevent unclean persons from entering the temple. Note the state of purity that must prevail for the theophany in Exod 19:10–15.

[8]Cf. Judg 13:4, 7, 14 where Samson's mother is warned not to eat anything unclean. This is connected with the command that Samson be a nazirite from the womb (vv 5, 7). See also J. Milgrom, *Cult and Conscience: The Asham and the Priestly Doctrine of Repentance* (SJLA 18; Leiden: Brill, 1976) n. 240.

[9]See chap. 9, section 9.2.2.1.

study of the communicability of impurity that follows that the main reason for the exclusion or restriction of severely polluted persons from the profane is so that they will not contaminate other persons and objects which in turn would pose a danger to the sacred.

Before proceeding to a discussion of the exclusion and restriction of impure persons, I should observe that this discussion is concerned with how exclusion and restriction pertain to a habitation in which there is a sanctuary. The purity rules and customs in P, due to being set in a narrative concerning the wilderness camp where the Tabernacle is the center of the camp's structure and religious life, are mainly oriented toward a city or town with a sanctuary. Though some of P's purity laws may be construed as pertaining to habitations without sanctuaries (cf. the *ṣāraʿat* laws, especially 14:34), the corpus gives little indication about how impurity would be handled in habitations without sanctuaries. Presumably, impurities in such habitations would not be as rigorously restricted. It will be important to bear this observation in mind throughout this chapter and in the following chapter where I discuss the place of impurity.

8.3.1 The Exclusion of Impure Persons

Certain impure persons were to be completely removed from the camp according to Priestly prescription. Num 5:1–4, the fullest expression of this rule, state:

> God spoke to Moses: "Instruct the Israelites to send out of the camp anyone with *ṣāraʿat*, anyone with an abnormal sexual discharge, and anyone who is corpse-contaminated. Both male and female you shall send out—you shall send them outside of the camp—so that they will not defile the camp of those among whom I dwell." The Israelites did so and sent them outside the camp. Just as the Lord spoke to Moses, so the Israelites did.

According to this, three classes of persons—those with *ṣāraʿat*, those with irregular sexual fluxes, and those corpse-contaminated—are to be excluded. This stipulation, however, is found to be at odds with the larger picture of impurity regulations described in P. The passages giving the prescriptions regarding corpse-contaminated persons (Num 19) and those with irregular fluxes (Lev 15:2–15; 25–30) do not appear to require that those thus defiled be excluded from the camp.[10] A discussion of each of these impurities will follow in order to shed light on this difficulty.[11]

8.3.1.1 The Corpse-Contaminated Person

The strict law of Num 5:1–4 which excludes a corpse-contaminated person from the camp is reflected in Num 31:13, 19–24. Moses meets soldiers returning from war with Midian outside the camp and instructs them to purify themselves, their captives, and various utensils and articles from corpse contamination before entering the camp. These two passages contrast with Num 19 where nothing is said concerning the stay of a corpse-contaminated person outside the camp. It is true that the ashes of the Red Cow are prepared (vv 2–8) and stored (vv 9–10) outside the camp, but in the last part of the chapter which delineates how the ashes are to be used on the corpse-contaminated there is no hint that the polluted person is outside the camp. In fact, it seems that the pericope assumes the person to be inside the camp. Most telling is the lack of any stipulation that the person may enter the camp after he has been purified. Such a statement always accompanies those rites that deal with the purification of persons that are expressly outside the camp.[12] Furthermore, when the passage prescribes the sprinkling of the water of purgation, it lists the various recipients without any distinction whether

---

[10]Rabbinic interpretation solved the contradiction in these passages by saying that the persons in Num 5 were restricted from different camps. A corpse-contaminated person could not enter the Tabernacle area, a *zāb* could not enter the Levitic camp around the Tabernacle, and a person with *ṣāraʿat* was excluded from the entire Israelite camp (see Rashi to Num 5:2; *b. Pesaḥ.* 67a; cf. *m. Kelim* 1:8; Maimonides, *MTor,* ʿAboda, Bet habBeḥira 7:11; Biʾat hamMiqdaš 3).

[11]J. Milgrom has interpreted the discrepancies between the various passages on corpse contamination as evidence of different historical levels of P's view of the power of impurity ("Studies," 515–16; "The Paradox of the Red Cow (Num. XIX)," *VT* 31 [1981] 70–72; "The Graduated *Ḥaṭṭāʾt* of Lev 5:1–13," *JAOS* 103 [1983] 249–54).

[12]Lev 14:8; 16:26, 28; Num 19:7; especially Num 31:24 (see below). Cf. Deut 23:12.

they are in the camp or not: "and he shall sprinkle on the tent, and on all the objects, and on the people that were there, and on the one who touched a bone, a slain body, a corpse, or a grave" (v 18).[13]

How are these conflicting rules to be judged? A clue to the solution is found in the account and prescription of the soldiers' purification in Num 31. The rites prescribed there are clearly dependent from a literary point of view, and hence a chronological point of view, upon Num 19. Note the following similarities: (a) The verb *hitḥaṭṭā'* is used in both passages to describe purifying (19:12, 13, 20; 31:19, 20, 23). (b) The people are to purify themselves on the third and seventh days (19:12, 19; 31:19, 24). (c) The *mê niddâ* are used (19:13, 20, 21; 31:23). (d) Both use the term *ḥuqqat hattôrâ*, found only in these passages (19:2; 31:21). (e) Both people and objects are purified (19:14–15, 18; 31:19–24). (f) The people are to bathe and launder[14] on the seventh day (19:19; 31:24).[15] But despite this dependence on Num 19, Num 31 does not adopt the apparent leniency of Num 19 in allowing the soldiers to enter into the camp while impure. The statement allowing entrance into the

---

[13]For other reasons why the person appears not to be excluded according to Num 19, see the literature in n. 11.

[14]See n. 38, below.

[15]There are also minor differences, most of which are to be attributed to the adaptation of rules in Num 19 to the war situation. Num 31, however, has a major innovation. All articles are to undergo two purifications for corpse contamination: the sprinkling of the water of purgation and an immersion in water or fire. I have argued elsewhere that the addition of the fire/water immersion is a logical expansion of the prescription of Num 19. Persons in Num 19 undergo both the sprinkling of the water of purgation and bathing and laundering (vv 18–19). Num 19, however, mentions only sprinkling for the corpse-contaminated objects (v 18). It lacks any mention of vessel washing which would correspond to the bathing and laundering of persons. The inclusion of a water or fire purification in Num 31 is therefore to be seen as a supplement to Num 19 making clear that the objects, as well as persons, have two aspects or parts to their purification. The use of fire for cleansing some of the implements instead of water is to be attributed to the severity of the contamination. In Lev 11:32, *šereṣ*-contaminated articles are purified by water. Since human corpse contamination is a more serious contamination, fire is chosen to purify those articles which could endure it. See my article, "Purification from Corpse-Contamination in Numbers XXXI 19–24," *VT* 35 (1985) 213–23.

camp only after purification, conspicuously absent from chapter 19, is found in chapter 31 (v 24).

The stricture in Num 5 and 31 is to be explained by the character of the wilderness camp. It is a hybrid cross of a regular community and a war camp.[16] It is well known from non-Priestly material that a war camp was under stricter conditions of purity than the normal community. According to Deut 23:10–15, when the Israelites go out to war, one suffering a seminal emission is to stay outside the camp until he bathes and evening comes. Moreover, defecation is to take place outside the war camp. The reason is given: God moves throughout the camp so that he might grant victory to the soldiers. The camp must be holy for God's presence to continue there (v 15). Similarly, David and his troops are allowed to eat holy bread since they, as soldiers on a holy mission, had kept themselves from women and are thus pure (1 Sam 21:4–7). Num 5 and 31 are exclusively connected with the Israelite wilderness camp and are not necessarily reflections of how postconquest settled communities are to deal with these impurities. Num 5:1–4 come at the end of the description of the structure of the wilderness camp, a structure which obviously only applies to the wilderness march. Num 31 recounts an event occurring in the wilderness period. Hence, these two passages, which contain the rigorous rule of excluding the corpse-contaminated, must be expressions of the ideal of the wilderness camp. On the other hand, Num 19, though it is set as a revelation received and applied in the wilderness, is a more generalized prescription and has less specific connection with the wilderness camp. It is to be a permanent law (*lĕḥuqqat ʿôlām*, vv 10, 21). It is thus conceived of as applying not only to the wilderness war camp, but to later settled communities not under the rigor of the wilderness camp ideal.

---

[16]The military character of the wilderness camp is observed in the arrangement of the camp and its march (cf. Num 2, 10), the use of the ark in war (Num 10:35–36), the use of trumpets (Num 10:9), the use of the term *ṣābāʾ* (cf. 1:3, etc.; 2:4, etc.; 10:14, etc.), and the battle situations the Israelites found themselves in during their whole march. Cf. R. de Vaux, *Ancient Israel* (London: Darton, Longman, and Todd, 1961; reprint, 2 vols., New York: McGraw-Hill, 1965) 1. 214; F. M. Cross, "The Priestly Tabernacle," *The Biblical Archaeologist Reader, 1* (ed. G. E. Wright and D. N. Freedman; Missoula: Scholars, 1975) 213. Milgrom ("The Graduated *Ḥaṭṭāʾt*," 252b) argues that God's presence was "coextensive with the entire camp" thus making it entirely holy as opposed to the later view that holiness is restricted to the sanctuary area.

A final word on the nature of the Israelite wilderness camp is necessary. Since it was a community of men, women, and children, it was not a military camp in the pure sense.[17] The fact that Num 5:1–4 need to mention at all the exclusion of those with *ṣāraʿat*, corpse-contaminated persons, and those with severe sexual fluxes is evidence of the broad social composition of the camp. Deut 23:10–15 do not need to speak of these severer impurities since they are excluded from the army from the beginning. Only the impurities which might befall a soldier during the campaign, such as an emission, are discussed. There is thus a compromise in the rules that cover the wilderness camp in Num 5 and 31. It is more rigid than a normal community in removing the corpse-contaminated and one with a severe flux, but less rigid than a true military camp in allowing other impurities, including menstruants, parturients,[18] men with emissions, and all noncommunicable impurities, to remain in the camp.

8.3.1.2 The *Zāb*

A conflict similar to that regarding corpse contamination exists in the passages on the *zāb* and the *zābâ*, those with irregular sexual fluxes.[19] Num 5:2–3 state that these persons must be excluded from the

---

[17]G. Gray (*A Critical and Exegetical Commentary on Numbers* [ICC; Edinburgh: T. and T. Clark, 1903] 40) notes that the mention of women in Num 5:3 does not support the idea that the stricture of Num 5:2–4 is based on war camp conceptions. I do not agree that war camp ideology must be ruled out entirely. It is only modified.

[18]A legitimate question may be whether menstruants and parturients are included among the females in Num 5:3 who are excluded. In Lev 15:19, the case of the menstruant is introduced using the words *zābâ* and *zôbāh* to describe her condition. This may suggest that she is included in the exclusion of the *zāb* in Num 5. Also, since the parturient is like the menstruant in her first stage of impurity (see Lev 12), she would be excluded also. In my opinion, menstruants and parturients are not included in the rule of Num 5 since it does not mention them explicitly. Further, v 2 mentions only the *zāb* and v 3 states that the female equivalent of the *zāb* be sent out of the camp. The true female equivalent of the *zāb* is the woman who has a flow of blood beyond or outside her normal menstrual period since her impurity is indefinite and she brings the same sacrifices as the *zāb* when she is well (Lev 15:2–15, 25–30).

[19]See Milgrom, "The Graduated *Ḥaṭṭāʾt*," 252–53.

camp, while Lev 15:2–15, 25–30 do not. Indeed, Lev 15 seems to assume that the *zāb* and *zābâ* are in the camp, particularly when it discusses all the many possible impure contacts these persons may have. Such contacts would not be likely to occur if those with this impurity were excluded.[20] Moreover, permission to enter the camp after purification is absent here as it was in Num 19.

The solution to this problem must be the same as it was in the case of the passages on corpse contamination. Lev 15 is a law which reflects the conditions of settled life and not the wilderness camp. The chapter, like Num 19, does not have any special connection with the wilderness march.

To summarize thus far, the laws about the corpse-contaminated and one with a severe sexual flux reflect two situations. The first is that of the wilderness camp where one who is corpse-contaminated and one with an irregular sexual flow are excluded. The other is that of settled communities where one corpse-contaminated and one with a severe sexual flow are allowed to remain in the habitation. In both cases, a person with *ṣāraʿat* is excluded from the community. Attention will now be given to this latter impurity.

8.3.1.3 The Person with *Ṣāraʿat*

Priestly prescriptions about persons with *ṣāraʿat* are unanimous about excluding them from the community. In addition to Num 5:2–3, Lev 13:46 stipulates that those with the disease must dwell alone outside the camp as long as they are affected. When they recover from the disease, they cannot enter the camp until certain preliminary rites have been performed. The priest must go outside the camp to the healed person to perform these rites (Lev 14:3, 8).

In contrast to the silence in narrative sources about the relation of one who is corpse-contaminated and one who has a sexual flow to society,[21] we find in these writings quite a bit about the exclusion or seclusion of one with *ṣāraʿat*. Miriam, shamed by being smitten with *ṣāraʿat* for her

---

[20]Note that the Bible nowhere discusses the effect of the impurity of one with *ṣāraʿat* on other persons and things. This may be attributable in part to this person's exclusion from the community which would preclude contact with others. See section 8.3.2.1, j, below.

[21]Cf. 2 Sam 3:29 where the serious nature of the *zāb*'s and *ṣāraʿat*-infected person's impurity is indicated.

rebellion against Moses, is shut up (*tissāgēr*) outside the camp for seven days (Num 12:14–15).[22] Elsewhere, four *ṣāraʿat*-afflicted men who discovered a deserted Syrian camp during Samaria's famine dwelt outside the gate of the city (2 Kgs 7:3–4).[23]

More difficult to understand is Uzziah's dwelling in the *bêt haḥopšît* after being afflicted with *ṣāraʿat*, for encroaching on priestly prerogatives by burning incense in the temple (2 Kgs 15:5, cf. 2 Chr 26:21).[24] The meaning of the problematic *bêt haḥopšît* is widely disputed.[25] Philo-

---

[22]This passage is generally accepted as E, or mostly so (G. Gray, *Numbers*, 120; S. R. Driver, *An Introduction to the Literature of the Old Testament* [(6th ed.); Edinburgh, T. and T. Clark, 1897; reprint, Gloucester: Peter Smith, 1972] 62; E. Sellin and G. Fohrer, *Introduction to the Old Testament* [Nashville: Abingdon, 1968] 154; O. Eissfeldt, *The Old Testament: An Introduction* [New York: Harper and Row, 1965] 201; interestingly J. Neusner, [*The Idea of Purity in Ancient Judaism* (SJLA 1; Leiden: Brill, 1973) 24] calls it Priestly). However, the use of the verb *hissāgēr* suggests that some Priestly influence is present. Persons or things suspected of *ṣāraʿat* are "quarantined" (*hisgîr*, Lev 13:4, 5, 11, 21, 26, 31, 33, 50, 54; 14:38, 46) for seven days. Miriam is similarly quarantined (*tissāgēr*) for seven days. If Priestly legislation can be presumed in this example, then it appears Miriam is being quarantined as a person *suspected* of the condition (rabbinic *musgār*) and not as one *diagnosed* as having it (*muḥlaṭ*). Only after this period is she healed from *ṣāraʿat* (interpreting the verb *ʾsp*, vv 14–15, as "be healed [from *ṣāraʿat*]" as in 2 Kgs 5:3, 6, 7, 11; P, however, uses *rpʾ* for recovering from the disease, Lev 13:37; 14:3, 48). Not having been diagnosed as having the condition, she is not required to go through a purification period or bring any offerings. If the passage is interpreted this way, an anomaly appears in that Miriam is quarantined "outside the camp," while in Lev 13 there is no indication of removing a suspected person from the camp. Interestingly, the Mishnah pictures both suspected and diagnosed persons as being excluded from the camp (*m. Meg.* 1:7; so interpreted by *b. Meg.* 8b and Bertinoro and Maimonides on the Mishnah passage). No support is given for this view in the Mishnah. It may be that this passage about Miriam is the basis for it.

[23]*Petaḥ haššāʿar* means outside the gate of the city, cf. Josh 8:29; 20:4; Judg 9:35, 44; 2 Kgs 10:8 (cf. Deut 17:5; 22:24; see also Rashi, Kimhi, Altschuler on 2 Kgs 7:3–4).

[24]On Uzziah's sin as sacrilege against God and its connection with *ṣāraʿat*, see Milgrom, *Cult*, 80–82; J. Morgenstern, "Amos Studies II: The Sin of Uzziah," *HUCA* 12–13 (1937–38) 1–20.

[25]There is no consensus about the interpretation of the term *byt hḥpšyt*. For over fifty years (since C. Virolleaud, "La lutte de Mot, fils des

---

dieux et d'Aleïn, fils de Baal," *Syria* 12 [1931] 224) scholars have usually drawn upon the parallel Ugaritic term *bth pṯt* (*UT* 51.viii.7; 67.v.15) to help clarify the Hebrew. Unfortunately, the Ugaritic term (generally divided *bt h pṯt* due to the Hebrew, but cf. T. Gaster, "The Canaanite Epic of Keret," *JQR* 37 [1946–47] 292, who divides it *b-th pṯt*) is just as obscure as the Hebrew term. All that can be said with certainty is that it is a term for the nether world. The attempts at interpreting the Hebrew term can be sorted out into six categories: (1) *Ḥpšyt* is an abstract nominal formation related to the adjective *hopšî* "free." Thus *byt hḥpšyt* means "house of freedom." Kimhi (on 2 Kgs 15:5) understands it to be a place where the king stayed having been released or freed from his royal service (similarly N. Lohfink, "*Ḥōpšî*," *TWAT* 3 [1982] 125). J. A. Montgomery ("Soul Gods," *HTR* 34 [1941] 321; cf. J. A. Montgomery and H. S. Gehman, *A Critical and Exegetical Commentary on the Book of Kings* [ICC; New York: Charles Scribner, 1951] 448) perceives it more abstractly as "'house (= state?) of exemption,' i.e., from royal duties." (2) *Byt hḥpšyt*, still connected with *ḥōpšî* or other Semitic cognates, is a special place for those with *ṣāraʿat*. Ralbag (on 2 Kgs 15:5) says the place was called such because those with this disease were secluded and thus free from contact with other people. O. Loretz ("Ugaritisch-hebräisch *ḪB/PṮ, BT ḪPṮT—ḤPŠJ BJT HḤPŠJ/WT*," *UF* 8 [1976] 129–31; cf. "Die hebräischen Termini *ḤPŠJ* 'Freigelassen, Freigelassener' und *ḤPŠH* 'Freilassung,'" *UF* 9 [1977] 165), connecting it with Akkadian *h upšu* "a member of one of the lower social orders" (CAD Ḫ, 241a), interprets both the Ugaritic and Hebrew terms as "Haus der *Ḫupšu*-Mannschaft." The place where these lower classes of society lived is applied to the underworld in the Ugaritic texts. In the Bible, according to him, a *h upšu* house continued to exist where those with *ṣāraʿat* stayed after the *h upšu* class died out. U. Cassuto (*The Goddess Anath: Canaanite Epics of the Patriarchal Age* [Jerusalem: Magnes Press, 1971] 23; "*Bêt haḤopšît*," *EM* 2 [1954] 75–76) refers to Ps 88:6 and Job 3:19 to show that there was a tradition that the dead were considered "free." Hence the Ugaritic and Hebrew terms designate the underworld "house of freedom" meaning "house of the dead." The Hebrew term was applied to the place those with *ṣāraʿat* lived since they were considered as dead (cf. *b. Ned.* 64b; *b. Sanh.* 47a; Num 12:12; E. Feldman, *Biblical and Post-Biblical Defilement and Mourning: Law as Theology* [New York: Ktav and Yeshivah University, 1977] 37–38; for this view, see S. B. Gurewicz, "Some Examples of Modern Hebrew Exegesis of the Old Testament," *Australian Biblical Reviews* 11 [1963] 22).W. Rudolph (*Chronikbücher* [HAT 1/21; Tübingen: J. C. B. Mohr, 1955] 284; "Ussias 'Haus der Freiheit,'" *ZAW* 89 [1977] 418) treats the term in Hebrew and Ugaritic as a euphemism for "house of isolation" (cf. Morgenstern, "Amos Studies," 1, n. 1). (3) J. Gray (follow-

logically, it appears preferable to connect *ḥopšît* with Hebrew *ḥopšî* "free" and *ḥupšâ* "freedom," yielding "house of freedom, release."[26] It makes more sense to view such a building as a house for the king's retirement rather than a place where those with *ṣāraʿat* stayed, since the king, though afflicted with the disease, presumably would still be treated with respect and would thus be kept apart from common people with *ṣāraʿat*.[27] Moreover, though it is possible that the *bêt haḥopšît* was some type of royal residence outside the city,[28] there is no real evidence that Uzziah was made to stay outside the city. Yet, despite the possibility that Uzziah may have remained in the city—and I would stress that if he did, it would have been an exception due to his royal

---

ing Klostermann) emends the text to *bêtōh ḥopšît* "his house freely" (i.e., released from obligations) (Gray, *I and II Kings: A Commentary* [2d ed., OTL; Philadelphia: Westminster, 1970] 618, n. b; 619–20). Gray does not connect the Hebrew term with the Ugaritic. See his "Feudalism in Ugarit and Early Israel," *ZAW* 64 (1952) 53, and his *Legacy of Canaan: The Ras Shamra Texts and Their Relevance to the Old Testament* (VTSup 5; Leiden: Brill, 1957) 46. (4) W.F.Albright ("The North Canaanite Poems of *Alʾeyan Baʿal*," *JPOS* 14 [1934] 131 and n. 162) connects the Hebrew with Arabic *ḫbṯ* "be low, base" and interprets it as "subterranean house, basement." (5) P. Grelot ("*Ḥofšî* [Ps LXXXVIII 6]," *VT* 14 [1964] 256–63) seeks to establish two separate Hebrew roots, *ḥpš* I ("free") and *ḥpš* II. For *ḥpš* II (attested for him in *byt hḥpšyt* and in Ps 88:6) he proposes two possible meanings. The first is derived from Arabic *ḫabaṯa/ḫabuṯa* denoting corruption or impurity. Both the Hebrew and Ugaritic terms connected with this second root would mean "place of putrefication, rottenness." (6) Grelot alternatively connects the Hebrew term with *ḥbš* "tie up, bind, incarcerate.," thus Hebrew *byt hḥpšyt* means "place of confinement." He admits that the Ugaritic *btḫpṯt* cannot be adapted to this interpretation for phonological reasons. (I note in passing that popular Jewish tradition called the burial cave of the Bene Hazir in the Kidron Valley the *bêt haḥopšît*; see N. Avigad, *Monuments of the Kidron Valley [Maṣṣebot Qedumot beNaḥal Qidron]* [Jerusalem: Bialik Institute, 1954] 4.)

[26]On *ḥopšî*, see the excellent remarks of de Vaux, *Ancient Israel*, 88 and P. K. McCarter, *I Samuel: A New Translation with Introduction, Notes and Commentary* (AB 8; Garden City: Doubleday, 1980) 304. They caution against reading too much into this root from Near Eastern cognates.

[27]Note the respect that the diseased Naaman is given; see below.

[28]Y. Aharoni ("Excavations at Ramat Raḥel," *BA* 24 [1961] 116–18) once thought that a small palace excavated at Ramat Rahel on a hill, between Jerusalem and Bethlehem, was Uzziah's place of seclusion. But it turned out to be later than Uzziah (cf. Gray, *Kings*, 619).

position—he was clearly severed from any contact with cultic matters. He was "cut off from the temple" (2 Chr 26:21).[29] Herein may be part of the reason why his son, Jotham, took the throne. Uzziah could not function as king whose duties included participation in public and royal sacrifices and festivals at the temple. Finally, it is a reasonable conjecture that if he did remain in the city, he would have been subject to certain social restrictions as would pertain to any severely impure person.

Another story, that of Naaman's cure from *ṣāraʿat*, in contrast to the preceding examples, does not indicate that the Syrian general is denied any type of social access due to his disease (2 Kgs 5). He is able to act in his military responsibility (vv 1–2), he can approach Israel's king (v 6), and he can go to Elisha's house (v 9). This situation has caused some to believe that Naaman's *ṣāraʿat* was of a less serious nature than that described in Lev 13, 14 and other places, hence allowing him social freedom.[30] Though this explanation is tempting, a distinction of different types of *ṣāraʿat* is not really evident in the Bible. Naaman's apparent free access must be explained differently. First of all, the writer of this passage does not necessarily have to share the same concerns as the ideal Priestly law or even the social customs of his contemporaries that those with *ṣāraʿat* must be excluded. Perhaps at his time there was not an absolute requirement that those with this condition must stay outside the camp. Yet, I think that the real reason for the difference in how Naaman is treated is to be found in the political situation surrounding the story. Naaman is a foreigner and a high official in a nation that had superiority over Israel. In view of this, it would be unlikely that he would observe Israelite custom.[31] It would also be politically unthinkable to deny him access to Israelite society.[32]

[29]*Bêt Yhwh* means the whole temple complex. Cf. Milgrom, *Levitical Terminology*, n. 47.

[30]Cf. Montgomery and Gehman, *Kings*, 373–74; J. Gray, *Kings*, 504; R. K. Harrison, "Leprosy," *IDB* 3 (1962) 113b; J. Michman, "Leprosy," *EncJud* 11 (1972) 33.

[31]E. V. Hulse ("The Nature of Biblical 'Leprosy' and the Use of Alternative Medical Terms in Modern Translations of the Bible," *PEQ* 107 [1975] 101) suggests that since Naaman was a non-Israelite, Lev 13–14 did not apply to him.

[32]On this passage, see the stimulating literary study by R. Cohn, "Form and Perspective in 2 Kings V," *VT* 33 (1983) 171–84. For more on the restriction or exclusion of persons and things with *ṣāraʿat*, see D. P. Wright and R. Jones, "Leprosy," *ABD*, forthcoming.

8.3.1.4 Summary

To summarize the foregoing discussion, the Priestly writings express two views about the exclusion of impure persons from society. According to the ideal of the wilderness camp, one with *ṣāraʿat*, a *zāb* and *zābâ*, and one who is corpse-contaminated were excluded. In the settled postconquest communities, only a person with *ṣāraʿat* was excluded. Why did the latter remain excluded? Clearly because this impurity was the one most loathed. Aaron's request to Moses to heal Miriam indicates this: "Don't let her be like a dead (fetus) which, when it comes out of its mother's womb, half of its flesh is consumed!" (Num 12:12). Also, of the three impurities mentioned in Num 5:2–3, *ṣāraʿat* requires the most extensive purification rites (Lev 14:1–32). Moreover, *ṣāraʿat* may have been the most abhorred since it was the most visible.[33]

---

[33]The Temple Scroll has developed a more stringent scheme of restriction and exclusion than that found in the Bible. The Scroll distinguishes between the purity and holiness of the temple city versus other cities. All impurities are excluded from the temple city. Mentioned specifically are: one who has intercourse (45:11–12), a blind or otherwise defective person (45:12–14; see n. 5, above), one with *ṣāraʿat*, a *zāb* (until the seventh day of his purification), one who is corpse-contaminated (until after his seven day period; cf. Milgrom, "Studies," 514; TS 45:17–46:1, 16–18; for a different understanding of these last lines, see Yadin, *Temple Scroll*, 1. 236), unclean birds (while alive!; 46:1–4), defecation (46:13–16; cf. Deut 23:13), impure wine, oil, food, and drink (47:6), and impure animal skins (47:7–18). The person who has an emission is to be excluded also (a place is set apart for him outside the city where he stays while impure, 46:16–18; the Scroll prescribes in a general way that "everyone in its [i.e., the temple city's] midst shall be pure," 47:5–6), but his exclusion appears to be mitigated somewhat since he may return to the city after his first ablution. Still he must not enter the temple area until after the passage of three days (45:7–10; on the problems of this apparent exception, see Yadin, *Temple Scroll*, 1. 221–23; B. Levine, "The Temple Scroll: Aspects of its Historical Provenance and Literary Character," *BASOR* 232 [1978] 14–18; Milgrom, "'Sabbath' and 'Temple City' in the Temple Scroll," *BASOR* 232 [1978] 26–27; "Studies," 513–15; J. M. Baumgarten, "The Pharisaic-Saducean Controversies about Purity and the Qumran Texts," *JSS* 31 [1980] 159, n. 11). From the regular city are excluded: a grave (48:10–14), those with *ṣāraʿat*, *zābîm*, menstruants, and parturients (48:14–17). (I agree with Yadin that all these were to be excluded; Milgrom ["Studies," 516–17]

8.3.2 The Restriction of Impure Persons

Though impure persons like the *zāb* and corpse-contaminated were allowed in the community in the period of settlement, there is evidence that they and others who had severe impurity were restricted in their social mobility. Before we can broach the question of the extent of this restriction and the reason for exclusion and restriction of certain impurities, we need to digress to examine the communicability of impurity generally in the Priestly writings.

8.3.2.1 Excursus: The Communicability of Impurity

In the P system, certain impurities can cause other profane persons or objects to become secondarily polluted. Some of these secondarily polluted persons or objects can, in turn, pollute yet other profane persons and things. This excursus seeks to determine just how long or extensive such chains of impurity can be. It charts and describes the extent of pollution from major sources of pollution to secondarily polluted persons and objects. It also provides information about the duration of secondary impurities.

To describe fully the communicability of impurities it will be necessary to reconstruct to some extent the often laconic prescriptions found in P. While much of this deduction is rather straightforward, it is sometimes not clear how the larger prescriptive picture is to be fleshed out. The choice of solutions may be ambiguous or semantic and textual

---

understands the passage to mean that *zābîm*, menstruants, and parturients were allowed in the city, but were restricted therein.) A corpse-contaminated person and one who has had an emission may stay inside the regular city since they bathe themselves on the first day and thus become innocuous to society (see Milgrom, "Studies," 514–15). The restriction of impurities from the temple city reflects the stricture of the war camp in Deut 23 where all impurities are removed. (On the purity necessary for Qumran's war camp, see Milgrom, "Studies," 514.) In fact the stipulation that one who has had an emission or who has had intercourse is impure three days instead of the biblical one day duration (Lev 15:16, 18; Deut 23:11–12) shows a greater rigor than Deuteronomy's camp. Yadin (*Temple Scroll*, 1. 223) relates the austerity in the Temple Scroll to the three day preparation for the Sinaitic revelation (Exod 19:10–15; cf. Milgrom, "Studies," 513).

questions may obscure the path to the broader meaning of a regulation. Also, the fact that the text is composite, resulting from several stages of reediting and reinterpretation, leads to confusion about how the prescriptions are to be understood. Thus the reader should be aware that there is some deal of speculation involved here. In order to overcome some of the difficulty, I will treat the impurities that receive extensive treatment in the biblical text first in order to set down principles that will elucidate other impurities incompletely treated by the Bible. This means that the order of the presentation here is not based on some systematic principle of ordering, such as the severity of the impurities or classes of impurities (though it reflects this to a certain extent), but rather on a practical and somewhat *ad hoc* rationale.

I have devised "trees" to illustrate the communicability of impurity so that it may be comprehended at a glance. Each tree consists of the "father" of uncleanness, to use rabbinic terminology, with branches showing the "offspring" of impurities. Sigla are used to denote whether an offspring is human or inanimate, in what way the person or object was contacted, the manner in which impure persons or objects are purified, and the duration of the impurity. Deductions are bracketed and deduced branches occur with shaded lines. Each of the main branches stemming from the "father" (numbered 1, 2, 3, etc., from the left) is fully discussed in the sections in which the trees occur.

The meanings of the sigla are as follows:

a	denotes the "father" contacting the "offspring" in the described manner
b	denotes the "offspring" contacting the "father" in the described manner
B	a bed (*miškāb*)
br	breaking, of earthenware vessels
c	contact by carrying
e	contact by eating
F	purification of metal utensils by fire
i	contact by sexual intercourse
l	contact by lying on something
L	laundering one's clothes (*kibbēs*)
o	overhang, contracting impurity by being in the same enclosure with an impurity
P	a person
r	contact by riding

s	contact by sitting
sp	contact by spitting
spr	contact by sprinkling
S	a saddle (*merkāb*)
T	a thing, object
t	contact by touch
u	contact by something being under someone
W	washing: bathing for people, rinsing or immersing for utensils
wp	purification by the water of purgation
x	indefinite length of impurity
( )	in parentheses are the requirements for purification and the duration of the impurity
(1)	a one day impurity
(7)	a seven day impurity
[ ]	brackets indicate a deduction
∞∞∞	a shaded line indicates a deduced branch

a. The *Zāb*

See fig. 8.1.

Sources: Lev 15:2–15; cf. 22:4–6.; Num 5:2–3; 2 Sam 3:29.

Branch 1: A clean person who touches a *zāb* (Lev 15:7[34]), is touched

---

[34]The meaning of *bāśār* "flesh" in 15:7 is disputed. The word can mean "genitalia" (cf. Exod 28:42; Lev 6:3; 15:2; Ezek 16:26; 44:7, 9, of a male; Lev 15:19, of a female; Ezek 23:20, of animals) or it can mean flesh in general (cf. Lev 15:16; see the lexicons). Since the person's unclean flux comes out of his *bāśār* (15:2), it may be logical to think that v 7 refers to touching only his genitals and not his whole body (cf. K. Elliger, *Leviticus* [HAT 1/4; Tübingen: J. C. B. Mohr, 1966] 191, translation). This might be further supported by the observation that the text states specifically *bibśar hazzāb* as opposed to the more simple and expected *bazzāb* or *bô* (cf. v 19) in the case of general touch. Other considerations, however, lead to the conclusion general flesh or body is meant here. The menstruant is a lesser impurity than the *zāb* (as her requirements of purification show). If general contact with her brings impurity on another (v 19), so should general contact with a *zāb*. V 7 with *bāśār* in the general sense would give the rule which corresponds to v 19. On the other hand, to limit basar in v 7 to mean genitals would cause doubt about whether general contact with the *zāb* brought impurity

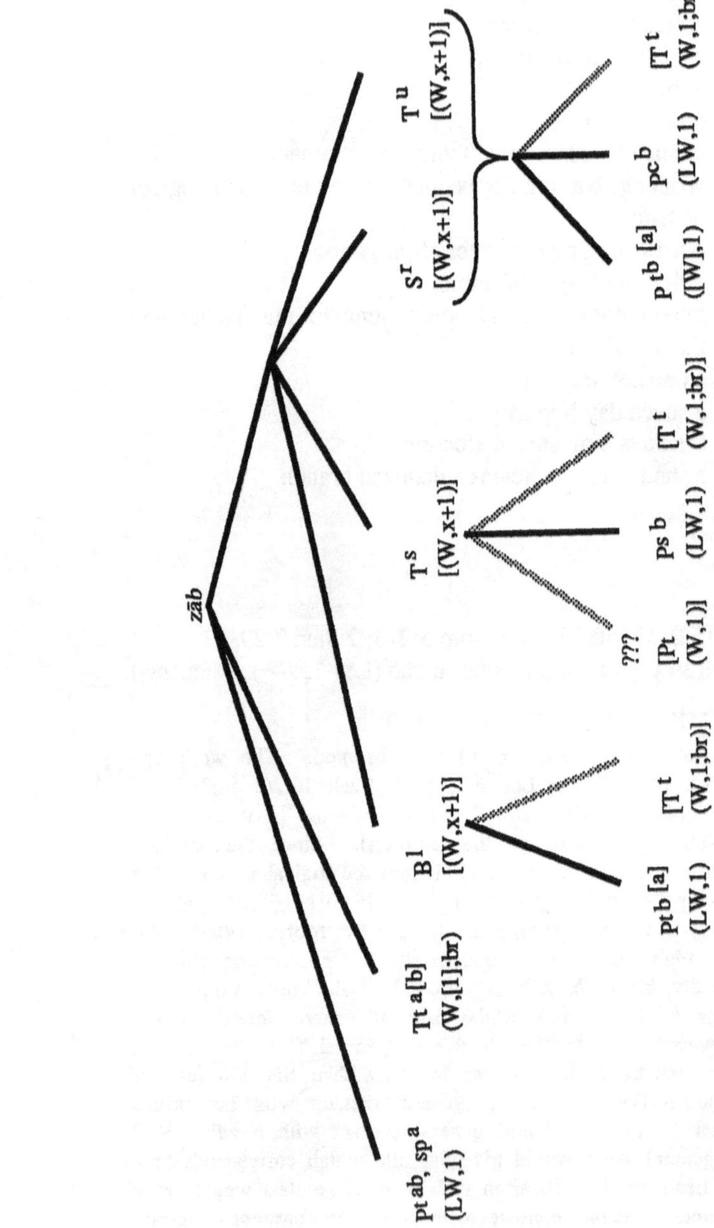

Fig. 8:1: The *Zāb*'s Pollution

by a *zāb* with unwashed hands (v 11[35]), or is spat upon by a *zāb* (v 8) receives a one day impurity requiring the person to launder his clothes and bathe his body. This secondarily polluted person, because of the silence of the text and the picture of evidence in the larger system, does not appear to be able to pollute other profane persons and objects.

---

or not. Finally, v 13 rules that a *zāb*, when pure, is to wash his *bāśār*. Again the meaning of the word here could be open to doubt, but it is clear from the washing of one who is semen contaminated (v 16), a lesser impurity, that entire bathing is meant (Elliger, *Leviticus*, 194; D. Hoffmann, *The Book of Leviticus [Seper Wayyiqraʾ]* [2 vols.; Jerusalem: Mossad Harav Kook,1953] 1. 293). The meaning of *bāśār* in v 7 should be defined by the meaning in vv 13, 16, rather than by that in v 2.

When *bāśār* is understood as general flesh, it is notable that v 7 should talk only of touching the *flesh* of the *zāb* and not his person in general, including his clothes. My supposition is that not only touching the *zāb*'s body, but also his clothes, brings pollution as indicated by branch 1. This can be concluded from two different arguments. One can argue that by "flesh" the law implicitly includes clothing, an extension of a person's body. That this may be so, see n. 39, below, and H. Christ, *Blutvergiessen im Alten Testament: Der gewaltsame Tod des Menschen untersucht am hebräischen Wort* Dām (Basel: Friedrich Reinhardt Kommission, 1977) 166, n. 167. Also, v 19 which talks of touching a menstruant, an impurity similar to that of a *zāb*, does not talk specifically of touching her "flesh"; the object is simply "her." This suggests, perhaps, that "flesh" in v 7 is not to be taken literally or in such a specific way. The conclusion, however, may be reached a different way. Since the *zāb*'s clothing is in constant contact with his body, it may be argued that his clothing is as impure as a bed upon which he sits (cf. branch 3). Just as touching a bed requires the polluted person to launder, bathe, and wait until evening, so would touching the *zāb*'s clothes. Note that the pollution effect and purification requirements deduced here are exactly the same as those for touching the *zāb*'s flesh. Thus, in whatever way "flesh" is understood (including clothes or not), the conclusion about the effect of touching the *zāb*'s clothing is the same. (I thank my student Morgan W. Tanner for bringing this issue to my attention.)

[35]The reason behind the leniency of the *zāb*'s touch when his hands are washed seems clearly to lie in the physical nature of the impurity. Before his hands are washed, it is assumed that they have been dirtied by contact with his genitalia, e.g., during micturition. Washing removes the physical impurity and his touch is clean until his hands are dirtied again.

Branch 2: An object merely touched by the *zāb*, as opposed to being contacted in a more severe way such as sitting, lying, and riding (see branch 3), becomes uncommunicably impure (v 12). However, if the *zāb*'s hands are washed, the contact probably does not pollute as in the case of contact with a person (v 11). Earthenware thus polluted is broken, other items are rinsed.[36] The time period of the impurity is not stated, but it is certainly one day as in the case of the person (v 11) and other polluted utensils (11:32). In the diagram I have included not only the notation "a" which indicates that pollution results when the *zāb* initiates the contact, but also the sign "[b]" to indicate that impurity occurs when an object comes in contact with the *zāb* without his agency, such as when another person carries an object and it touches the *zāb*. The latter form of contact is not described by the text, but is implied by the case of the person in 15:7.

Branch 3: When the *zāb* lies on a bed or sits on a chair, the pieces of furniture become communicably impure (v 4). It is not stated how long these objects remain impure. Since they would generally be his personal items, they probably suffer an indefinite impurity with the *zāb* until they are purified. To be purified, they, like articles in other cases of impurity (cf. v 12; 6:21; 11:32; 15:17), are probably immersed or rinsed with water and become clean at evening. Interestingly, the LXX gives the length of impurity in the case of the saddle as "until evening" (v 9).

The person who touches the bed (v 5) or sits on the chair (v 6) becomes impure and requires laundering, bathing, and waiting until evening.

The related regulations in vv 9–10 are somewhat confusing. A saddle on which the *zāb* rides becomes unclean (v 9). One expects that a person contacting the polluted saddle would be as impure as if he contacted a bed (v 5). But no specific statement regarding purification is given in v 9. Instead, a general and contradictory rule follows which, by its juxtaposition to v 9, appears to pertain to the case of the saddle, as well as to cases of other, unlisted objects (v 10). It distinguishes between different types of contacts occurring with things under the *zāb*. One who merely touches what was under the *zāb* [37] suffers a one day impurity

---

[36]The wooden and earthen utensils are stated here as borderline cases. Other utensils are implied along with wooden ones. See chap. 4.

[37]*Taḥtāw* (v 10) means under the *zāb* (cf. *Sipra*, Meṣoraʿ, Zabim, 4:1, 2). This is the most natural meaning. Other interpretations of the pro-

needing only bathing,[38] while one who makes a more active and aggressive form of contact, i.e., carrying, needs both laundering and bathing.[39] This appears to contradict v 5 where merely touching a *zāb*'s bed brings an impurity that requires both laundering and bathing. I have drawn branch 3 in fig. 8.1 retaining this contradiction. Indeed, this is

---

noun (e.g., Ibn Ezra "under the saddle"; the Rabbis "anything which the *zāb* is under" [taking *zāb* as the subject of *yihyê*], yielding evidence for *maddāp* uncleanness [*b. Nid.* 32b–33a; Hoffmann, *Leviticus*, 1. 290; on the derivations of *maddāp* uncleanness, see Neusner, "The Scriptural Origins of Mishnah's Conception of *Maddaf*-Uncleanness: An Exercise in Analogical Contrastive Exegesis," *Method and Meaning in Ancient Judaism, Second Series* [ed. J. Neusner; Chico: Scholars, 1981] 187–96) are attempts to make sense of the less stringent stipulation in v 10 vis-à-vis v 5. That part of Jewish tradition which understood the pronoun to refer to the *zāb*, limited *kōl ʾăšer* in v 10a to the saddle (see *Sipra*, Meṣoraʿ, Zabim, 4:1, 2; *m. Zabim* 5:6, 8, 10; Rashi on v 10). Thus, touching the *zāb*'s bed and chair cause a greater impurity requiring laundering and bathing than just touching the saddle requiring only bathing.

[38]Bathing or washing appears to be a basic requisite for purification from all impurities. Whenever the diagnosis "he shall be unclean until evening" is found, or whenever laundering is mentioned without the mention of bathing, ablution is implicit. Several examples make this clear: (a) Lev 11:40 states that one who eats of the carcass of improperly killed clean animals must "launder his clothes and be unclean until evening." A parallel law (Lev 17:15) says that whoever eats such carcass must "launder his clothes, bathe in water, and be unclean until evening." (b) If washing of a *šereṣ* contaminated utensil is necessary (Lev 11:32), the same should be necessary for people who touch the *šereṣ* (vv 31, 36). (c) A priest who touches certain impurities "becomes unclean until evening" (Lev 22:6). Scripture adds an explanation, lest there be any mistake: "He shall not eat of the holy things unless he has bathed his flesh in water." (d) Num 31:24 omits bathing, but it is clearly required from Num 19:19. (e) Bathing for the gatherer of the Red Cow ashes is missing (Num 19:10), but is certainly required as it is explicitly with the priest and the burner who also participate in the rite (vv 7, 8). (f) No ablution is mentioned for the *zābâ*'s purification (Lev 15:28–30), but it is surely to be supplied from the parallel case of the *zāb* (v 13). (g) Ablution is often assumed and thus omitted as it seems in the cases of the menstruant (see n. 44, below), parturient, and the corpse-contaminated nazirite. (I thank J. Milgrom for several of these points.)

[39]Several passages show a distinction in the impurity acquired by different modes of contact: (a) Lev 11:24–25, 27–28: *touching* carcasses

of certain unclean animals requires bathing (implied, see n. 38) and waiting until evening, while *carrying* them requires laundering, bathing (implied), and waiting until evening. (b) Lev 11:39–40: *touching* the carcass of a clean animal requires bathing (implied) and waiting, while *eating* or *carrying* it requires laundering, bathing (implied), and waiting. (c) Lev 14:46–47: one who *enters* a quarantined house requires bathing (implied) and waiting, while *lying* or *eating* in the house requires laundering, bathing, and waiting (these last two implied). (d) Num 19:21: one who *touches* the water of purgation needs bathing (implied) and waiting, while one who *sprinkles* needs laundering, bathing, and waiting (these last two implied).

The reason for the requirement of laundering cannot simply be that the clothes have contacted the impurity. The prescriptions do not give this as a reason for laundering. Indeed, we would expect the rules to be more direct on this matter if clothing needed washing because it has touched the impurity. Furthermore, the forms of contact that require laundering do not necessarily imply that contact with clothing has been made. Conceivably, one could carry a dead mouse by its tail without touching clothing and one could eat impure meat without spilling it on clothing. Most decisive, however, is the rule about entering a *ṣāraʿat* infected house. If the requirement to launder was based purely on the contact of clothing with the impurity, then the clothing on the person who merely enters the house should become impure by overhang as the person does when he enters and should, consequently, require laundering. But this is not the case. Laundering is required only in the case of eating or lying down in the house. This suggests that the reason for laundering is more abstract than mere contact with the clothes. In my view, the requirement to launder is due to a more aggressive or longer lasting form of contact which the person makes with the impurity. His clothes do not need to touch it to require laundering. In other words, the more extensive the contact, the more complete the pollution of the person. Consequently, both bathing and laundering are required.

The Rabbis understood the requirement of laundering to be based on staying in the *ṣāraʿat* infected house for a longer period of time (cf. *m. Neg.* 13:9–10; *Sipra*, Meṣoraʿ, 5:4–6). Otherwise, the Rabbis understood the laundering requirement as deriving from the intensive impurity that persons suffer while in contact with the source of impurity. With certain impurities (those in the Bible requiring laundering), persons become highly charged with impurity while touching the impure source. Momentarily thus charged, they pollute the clothes they are wearing and can pollute other articles and persons (J. Neusner, *Zabim* [SJLA 6, HMLP 18; Leiden: Brill, 1977] 39–42, 86–90; cf. *m. Zabim* 2:4; 5:1, 6–10; *t. Zabim* 5:2–5; *m. Tohar.* 1:1; Maimonides, *MTor*, Ṭohora, Meṭammeʾe Miškab 6:1–2).

how the Rabbis would have drawn the branch. However, they obviate the contradiction by taking the text very literally. For them, a *zāb*'s bed and chair carry an impurity which can contaminate a person's body and clothes by mere contact, while the saddle (with v 10 referring specifically to the saddle) has a lesser impurity which can transmit impurity to clothes only when carried (see n. 37). A possible critical solution is to view v 10 as originally consisting of only parts aα and bβ.[40] The verse would have run: "Anyone touching anything which is under him shall launder his clothes, bathe with water, and be unclean until the evening." V 10 in this form would be giving a general rule about the impurity of objects under the *zāb* which agrees with vv 5 and 6. Any contact with the furniture requires both laundering and bathing. Support for this possibly original form of the law is found in the case of the menstruant (vv 21–22) and the *zābâ* (v 27, MT; but cf. the LXX; see n. 48) where merely touching their beds or chairs brings an impurity that requires both laundering and bathing. The expansion of the verse by the addition of parts aβ, bα altered the prescription to agree with the tenor of Lev 11 where touching or carrying various impure animals bring impurities that need only bathing or both bathing and laundering, respectively (see n. 39). Presumably, from the point of view of the expander of v 10, "touching" in v 5 would be explained as a more severe form of touching—perhaps "lying" or the like—in order to account for the requirement of laundering. This explanation would, for the expander, be supported by v 6 where sitting, not simply touching, is the form of contact. According to this revised understanding supplied by the expansion of v 10, the third branch (omitting pollution of objects which remains the same) appears as in fig. 8.2.

If this historical explanation is accepted, a difficulty remains in that the cases of the menstruant and the *zābâ* (cf. vv 21–22, 27) have not been edited to show a similar distinction in lighter and more severe contacts and respective requirements of bathing or of bathing and laundering. It may be that the editor perceived the impurity of an abnormal discharge in a male to be less severe in some way than that of a blood flow—normal or irregular—in a woman and hence did not change those prescriptions.[40a]

---

[40]This solution was suggest by J. Milgrom. One may alternately argue, however, that v 10 or vv 9–10 are altogether additions and still follow the substance of the historical reconstruction offered here.

[40a]From J. Milgrom (private communication).

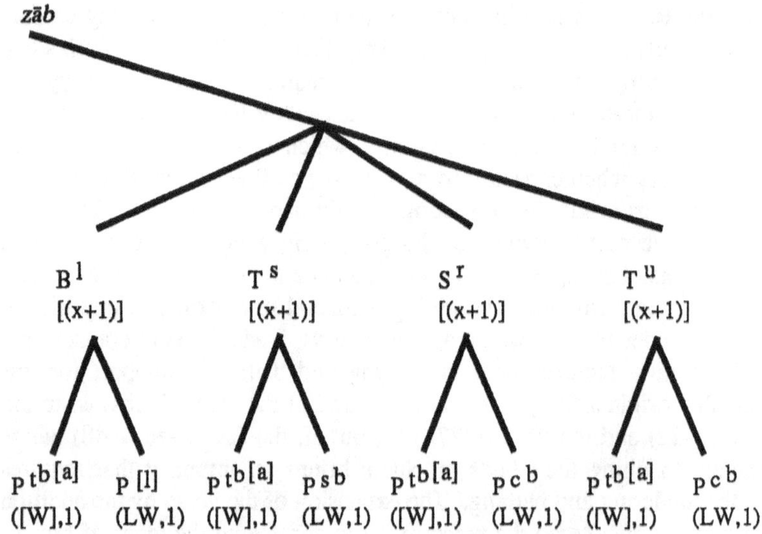

Fig. 8.2: Revised Third Branch of the *Zāb*

Another solution to why only the *zāb* law was amended—one more attractive to me—is that the editor was reinterpreting the original *zāb* rule or making explicit an implication in it. Note that the *zāb* rules in vv 5–6 talk of *touching* a bed and *sitting* on a chair, while the menstruant and *zābâ* rules talk of *touching* a bed and *touching* a chair (vv 21–22, 27). That the *zāb* rule has sitting as the form of contact for the chair may have indicated to the editor, if the text did not originally have this implication, that a form of contact less severe than sitting, i.e., just touching, had a less severe impurity requiring only bathing. This distinction he made explicit in v 10. Since the cases of the menstruant and *zābâ* give no indication of such a distinction, the editor made no change there. I have noted the possible implication of vv 5–6 on fig. 1 by the "T^s" branch with question marks.[41]

---

[41]Of course, one can raise the questions that if v 6 actually carried the implication that touching brought a lighter form of impurity requiring only bathing, why is it necessary to view part of v 10 (or all of it, or both vv 9–10) as an editorial addition? There are reasons to consider it still editorial: (a) a contradiction is still retained between v 5 and v 10. It

Finally in regard to branch 3, it is not explicitly stated that other objects become impure by touching the items made impure by the *zāb*'s lying, sitting, or riding. However, it is logical to suppose that impurities which pollute persons can pollute objects for the same length of time. We have already observed this in branches 1 and 2 where a *zāb*'s touch pollutes both persons and things for one day. Therefore, objects which contact the furniture of a *zāb* become unclean for one day like persons who contact his furniture. The means of purification for these objects would be the same as for other objects polluted for one day.

b. The Menstruant

See fig. 8.3.

Sources: Lev 15:19–24, 33; cf. Gen 31:35; Lev 12:2, 5; 15:25–26; 18:19; 20:18; 2 Sam 11:4; Isa 30:22; Ezek 7:19–20; 18:6; 22:10; 36:17.

Branch 1: A clean person who touches a menstruant becomes unclean until evening (Lev 15:19). Bathing is presupposed in the time requirement of v 19 (see n. 38). The question arises, however, if laundering is also required. A person who touches the *zāb* requires both, which suggests both are needed here (see, the *zāb*, branch 1). Moreover, since something upon which the menstruant lies or sits pollutes a person by simple contact so that the person needs laundering and bathing (see branch 3), directly touching her should all the more require both laundering and bathing.[42] Also, if she touches or spits on a person, that person probably becomes unclean, as in the case of the *zāb*.

---

is difficult to explain why touching a *zāb*'s bed would require laundering and bathing as opposed to touching other furniture pieces. Is it because the *zāb* is in more contact with the bed? But then why is there no corresponding change in the menstruant's and *zābâ*'s rules? (b) On a systematic level, one would expect the *zāb*'s rule to be parallel to the menstruant's (vv 21–22) and *zābâ*'s rule (v 27). Discerning different levels in the *zāb*'s law with different meanings would allow for this at one historical level of the text. (c) If vv 5–6 and 9–10 were written together with a distinction in the pollution of a bed versus other items, why were not the verses and cases arranged in a way which better expressed this? The confusion that the rules present for interpretation suggest that more than one hand has been involved.

[42]*Sipra*, Meṣoraᶜ, Zabim, Par 4:9 (cf. *m. Zabim* 5:6; see Hoffmann, *Leviticus*, 1. 293–94).

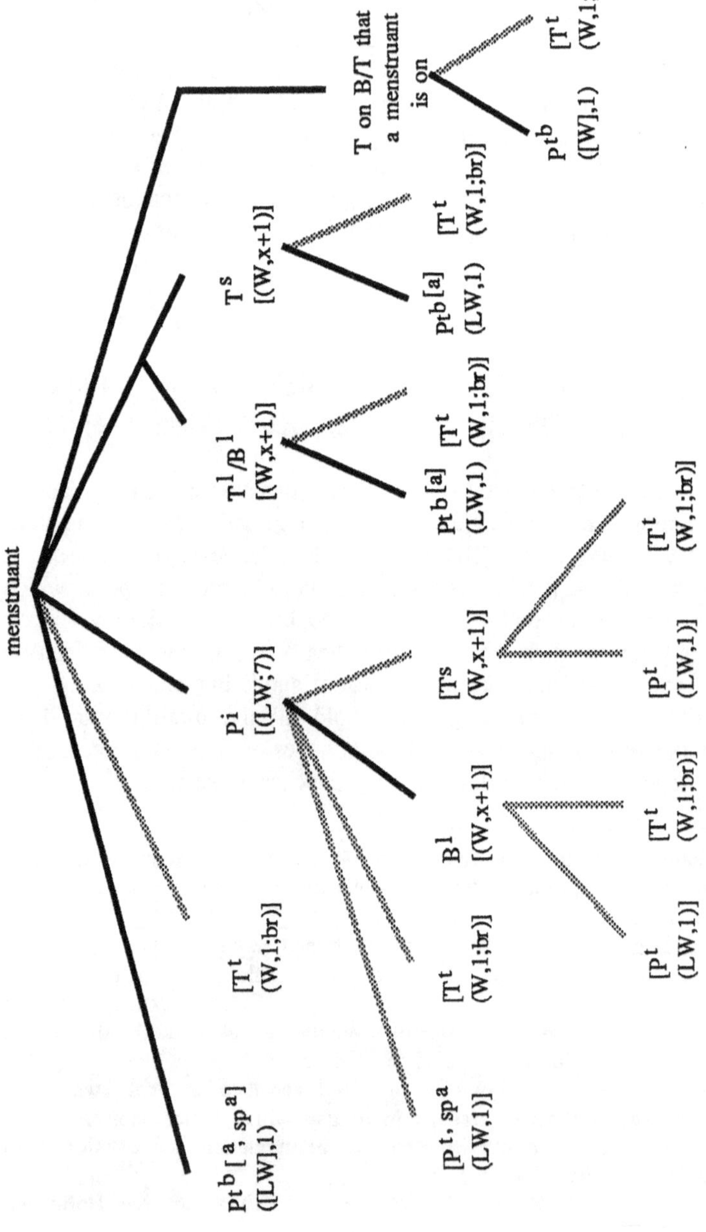

Fig. 8.3: The Menstruant's Pollution

Branch 2: It is not said how a menstruant affects various objects. This, however, can be supplied from the *zāb*'s case (15:12; see the *zāb*, branch 2).

Branch 3: A man who has intercourse with a menstruant acquires her menstrual impurity in the same degree. He is unclean seven days and pollutes persons and things as she does (v 24; see branch 4).[43] He would probably purify by laundering and bathing on the seventh day, as is probably the case with the menstruant.[44]

Branch 4: Whatever a menstruant lies or sits on becomes unclean (v 20). As the *zāb*'s furniture becomes indefinitely impure until it is purified, so also the menstruant's furniture (see the *zāb*, branch 3). The person who touches her bed or chair becomes unclean for one day and requires laundering and bathing (vv 21–22; cf. the *zāb*, branch 3). This rule agrees with 15:5 where merely touching a *zāb*'s bed requires laundering and bathing. We have seen that vv 9–10 pose a contradiction to v 5 and that v 10aβ, bα may be a supplement to v 5–6 distinguishing between mere touch and more aggressive contact such as carrying. Since the menstruant's case has not been revised as has been the *zāb*'s case, I doubt that the editor intended the revision of the latter to apply here.

---

[43]The phrase *wĕkōl hammiškāb ʾăšer yiškab ʿālāw yiṭmāʾ* (v 24) is a reference to the larger series of contacts in the case of the menstruant (cf. v 20). It is to remind the reader of all that was said there and the consequences of this impurity (vv 21–23). The Rabbis determined that the one who has intercourse with a menstruant causes a lesser impurity to fall upon beds and chairs than the menstruant. His furniture does not transmit impurity to other people (*m. Zabim* 5:11 and compare mishnah 6; *Kelim* 1:3; see the argument for deducing this rule in *b. Nid.* 33a; see also Maimonides, *MTor*, Ṭohora, Meṭammeʾe Miškab 3:2).

[44]Circumstantial evidence shows that the menstruant at least needs to launder and bathe at the end of her seven day impurity: (a) Since those with minor, noncommunicable impurities require at least bathing, so the menstruant whose impurity is seven days and is communicable should at least be required to bathe. (b) If persons who touch her or her furniture require laundering and bathing, we would expect her, the source of these impurities, to launder and bathe. (c) Other seven day periods of impurity are followed by laundering and bathing (the *zāb*, v 13; the person who has recovered from *ṣāraʿat*, 14:8–9; a corpse-contaminated person, Num 19:19, cf. 31:24; of course these impurities are significantly different from the menstruant's in having much more extended purification requirements). We may expect her seven day impurity to require laundering and bathing like these other impurities.

Branch 5: The pollution chain indicated by this branch is found in v 23 which is difficult. I concur with Ibn Ezra[45] that the pronoun *hûʾ* refers to a vessel or object. Its antecedent is apparently, though awkwardly, *kĕlî* in the phrase *wĕkol hannōgēaʿ bĕkol-kĕlî* in v 22. V 23 says that if this *kĕlî* which is touched "is on the bed (meaning on the bed on which the menstruant is lying) or on the *kĕlî* on which she is sitting when he touches it (i.e., touches the *kĕlî* which is lying on these objects), he is unclean until the evening." Note that the participle *yōšebet* appears to mean that the woman needs to be on the bed or chair when the other person makes contact with the object on the bed or chair. This law thus deals with the case of touching an object which is on furniture on which a menstruant is contemporaneously lying or sitting, where the woman is not directly touching the polluting object. One only needs to bathe, not launder as in vv 21–22, because the pollution is less direct.[46]

Though nothing is said about objects touching the object on the bed or chair, presumably they would become impure for a one-day period.

The impurity chain of branch 5 is complex: it has one more intervening member than the "two-generation" chain of branch 4, i.e., the object that is on the bed or chair. But at the same time the chain is not a pure "three-generation" chain as in branch 3. That is, in branch 5 the woman must be on the bed or chair for an object which is on these furniture pieces to pollute. Hence I draw the branch in a position between the two- and three-generation impurities to show this ambivalent or intermediate characteristic.

---

[45]And with J. Milgrom (private communication); Elliger, *Leviticus*, 199; *JB*; *AV*.

[46]Other solutions to v 23 are less satisfactory: (a) The LXX reads (taking *hwʾ* as *hîʾ* rather than *hûʾ*): "And if it is when she is on the bed or on the object upon which she may sit when he touches her, he shall be unclean until evening" (*ean de en tę̄ koitę̄ autēs ousēs ē epi tou skeuous, hou ean katisē ep' autǭ en tǭ haptesthai auton autēs, akathartos estai heōs hesperas*). It appears that the Greek understood v 23 as a contrast to v 24. Hoffmann (*Leviticus*, 1. 294–95) takes vv 23 and 24 as contrasting stipulations: "If he is on the bed or on the object on which she is sitting when he makes contact with it, he is unclean until evening. But if a man has intercourse with her, her menstrual impurity shall be on him. He shall be unclean seven days. Any bed on which he lies becomes unclean." The time stipulation in v 23, "be unclean until evening," serves to

c. The *Zābâ*

See fig. 8.4.

Sources: Lev 15:25–30, 33.

The *zābâ,* whose symptoms are an irregular blood flow beyond or outside the normal catamenial period, is similar to the menstruant and *zāb* in the effect of her impurity. Her impurity is described as being like menstrual impurity (Lev 15:25, 26) and her purification requirements (vv 28–30) are like those of the *zāb* (vv 13–15).[47] Thus the information about the communicability of impurity explicit with the *zāb* and menstruant helps flesh out this case.

Branch 1: This branch is supplied from the *zāb,* branch 1, and the menstruant, branch 1. It is implied from the fact that the *zābâ* can pollute objects which can, in turn, pollute persons (see branch 4). Thus she must be able to pollute persons directly.

---

contrast a short-lived one-day impurity with the longer seven-day impurity rather than to indicate that only bathing, not laundering, is necessary. The purification required for being on furniture items with the menstruant would be the same as in vv 21–22. (b) Some read *hûʾ* as *hîʾ* (cf. the Samaritan): "If she is on the bed or on the object she sits on when he touches it, he shall be unclean." This, however, would be superfluous to vv 21–22, unless one understands "unclean until evening" as excluding laundering. But then the difficulty lies in determining how a lighter impurity is transmitted when she is on the chair versus a more severe impurity when she is not. (c) Some say *hûʾ* refers to blood (see Hoffmann, *Leviticus,* 1. 294). (d) The *Sipra* (Meṣoraʿ, Zabim, Par 4:15; see Rabad on the *Sipra* passage; cf. Rashi and Rashbam on Lev 15:23) uses the principles deduced from vv 5–6, 9–10 to solve the problem of the lack of the mention of laundering (see n. 37). *Wĕʾim ʿal hammiškāb hûʾ* is separated conceptually from the rest of the verse. The person on the bed becomes unclean and needs laundering, bathing, and waiting. *Hakkĕlî ʾăšer hîʾ yōšebet ʿālāw* refers to a saddle. Touching a saddle (*bĕnogʿô bô*) requires only bathing (implicit in "unclean until evening"), but no laundering (cf. v 9–10).

[47]There are minor differences, the most significant being the lack of the mention of laundering and bathing in the passage about the *zābâ* (v 28; cf. v 13). The stipulations for the *zābâ's* purification have been abbreviated with laundering and bathing implicitly understood from v 13 (see n. 38). The other minor variations are due to stylistic concerns.

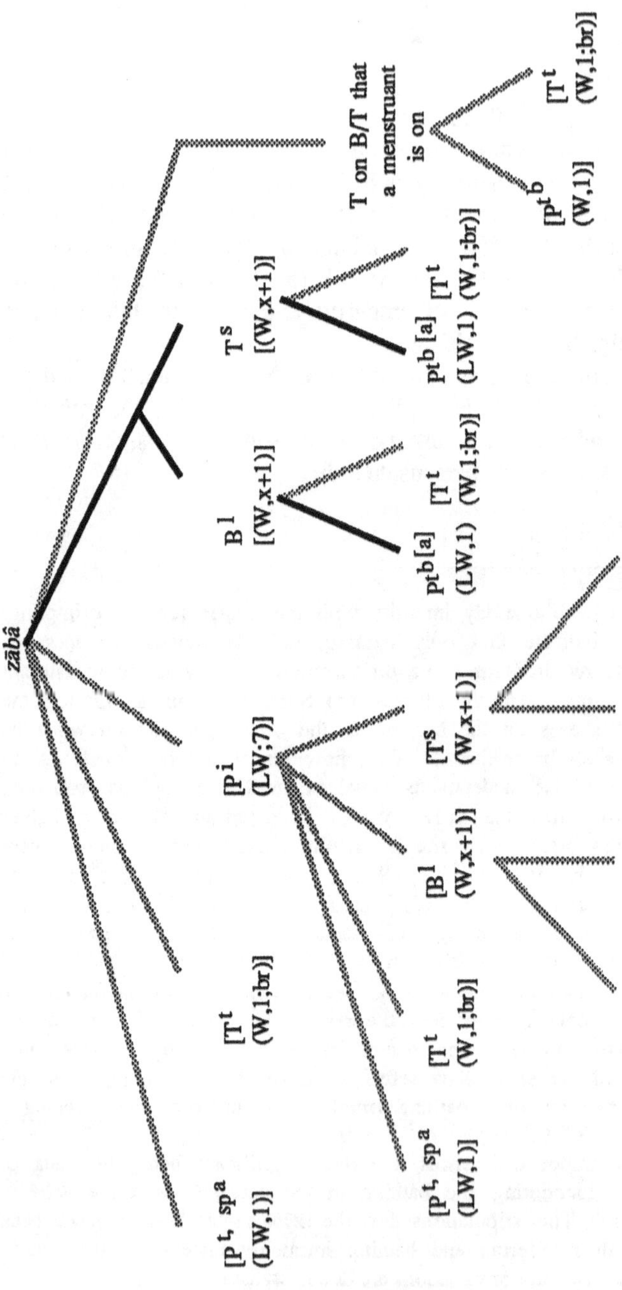

Fig. 8.4: The *Zābâ*'s Pollution

Branch 2: This is supplied from the *zāb*, branch 2. Cf. the menstruant, branch 2.

Branch 3: This is supplied from the menstruant, branch 3. A question in regard to the *zāb* may be brought up at this point. If it seems logical to apply the pollution that sexual intercourse with a menstruant causes to the case of the *zābâ*, is it not logical to apply it also to the case of the *zāb*? I do not think this question can be decided. On the one hand, the pollution effect of all three cases otherwise is very similar. This may suggest that intercourse with a *zāb* brings pollution as in the case of the menstruant. On the other hand we noticed earlier (see above the discussion on the *zāb*, branch 3) that the pollution of the *zāb* may be considered slightly less severe (in some way) than that of the menstruant and *zābâ*. If this is so, then perhaps the prescriptions may not intend that a *zāb* can pollute like a menstruant by sexual intercourse.

Branch 4: In essence, this (vv 26–27) is exactly like the stipulations with the menstruant (vv 20–22, see the menstruant, branch 4).[48] The *zābâ* pollutes a bed or chair by lying or sitting, which then pollute persons by touch giving the persons an impurity of one day requiring laundering and bathing. The qualifications made by vv 9–10 in the *zāb*'s case are probably not to be made here (see the *zāb*, branch 3; the menstruant, branch 4).

Branch 5: This is brought over from the case of the menstruant (see the menstruant, branch 5).

d. The Parturient

Sources: Lev 12.

The first stage of the parturient's impurity (seven or fourteen days) is like menstrual impurity (Lev 12:2, 5). Refer to the section on the menstruant (above, see fig. 8.3) for a description of this impurity. In the second stage of her impurity (33 or 66 days; vv 4–5), she does not contaminate profane items at all.[49] Therefore, no tree can or needs to be drawn for this stage.

---

[48]The LXX and a few Hebrew MSS (cf. *BHS*) have *bâ* instead of *bām* in v 27. The MT appears to be correct, being parallel to vv 20–22.

[49]See section 8.3.2.2, below.

e. Semen

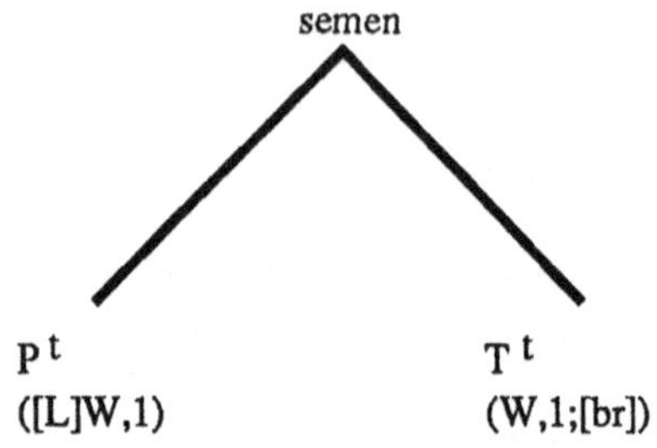

Fig. 8.5: The Pollution of Semen

See fig. 8.5.

Sources: Lev 15:16–18, 32; cf. Exod 19:10–11, 14–15; Lev 22:4–7; Deut 23:10–15; 1 Sam 20:26; 21:4–7; 2 Sam 11:11; Isa 13:3.

Branch 1: Semen pollutes the man who emits it (Lev 15:16) and the woman with whom he has intercourse (v 18). They are impure for a day and require bathing. Theoretically, laundering would be necessary too, but here, the laundering prescription has been separated from the bathing requirement in order to expand it to include all bedding and clothing which semen has touched.

Branch 2: Objects become contaminated by semen (v 17). Here only clothing and bedding are mentioned, but logically all articles that come in contact with semen would be impure. Earthen vessels would almost certainly require breaking.

f. A Corpse

See fig. 8.6.

Sources: Num 19; cf. Lev 10:4–5; 21:1–4, 10–12; Num 5:2–3; 6:6–12; 9:6–14; 31:13–24; Isa 65:4; Ezek 39:11–16; 43:7–9; 44:25–27; Hag 2:13, and see Chapter Five of this work.

Branch 1: Persons who make contact with a corpse, touching it directly (Num 19:11, 16, 18, including touching a human bone or grave) or being in the same enclosure with it (vv 14, 18), become unclean for seven days. They become pure by having the water of purgation (*mê*

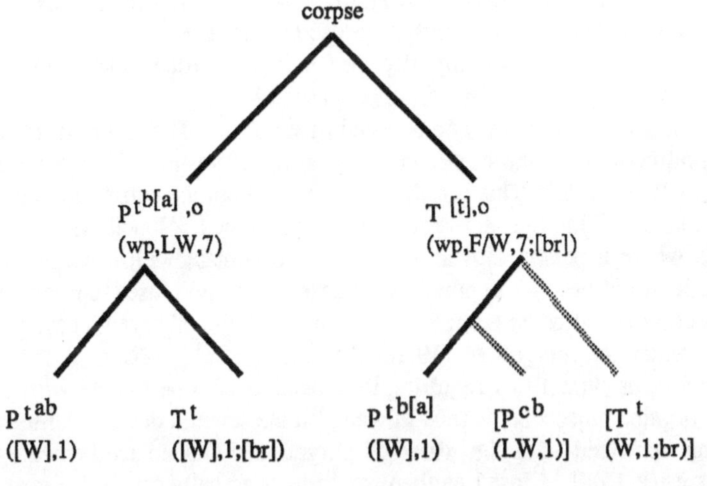

Fig. 8.6: The Pollution of a Corpse

niddâ,[50] vv 9, 13, 20, 21; cf. 31:23) sprinkled on them on the third and seventh days of their impurity (Num 19:12, 18–19; 31:19) and by laundering, bathing, and waiting till evening on the seventh day (19:19; 31:24). Those clean are polluted when corpse-contaminated persons touch them (19:22a[51]) or when they touch those contaminated (v 22b[52];

---

[50]*Niddâ* means "purification, purgation" in this phrase (cf. Zech 13:1). See J. Milgrom and D. Wright, "*Niddāh*," *TWAT* 5 (1984) 250–53.

[51]The phrase *wĕkol ʾăšer yiggaʿ bô haṭṭāmēʾ yiṭmāʾ* in Num 19:22a should be construed "and every (person or thing) that the (corpse) contaminated touches becomes impure" (cf. Rashi, Ibn Ezra; see the next note).

[52]The two phrases in Num 19:22 form a reciprocal relation. V 22a deals with the corpse-contaminated person touching the pure person or object, while v 22b concerns the pure person touching the corpse-contaminated person: "and the person who touches (the corpse-contaminated) becomes unclean until evening" (cf. Rashi). G. Gray (*Numbers*, 255) is not correct in interpreting v 22b to mean that a person who touches the thing that the corpse-contaminated has touched becomes unclean for a day. Our analysis, below, will show that an object suffering a minor, one day impurity, such as something or someone touched by a corpse-contaminated person, does not have power to pollute the profane sphere.

Lev 22:4[53]; cf. the *zāb*, branch 1). The impurity lasts for one day and requires bathing.[54] Similarly, corpse-contaminated persons pollute objects with a one day impurity (see n. 51). Earthenware would be destroyed; nonearthenware would be washed.[55]

Branch 2: Objects may be polluted by a corpse. The text only speaks of pollution when the object is in the same enclosure with the corpse (Num 19:14–15).[56] This is only logical since both the corpse and object are inanimate and thus active touching is precluded. Nonetheless, in the case where a person moved an object into contact with a corpse, the object would become impure. Nonearthenware and closed earthenware objects are purified by being sprinkled on the third and seventh days with the water of purgation (19:18–19; 31:20, 23). Num 31:21–23 supplement Num 19 by requiring that metal vessels be purged with fire and organic objects be washed in water on the seventh day in addition to being sprinkled with the water of purgation.[57] Open earthenware is broken (v 15).[58] Closed earthenware which actually touched a corpse would probably be destroyed.[59] A person who touches a corpse-contaminated object becomes unclean for one day and requires bathing (Lev 22:4–6).[60] It is highly likely that if a more aggressive form of contact occurred (e.g., carrying), laundering would also be required.[61] Finally, things that touch a corpse-contaminated object would suffer a

---

[53]Lev 22:4b should be construed: "whoever touches any (person or thing) that is corpse-contaminated."

[54]In Num 19:22b, the phrase *tiṭmāʾ ʿad hāʿāreb* includes bathing (Ibn Ezra, see n. 38). The sense of the time stipulation in v 22b applies to *yiṭmāʾ* in v 22a. Moreover, Lev 22:4–6 shows that bathing is required. Vv 4b–5 give a series of impurities which a priest might suffer: touching a corpse-contaminated person or object, having an emission, touching a (dead) *šereṣ* or any polluting person. V 6 sums up these contacts by a general statement: "A person who touches such" (semen contamination appears to be included, even though it is described in v 4b as not being contracted by touch). Then follow purification requirements. The impure person must (at least) bathe and wait until evening (vv 6–7).

[55]See chap. 4, section 4.2.

[56]On the understanding of vv 14–15, see section 4.2.

[57]See n. 15, above.

[58]See section 4.2 and nn. 12 and 13 to chap. 4.

[59]See section 4.2.

[60]See n. 53, above.

[61]See n. 39, above.

one day impurity and need washing, or in the case of earthenware, be broken. This may be deduced from the impurity that objects receive from coming in contact with a corpse-contaminated person (see branch 1).[62]

---

[62]The rabbinic system exhibits a more extensive chain of contamination due to certain principles deduced from the text. The rabbinic tree (leaving out the sigla referring to purification requirements) would appear as drawn in fig. 8.7.

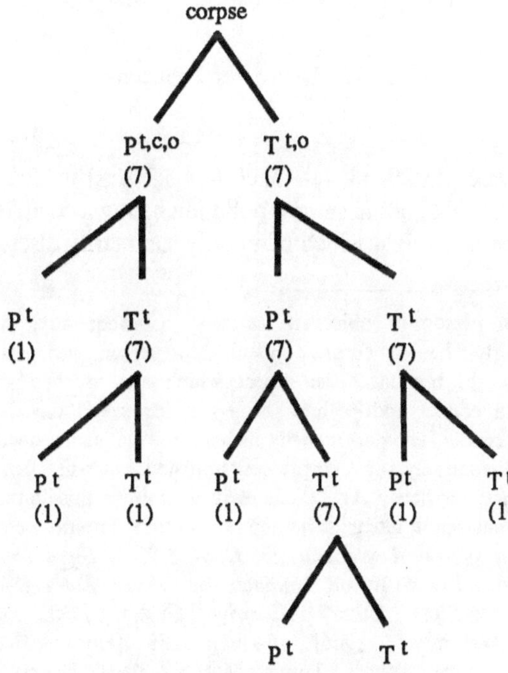

Fig. 8.7: Rabbinic View of Corpse Pollution

The principle leading to such extensive impurity is that any utensil polluted by a corpse becomes a father of uncleanness equal to the corpse. This principle is derived from Num 19:16 where the mention of a sword is taken to mean that touching a sword, hence any utensil that is corpse-contaminated, pollutes as the corpse itself. From this principle, another is derived: a utensil suffers the same degree of impurity as the corpse-

g. Carcass of Eight Types of Land *Šereṣ*

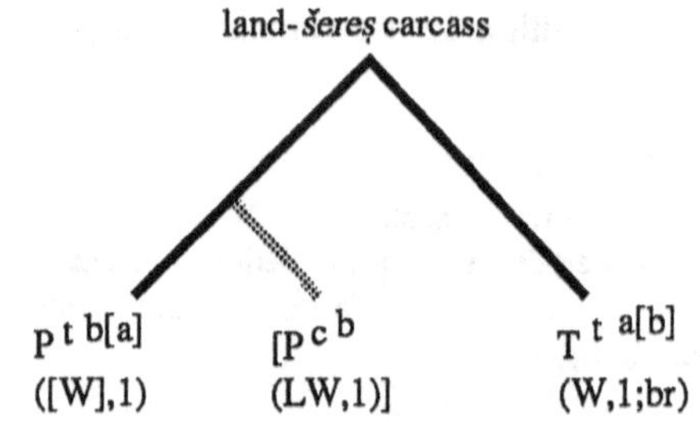

Fig. 8.8: Land-*Šereṣ* Pollution

See fig. 8.8.

Sources: Lev 11:29–38, 41–45; cf. Lev 5:2; 7:21[63]; 22:5–6.

The laws about animal carcass pollution betray a complex history and development of thought which I can only summarily discuss here. This

---

contaminated person or object it touches. Consequently, in branch 1, a utensil that touches a corpse-contaminated person becomes unclean for seven days. In branch 2, an object which has touched a corpse is as unclean as a corpse and pollutes a person for seven days. In turn, this person can render another utensil unclean to the same degree, for seven days. Alternatively, a corpse-contaminated utensil can contaminate another utensil for seven days. There is a limit to this impurity, however. After a certain point, utensils no longer contract impurity equal to that of the object or person they touch (*m. Ohol.* 1:2, 3; *Sipre Num* 127 [H. S. Horovitz, ed., *The Sifre on Numbers and Sifre Zutta [Sipre ʿal Seper Bammidbar weSipre Zuttaʾ]* [Leipzig: Gustav Fock, 1917; reprint, Jerusalem: Wahrmann, 1966] 164–65]; 158 [Horovitz, 214: 10–14]; Maimonides, *MTor,* Ṭohora, Ṭumʾat Met 5:2–5; H. Danby, *The Mishnah* [Oxford: Oxford University, 1933] 649–50, n. 3; and see Maimonides, *MTor,* Ṭohora, Ṭumʾat Met chaps. 1 and 5 in general).

[63]*Šeqeṣ* "abomination" in this verse is suspicious because of the similarity of the consonant chain *šqṣ*/*šrṣ* and the near parallel in Lev 5:2 which has *šereṣ*. Some Hebrew MSS, the Syriac and *Tg. Onq.* have *šereṣ* or its translated equivalent (also see A. B. Ehrlich, *Randglossen zur hebräischen Bibel* [7 vols.; Leipzig: J. C. Hinrichs, 1908–14] 2. 24 where he observes that *šeqeṣ ṭāmēʾ* is a tautology). Nevertheless, if *šeqeṣ* be the correct reading, the term includes *šereṣ* animals (Lev 11:41–42, 44, used of land *šereṣ*; cf. 11:10, 11, 12, of sea life).

is most readily seen in Lev 11. A close reading of this chapter makes one realize that the text is not a unity. My judgement is that it consists of three sections stemming from different periods and authors or editors (not including introductory and concluding formulae: vv 2b–23, 24–40, 41–45).[63a] (I am leaving out of consideration here the more minute critical judgements that certainly can be made.) This three-fold division is mainly determined by the style and legal perspective of the sections. Vv 2b–23 focus on prohibitions against eating certain animals. Though vv 4–8 talk of the impurity of four specific large animals with a command not to touch their carcasses, nothing is said about impurity in regard to the animals discussed in vv 9–23, and in vv 4–8 we find no discussion about the nature of the impurity that the animals listed here cause and purification requirements for pollution. In contrast to the tenor of vv 2b–23, vv 24–40 do not mention the prohibition of eating but center instead on the nature of the impurity caused by touching or carrying various animals and how to purify from that contamination. It should be noted that the differences in vv 24–40 in comparison to vv 2b–23 cannot be harmonized by saying vv 24–40 recapitulate the cases discussed in vv 2b–23 from the perspective of purification requirements. Vv 24–40 are not only different in theme, but also deal with different animals (2b–23 deal with large land animals with specific mention of the camel, hyrax, hare, and pig, and with sea and air animals; 24–40 deal with large land animals like the horse, bear, and dog and with eight types of *šĕrāṣîm*, small land animals). The difference in orientations and concerns in these two sections show that they stem from different periods and authors, with vv 24–40 being subsequent to vv 2b–24. The third section, vv 41–45, appears to be an addition from a still later period because of the difference in its concerns (especially the issue of holiness) as opposed to the preceding sections and because of its character as a supplement to vv 29–38. (In passing I note that vv 39–40 may actually be compositionally separate from vv 24–38.)

It is relatively easy to sort out these three blocks of material, but it is much harder to understand how they relate to one another. It can be argued that vv 24–40 are a sort of commentary or clarification to vv 2b–23, and that vv 41–45 are a commentary on the all of the preceding verses, particularly vv 29–38. But the meaning of each block and how

---

[63a]This interpretation grows out of discussions with J. Milgrom. The bulk of the interpretation, however, is independent of his ideas.

each is to be interpreted in the larger context is hardly patent. Only tentative and speculative answers can be given. Two solutions are plausible to me.

The first is what I term the "restrictive" interpretation. According to this, vv 2b–23, before the addition of the other blocks, were mainly concerned with prescribing that certain animals not be eaten. Though it may be argued that this original section presupposes the idea that eating these animals causes some type of pollution, the section shows no concern about impurity resulting from simple contact with the animals discussed in it, except perhaps in the case of the four large quadrupeds listed in vv 4–8. Apart from these, it would seem that none of the animals in this original section was thought to cause impurity by simple touch or carrying. It is assumed here that the use of the root *šqṣ* with the animals in vv 9–23 does not refer to their being able to pollute by touch, only their abhorrent nature in regard to eating.

The addition of vv 24–40 expanded only slightly the range of animals that could pollute by simple touching or carrying. Vv 24–28 by considering the criteria in vv 2–3 made explicit other cases of large quadrupeds, such as horses, bears, and dogs, that could pollute by touching or carrying. This is certainly not a radical transformation of the sense of the earlier section. The main contribution of vv 24–28 is their explanation of the nature of pollution caused by large quadrupeds and purification requirements when pollution occurs. It would seem that these verses not only prescribed the pollution effect and purification procedures for impurities caused by animals described explicitly in them, but also implicitly intended to supply a description of the impurity of the animals in vv 2–8 and the method for purifying from it. The larger section (vv 24–40) also added to the list of animals that could pollute by touch in a limited way when it prescribed that eight[64] types of *šereṣ* animals (types of reptiles and rodents) could pollute (vv 29–38). These verses parallel vv 24–28 in their description of the effect of the animals' impurity and purification procedures. Vv 29–38 contain no prohibition against eating the small land animals. Finally, the section also legislated that edible animals that had been improperly killed caused pollution by touch and carrying (vv 39–40; pollution by eating is also

---

[64]That only eight are mentioned may be due to the fact that these are the most prevalent in a person's household (cf. Milgrom, "Graduated *Ḥaṭṭāʾt*," 253, n. 37).

mentioned). These verses give purification procedures similar to those in vv 24–38.

To these blocks was added the third block, vv 41–45. This section came mainly as a response to vv 29–38. Vv 29–38 spoke of small land animals that could pollute by touch. This section, however, did not prohibit the eating of these small land animals (though such a prohibition seems latent in the criteria in vv 2–3). Vv 41–45 make up for this lack by adding the stipulation that no small land animals, not just the eight discussed in vv 29–38, are to be eaten.

In sum, according to the restrictive interpretation of Lev 11, though many animals are not to be eaten (all told, large land animals that do not fit the criteria in vv 2–3, cf. vv 4–8, 24–28; sea animals that do not fit the criteria in 9–12; the birds listed in vv 13–19; flying insects that do not fit the criteria in vv 20–23; and all small land animals, vv 41–45), only large land animals and eight types of small land animals are able to pollute by touch and carrying. Though only a limited number pollute by touch and carrying, it is assumed that all the prohibited animals pollute when eaten (at least according to the final form of the text).

The second explanation of the relation of the sections of Lev 11 is what I call the "expansive" interpretation. According to this, vv 2b–23 are interpreted as in the previous explanation, but vv 24–40 are viewed as explaining the impurity of not only large land animals, but sea and air animals as well. In this interpretation, the term *ule᾽ēlê* in v 24 is taken to refer to all the animals that precede as well as those that follow (in the previous interpretation this term only refers to what follows). Hence not only the large land animals discussed in vv 24–28 pollute by touch and carrying; all those prohibited animals in vv 2b–23 pollute by these means as well. Only one limitation would be found in the text made up of vv 2b–23 and 24–40: only the eight types of small land animals listed in vv 29–38 would pollute by touch or carrying; all other small land animals would not pollute this way. To these sections was added vv 41–45 which not only legislated that no small land animals were to be eaten, but by talking about *all* small land animals (note the term *kol* throughout) and requiring the Israelites not to become polluted by them (vv 43–44) they seemed to legislate that all small land animals, not just the eight types in vv 29–38, could pollute by touch and carrying, as well as by eating.

In sum, the expansive interpretation views all animal carcassess (including the smallest insects), except those of properly killed edible animals, as being able to pollute by simple contact. One can immediately see the vast difference between the restrictive and expansive interpretations and perceive the former to be a more practical way of understanding the legislation.

This discussion of the effect of animal carcass impurity here follows the restrictive interpretation. The trees will only describe the impurity of land *šereṣ* and (in the next section) that of large land animals. If the expansive interpretation of Lev 11 be accepted, then the trees drawn here would apply to all animals that pollute by simple contact according to that understanding. I noted, above, that though certain animals may not have been viewed as polluting by simple contact, all the prohibited animals, even in the restrictive interpretation, probably polluted by eating. Surprisingly, however, no passage in Lev 11 speaks of what the effect of pollution and purification requirements for eating prohibited animals would be, except for vv 39–40 (cf. 17:15–16), which, since they deal with animals that are of an edible class but improperly killed, are not a direct statement on the matter. It would seem, however, that, at least for the final form of the text, the prescriptions in vv 39–40 would describe analogically the impurity and purification procedures for eating any of the prohibited animals. Only the case of eating described by vv 39–40 will be charted on the tree diagrams here.

Branch 1: Persons touching a land *šereṣ* carcass become unclean for a day and need bathing (Lev 11:31, 36b; cf. 5:2; 7:21; 22:5).[65] If they carry the carcass, they also need laundering.[66] This last item is derived from the regulations concerning contact with large land animals (Lev 11:24–25, 27–28, 39–40 and see the next section).[67] One may argue that since these other cases deal with large animals, the requirements may not apply in the case of smaller *šereṣ* animals. But there is nothing except the silence of the *šereṣ* prescription to support this idea.

---

[65]See n. 38, above.

[66]The Temple Scroll stipulates that both laundering and bathing are necessary for simple contact and carrying (51:2–5; cf. Yadin, *Temple Scroll*, 1. 261). Rabbinic tradition says that carrying a *šereṣ* carcass (when direct contact is not made with the impurity) does not pollute (*m. Kelim* 1:1; Maimonides, *MTor*, Ṭohora, Šeʾar ʾAbot haṭṬumʾot 4:2; 6:2). This understanding arises from imputing significance to the silence about carrying the *šereṣ* in Lev 11 (see *Kesep Mišna* on the Maimonides passage).

[67]See n. 39, above.

Branch 2: Objects touched by the *šereṣ* carcass become unclean. Nonearthenware utensils become clean by immersing in water and waiting until evening. Earthenware, including stoves and ovens, cannot be purified and are consequently broken (vv 31–35).[68] Food that has water on it and liquids become unclean and must be thrown away (v 34, 37; cf. v 33).[69] Water sources and dry seed remain clean (vv 36–38).

h. Large Land Animal Carcass

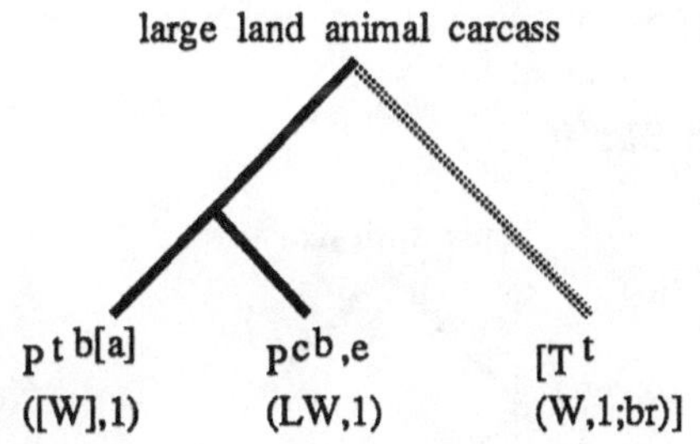

Fig. 8.9: Large Land Animal Carcass Pollution

See fig. 8.9.

Sources: Lev 11:24–26, 27–28, 39–40; 17:15–16; cf. Gen 7:2–3, 8–9; Exod 22:30; Lev 5:2; 7:21; 11:2–8; 22:8; Deut 14:3–21; Judg 13:4, 7; Ezek 4:12–13; Isa 66:17.

Four passages give detailed information about the extent or duration of the impurity caused by carcasses of large land animals (see above): (a) Lev 11:24–26, concerning the carcass of an animal which "has hoofs but does not have a cleft hoof nor chews the cud" (e.g., a horse); (b) 11:27–28, concerning the carcasses of animals that walk on paws (i.e., without hoofs; e.g., bears, dogs); and (c) 11:39–40 and (d) 17:15–16, both concerning the carcasses of improperly killed clean animals. Other passages, listed above, give less detailed information about the pollution of large land animals (but cf. in particular Lev 5:2; 7:21; 11:2–8; 22:8).

---

[68] See chap. 4.

[69] The term *yiṭmāʾ* with no time stipulation can indicate that the impure item is to be disposed of (vv 33, 34) or suffer and indefinite impurity. See chap. 4, n. 13.

Branch 1: A person touching these carcasses becomes unclean for a day and needs bathing (Lev 11:24b, 26b, 27b, 39b),[70] while one carrying them needs also laundering (vv 25, 28, 40b).[71] The case about a clean animal which has been improperly killed adds that one who eats its carcass needs laundering, bathing (implied), and waiting until evening (v 40a). Similarly, Lev 17:15–16 requires bathing, laundering, and waiting for a day after eating an improperly killed animal.

Branch 2: This branch is supplied from the land *šereṣ* carcass, branch 2. As the impurity affects persons the same in the case of land *šereṣ* and other animal carcass, so it must affect objects similarly.

i. A House with *Ṣāraʿat*

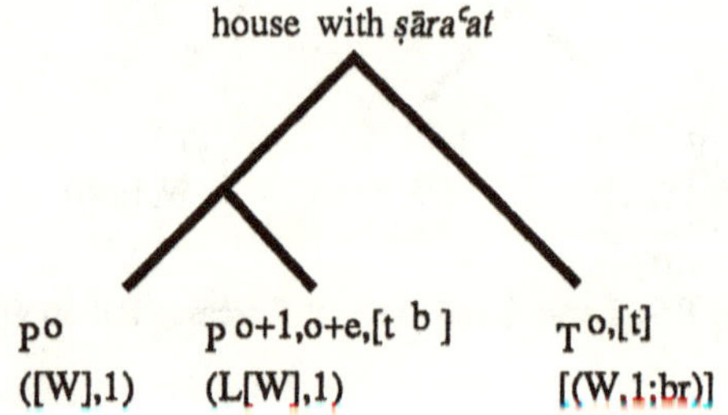

Fig. 8.10: Pollution of a House with *Ṣāraʿat*

See fig. 8.10.

Sources: Lev 14:33–53.

Branch 1: Anyone who is simply in a quarantined house suspected of having *ṣāraʿat* or in a house diagnosed as infected with it[72] becomes

---

[70]See n. 38, above.

[71]See n. 39, above.

[72]That a house suspected of *ṣāraʿat* pollutes, and not just one that has been diagnosed, is clear from the prescriptions in Lev 14. Before the priest comes to examine the plague, the house is to be cleared. This is to prevent the household items from becoming unclean (v 36). It appears that impurity begins at the time the priest makes his initial inspection and finds suspicious greenish or reddish spots (v 37). From this initial inspection until the house is demolished (vv 43–45) or purified (vv 48–53)—that is, while the house is shut up for diagnosis—it pollutes.

unclean for one day and needs to bathe[73] (Lev 14:36,[74] 46).[75] If a person tarries in the house, lying or eating there, the person also needs laundering (v 47).[76] Though unexpressed, directly touching an infected house would contaminate a person.[77] Since touching is a more direct form of contact than overhang, laundering as well as bathing would probably be necessary.

Branch 2: An object in an infected house becomes unclean (14:36 [see n. 74]). Though not specified by the text, the duration of the impurity is clearly one day as in the case of people (branch 1). The rules concerning corpse contamination can be used carefully to round out the understanding of the effect of the impurity of *ṣāraʿat* on objects, since a corpse pollutes by overhang like a *ṣāraʿat* infected house. In the case of corpse contamination, all vessels, except open earthenware, may be purified. This rule may apply here. But note that the impurity of a *ṣāraʿat* infected house is less severe than corpse contamination. The former causes only a one-day pollution while the latter causes a seven-day pollution. Thus it is possible that the effect of *ṣāraʿat* impurity on objects is less than what we see in the case of corpse contamination.[78] Though the effect of pollution for objects exposed to *ṣāraʿat* may follow the case of corpse contamination, the purification of those objects,

---

This is also apparent from vv 46–47 which say that a person who enters a quarantined (and presumably undiagnosed) house becomes unclean. Support for the idea that a quarantined house is impure and can pollute comes from the impurity that a person suspected of *ṣāraʿat* suffers (see section 8.3.2.1, k).

[73]See n. 38, above.

[74]Lev 14:36a should be translated: "so that no (one or thing) in the house will become impure."

[75]Though these verses deal with a house that is quarantined and not yet diagnosed as an infected house, a diagnosed house about to be dismantled would similarly pollute.

[76]See n. 39, above.

[77]Rabbinic interpretation makes a distinction between the quarantined house and the diagnosed house. The quarantined house only pollutes on the inside while the diagnosed house pollutes on the outside also by contact. See *m. Neg.* 13:4; *t. Neg.* 7:4; Maimonides, *MTor,* Ṭohora, Ṭumʾat Ṣaraʿat 16:2.

[78]The Mishnah (*Neg.* 13:12; cf. *t. Neg.* 7:13) gives some opinions that show sensitivity to the question of the communicability of impurity

however, cannot follow the requirements of that case, since the water of purgation is not used for *ṣāraʿat* and since purification by fire is unique and only applicable to corpse-contaminated metal utensils. Because the impurity of *ṣāraʿat*-contaminated objects lasts only one day, it is reasonable to suppose that polluted objects would be purified by washing as are other utensils which are impure for the same duration (Lev 6:21; 11:32; 15:12) and also as the people who are contaminated by an infected house (see branch 1). Polluted open earthenware is presumably destroyed.

j. The Person with *Ṣāraʿat*

See fig. 8.11.

Sources: Lev 13; cf. Exod 4:6–7; Lev 14; 22:4; Num 5:2–3; 12:10–15; Deut 24:8; 2 Sam 3:29; 2 Kgs 5; 7:3–10; 15:5 (= 2 Chr 26:16–21).

Branch 1: One of the most surprising facts a student of biblical purity learns is that the Bible does not give any information about the effects of the impurity of a person with *ṣāraʿat.* We can only speculate about how extensively such a person may have polluted other persons and objects. The impurity of a house infected with *ṣāraʿat,* since it is the same type of impurity, offers an example from which to deduce some aspects of the infected person's communicability. We can assume that just as an infected house pollutes for one day by overhang, an infected person who is in an enclosure pollutes other persons and things in the enclosure for

---

in a tent containing a corpse and in a house with *ṣāraʿat.* Rabbi Meir is of the opinion that whatever protection tightly sealed (*ṣāmîd pātîl,* Num 19:15; cf. *m. Kelim* 10:1) or covered vessels receive in a tent with a corpse, the same protection is afforded in the infected house. The Tosefta adds to his view: "The infected house is like the tent with a corpse." R. Yose diverges from Meir, no doubt due to the lesser impurity of an infected house, and says whatever is protected by a tightly sealed lid in a tent with a corpse is protected by a mere cover in an infected house, and whatever is protected by a cover in a tent with a corpse is safe if uncovered in an infected house (cf. *m. Ohol.* 5:6; *t. Neg.* 7:12; H. Albeck, *The Six Orders of the Mishnah [Šiša Sidre Mišna]* [6 vols.; Jerusalem and Tel-Aviv: Bialik Institute and Dvir, 1957–59] 6. 245; Maimonides, *MTor,* Ṭohora, Ṭum'at Ṣaraʿat 16:9; J. Neusner, *Negaim, Mishnah-Tosefta* [SJLA 6, HMLP 6; Leiden: Brill, 1975] 263–65).

one day.[79] If people merely enter an enclosure where an infected person is, they need only to bathe and to wait until evening. If they tarry there, for example by lying down or eating, they need to launder too.

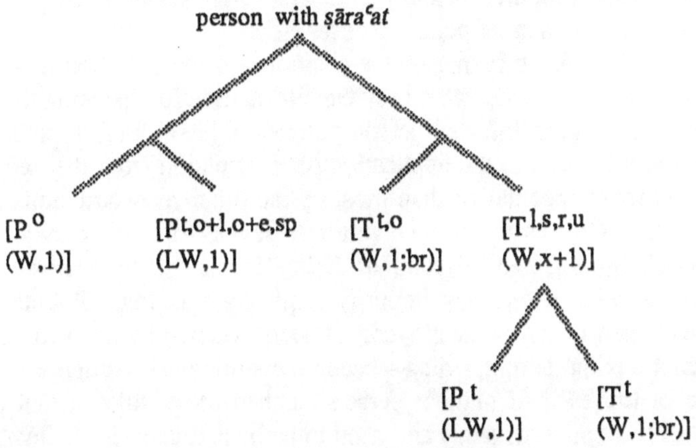

Fig. 8.11: Pollution of a Person with *Ṣāraʿat*

Though the communicability of an infected house provides help in determining the effect of an infected person's impurity, it is not fully adequate since the person appears to carry a much more serious impurity than the house. This is indicated by the difference in purification rites they undergo. The house is purified only by the rite using a dispatched bird (see Chapter Three; Lev 14:48–53), while the person requires not only this, but other additional purification rites including sacrifices at the sanctuary (Lev 14:2–32). Moreover, after the bird rite, the person still carries a communicable impurity that requires social restriction (see the section on the person purifying from *ṣāraʿat*, below). It seems reasonable to suppose, as the Mishnah does,[80] that an infected person

---

[79]In rabbinic tradition, the person with *ṣāraʿat* polluted by overhang (*m. Neg.* 8:8; 13:7, 11; *Kelim* 1:4; *t. Neg.* 7:11; Maimonides, *MTor*, Ṭohora, Ṭumʾat Ṣaraʿat 10:12).

[80]The Mishnah equates persons with *ṣāraʿat* with a *zāb*, *zābâ*, menstruant, and parturient in the effect of their impurity when one touches them (*m. Zabim* 5:6; cf. *t. Zabim* 5:3). Similarly, the bed or chair of those with the disease are impure like the furniture of sexually impure

polluted much like a *zāb*. Thus an infected person would pollute persons by contact and by spitting, requiring them to bathe and launder. Finally, the requirement that infected persons cover their mouths (Lev 13:45) may indicate that their breath pollutes those on whom it falls. I am not convinced of this latter point, however.[81]

Branch 2: As in branch 1, the examples of the pollution of a *ṣāraʿat* infected house and the *zāb* supply the information for deducing the extent to which a *ṣāraʿat* infected person pollutes objects. Before proceeding, one should note that the application of information from the *zāb*'s case here is more speculative than most of the other reconstructions in this excursus. Objects which receive a less severe form of contact—being touched by infected persons or being in the same enclosure with them—receive a one day impurity requiring washing. Polluted open earthenware would be destroyed. Objects polluted by a severe form of contact—lying, sitting, riding—become communicably impure as in the case of the *zāb*. If another person touched these objects, that person would be impure for a day and need to bathe and launder. Other objects contacting these impure objects would require washing, or breaking if earthenware.

k. The Person Suspected of *Ṣāraʿat*

An obscure impurity is that of one suspected of having *ṣāraʿat* (*hammusgār*, in rabbinic terminology) who is shut up for seven days in order to determine if in fact the disease is *ṣāraʿat* (Lev 13:4, 5, 21, 26, 31, 33). That such persons are quarantined[82] shows that they are being restricted from society due to impurity; it is a temporary sort of banishment.[83] Their impurity is also reflected in the requirement that they launder after being shut up (13:6, 34).[84] Moreover, just as a quarantined house not yet diagnosed as having *ṣāraʿat* can pollute

---

persons (cf. Albeck, *Mishnah*, 6. 451–52; the translation of Danby, *Mishnah*; Maimonides, *MTor*, Ṭohora, Ṭumʾat Ṣaraʿat 10:11).

[81]Suggested by J. Milgrom (private communication). Cf. the practice in mourning customs, Ezek 24:17, 22; Mic 3:7.

[82]*Hisgîr* means to quarantine the person so he does not circulate (see Hoffmann, *Leviticus*, 1. 257).

[83]See n. 22, above.

[84]Bathing may be implied here; see n. 38, above.

(14:46–47),[85] so quarantined persons must be able to pollute. It is possible that while in this quarantined status, these persons polluted as if they were diagnosed as having *ṣāraʿat*.[86]

This is not entirely clear, however, since the Bible reveals a distinction between different types of persons suspected of having the condition. There are four sections in which quarantine is stated: vv 2–8, 18–23, 24–28 and 29–37. In the first and the last, two quarantine periods are possible. If a white *baheret* is not "deeper" than the skin and hair in it has not turned white, the person is shut up seven days (v 4). The priest inspects the affection again. If it has not spread, the person is shut up for a second seven days (v 5). If after this it has faded and not spread, the patient is pronounced clean and must launder (v 6). In the last case (vv 29–37), a person who has a *neteq* affection which is not "deeper" than the skin and has no black hair in it is shut up seven days (v 31) after which the priest inspects it (v 32). If the *neteq* has not spread, has no yellow hair, and is not "deeper" than the skin, the patient is to shave (except for the place of the lesion) and be quarantined again for seven days (vv 32–33). The priest then inspects the affection and if it has not spread and is not "deeper" than the skin, the patient is pronounced clean and must launder (v 34). These two cases have two quarantine periods, the last of which is followed by laundering (see n. 84).

The other two cases (vv 18–23, 24–28) are different. In vv 18–23, a white eruption (*śĕʾēt lĕbānâ*) or a reddish-white *baheret* develops in the place of a healing boil (*šĕḥîn*). When the priest inspects it, if there is no white hair in the lesion, if it is not "deeper" than the skin, and if it is pale, the patient is shut up seven days (v 21). If after this the *baheret* has not grown, the person is clean (v 23). No laundering requirement is mentioned. Similarly in vv 24–28, a person who has a burn that develops a reddish-white or white *baheret* which has no white hair, is not "deeper," and is pale is shut up for seven days (v 26). If after this the *baheret* has not spread and is pale, the person is clean (v 28). Again, no laundering is mentioned. In these last two cases, only one quarantine period is prescribed and no laundering.

---

[85]See n. 72, above.

[86]The Rabbis understood the suspected person to have the same effect as the diagnosed person (*m. Meg.* 1:7; *Kelim* 1:5; *Neg.* 8:8; *t. Meg.* 1:12; *b. Meg.* 8b; cf. Bertinoro on *m. Meg.* 1:7; Maimonides, *MTor*, Ṭohora, Ṭumʾat Ṣaraʿat 10:11).

From these different prescriptions it appears that there is a distinction in the degree of impurity associated with the number of quarantine periods. A person who has been shut up for two periods suffers a greater degree of impurity, requiring laundering, than a person who has been shut up for only one seven day period and who does not require laundering. Consequently, to simply say that the quarantined person contaminates like a diagnosed person may not be correct.

Other questions still exist. Was the suspected person quarantined for only one week required to bathe? This is a possibility since the requirement for ablution is often left unsaid.[87] A further complication is the lack of the requirement of waiting until evening (13:6, 23, 28, 34). It is not clear whether this is to be implicitly understood or if there is an exception to this rule in the case of the suspected person. With these unanswerable questions, I am reticent to conclude anything definite about the impure effect of the quarantined persons, other than to say that at most they would pollute like those diagnosed as having *ṣāraʿat.*

l. The Person Purifying from *Ṣāraʿat*

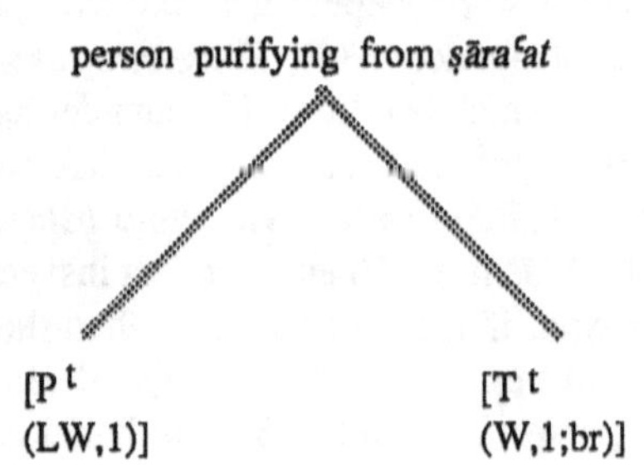

Fig. 8.12: Pollution of Person Purifying from *Ṣāraʿat*

See fig. 8.12.

Sources: Lev 14:8–10.

Persons who have recovered from *ṣāraʿat,* after undergoing purification rites using birds and laundering, shaving, and bathing, enter a period of seven days awaiting rites that complete the purification process (Lev 14:8). The effect of these persons' impurity during this period has been reduced as is evidenced by the stipulation that they may

---

[87]See n. 38, above.

enter the camp after the preliminary rites and by the fact that they experience initial purificatory acts that culminate in a declaration of purity (*wĕṭāhēr*, v 8).[88] The question is, how much has their impurity been reduced? A clue to the answer lies in the restriction that purifying persons must abide outside their tents for the seven day term. It may be thought that this requirement shows that they contaminate by overhang and thus cannot enter their tents lest they pollute other persons and objects. However, this idea is to be dismissed. Contamination by overhang is an effect of only the severest impurities (of a corpse and *ṣāraʿat* infected items). Other impurities pollute only by contact. Being the most external effect of the impurity, overhang contamination, like radiated heat from a fire whose energy has been reduced, would be the first effect to disappear. We are thus forced logically to view overhang pollution as the effect that has been reduced in the preliminary rites of the healed persons' purification. In that case, what does the stipulation that they must stay outside their tents mean?[89] It may be argued that to stay outside one's own tent means also not to come into other persons' tents. This rule would then signify that purifying persons are to be restricted in all their social contacts, implying that they can still pollute others by contact. The conclusion I would draw is that the healed persons during this period have lost the power to pollute by overhang, but retain the power to pollute by contact.[90] The person who makes contact with a purifying person would require laundering, bathing, and waiting until evening as with the *zāb* (Lev 15:7, 11). Articles would need washing, or, if earthenware, breaking. The impurity lasts only one day, since contact with a person who is still infected gives only a one day impurity.

---

[88]The text says "then he shall be clean" *wĕṭāhēr* (v 8). It is clear from the context that only a level of purity has been granted to the person, not complete purity. Other levels of purification are indicated in this rite by this verb (vv 9, 20).

[89]Rabbinic tradition interprets this to include that he is forbidden to have sexual relations with his wife (*m. Neg.* 14:2; *t. Neg.* 8:6; *Sipra*, Meṣoraʿ, Par 2:11; *Tg. Ps.-J.*; Rashi).

[90]The rabbis say that the purifying person's impurity has been reduced to that equal to a *šereṣ* carcass (*m. Neg.* 14:2; cf. *Zabim* 5:10 and mishnah 6; *Kelim* 1:1; see n. 66, above). As it turns out, this is essentially my conclusion, though simple contact requires laundering and bathing in my reconstruction like simple contact with the *zāb* and menstruant.

m. The Bird and Bird Blood of the *Ṣāraʿat* Purification Rite

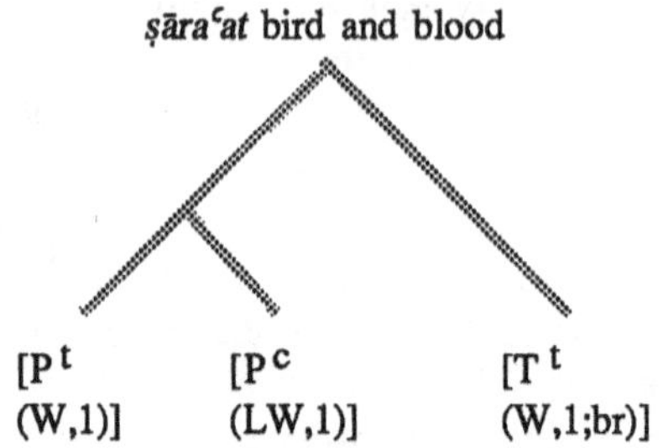

Fig. 8.13: Pollution of *Ṣāraʿat* Bird and Blood

See fig. 8.13.

Sources: Lev 14:2–7, 48–53.

There is no explicit evidence that the live bird or the blood used to purify from *ṣāraʿat* pollutes (cf. Lev 14:2–7, 48–53). This pollution can only be deduced circumstantially and therefore it must be held tentative. It appears that since the bird and blood are used to remove contagious impurity from a person who has recovered from the disease (see the foregoing section and Chapter Three), they probably acquire the power to pollute others. This assumed impurity would exist after the cathartic materials have been used on the person to remove the impurity. Since they do not remove all the person's impurity (the person is still impure to a certain extent after the bird rites), they probably do not pollute by overhang but only by contact. The most telling indication that the bird can pollute is the requirement to send it into the field outside the city (v 53; cf. v 7). This is similar to the disposal of other communicably impure items, especially the scapegoat. Another hint of the ability of the blood to pollute is found in the requirement to use an earthenware vessel for the water-blood mixture so that, implicitly, it may be broken after the rite.[91]

Branches 1 and 2: I would judge the bird and blood to have an impurity no stronger than an animal carcass whose impurity is one of the most minor of the communicable impurities. Thus I reproduce here the basic information from the trees for land *šereṣ* and large land animal carcasses.

---

[91]See chap. 4, n. 14.

Below, in the sections on the impurity of the *ḥaṭṭā't* sacrifice and the scapegoat, we will find that priests involved in these rites do not become polluted. Only laypersons employed in auxiliary functions or who are not involved at all become polluted. It is possible that here too, the priest officiating in the *ṣāraʿat* purification rite does not become impure from the bird and blood. These materials would only directly contaminate nonpriestly persons indirectly involved in the rite. This assumption about the priest's purity is based also in part on the silence of the text about purification rites necessary for the priest. But we should keep in mind that priests involved in purification rites are not totally immune from the effects of impurity. For example, the priest who prepares the Red Cow becomes impure and must launder and bathe (Num 19:7). It may be that here an officiating priest would suffer pollution because the bird rite is performed outside the sanctuary area as is the Red Cow ritual.

n. Fabrics with *Ṣāraʿat*

Sources: Lev 13:47–59.

Nothing is said about the polluting effect of fabrics infected with *ṣāraʿat* (Lev 13:47–59). From the analogy of the infected house, we may theorize that infected fabrics contaminate the same way when they are quarantined (Lev 13:50, 54) and when they are declared unclean prior to disposal (vv 51–52, 55, 57) by overhang and contact.[92]

o. The Water of Purgation

See fig. 8.14.

Source: Num 19:11–22.

Branch 1: Paradoxically, the water used for purification from corpse contamination pollutes those who touch it with a one day impurity.[93] The person who sprinkles it, a more aggressive form of contact,[94] needs

---

[92]In the rabbinic view, infected fabrics pollute like an infected person (*m. Neg.* 13:8; *t. Neg.* 7:6; *b. Yebam.* 103b; Maimonides, *MTor,* Ṭohora, Ṭum'at Ṣaraʿat 13:13–14; Hoffmann, *Leviticus,* 1. 270).

[93]On the paradox, see Milgrom, "Paradox."

[94]See n. 39, above.

laundering and bathing, while one who merely touches it needs only bathing (v 21).[95]

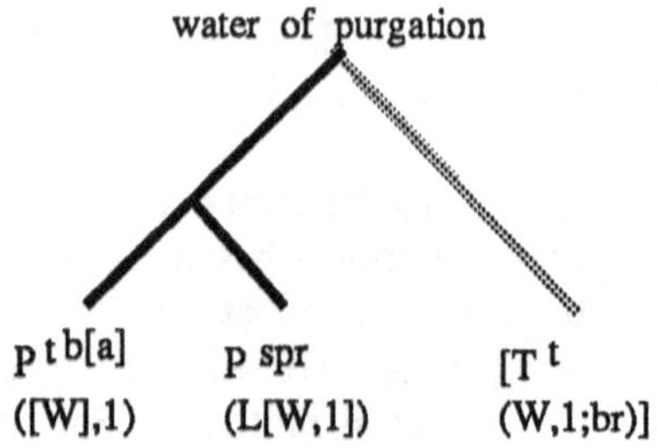

Fig. 8.14: Pollution of the Water of Purgation

Branch 2: Though not said, objects are certainly contaminated by the water. Nonearthenware would be washed (cf. Lev 6:21; 11:32; 15:12) while earthenware would be broken.[96] The extent of pollution is like that of animal carcasses.[97]

p. The Red Cow and its Ashes

See fig. 8.15.

Sources: Num 19:2–10.

Branch 1: As one who sprinkles the water of purgation becomes impure, so the persons who prepare the ashes—the priest, the one who burns the cow, and the one who gathers the ashes—become impure for one day and require laundering and bathing (vv 7, 8, 10).[98] V 7 states that the priest may enter the camp after laundering and bathing. This is implicitly understood in the other two cases (vv 8, 10).

---

[95]See n. 38, above.

[96]See chap. 4, n. 14.

[97]Rabbinic interpretation reduces the effect of the impurity of the water of purgation. Only those touching the water for purposes or at times other than for purification become impure. (Maimonides, *MTor,* Ṭohora, Para ʾAdumma 15:1; cf. *m. Kelim* 1:2; *b. Nid.* 9a; Maimonides, *MTor,* Ṭohora, Šeʾar ʾAbot haṭṬumʾa 6:13.

[98]In v 10, bathing is not mentioned, but it is implied from vv 7, 8. See n. 38, above.

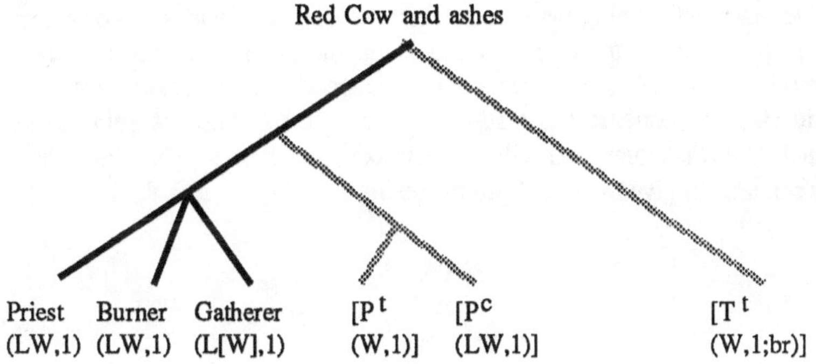

Fig. 8.15: Pollution of Red Cow and Ashes

The ashes of the Red Cow in their stored state, between the time that they are prepared and the time that they are used, are communicably impure. This is indicated by the fact that they are stored outside the camp (v 9), that the ash gatherer becomes impure, and that the ash-water mixture pollutes (v 21). Following the rules with the water of purgation, a severe form of contact with the ashes, such as carrying them, would require bathing and laundering, while simple touch would require only bathing. The idea that severe contact with the ashes requires laundering as well as bathing is confirmed in the requirement that the ash gatherer must launder.

Branch 2: Objects would become impure from these sources of impurity as well as persons. The length of impurity and requirements for purification would be the same as in the case of pollution by the water of purgation.

q. The Scapegoat

See fig. 8.16.

Source: Lev 16:26; cf. vv 8–10, 20–22.

Branch 1: The person who dispatches the scapegoat becomes polluted and must launder and bathe before entering the camp (Lev 16:26). Surprisingly, the time stipulation "until evening" is not given. It is likewise absent in the case of one who burns the *ḥaṭṭā'ṯ* sacrifice (v 28). Does this mean that their impurity ends when they bathe and launder? Probably not. J. Milgrom has explained that the absence of the time stipulation is due to the fact that it is not relevant here and so is left out.

The reasons for being pure are to enter the sanctuary and to eat of sacred offerings. Since the duties of the scapegoat dispatcher and the *ḥaṭṭāʾt* burner are complete after removing the scapegoat and carcasses, and since the Day of Atonement is a fast day, these persons are not going to go back to the sanctuary nor will they partake of sacrifices. Therefore, there is no need to give the time limit of the impurity.[99]

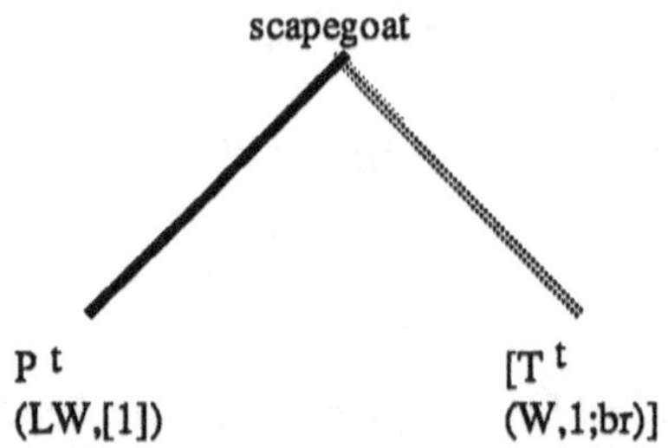

Fig. 8.16: Pollution of the Scapegoat

It is important to note that the high priest is not polluted by the scapegoat.[100] Similarly, priests performing and eating *ḥaṭṭāʾt* sacrifices are not polluted by them. That the ritual officiants do not become impure when performing these rites is to be viewed as a concession or exception so that ritual goals will not be obstructed or frustrated.

Branch 2: If the goat comes in contact with other objects, they would receive an impurity similar to that of a person.

---

[99]J. Milgrom (private communication), following the suggestion made by L. Finkelstein, *The Pharisees: The Sociological Background of their Faith* (3d ed., 2 vols.; Philadelphia: Jewish Publication Society of America, 1962) 2. 670–71.

[100]That the high priest bathes (v 24) does not mean he is impure. This is to be viewed as a rite of transition between different parts of the rite (Milgrom, private communication). Rabbinic tradition solves the question of the high priest's possible impurity by concluding that the scapegoat does not pollute until it has gone outside Jerusalem's wall (or, according to another opinion, from the time it is pushed down the ravine; *m. Yoma* 6:6; *b. Yoma* 67b) and that the *ḥaṭṭāʾt* remnants do not pollute until they leave the temple court area (or, according to another opinion, until they start to burn; *m. Yoma* 6:7; *Zebaḥ.* 12:6). Thus, the high priest who remains in the temple precincts does not become impure.

r. The *Ḥaṭṭā˒t* Sacrifice

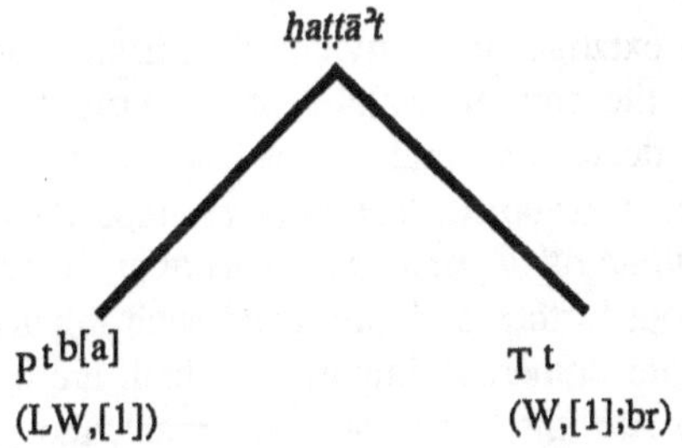

Fig. 8.17: Pollution of the *Ḥaṭṭā˒t*

See fig. 8.17.

Sources: Lev 16:27–28; 6:20–21; cf. Lev 4, and see Chapters Six through Seven of this work.

Branch 1: One who burns *ḥaṭṭā˒t* carcasses outside the camp becomes impure and needs laundering and bathing (Lev 16:27–28).[101] This impurity implicitly lasts only one day.[102] As noted in the previous section on the impurity of the scapegoat, the priests who perform the *ḥaṭṭā˒t* rites and eat *ḥaṭṭā˒t* portions do not become unclean.

Branch 2: Objects that contact *ḥaṭṭā˒t* meat and blood become impure. Vessels in which the edible *ḥaṭṭā˒t* is cooked must be purified (Lev 6:21). Earthenware is destroyed; metal pots are purified by rinsing and scouring. Clothing that has been spattered with *ḥaṭṭā˒t* blood is purified by washing (6:20). The time limit of the impurity of these objects is not mentioned in Lev 6. It would make sense that the pots are pure as soon as they are washed. Then they may be used again for other sacrifices on the same day. Similarly, it would make sense that a garment spattered with blood, which was more often than not that of a priest and which was cleansed in the sanctuary area, would be pure as soon as it was washed. Nevertheless, if the carcass or blood came in contact with objects outside the sanctuary area, we assume they would be impure until the evening.

---

[101]On the impurity of the *ḥaṭṭā˒t* sacrifice, see chap. 6, section 6.2.

[102]See the previous section on the impurity of the scapegoat (8.3.2.1, q) for a discussion of the reason why a time limit is not given in the Day of Atonement prescription.

8.3.2.2 The Restriction of Impure Persons (Continued)

The preceding excursus has provided data from which we can draw conclusions about the communicability of impurities. In every case, communicability decreases and stops at a particular point.[103] Specifically, *a person or object that receives impurity which lasts only one day cannot pollute other persons or objects in the profane sphere.*[104] P says nothing about further pollution from such impurities.[105] On the other hand, there are numerous impurities which are communicable to others: that of the *zāb*, the *zābâ*, the menstruant, the parturient in her first stage, the person who has had intercourse with one of these women,

---

[103]There appears to be no perpetual pollution in the profane sphere. The only possible case is where a person becomes as impure as a menstruant or *zābâ* when he has intercourse with them. It might be thought that he would be able to repollute a woman for seven days after she has become pure and that this pollution might be given back and forth indefinitely. Nevertheless, in view of the lack of other cases of perpetual pollution in the profane sphere, the Priestly legislation probably does not intend it in the case of one who has intercourse with one of these women. See how the Rabbis have lessened the impurity of the *bôʿēl niddâ* in n. 43.

In contrast, it appears that perpetual pollution may occur in the sacred sphere. Holy food which becomes impure can pollute other holy food which can in turn pollute other holy food, and so on, indefinitely. This requires greater care in controlling impurity in sacred matters. In the rabbinic system, perpetual impurity is possible with profane foods and vessels due to the higher susceptibility of these items to impurity (cf. *m. Para* 8:7; *Ṭohar.* 1:9; 2:6; Maimonides, *MTor,* Ṭohora, Šeʾar ʾAbot haṭṬumʾa, chaps. 7 and 10).

[104]The only possible exception is the bed, chair, etc., of those with sexual flows and the one with *ṣāraʿat,* which, theoretically, can be washed the same day they become impure and become pure at evening. But the impurity of these objects is really different than other one-day impurities. Their impurity comes from severe contact with those with sexual fluxes, by lying or sitting. Thus they are capable of polluting. Further, in sections 8.3.2.1, a–c, it was noted that in reality, the impurity of these items lasted indefinitely, as long as the impure people used them.

[105]It has been suggested that ablution effects a decrease in a person's impurity apart from the regulation to wait until evening. That is, before ablution, one pollutes profane persons and things, but afterward he does

not (Milgrom, private communication; cf. "Studies," 513). The Bible does not appear to make such a distinction: (a) Nowhere does it indicate a change in the purity status after ablution nor does it say that profane items or persons coming in contact with a preablution impure person or object become unclean. (b) In fact, ablution seems tightly bound up with the prescription to wait until evening. We have seen that the prescription requiring ablution is often left unsaid (see n. 38, above). If ablution effected a change in status, we would expect the requirement to be always stated. (c) Furthermore, certain passages tie the bathing (and laundering) and waiting till evening rules together as having a collective effect and purpose (see Lev 17:15–16; 22:6–7). Especially noteworthy is Deut 23:12. Though not a Priestly passage, it allows a glimpse of how one ancient Israelite school of thought viewed ablution in regard to waiting till evening. When one has an emission, he dwells outside the camp. *Towards evening,* he bathes and when the sun sets, he may enter the camp. The two requirements are temporally juxtaposed and are thus to be viewed as a ritual unit. (d) Other rituals have a series of rites which are not of individual effect, but which each contribute to a larger unified goal, such as sprinkling on the third and seventh days for purification from corpse contamination (Num 19). I consequently submit that there is no distinction in the state of one's impurity before and after ablution and that the series of bathing, laundering, and waiting is to be taken as a ritual unit.

There are some passages in the Bible, however, that suggest indirectly a distinction in pre- and postablution impurity. Lev 15:11 says that a *zāb* does not pollute others by touching if his hands have been rinsed. This does not refer to ablution at the end of his impurity, but simple hand washing while he is fully impure (see n. 35, above). Thus it cannot be used as proof for an impurity change caused by ablution in the sense that we are discussing. Num 19:7 says that the priest who burns the Red Cow must bathe and launder before entering the camp, but that he remains unclean until evening. This seems to imply that the priest suffers an impurity which excludes him from the camp, i.e., he can pollute others. Only after ablution may he enter. However, taken in the larger context of the present study of personal impurity and other passages which require ablution before entering the camp, the ablution here can be understood otherwise. The impurity suffered by one participating in the Red Cow rite in comparison with all the other possible impurities is not very severe. It only lasts one day. As other one-day impurities are not communicable to others, so this one should not be communicable. Furthermore, in all other cases where it is said that a person who is purifying may enter the camp, ablution and laundering are required before they may enter (Lev 14:8; 16:26, 28; Num 31:24; cf. 19:19). This suggests that preentrance

the person with *ṣāraʿat*, the beds, chairs, etc., of any of the foregoing persons, a corpse, a corpse-contaminated person or thing, a house infected with *ṣāraʿat*, fabrics infected with *ṣāraʿat*, a person suspected of *ṣāraʿat*, a person healed from *ṣāraʿat* in the seven day purificatory period, the bird and blood used in the *ṣāraʿat* purification rite, various animal carcasses, semen, the water of purgation, the Red Cow while being prepared and the resulting ashes, the scapegoat, and *ḥaṭṭāʾt* sacrifice carcasses and blood.

With this understanding of communicable and noncommunicable impurities we can return to the discussion we began earlier about the restriction of impure persons. We have already seen that a person with *ṣāraʿat*, the *zāb*, *zābâ*, and corpse-contaminated person are excluded from the community according to the Priestly war-camp ideal, and that a person with *ṣāraʿat* was also excluded from the settled communities according to all biblical sources.

There is also evidence of the restriction of persons with communicable impurities within the community. A prime example is the case of the parturient (Lev 12). As outlined in section 8.2, above, there are three stages in her impurity and purification: (1) the first, immediately after birth for seven or fourteen days when the woman is as impure as a menstruant (vv 2, 5; cf. 15:19–24; see section 8.3.2.1, impurities b and d, above); (2) the second, a period of lighter impurity, lasting 33 or 66 days when the woman no longer pollutes the profane (vv 4, 5); and (3) the third stage when sacrifices are brought and full

---

ablution is a general requirement for all impure persons before they enter the camp, but not necessarily to reduce the impurity in every case. This requirement of ablution before entrance is probably to insure that purification is performed so that impurity would not be prolonged.

Finally, we may note that the Sages who recognized a distinction in the state of impurity before and after ablution (*m. Kelim* 1:5, 8; see Albeck, *Mishnah*, introduction to *Tebul Yom*, 6. 457) did not consider a person with a minor one day impurity contagious to other persons and utensils. Before ablution, such a person had a first degree impurity and after ablution, a second degree impurity (*m. Zabim* 5:6–12; see Albeck, *Mishnah*, on these mishnayot; *b. B. Qam.* 2a, b; Maimonides, *MTor*, Ṭohora, Ṭumʾat Met 5:7–8; Šeʾar ʾAbot haṭṬumʾot 6:10–16.). On the question of ablution and its effect at Qumran, see Milgrom, "Studies," 513–15; Yadin, *Temple Scroll*, 1. 262; Baumgarten, "Controversies," 157–61.

purity is attained (vv 6–8). These stages appear to be accompanied by different degrees of cultic and social access.

The key verse here is v 4 which states that during the second stage the parturient is not to make contact with anything holy and is not to go to the sanctuary.[106] This statement of restriction in the second stage seems to imply that *some* freedom has been given to her in relation to the first stage, but not complete freedom. It is thus possible that the parturient was to be placed under certain restrictions within the community barring her from contacts with the profane during the initial communicable stage of her impurity. V 4 tells us by implication that in the second stage those restrictions have been lifted since she no longer pollutes the profane communicably. At the second stage, therefore, she can mix freely with others and even have sexual intercourse with her husband.[107] She is only kept from the sancta since her impurity, though lighter, remains a threat to them.

From the example of the parturient's restriction, we can easily deduce that the menstruant[108] and *zābâ* were also restricted within the settled community since their impurities likewise derive from feminine blood flows and have similar strength. From here it is only a step away to say that the *zāb* and one who has intercourse with one of the women just listed were also restricted since their impurity is similar to that of the women.

---

[106]J. Milgrom made me aware of the implications of this verse.

[107]There is a Karaite and Rabbinic dispute whether the woman in this second period may have intercourse with her husband. The Rabbinic view is that she has complete freedom except contacting the sancta. This view is clearly correct in this particular. See Hoffmann, *Leviticus,* 1. 250–51. Ehrlich (*Randglossen,* 2. 40–41; followed by J. Döller, *Die Reinheits- und Speisegesetze des Alten Testaments in religionsgeschichtlicher Beleuchtung* [ATAbh 7/2–3; Münster: Aschendorff, 1917] 11), thinks that the verb *tēšēb* "she sits, remains" means she is not to have intercourse.

[108]On aversion to menstruants, see Isa 30:22. There is some evidence outside the Bible that in Second Temple times menstruants and others like her were restricted during their periods. *M. Nid.* 7:4 speaks of a *bêt ṭumʾôt* "place/house of impurities" (or according to another text, *bêt ṭĕmēʾôt* "house for impure women"; see Albeck, *Mishnah,* 6. 397) in which menstruants were to have stayed during their impurity (cf. Bertinoro and Albeck; Rashi explains *ḥădārîm* [some take this as a mistake for *ḥrrym* "holes," cf. J. Neusner, *Niddah Commentary* (SJLA 6, HMLP 15; Leiden: Brill, 1976) 107; cf. Maimonides, *MTor,* Ṭohora, Meṭammeʾe

The Bible shows that other personal impurities were restricted too. In the excursus (section 8.3.2.1, k), it was noted that the person suspected of *ṣāraʿat* is quarantined for a seven day period. Though it is not clear what the extent of this impurity is, it is probably a communicable impurity and is therefore quarantined.

Another example of restriction is found with the person purifying from *ṣāraʿat* in the seven day period of purification. When he enters the camp after the preliminary rites, he must dwell seven days outside his tent (Lev 14:8). In the excursus (section 8.3.2.1, l), we determined that to dwell outside one's tent meant to be restricted in one's social movements during the seven day period.

8.4 THE CORRELATION OF THE EXCLUSION AND RESTRICTION OF IMPURITIES AND THE COMMUNICABILITY OF IMPURITY

In the foregoing section (8.3) we found direct evidence or deduced logically that all the personal communicable impurities were excluded or restricted: the *zāb*, the *zābâ*, the menstruant, the parturient in her first stage, the person who has intercourse with one of these women, a corpse-contaminated person, a person with *ṣāraʿat*, one suspected of this condition, and one who has healed from *ṣāraʿat* and is in a seven-day purification period. In contrast, there is no evidence of the restriction of a person suffering a noncommunicable one-day impurity from the

---

Miškab 4:10 who has *ḥôrîm*] as rooms especially for menstruants). The Tosefta (6:15) has "washing places of women" (*mrḥṣʾwt šel nāšîm*) instead of *bêt ṭumʾôt* (see Albeck, *Mishnah*, 6. 397). Josephus (*Ant.* 3.11.3 §261) says that the menstruant was restricted during the seven days of her impurity. (It is not clear here if Josephus is giving an interpretation of scripture or if he is reflecting Second Temple practice. G. Alon [*Studies in the History of Israel in the Days of the Second Temple and in the Period of the Talmud and Mishnah (Meḥqarim beToledot Yiśraʾel Bime Bayit Šeni ubiTequpat hamMišna wehatTalmud)* (2 vols.; Tel-Aviv: Hakkibutz Hameuchad, 1967) 1. 170–71], Yadin [*Temple Scroll*, 1. 227, 237–38], and J. Milgrom ["Studies," 515–16] believe Josephus is reflecting the practice of his time.) Elsewhere Josephus says that menstruants were only restricted in their access to the temple (*J. W.* 5.5.6 § 227). On this issue, see also Y. Dinari, "Customs Regarding the Menstruant's Impurity: Their Sources and Development," *Tarbiz* 49 (1980) 302–24 (Hebrew).

profane sphere. This leads to the conclusion that *the reason for the exclusion of certain impure persons is because their impurity is communicable to the profane sphere.*

This conclusion is given further support from the fact that communicably impure objects are also disposed of or deposited outside of the habitation, restricted within it, or made innocuous in some way. The scapegoat and birds used in the *ṣāraʿat* purification rites are sent away outside the habitation.[109] Building materials infected with *ṣāraʿat* are dumped outside the camp.[110] Corpses are removed from the habitation and buried.[111] *Ḥaṭṭāʾt* carcasses are taken outside to be burned.[112] The Red Cow rite is performed outside the camp and its ashes are stored there.[113] We can assume that since the bird rite for purification from human *ṣāraʿat* is performed outside the habitation, the birds's blood and carcass are discarded there.[114] We can also suppose that animal carcasses, in analogy to human corpses, are disposed of outside the habitation, though the Priestly literature gives no indication of this. Also, as corpse-contaminated persons are restricted (according to the rule that would prevail in the settlement), so corpse-contaminated objects must also be restricted. Similarly, the bed, chair, etc., of those with severe sexual impurities and the person with *ṣāraʿat* would also be restricted. Fabrics infected with *ṣāraʿat*, *ḥaṭṭāʾt* blood, and semen are not disposed of outside the habitation or restricted in it, but are destroyed or removed to make them ineffective by burning, pouring out at the base of the altar, or washing out, respectively.

The only apparent exception to this general scheme of removing impure items from the habitation or restricting them in it is the use of the water of purgation within the habitation. Since a corpse-contaminated person (according to the rule prevailing in settled communities) and the tent or house in which a corpse was are inside the

---

[109]See chaps. 1 and 2.

[110]See chap. 3.

[111]See chap. 5.

[112]See chap. 6.

[113]See section 8.3.2.1, p.

[114]See chap. 2 and chap. 8, section 8.3.2.1, m. It is less clear what is to be done with a bird used to purify a house, which presumably is in the area of the habitation. One imagines it would have been disposed of outside the habitation.

habitation, the ashes which are stored outside have to be brought in to perform the purification. This seems to be opposite of the general tendency to remove communicable impurity from the habitation. But this is clearly a necessary exception since the ashes and the water serve to remove a more serious impurity. We can assume that though the ashes and water were used in the habitation, they were under restriction like other communicable impurities.

In contrast to these examples of the disposal, exclusion, or restriction of communicably impure items, noncommunicably impure items were not restricted or disposed of. The only exception is the breakage of impure earthenware and the implicit disposal of impure foods.[115] These must be discarded even if they have contracted only a noncommunicable impurity. This allows us to supplement the rule that communicable impurities must be excluded or restricted from the profane sphere: *non-communicably impure items that are irretrievably impure are destroyed.*

To help in comprehending the foregoing data and conclusions, here is a summary of the personal and impersonal communicable impurities with a brief description of what is to be done with them to make them innocuous. The list is arranged according to the strictness of the treatment of the impurity in regard to the habitation:

ITEM	PLACE OR MANNER OF TREATMENT (An * indicates a deduction)
PERSONS:	
one with *ṣāraʿat*	excluded from habitation
zāb	excluded from or *restricted in habitation
zābâ	excluded from or *restricted in habitation
corpse-contaminated	excluded from or *restricted in habitation
menstruant	*restricted in habitation
parturient in her first stage	restricted in habitation
one who has intercourse with a *zābâ*, menstruant or parturient in the first stage	*restricted in habitation

one suspected of *ṣāraʿat*	restricted in habitation
one purifying from *ṣāraʿat*	restricted in habitation

NONPERSONS:

scapegoat	sent out of habitation
ṣāraʿat bird	sent out of habitation
ṣāraʿat infected building materials	dumped outside habitation
corpses	buried outside habitation
ḥaṭṭāʾt carcasses	burned outside habitation
Red Cow materials and ashes	rite performed and materials stored outside habitation
ṣāraʿat bird blood and carcass	*discarded outside habitation
animal carcasses	*taken out of habitation
water of purgation	*restrictedly used inside habitation
corpse-contaminated item	*restricted within habitation
bed, chair, etc., of those with a severe sexual impurity or of a person with *ṣāraʿat*	*restricted within habitation
fabrics infected with *ṣāraʿat*	burned
ḥaṭṭāʾt blood	poured at base of altar
semen	washed out

To conclude, there is more behind the restriction of communicably impure persons and things from the profane sphere than a mere social aversion to impurity. Indeed, underlying this entire phenomenon is ultimately a theological concern. If communicably impure persons and objects were allowed full access to the community, other persons and objects would become contaminated. This would in turn threaten cultic matters. With severe impurities running loose, the average impurity of the community would increase, causing a greater chance of defiling sancta. Consequently, severe impurities are restricted. The disposal of items with incorrigible, though noncommunicable, impurities stems from this same reasoning. If they were allowed to remain, the chance of defiling sancta would be increased. Therefore, the underlying rationale for restricting or excluding communicable impurities, or for destroying permanent impurities, is to protect the sancta from defilement.

Part Three

Conclusions

9

The Place of Impurity

9.1 INTRODUCTION

Having finished the study of the phenomenon of disposal of impurity, the restriction of human impurities, and the communicability of impurity in the Priestly writings, we are in a position to study the idea of the *place* of impurity in this corpus. We will take two approaches to this subject.

The first approach is an examination of the internal Priestly system regarding the place of impurity. In the foregoing chapters we saw the Priestly writings' concern to put impurity in its proper place. When this corpus is studied further, one finds that there is a similar concern about the proper places for holiness and purity. The information about places of holiness, purity, and impurity, as a whole, reveals a larger system of what may be called "cultic topography." It is a graduated system: the sanctuary at the middle of the habitation is holy; the habitation surrounding the sanctuary is generally pure though some impurities (noncommunicable and restricted communicable impurities) are tolerated there; and the area outside the habitation is both pure and impure and is the place where most irretrievable and communicable impurities are located. The first half of this chapter describes this cultic topography. This is done by studying the terms "holy place," "pure place" and "impure place" and determining where these places are located and what activities occur in them. This leads to charting a "map" of cultic topography which is a correlation of information from the study of holy, pure, and impure places and information gleaned from earlier chapters about the places of the disposal, exclusion, and restriction of impurities.

The second approach to the Priestly conception of the place of impurity, found in the second half of this chapter, consists of examining the methods and places of disposal in Mesopotamian and Hittite literature and then contrasting these with the Priestly phenomena and conception. There are many similarities between P and these other literatures, but there are significant differences: P uses a more limited repertoire of elimination rites than the rites in the other literatures; the goal of P's purification rituals is to protect the sanctuary from pollution as opposed to the more individualistic goals of the other rites; and P lacks a demonic and underworld conception of impurity found in the other literatures.

9.2 HOLY, PURE, AND IMPURE PLACES

Priestly legislation often uses the terms "holy place," "pure place," and "impure place" to define the locale of certain ritual activities. Defining where these places are and the activities that go on in each will give an approximate idea of the ideal qualities that, according to Priestly thought, should prevail in various parts of the Israelite sanctuary community.

9.2.1 The Holy Place

Several different cultic acts are to occur "in a holy place" (*bĕmăqôm qādôš*) or "in the area of the sanctuary (forecourt)" (*bimqôm haqqōdeš*). These include the consumption of the most holy offerings[1] by the priests (*bĕmăqôm qādôš*, Lev 6:9, 19; 7:6; 10:13; 24:9; *bimqôm haqqōdeš*, Lev

---

[1]The most holy offerings that are eaten are the *ḥaṭṭāʾt* (Lev 6:18, 22, 23; 10:17), *ʾāšām* (7:6), and *minḥâ* (2:3; 6:9–10; 7:9–10; 10:12) including the bread of presence (24:9). Not all *ḥaṭṭāʾt* sacrifices are eaten (see chap. 6). Not all cereal offerings are eaten. The priest's *minḥâ* is to be totally burnt (6:16) and perhaps other *mĕnāḥôt* are to be totally burnt (cf. *m. Menaḥ.* 6:1, 2). The *ʿōlâ* which is also most holy is not taken into consideration here because it was totally burned (cf. Lev 1). The rule for eating the ram of consecration, though a *šĕlāmîm* type of offering (compare the use of its fat parts and the priestly dues taken from it in Exod 29:22–28 and Lev 8:25–29 with the rule about the *šĕlāmîm* in Lev 3 and 7), is like the most holy offerings in that the offering must be eaten in one day by the priestly initiates in a holy place (Exod 29:31–34; Lev 8:31–32). Rabbinic tradition says that *šĕlāmîm* offerings for the Feast of Weeks are to be eaten in one day in the court by the priests (Lev 23:19; *m. Zebaḥ.* 5:5; *t. Zebaḥ.* 6:16 calls these particular *šĕlāmîm* "most holy").

10:17), cooking the priestly initiates' ram of consecration (*bĕmăqôm qādôš*, Exod 29:31), slaughtering the *ʾāšām* lamb and other offerings of a person recovered from *ṣāraʿat* (*bimqôm haqqōdeš*, Lev 14:13), washing *ḥaṭṭāʾt* blood out of a garment (*bĕmăqôm qādôš*, Lev 6:20), and the bathing of the high priest on the Day of Atonement (*bĕmăqôm qādôš*, Lev 16:24). This section will determine which locale or locales these terms refer to and to what extent they are synonymous. We will first treat *māqôm qādôš*, then *mĕqôm haqqōdeš*.

Māqôm qādôš refers to the area within the Tabernacle court enclosure. It is a term which appears to designate the quality of area in these confines and not necessarily a specific place within the sanctuary precincts as opposed to *bimqôm haqqōdeš* (see below). All this is indicated by several data: (a) The phrase is always indefinite "a holy place," never "the holy place." This suggests an indefinite locale. (b) In Lev 10:12–14, the term is used of the place of eating most holy offerings in contrast to a *māqôm ṭāhôr* "a pure place" where lesser holy offerings are eaten. As the latter term is nonspecific and only designates the quality of area in which lesser holy offerings may be eaten, so the former phrase must be nonspecific and indicate the quality of place where the most holy offerings are consumed. (c) The rationale is often given to eat most holy offerings in a holy place because they are most holy (Lev 7:6; 10:12, 17; 24:9; cf. Exod 29:33). This rationale intimates that *māqôm qādôš* refers to the quality of the place of eating, rather than to a specific locale. (d) The book of Ezekiel places the chambers in which the priests eat the most holy offerings to the rear of the temple building, on the north and south sides (42:1–14; 46:19–20).[2] It justifies this position of the chambers by stating that "the place is holy" (42:13). In using this phraseology the book shows a possible familiarity with the P term *māqôm qādôš*. If so, it seems to understand it in a general way referring to the quality of place in which the offerings are to be eaten, not to a specific locale in the sanctuary area.[2a]

---

[2]See K. Elliger, "Die grossen Tempelsakristeien im Verfassungsentwurf des Ezechiel (42, 1ff.)," *Geschichte und Altes Testament* (ed. W. F. Albright, BHT 16; Tübingen: J. C. B. Mohr, 1953) 79–103; W. Eichrodt, *Ezekiel: A Commentary* (OTL; Philadelphia: Westminster, 1979) 537.

[2a]There are two ambiguous pieces of data on this question: (a) In Lev 6:9, 19, the text has after *bĕmāqôm qādôš* the adverbial phrase "in the court of the Tent of Meeting." It is not clear if this is equating *māqôm qādôš* with the court, or if it seeks to limit *māqôm qādôš* which is under-

Mĕqôm haqqōdeš is a near synonym of *māqôm qādôš*, but it is more specific in defining a locale than *māqôm qādôs* since *qōdeš* in this phrase means the sanctuary court, specifically the forecourt. This is evident in the use of *mĕqôm haqqōdeš* in Lev 10:17 as the place of eating the *ḥaṭṭāʾt* sacrifice. Elsewhere, we learn that most holy sacrifices were eaten in the court, or more specifically the forecourt,[3] and so *mĕqôm haqqōdeš* in Lev 10 would apparently refer to this area. Similarly, Lev 14:13 says that the *ʾāšām* of a person purifying from *ṣāraʿat* is to be slaughtered "in the place where the *ḥaṭṭāʾt* and *ʿōlâ* are slaughtered," that is, "*bimqôm haqqōdeš.*" Since other prescriptions locate slaughtering of animals "at the door of the Tent of Meeting,"[4] the forecourt (see n. 3), *mĕqôm haqqōdeš* seems to refer to the forecourt of the sanctuary.

---

stood as a more general term. (b) Similarly, in Exod 29:31 Moses is commanded to cook the ram of consecration *bĕmāqôm qādôš.* The fulfillment passage in Lev 8:31 says that the cooking is to be done "at the door of the Tent of Meeting." It is not clear if the phrase in Lev 8 is to be taken as an equivalent to *bĕmāqôm qādôš* or as a limiting definition.

[3]Lev 6:9, 19 specify that the consumption of the *minḥâ* and *ḥaṭṭāʾt* is to occur in the "court of the Tent of Meeting." Lev 10:12 says that the *minḥâ* is to be eaten "near the altar." These data imply that the offerings may be eaten anywhere in the sanctuary forecourt. The prescription about eating the ram of consecration places consumption in the *petaḥ ʾōhel môʿēd* "the door of the Tent of Meeting" (Exod 29:31–32; Lev 8:31). If this phrase is understood to refer to the area between the altar and court entrance (J. Milgrom, *Studies in Levitical Terminology, I: The Encroacher and the Levite; the Term* ʿAbodah [UCPNES 14; Berkeley: University of California, 1970] 17–18) then the place of eating the ram of consecration differs from the place of eating other priestly portions. This difference can be explained by noting that Aaron and his sons at the time of consuming the ram are not yet fully priests. This status is achieved at the end of the seven day period. Hence, they partake of offerings in the forecourt where laypersons eat and perform their sacrificial rites (Milgrom, *Levitical Terminology*, 17–18, and private communication).

[4]Exod 29:11, 42; Lev 1:3; 3:2; 4:4; 12:6; 14:11, 23; 15:14, 29; 16:7; 17:4, 5, 9; 19:21; Num 6:10, 13. Another passage, Num 18:10a, is sometimes construed as referring to the place of eating most holy offerings (cf. *AV*, *RSV*, G. Gray, *A Critical and Exegetical Commentary on Numbers* [ICC; Edinburgh: T. and T. Clark, 1903] 223; "in a most holy place"). The preposition *b-* should be understood as a *beth essentiae* so that the phrase is understood: "as most holy offerings you shall eat it" (cf. A. B. Ehrlich, *Randglossen zur hebräischen Bibel* [7 vols.; Leipzig: J.

Confirmation of the meaning of *qōdeš* in *mĕqôm haqqōdeš* as "sanctuary forecourt" comes from Lev 10:18 which says that the *ḥaṭṭāʾt* sacrifice is to be eaten *baqqōdeš*. This can only mean "in the sanctuary forecourt."

But though *mĕqôm haqqōdeš* is specific, it, like *māqôm qādôš*, also refers to the quality of area in which cultic acts occur. This appears from the use of the motive clause in Lev 10:17: "Why did you not eat the *ḥaṭṭāʾt* in the *mĕqôm haqqōdeš*, since it (i.e., the *ḥaṭṭāʾt*) is most holy?"

9.2.2 The Pure Place

Several different ritual acts are to occur in a pure place. The most important of these is the consumption of lesser holy offerings[5] (Lev

---

C. Hinrichs, 1908–14] on Num 18:10; P. P. Joüon, *Grammaire de l'Hebreu biblique* [2d ed.; Rome: Institut Biblique Pontifical, 1947] §133c; *NJPS*; *NEB*; BDB, 88–89). Ramban (on 18:10), with almost similar results, understood the phrase as meaning "in a most sacred state" (cf. J. Milgrom, *Cult and Conscience: The Asham and the Priestly Doctrine of Repentance* [SJLA 18; Leiden: Brill, 1976] 36, n. 134).

[5]The following criteria distinguish the lesser holy offerings: they may be eaten by nonpriests (some may only be eaten by the priests' households, others by laypersons) and they may be eaten outside the sanctuary precincts, as will be shown. The lesser holy offerings that laypersons may eat are their own *šĕlāmîm* (Lev 7:16–18; 19:5–8; cf. Deut 12:6–7, 11–12, 21–22), *tôdâ* (Lev 7:15; 22:29–30), and *pesaḥ* (Exod 12:1–14; cf. Deut 16:5–7) offerings. The items that the priests and their households may eat are the breast and thigh from the Israelites' *šĕlāmîm* offerings (Exod 29:26–28; Lev 7:32–34; 10:14–15; Num 18:11), the entire first born animal given by the Israelites (Num 18:15–18; cf. Exod 13:12–13; 22:28–29; 34:19; Neh 10:37; in Deut 15:20 it belongs to the layperson who brings it; see S. R. Driver, *A Critical and Exegetical Commentary on Deuteronomy* [ICC, 3d ed.; Edinburgh: T. and T. Clark, 1901] 186–87; J. Milgrom, "First-born," *IDBSup* [1976] 338a), the first ripe produce (*bikkûrîm*; Num 18:13; cf. Exod 23:19; 34:26; Neh 10:37; Ezek 44:30; Deut 26:2, 10 use *rēʾšît (kol) pĕrî hāʾădāmâ* to mean *bikkûrîm* [cf. J. Milgrom, "First-fruits," *IDBSup* (1976) 336]), the first processed produce (*rēʾšît;* Lev 2:12; 23:10; Num 15:20–21; 18:12; cf. Deut 18:4; Ezek 44: 30; Neh 10:38; 12:44; 2 Chr 31:5; on the difference between *rēʾšît* and *bikkûrîm*, see Milgrom, "First-fruits"), items dedicated as *ḥērem* (Lev 27:28; Num 18:14; cf. Josh 6:17–19; Lev 27:28 calls *ḥērem* "most holy," but this appellation may be used only for emphasis because *ḥērem* is not redeemable; technically it is not most holy as Num 18:14 shows;

10:14).[6] The term *māqôm ṭāhôr* "pure place" indicates a place outside the sanctuary area. This is evident from the contrast of v 14 with vv 12-13 which say that the most holy offerings must be eaten in a holy place, near the altar. Moreover, the fact that the entire priestly household is allowed to eat these portions (v 14) implies that the items are taken home and consumed there (cf. Lev 22:10–16; Num 18:11, 13, 19; see n. 6).

---

see Milgrom, *Cult*, 18 and nn. 59, 187, 236 there), animals and produce otherwise dedicated to the sanctuary (*heqdēš*; see Lev 27; cf. J. Milgrom, "Sacrifices and Offerings, OT," *IDBSup* [1976] 770b; "Sanctification," *IDBSup* [1976] 783b; *Cult*, 39–40, n. 150), the animal tithe (Lev 27:32-33; cf. 2 Chr 31:6), and the produce tithe (Lev 27:30–31). The history of the tithe as manifested in various sources at different levels cannot be pursued here. We need only note schematically the insightful reconstruction offered by Milgrom (*Cult*, 66, n. 235; *Levitical Terminology*, 67, n. 246; see also the excursus in *Cult*, 55–58). Originally, according to Lev 27:30–33, the animal and produce tithe went to the priests. Later the produce tithe was transferred to the Levites (Num 18:25–32; cf. Neh 10:38-39; 12:44; 13:5, 12) who were to give one tenth of this to the priests. At this later level the animal tithe appears to have fallen into desuetude. (In Deuteronomy, laypersons and their dependents and the levite eat the produce tithe; 12:6–7, 11–12, 17–18; 14:22–23, 28–29; 26:12).

In connection with the tithe and the place of eating we need to comment on Num 18:31 which says that the tithe may be eaten in "any place." Originally, the animal and produce tithes were both considered holy (Lev 27:30, 32) and would have been consumed by priests in a "pure place" as with other lesser holy offerings. When the produce tithe was transferred to the Levites, it was, in effect, desanctified. Only the tenth which was to be given to the priests remained holy (Num 18:32). When the Levites removed this tenth from the tithe they received, their tithe became profane, just as the produce of the Israelites from which the tithe has been taken (vv 27, 30). Consequently, it could be eaten in any place, even in a graveyard, as Rashi (on Num 18:31) says (cf. Milgrom, *Cult*, 57; "The Alleged 'Demythologization and Secularization' in Deuteronomy," *IEJ* 23 [1973] 157 and n. 3; G. Gray, *Numbers*, 236).

[6]Lev 10:14 speaks only of the breast and thigh of the *šělāmîm* offering in Lev 9:4, 18–20. That all lesser holy offerings are eaten in a pure place must be deduced from the passages stating that lesser holy offerings may be eaten by the priests and their households (Lev 22:10–16 [*qōdeš* here refers to lesser holy offerings; Milgrom, *Cult*, 65–66]; Num 18:11–19, 25–29). As in Lev 10:14 the breast and thigh are eaten by the priests' households in a pure place, so the other holy offerings eaten by the priests' households are consumed in a pure place.

9.2.2.1 Excursus: The Place of Lay Sacrificial Consumption

Lev 10:14 only speaks of the place where priests and their households eat the *šĕlāmîm* portions, which, by our argument above, was outside the sanctuary. This leads to the question whether P also allows laypersons to eat their portions of the lesser holy offerings outside the sanctuary. Circumstantial evidence indicates that laypersons generally eat at the sanctuary but are not required to do so; they can on occasions eat outside the sanctuary precincts or in their homes.

Three points demonstrate that the normal and logical place of laypersons' eating is in the sanctuary area. First, there are examples of eating sacrifices at the sanctuary. The pericope about the nazirite implicitly places sacrificial consumption within the sanctuary confines. Among other offerings he brings is a ram for a *šĕlāmîm* offering (Num 6:14, 17) which is cooked at the sanctuary.[7] Cooking the sacrifice at the sanctuary suggests that eating the sacrifice is also done there. 1 Samuel also has examples of eating sacrifices at the sanctuary (1 Sam 1:4, 7–9, 18–19; 2:13–17; 9:12–25; see below).

A second reason for believing that laypersons could eat their portions at the sanctuary is the architecture of the Tabernacle court. Though the Tabernacle as described in P is not entirely historical, its structure as described is part of P's total prescriptive picture and can therefore be understood as reflecting P's larger system of thought. The exact layout of the Tabernacle and the furniture within the court is not detailed, but the most logical reconstruction divides the court, which measures one hundred by fifty cubits, in half into two squares, each fifty by fifty cubits, with the Tent in the rear half. The ark in the most holy place would be in the exact center of the rear half of the court and the burnt offering altar would be in the exact center of the forehalf.[8] If we assume that laypersons are restricted to the area of the forecourt between the

---

[7]The whole context definitely shows that cooking was done in the court. The nazirite shaves his hair at the Tent door and then places it on the fire which is cooking the *šĕlāmîm* (v 18). The priest takes the cooked shoulder and some breads and performs *tĕnûpâ* with them "before the Lord," i.e., before the sanctuary (vv 19–20). That the Second Temple had a room specially set apart for cooking the nazirite's offering indicates that this passage places the cooking in the court (cf. *m. Mid.* 2:5).

[8]I. Abrahams, "Tabernacle," *EncJud* 15 (1972) 682; G. H. Davies, "Tabernacle," *IDB* 4 (1962) 501; M. Haran, *Temples and Temple-Service*

altar and the court entrance, that gives an area twenty-five cubits by fifty cubits (37.5 feet by 75 feet) in which Israelites can gather. This area would be large enough to hold a significant number of people and, consequently, implies that sacrificial meals can be held there.[9]

Thirdly, the nature of sacrificial worship implies that the proper and logical place for laypersons to eat their portions is at the sanctuary. Deuteronomy shows the intimate relation of eating sacrifices to the rest of sacrificial worship when it requires the Israelites to come to the one sanctuary and rejoice and eat before the Lord.[10] It is reasonable to suppose that in Priestly thought too, eating at the sanctuary is an integral part of the joyful expression of sacrifice. Indeed, it would be most anticlimactic for a person to bring an offering and then return home in order to eat it.

Hence there is clear reason to believe that laypersons would consume their sacrificial portions at the sanctuary. But this conclusion must be qualified by data indicating that laypersons are not obligated to eat their portions in the sanctuary. First, the two-part prohibition that the parturient not contact any holy thing nor go to the sanctuary (Lev 12:4) indicates that holy things exist in two places: in the community and at the sanctuary. The lesser holy offerings of laypersons that are consumed at home may be part of the holy items that are extant in the community from which the parturient is restricted.[11] Secondly, Lev 7:20–21 warns against allowing impurity to come in contact with the *šĕlāmîm* portions, a situation most likely if the meat is outside the Tabernacle

---

in Ancient Israel: An Inquiry into the Character of Cult Phenomena and the Historical Setting of the Priestly School (Oxford: Clarendon, 1978) 150–55; B. Janowski, *Sühne als Heilsgeschehen: Studien zur Sühnetheologie der Priesterschrift und der Wurzel* KPR *im Alten Orient und im Alten Testament* (WMANT 55; Neukirchen: Neukirchener, 1982) 223.

[9]If we calculate one square yard per person, the area between the altar and court entrance would hold 312.5 persons. This gives a rough idea of the capacity of the front half of the forecourt.

[10]See the instances in Deuteronomy mentioned in n. 31, below.

[11]Other holy things susceptible to impurity in the community besides the priests' or laypersons' portions taken home from the sanctuary would be materials that have been dedicated to God before they are brought to the sanctuary such as produce tithes, first ripe produce, first processed produce, cereal offerings, and various other dedicated items (*ḥērem* or *heqdēš*; cf. n. 5, above). See Milgrom, *Cult*, 39–40, n. 150; "Sanctification," 783b.

where impurities are allowed to exist.[12] Finally, the silence of the Priestly writings concerning where the laypersons may eat their offerings is significant. As observed in the foregoing section on the holy place, the text often prescribes where the most holy offerings are to be eaten. In contrast, nothing is said about where the laypersons eat the lesser holy offerings. If it were necessary for them to eat in the sanctuary precincts, it probably would have been stated. The silence therefore implies that the offerer may eat the sacrifices outside the sanctuary. He or she is only warned to keep them from impurity (Lev 7:20–21).

Thus we see that laypersons do not have to eat their portions in the sanctuary though the logical place of eating from the point of view of sacrificial worship is at the sanctuary. Why would laypersons ever need or want to eat outside the sanctuary? Why would Priestly legislation allow this? Perhaps allowing the laypersons to eat outside the sanctuary stems from the necessary expansion of the place of eating during large assemblies as on festivals. The Tabernacle court would not be able to hold the crowds that would be gathered and, hence, sacrifices would need to be consumed outside the court in the camp area. Also, we can suppose that when small sacrificial groups would congregate at the sanctuary, the participants would take the remnant of the meat home to finish after initial feasting at the sanctuary. This would be expected in particular in the case of the regular *šĕlāmîm* which was eaten over two days.[13]

Before leaving the subject of the place of eating sacrifices, it is instructive to compare the historical picture of the place of eating in the Priestly literature with that of Ezekiel and later Jewish theory and practice. In the Priestly writings, there are two distinct pictures of the place of eating lesser holy offerings which appear to reflect and derive from different historical conditions.[14] The earlier situation is found in the prescriptions for the nazirite in Num 6 which, as we have already observed, appear to require that he eat his *šĕlāmîm* in the sanctuary precincts. This place of sacrificial consumption accords with early non-

---

[12]Ideally, no impurity may exist in the sanctuary. See chap. 8, section 8.2. J. Neusner (*The Idea of Purity in Ancient Judaism* [SJLA 1; Brill, 1973] 18) says with reference to Lev 7:19–21: "The Temple is presumed to be clean; therefore the reference to uncleanness and the unclean person suggests the sanctuary is not the location of the meal."

[13]See chap. 6.

[14]See Milgrom, "Sacrifices," 769b.

Priestly instances in which sacrificial meals were held at sanctuaries. For example, Elkanah and his family made a yearly pilgrimage to the sanctuary at Shiloh (1 Sam 1, 2). There they would rejoice and eat their sacrificial meals (1:4, 7–9, 18–19). At Shiloh, sacrifices were to be cooked at the sanctuary and the priest would receive his portion from the cooked meat (1 Sam 2:13–17).[15] This implies, as in the case of the nazirite in Num 6, that eating was done at the sanctuary. Samuel, Saul, and other invited guests ate a sacrifice at a *bāmâ* (1 Sam 9:12–25). There was a chamber (*liškâ*, v 22) at this sanctuary where the food was consumed.[16]

This custom contrasts with the situation implied by other data in the Priestly writings—that offerings may be consumed outside the sanctuary. This appears to be a later development in custom. The latest stage of this trend toward eating outside the sanctuary precincts is put into prescriptive terms in the Mishnah. It stipulates that all lesser holy offerings may be eaten anywhere within the walls of Jerusalem, but they must not be removed from the city.[17] If they are, the meat becomes invalid and must be burned.[18] Moreover, if they are eaten outside the city, the offender incurs flogging.[19]

But though eating outside the sanctuary is clearly stated in the Mishnah, the expansion of the place of eating as reflected in the Priestly writings is not a late development. This becomes evident by an

---

[15]This is the proper custom that was to be followed, but was breached by Eli's sons (cf. Milgrom, "The *Šôq hatTĕrûmâ*," *Tarbiz* 42 [1973–74] 7–8 [Hebrew]; P. K. McCarter, *I Samuel: A New Translation with Introduction, Notes and Commentary* [AB 8; Garden City: Doubleday, 1980] 83; H. H. Rowley, *Worship in Ancient Israel: Its Form and Meaning* [London: SPCK, 1967] 114). It is not part of the negative behavior of the Elides as construed by some (H. W. Hertzberg, *I and II Samuel: A Commentary* [OTL; Philadelphia: Westminster, 1964] 34–35; see the literature cited in Rowley).

[16]Cf. M. Haran, "*Zeḇaḥ Hayyamîm*," *VT* 19 (1969) 11–22 on these last two examples.

[17]*M. Pesaḥ*. 3:8; 7:8, 9; *Meg*. 1:11; *Zebaḥ*. 5:6–8; *Kelim* 1:8. In contrast to the implicit meaning of Num 6:14–20, the Mishnah says the nazirite may eat his ram anywhere in the city (*Zebaḥ*. 5:6), though it is to be cooked in the court (*Mid*. 2:5).

[18]*M. Pesaḥ*. 7:8, 9; Maimonides, *MTor*, ʿAboda, Pesule hamMuqdašin 19:8.

[19]*M. Mak*. 3:3.

examination of the place of eating lesser holy offerings in the book of Ezekiel. The book does not state explicitly where lesser holy offerings are to be consumed, but it appears rather clearly to require them to be eaten in the outer temple court. In each of the four corners of the outer court there are enclosures,[20] each measuring forty by thirty cubits (46:21–22). Fixtures for cooking the people's sacrifices[21] are located in these enclosures (vv 23–24). In addition to these kitchens, there are thirty chambers in the outer court against the outer wall (40:17–18). The precise use of these chambers is not clear, but it is likely that one of their functions was to provide a place where people could eat their sacrifices.[22] These two architectural features—the kitchens and the chambers—plus the large outer court (500 by 500 cubits; 42:16–20), which would allow large crowds to gather, suggest strongly that Ezekiel intended the people to eat the lesser holy offerings within the confines of the outer court and not outside it. By enlarging the court to accomodate large crowds, Ezekiel may be giving testimony that the place of eating had by the time of these chapters expanded to areas outside the temple court. The book was possibly expanding the court area so that consumption would remain in the sanctuary precincts. In this detail, Ezekiel adopts or perpetuates the older, conservative usage instead of the more recent development in Priestly tradition. This tendency of Ezekiel to be more strict or conservative than Priestly regulation in the Pentateuch is evidenced in regard to other matters.[23] In Ezekiel, the clothes of the priests and the most holy offerings convey holiness to people (42:14; 44:19; 46:20), while in the Priestly material they do not.[24] For this reason the laity, even the civil ruler, cannot enter the inner court (46:1–3). Ezekiel also requires the corpse-contaminated

---

[20]Each enclosure is called a *ḥāṣēr*, 46:21.

[21]*Zebaḥ hāʿām* (v 24), i.e., their *šĕlāmîm* offerings.

[22]Besides serving as a place for eating sacrifices (cf. 1 Sam 9:22), they could be used as meeting rooms (cf. Jer 35:2, 4) and storage rooms for food and clothing (cf. W. Zimmerli, *Ezechiel* [BKAT 13/1, 2, 2 vols.; Neukirchen: Neukirchener, 1969] 2. 1005; Eichrodt, *Ezekiel*, 544).

[23]Milgrom, "Sacrifices," 765a; M. Greenberg, "The Design and Themes of Ezekiel's Program of Restoration," *Interpretation* 38 (1984) 196, n. 32; 205–06; J. Skinner, *The Book of Ezekiel* (ExBib; New York: A. C. Armstrong, 1895) 438.

[24]J. Milgrom, "Sancta Contagion and Altar/City Asylum," *VTSup* 32 (1981) 278–310, esp. 297–98.

priest to bring a *ḥaṭṭāʾt* (44:27) while the Priestly legislation does not (Num 19; Lev 21).[25]

Interestingly, the Temple Scroll exhibits the same stricture as Ezekiel, probably with an implicit polemic against the laxness in custom in Jerusalem as manifested later in the Mishnah. Laypersons must eat the lesser holy offerings within the confines of, at least, the outer court. It specifically mentions this rule with the passover,[26] *šĕlāmîm* offerings,[27] the first born,[28] and implies it with the second tithe.[29] This stricture may in part derive from the influence of Ezekiel, particularly from the architectural feature of the large outer court to facilitate large gatherings.[30] But the passages from Deuteronomy that require eating and rejoicing "before the Lord" and "in the place he shall choose" appear to have had the greatest influence on the Scroll's view. It understood these to mean that consumption was to take place in the sanctuary precincts.[31]

---

[25]J. Milgrom, "The Paradox of the Red Cow (Num. XIX)," *VT* 31 (1981) 71–72. The nazirite must bring a *ḥaṭṭāʾt* when he becomes corpse-contaminated (Num 6:10–11). This, with the requirement to eat the *šĕlāmîm* in the court, indicates that the law for the nazirite is quite ancient.

[26]TS 17:8–9. Cf. *Jub.* 49:16–21. The Scroll says the passover is in the "courts," showing that not just the outer court would be used.

[27]TS 21:3; 22:11–14; 52:13–21.

[28]TS 52:9. It is to be eaten in the place God chooses. Cf. 52:16.

[29]TS col. 43. Cols. 40–46 deal with the outer court. Thus eating of the tithe discussed in col. 43 is one of the things that happens in the court.

[30]On architectural similarities and differences of the Scroll's temple with that of Ezekiel, cf. J. Milgrom, "The Temple Scroll," *BA* 41 (1978) 114; Y. Yadin, *The Temple Scroll (Megillat hamMiqdaš)* (3 vols.; Jerusalem: Israel Exploration Society, 1977) 1. 146–48. The difference in the size of the outer courts of Ezekiel's (500 by 500 cubits) and the Temple Scroll's (about 1590 by 1590 cubits; cf. Yadin, *Temple Scroll*, 1. 195–96) temples perhaps indicates the architectural expansions thought necessary to accomodate an increasing number of participants.

[31]TS 21:3; 22:13–14 use the phrase "before the Lord" (cf. 52:9, 16 "before me") and add "in the outer court." 52:9 and 16 say "in the place I shall choose." *Jubilees* echoes the strict understanding of Deuteronomy's language (32:10, 15; 49:16–21). Yadin (*Temple Scroll*, 1. 80–81) notes that the Karaites required the passover to be eaten in the sanctuary. For eating and rejoicing before the Lord in Deuteronomy, see 12:6–7, 11–12, 17–18; 14:22–23, 26; 15:20; 16:7; cf. 16:11; 27:7.

9.2.2.2 The Pure Place (Continued)

In addition to eating lesser holy things in a pure place, we recall that carcasses of *ḥaṭṭā't* sacrifices whose blood was used in the Tabernacle were to be taken outside the camp and burned in a pure place (Lev 4:11–12; Cf. Exod 29:14; Lev 4:21; 6:23; 8:17; 9:11; 16:27). At this pure cultic dump site, called the "ash dump" (*šepek haddešen*), the ashes from the burnt offering altar were also to be deposited (Lev 6:4).[32] Finally, the ashes obtained from the Red Cow preparation were to be stored in a pure place outside the camp (Num 19:9).[33]

To summarize, pure places are located both within the habitation, as the requirements about eating the lesser holy sacrifices show, and outside it, as the examples of the disposal of *ḥaṭṭā't* carcasses and altar ashes, and the storage of Red Cow ashes show.

9.2.3 The Impure Place

The only example we have of an impure place (*māqôm ṭāmē'*) is in the case of the disposal of *ṣāra'at* infected building materials (Lev 14:40, 41, 45). All contaminated stones, timbers, and plaster are to be deposited outside the city in an unclean place.[34]

9.3 THE CORRELATION OF HOLY, PURE, AND IMPURE PLACES WITH THE COMMUNICABILITY OF IMPURITY

The instances of holy, pure, and impure places yield some evidence about how the Priestly school perceives the qualities of different areas of the sanctuary camp or town and its environs. The terminology clearly indicates that the sanctuary area is thought to be holy and that the area outside the camp is considered both pure and impure.[35] Unfortunately, the terminology does not allow us to determine what the quality of the area inside the habitation is perceived to be. All we know from it directly is that part of it is pure so that lesser holy offerings could be consumed there. This data is represented in fig. 9.1.

---

[32]See chap. 6, section 6.5.

[33]See chap. 8, sections 8.3.2.1, o and p.

[34]See chap. 3.

[35]It is important to notice that the area outside the habitation is not considered entirely impure. It has a mixed nature of pure and impure; in

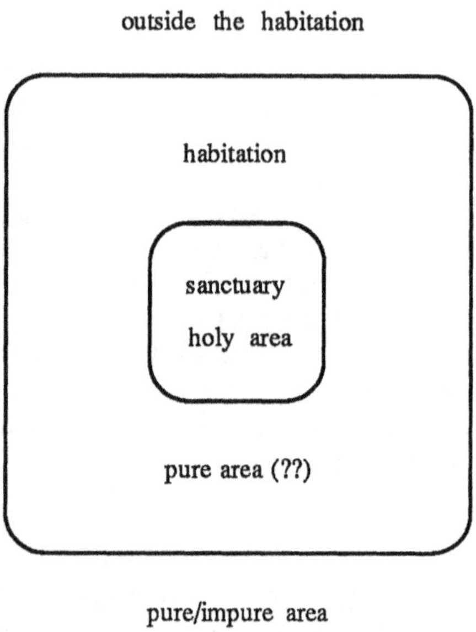

Fig. 9:1: Basic Data on the Places of Holiness, Purity, and Impurity

---

other words, it is neutral (J. Milgrom, "Two Kinds of *Ḥaṭṭāʾt*," *VT* 26 [1976] 334–35). The activities carried out there such as the disposal of sacrifices or the disposal of materials infected with *ṣāraʿat* will determine the quality of a particular locale outside the camp. This mixture of qualities outside the camp is somewhat startling. *A priori*, we might have expected that the Priestly system would consist of a logical tripartite division where the sanctuary area is holy, the habitation pure, and the area outside the habitation entirely impure. In fact, some, such as Y. Kaufmann (*The History of Israelite Belief: From Ancient Times Until the End of the Second Temple [Toledot haʾEmuna hayYiśreʾelit Mime Qedem ʿad Sop Bayit Šeni]* [4 vols.; Jerusalem and Tel-Aviv: Bialik Institute and Dvir, 1937–56] 1. 542–43) and D. Davies ("An Interpretation of Sacrifice in Leviticus," *ZAW* 89 [1976] 394) have worked according to a similar theoretical assumption. Such an assumption, however, cannot be supported by the evidence. Nevertheless, even with the mixed nature of the area outside the habitation, there is a descending order of qualities from the sanctuary outward. On concentric degrees of holiness, see J. Blenkinsopp, "The Structure of P," *CBQ* 38 (1976) 289.

The model in fig. 9.1 can be made more precise by imposing upon it another model constructed from the places of the disposal, exclusion, and restriction of communicable and noncommunicable impurities. This second model will corroborate the perception of the qualities that exist in the sanctuary and outside the camp in the first model and will allow us to determine the quality that is to exist within the habitation.

Chapter Eight, as well as the chapters before it, provided clear or implicit evidence of the exclusion of all communicable impurities from the habitation, the restriction of these impurities within the habitation, or the destruction of several of these impurities. We know explicitly or by deduction that the scapegoat, a bird used in *ṣāraʿat* purification rites, *ṣāraʿat*-infected building materials, corpses, *ḥaṭṭāʾt* carcasses, Red Cow materials (including the ashes), blood from the bird used in the *ṣāraʿat* purification ritual, and impure animal carcasses were disposed of or placed outside the habitation. Similarly, according to the ideal of Num 5:2–3, a person with *ṣāraʿat*, a *zāb*, a *zābâ*, and a corpse-contaminated person were excluded from the habitation. As discussed in Chapter Eight, this ideal exclusion of a number of communicably impure persons was relaxed in settled communities so that a corpse-contaminated person, *zāb*, and *zābâ*, as well as a menstruant, parturient, one who has intercourse with one of these women, those suspected of or purifying from *ṣāraʿat*, and communicably impure furniture might remain in the habitation with the provision that they be separated from the rest of society. Only a person with *ṣāraʿat* remained excluded. A few other communicably impure items—fabrics with *ṣāraʿat*, *ḥaṭṭāʾt* blood, and semen—were not discarded outside the habitation;[36] nevertheless, they were disposed of in a way that society would not be polluted.

In contrast to the restriction and exclusion of communicable impurities, there is no requirement for the restriction of noncommunicable impurities in the habitation. The only restriction placed on noncommunicable impurities, which of course applies to communicable impurities as well, is that they not come in contact with holy items, whether these be in the sanctuary area or in the community.

The foregoing examples of disposal, exclusion, and restriction can be summarized as follows: the sphere of the holy is to be kept separate from anything impure; noncommunicable impurities may remain in the

---

[36]Note Second Temple evidence that *ḥaṭṭāʾt* blood was channeled outside the habitation to the Kidron Valley (see chap. 7, section 7.3.2).

habitation unrestricted; most communicable impurities, according to the ideal of Num 5:2–3, are placed outside the habitation, but in the settled community, all humans bearing a communicable impurity, except one with *ṣāraʿat*, may remain in the habitation but under restriction.

This information helps in determining the quality of the habitation area. All communicable impurities are excluded from or restricted in it. This results in the limitation of impurity that exists there. Noncommunicable impurities are tolerated since they do not perpetuate themselves. Furthermore, noncommunicable impurities, which are allowed to exist in the community, are short-lived. They only last one day, as a glance over the trees in Chapter Eight will show. Sanctions against delaying impurity past the given time limit help insure that noncommunicable impurities are kept brief. Lev 5:2–3, 5–13 stipulate that a person who contracts a noncommunicable impurity by touching an animal carcass or a human impurity and forgets about it so that he does not purify by the end of the day must bring a *ḥaṭṭāʾt* sacrifice. Lev 17:15–16 gives sanctions against one who does not purify from pollution caused by eating impure animal carcass: "And if he does not launder and does not wash his flesh, he shall bear his penalty."[37] The requirement to destroy items that have become irretrievably though noncommunicably impure, such as clay pots and food, also reflects the desire to keep impurity in the habitation short lived. All of these rules—the exclusion or restriction of communicable impurities, sanctions against prolonging noncommunicable impurities, and the destruction of incorrigible impurities—suggest that the habitation in the sanctuary camp or town is to possess a status of general purity. The correlation of the diagram constructed from the instances of the terms holy, pure, and impure place with the model from the examples of the exclusion, restriction, or disposal of communicable and noncommunicable impurities appears in fig. 9.2.

The significance of this unified model of cultic topography is that it better defines the relationship between different parts of Israelite society as perceived explicitly or implicitly in Priestly thought. Notably we do not find here simple oppositions between holy and profane or between pure and impure. There is a three-fold opposition between holy, generally pure and pure/impure. Furthermore, and I believe this is most significant, there is a functional difference between types of impurity: commu-

---

[37]A similar sanction is found in Num 19:13, 20. One who does not purify from corpse contamination within a seven day period will suffer *kārēt*.

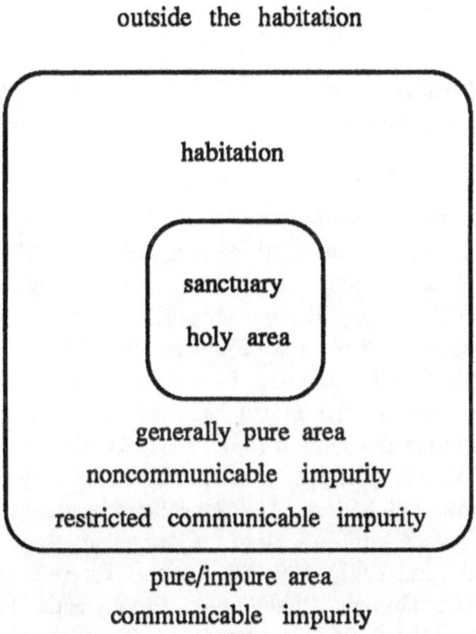

Fig. 9:2: Final Model of the Places of Holiness, Purity, and Impurity

nicable and noncommunicable. Hitherto, constructions of the theory of purity have generally dealt with impurity as a whole without differentiating clearly between its two potencies. Any further theoretical discussion of the matter will have to consider the interplay of these two impurities with society and the cult.

9.4 PLACES FOR THE DISPOSAL OF EVILS IN MESOPOTAMIAN AND HITTITE LITERATURE

In order to further elucidate the idea of the place of impurity in the Priestly writings, we turn to an examination of this concept in Mesopotamian and Hittite texts. The following studies are presented in sufficient detail so that they may serve not only the needs of the present chapter but also supply a more complete description of the nature of evils and their disposal in these literatures and thus provide supplementary information to the examples from these corpora cited in other chapters. At the end of these two studies, we will employ contrastive comparison in order to bring out the unique and salient features of the Priestly conception of disposal and the place of impurity.

9.4.1 Mesopotamian Texts

Impurity in Mesopotamian religion is characterized by its essentially demonic nature.[38] When a person sins[39] or suffers the spell of a

---

[38]On demons and demonic evil, see B. Meissner, *Babylonien und Assyrien* (2 vols.; Heidelberg: Carl Winter, 1925) 2. 199–200; C. Frank, *Lamastu, Pazuzu und andere Dämonen, ein Beitrag zur babyl.-assyr. Dämonologie* (*MAOG* 14/2; Berlin: Otto Harrassowitz, 1941); H. W. F. Saggs, *The Greatness that was Babylon: A Sketch of the Ancient Civilization of the Tigris-Euphrates Valley* (New York: Hawthorn Books, 1962) 302–05; E. Reiner, "La magie babylonienne," *Le monde du sorcier* (SOr 7; Paris: Éditions du Seuil, 1966) 78–81; G. Contenau, *Everyday Life in Babylon and Assyria* (London: E. Arnold, 1959; reprint, New York: W. W. Norton, 1966) 253–56; A. L. Oppenheim and E. Reiner, *Ancient Mesopotamia: Portrait of a Dead Civilization* (rev. ed.; Chicago: University of Chicago, 1977) 199–206. For texts referring to the attack of demons, see O. Gurney, "Babylonian Prophylactic Figures and their Rituals," *AAA* 22 (1935) 76–79; Shurpu iv 45–55; v–vi 1–22; vii 1–36; Maqlu ii 31–69; *DES*, passim. See the lexicons under the following demons and/or diseases: *aburriṣanu, aḫḫāzu, alluḫappu, alû, ardat lilî, arurtu, asakku, ašru, ašû, barīrītu, bennu, bibītu, dimītu, dīʾu, eṭimmu, gallû, gulūlu, ḫaʾattu, ḫāʾītu, ḫallulaja, ḫimṭu, ilu limnu, imḫullu, kattillu, kibbu, kilili, kinūnu, kiskilīlu, kišittu, kūbu, labaṣu, lamaštu, liʾbu, lillītu, lilû, māmītu, miqtu, mukīl rēs lemutti, mūtu, namtaru, qāt ili, rābiṣu, sibtu, šaggašu, šiptu, šūlu, šuruppû, ūmu, utukku, zaqīqu.* On the *sibitti*-demons, see L. Cagni, *The Poem of Erra* (SANE 1/3; Malibu: Undena, 1977) 18–19; on *eṭimmu* demons, see M. Bayliss, "The Cult of Dead Kin in Assyria and Babylonia," Iraq 35 (1973) 115–125.

[39]Shurpu is noted for its concern with rectifying evil caused by some unknown sin. Tablet ii gives a long list of sins a patient may have committed with the wish that the gods absolve him from his guilt (cf. also E. Reiner, "*Lipšur* Litanies," *JNES* 15 [1956] 136: 81–95; W. G. Lambert, "DINGIR.ŠÀ.DIB.BA Incantations," *JNES* 33 [1974] 278, 284, 286; OECT 6, 40–41, 72–73). Because of sin, demonic influence is present and must be exorcised (cf. Saggs, *Greatness*, 318–20). See Shurpu iv 45–55 where a list of affecting demons are listed in an incantation in order to release a patient from evil. A good example of the chain of causation involved in sinning and ensuing demonic attack is found elsewhere in Shurpu. Demons are said to encounter "the man from whom his god has withdrawn and covered him like a cloak" (vii 19/20). Sin may estrange one's protective personal god and thus leave him open to attack (Cf. E. E. Knudsen, "An Incantation Tablet from Nimrud," *Iraq*

sorcerer,[40] the person becomes susceptible to an onslaught of demons, described in terms of a terrible wind or storm,[41] an overwhelming flood,[42] a cloak which covers the person's whole body,[43] etc.,[44] and which cause mental distress[45] or physical disease.[46] Consequently, the main goal of numerous rituals is to exorcise these demons, to cast them out, and send them back to their proper abodes.[47] This exorcism may be performed by incantations which call upon beneficent deities to help remove the demons or by direct speech to the demons to get out.

[1959] 56: 13–14; Lambert, "DINGIR.ŠÀ.DIB.BA," 270; T. Jacobsen, *Treasures of Darkness: A History of Mesopotamian Religion* [New Haven: Yale University, 1976] 153; and particularly Janowski, *Sühne*, 34–37).

[40]The Maqlu series is concerned with annulling the effects of sorcery. Though much of the talk is about destroying the sorcerers, their sorcery, returning it to their own heads, and doing magic back on them, there is also a concern with demonic attack arising from their sorcery. See i 135–143 where models of various demons are burned. On sorcery as a cause of evil, see Saggs, *Greatness*, 316–18.

[41]*CT* 16.19: 1–15 (= *DES* 1. 88); 16.19: 30–34 (=*DES* 1. 90); 16.21: 145–53 (=*DES* 1. 98–101.).

[42]*CT* 16.12: 25 (= *DES* 1. 52); 16.21: 144 (= *DES* 1.98).

[43]Shurpu vii 19/20; *CT* 16.1: 30/31 (= *DES* 1. 4). Demons may be described as covering the patient "like a net" (cf. Knudsen, "Incantation Tablet," 56: 55, *sapāru;* 57: 23, *šuškallu*).

[44]Descriptions of fierceness are attached to demons, such as being like thrusting bulls (*CT* 16.14 iv 15 = *DES* 1. 68) or wild horses (*CT* 16.15 v 48 = *DES* 1. 76). See also Knudsen, "Incantation Tablet," 56: 44–57.

[45]Cf. J. V. Kinnier-Wilson, "An Introduction to Babylonian Psychiatry," *Studies in Honor of Benno Landsberger on his Seventy-Fifth Birthday, April 21, 1965* (Chicago: Oriental Institute of the University of Chicago, 1965) 289–98.

[46]Many demons are sicknesses and vice versa, see n. 38, above. Various passages speak of sickness and plague caused by demons (Shurpu vii 1–20; *CT* 16.2: 40–45 = *DES* 1. 6; 16.14: 40–45 = *DES* 1. 64–66) and also death that demons bring to men (*CT* 16.12: 30–35 = *DES* 1. 52; 16.14 iv 25–30 = *DES* 1. 70) and to their animals (*CT* 16.9 ii 15–25 = *DES* 1. 34).

[47]The sin, the cause of demonic attack, may be the object removed by these rites. See the "*Lipšur* Litanies" where a patient requests that a bird or fish take his sin (*arnu*) away (Reiner, "*Lipšur Litanies*, " 140: 22´; cf. 142: 37´ where *māmītu* "curse" is the object of removal). In Shurpu, it is hoped that the tablet which contains one's "sins, errors, crimes oaths,

Moreover, these incantations are accompanied by rites which physically embody the wishes expressed in the incantations. Certain objects may be used to represent the evils attaching themselves to the individual which are then thrown away. The concern in this section is to investigate the various areas where evils are thrown away. To do so, however, it is necessary to study the home of demons, for it will be seen that the place of disposal corresponds to the demons' home.

The home or source of demons are places which are removed from human habitation. Mythologically speaking, demons live in the nether world: *šú-nu bi-nu-ut a-ra-al-li-e*[48] *šú-nu* "they are the creatures of the underworld";[49] *ul-tu ir-ṣi-tu it-ta-ṣu-nu šú-nu* "they have come forth from the nether world";[50] *šú-nu iš-tu ap-si-i i*[*t-t*]*a-ṣu-ni šú-nu* "they have come forth from the abyss";[51] *iš-tu qí-rib ša-di-i ana ma-a-tum ur-du* "it (headache) descended from the midst of the mountains to the land";[52] *iš-tu* É É.KUR *it-ta-ṣu-ni šú-nu* "they have come forth from the house,

---

what was sworn (*arnišu ḫiṭātišu gillātišu māmâtišu tumamātišu*) be thrown into water (to dissolve)" (iv 79). These cases, however, are only expressions and not actual rites. More often, the gods are invoked to remove, release, or dispel the sins (cf. *CAD* A/2, 297), while the actual ritual performances are left to take care of removing the consequent evil that attends the sins.

[48] *Arallû* (a poetic name for the underworld) is characteristically the birthplace of demons, see *CAD* A/2, 227a.

[49] *CT* 16.12: 13 (= *DES* 1. 50).

[50] *CT* 17.41: 2 (= *DES* 2. 134). Cf. [*u*]*l-te i-rat* KI-*tim i-ši-ḫa ṭi-ʾ-i* "headache blew forth from the midst of the nether world" (*BWL*, 40: 52). See *CAD* E, 310–11 for a discussion and examples of *erṣetu* as nether world.

[51] *CT* 17.13: 18 (= *DES* 2. 50). Cf. *šu-ú-lu lim-nu it-ta-ṣa-a ap-su-uš-šú* "evil *šūlu*-sickness has gone forth from its *apsû*" (*BWL*, 40: 53); [ÉN AB]ZU.TA NAM.MU.UN.DA KU4.KU4 "Incantation: let them not enter from the *apsû*" (R. Caplice, "Namburbi Texts in the British Museum, V," *Or* 40 [1971] 169 vs. 8´); *di-me-tum ul-tu qí-rib ap-si-i it-ta-ṣa-a* "*dimētu*-disease came forth out of the *apsû*" (Shurpu vii 2). See *CAD* A/2, 195b for demons from the *apsû*. Also related to the waters as the place of evil is: *a-gu-ú ta-ma-tu šu-ru-up-pa-a ú-šam-ḫ*[*ir*] "he transferred *šuruppû*-disease to the sea-flood" (*BWL*, 52: 9).

[52] *CT* 17.12: 5 (= *DES* 2. 43); cf. *CT* 17.22: 157–58; also [*la-maš-tu ú-ri*]*-da ul-tu qí-rib* KUR-*i* "[the *lamaštu*-demon des]cended from the midst of the mountain" (*BWL*, 40: 55).

Ekur";[53] *im-ḫul-li* [*iš-tu i-šid*] AN-*e i-zi-qa* "a disease bearing wind has blown [from the ho]rizon";[54] [*ú-t*]*uk-ku lem-nu šá ina ṣe-e-ri il-la-ku* "the evil [*ut*]*ukku* that walks in the steppe";[55] *šu-bat-ka* É *na-du-ú ḫar-bu* "your dwelling is an uninhabited, wasted house";[56] *ina ni-gi-ṣi ir-ṣi-ti it-ta-na-aḫ-lal-lu* "they continually creep in the crevices of the earth";[57] UKU.MEŠ *mi-ta-tum... šá* URU.MEŠ-*ši-na* DUL.MEŠ "dead people... whose cities are ruins."[58]

When demons are exorcised, they are sent back to these places of origin: *gal-le-e šam-ru-ti a-na* KUR.NU.GI4.A *a-ṭar-rad-ma* "I will drive the savage *gallû*-demons to the Land of No Return";[59] *ana* GIDIM *a-ra-le-e li-ru-šú-nu-tim* "let him lead them (the demons) to the spirits of the underworld";[60] *mim-ma lim-nu ana* KI-*tim li*-[*tur*] "let whatever evil ret[urn] to the nether world";[61] [*uš-te*]-*rid ap-su-uš-šú šú-ú-lu lim*-[*nu*] "he sent down ev[il] *šulu*-disease to its abyss";[62] *is-kip la-maš-tu šá-da-a uš-te-e*[*š-šir*] "he sent away the *lamaštu*-demon, he dispatched [it] to the

[53]*CT* 16.1: 25 (= *DES* 1. 4); cf. *CAD* E, 70b. Cf. *di-ḫi-i iš-tu* É.KUR *it-ta-ṣa-a* "*diḫû*-disease left the Ekur" (*CT* 17.12: 3 = *DES* 2. 44); [*di-*ʾ]-*u ul-tu* É.KUR *it-ta-ṣa*-[*a*] (*CT* 17.25: 2 = *DES* 2. 86); [*u-tuk-ku l*]*a* [*ni*]-ʾ*i u-ṣa-a ul-tu* É.KUR "the irresistible [*utukku*] left the Ekur" (*BWL*, 40: 54). See *CAD* E, 70, generally.

[54]*BWL*, 40: 51; on *išid šamê* as "horizon," see *CAD* I, 240b.

[55]*CT* 16.37: 15 (= *DES* 1. 166). Cf. *utukku lemnu alû lemnu ina ṣēri tarbaṣa ib-ta-*ʾ*-u* "the evil *utukku*-demon (and) the evil *alû*-demon from the steppe have passed through the fold" (4 R, 18*, number 6:4–5, quoted in *CAD* Ṣ, 145b); *u-tuk-ku lem-nu e-dím-mu šá ina ṣe-e-ri šu-pu-u* "the evil *utukku* and *eṭimmu* which are extant in the steppe" (*CT* 16.32: 157); *mu-ru-uṣ qaq-qa-di ina ṣe-e-ri it-tak-kip* "headache knocks about in the steppe" (*CT* 17.19: 2). See *CAD* Ṣ, 145–46 for *ṣēru* as the haunt of demons (cf. *CT* 16.1: 29, 37 = *DES* 1. 4).

[56]*CT* 16.29: 99 (= *DES* 1. 138). Cf. *ina ni-du-ti er-ṣi-ti it-te-ni-*ʾ*-lu-ú* "in the desolate places of the earth they lie" (*CT* 16.44: 105).

[57]*CT* 16.44: 103 (= *DES* 1. 192)

[58]G. Castellino, "Ritual and Prayers Against 'Appearing Ghosts,'" *Or* 24 (1955) 246: 13.

[59]L. Cagni, *L'epopea di Erra* (Rome: Istituto di Studi del Vicino Oriente, Università di Roma, 1969) i 185.

[60]*LKA* 154 rs. 12–13 (cited in *CAD* A/2, 227a).

[61]O. Gurney, "Babylonian Prophylactic Figures," 86: 137; cf. *BWL*, 52: 5b.

[62]*BWL*, 52: 6.

mountain";[63] *ú-tu*[*k*]*-ku la ni-ʾi ú-tir é-kur-ri-*[*iš*] "he returned the irresistible *utukku* to the Ekur";[64] *mim-ma lim-nu* [*te-bi ú-ṣi*] *ana áš-ri* ᵈ*Eriškigalli* "whatever evil, [arise, go out] to the place of Erishkigal";[65] [*ud-da*]*p-pir im-ḫul-la a-na i-šid* AN-e "he dr[ove] the disease bearing wind to the horizon";[66] UDUG.ḪUL EDIN.NA.ZU.ŠÈ "evil *utukku*, to your steppe!";[67] [*u*]*-tuk-ku lim-nu ṣi-i ana ni-sa-a-ti* "evil utukku, go out to distant places";[68] *a-šib na-me-e ana na-me-ka at-lak* "you who dwell in the plain, go to your plain."[69]

The places where impure items are disposed of correspond to places where demons live or places connected with their habitations. The river is the most usual place for disposal. We remember that the ram's carcass that was used for cleansing Nabu's cella in the *akītu* festival is cast into the river.[70] In a namburbi ritual, the evil of creaking beams is put upon a fish in the form of dust and then the fish is apparently put back into the river.[71] The evil of bad omens may be disposed of by sweeping the affected house and throwing the sweepings into the river.[72] A clay figurine which represents an evil can be thrown into the river.[73]

---

[63]*BWL*, 52: 8.

[64]*BWL*, 52: 7.

[65]Gurney, "Prophylactic Figures," 86: 131.

[66]*BWL*, 52: 5.

[67]Caplice, "Namburbi Texts, V," 168:4´. Cf. (13) *u-tuk-ku lim-nu* (14) *a-na ṣi-ri-ka* . . . (16) *a-lu-ú lim-nu* (17) *a-na ṣi-ri-ka* . . . (19) *e-dím-mu lim-nu* (20) *a-na ṣi-ri-ka* . . . (22) *gal-lu-u lim-nu a-na ṣi-ri-*[*ka*] "evil *utukku*, to your steppe! Evil *alû*, to your steppe! Evil *eṭimmu*, to your steppe! Evil *gallû*, to your steppe!" (*CT* 17.8 vii 13–22 = *DES* 2. 26).

[68]*CT* 16.29: 93 (= *DES* 1. 138). On the meaning of *ni-sa-a-ti* as "Ferne," "distant places," see *AHw*, 781, under *nesû* I.

[69]*CT* 16.28: 57 (= *DES* 1. 134). Cf. [*a*]*-lu-ú lim-nu at-lak ana na-me-e* "evil *alû*, go away to the plain" (*CT* 16.29: 95 = *DES* 1. 138); *litbâ lištappidu na-me-e* "let (the demon) leave and run around in the steppe" (cited in *CAD* N/1, 251a).

[70]See chap. 1, section 1.5.1, lines 359–60.

[71]Caplice, "Namburbi Texts, V," 133: 6. See n. 132 in chap. I and chap. 2, section 2.2.

[72]Caplice, "Namburbi Texts, V," 135: 15´; 136: 3; 169 vs. 9´; *KAR* 72:6–7 (= E. Ebeling, "Beiträge zur Kenntniss den Beschwörungsserie Namburbi [Part 4]," *RA* 48 [1954] 182).

[73]R. Caplice, "Namburbi Texts in the British Museum, II," *Or* 36 (1967) 15 rs. 11; *KAR* 62 rs. 34–35 (= E. Ebeling, *Aus dem Tagewerk*

Breads used in a wiping rite may be thrown into the river.[74] Models of clay tongues are put into a model boat which is then thrown into the

---

eines assyrischen Zauberpriesters [*MAOG* 5/3; Leipzig: Otto Harrassowitz, 1931] 22). In this latter example, the figurine of a man riding an ox is "buried" (*temēru*) in the river.

[74]*KAR* 72: 5 (= E. Ebeling, "Namburbi [Part 4]," 182). Other objects disposed of in the river are: wiping material (*kupīrāti; LKA* 142: 17; *takpertu*, *TuL* 94: 37; on the disposal of other wiping material, see appendix 2); fingernails mixed with clay (*TuL* 98: 15–16); sand from a person's foot which is placed in a waterskin (R. Caplice, "Namburbi Texts in the British Museum, III," *Or* 36 [1967] 290: 26′–27′); a flour circle (*zisurrû*, *TuL* 94: 31); colored strings (*ulinnu*, *TuL* 94: 31); ashes in a vessel (Caplice, "Namburbi Texts, III," 289: 22′; thrown in A.MEŠ *pa-ši-ru-tú* "deep water"); a brazier (*garakku*, *TuL* 94: 30, 37); a *nappaṭu*-oven (*TuL* 119: 10); a censer (*nignakku*, Caplice, "Namburbi Texts, V," 168: 2′–5′); a dismantled offering arrangement (KEŠDA, Caplice, "Namburbi Texts, III," 290: 28′).

Some items thrown in the river are clearly not objects laden with or representing impurity, but are offerings to the river god which are made to enlist the god's aid in removing the impurity. Incantations recited to the river (see below) make this obvious. Such offerings include *maṣḫatu*-flour and *miḫḫu*-beer (Caplice, "Namburbi Texts, III," 290: 27′; cf. 289: 22′). These offerings accompany the dipsosal of impure items. The example in line 27′ is accompanied by an incantation to the river. For offerings of bread and *maṣḫatu*-flour, see *TuL*, 56: 27. One namburbi rite prescribes that a patient put seven grains of silver and a plant in his mouth, go to the river, and immerse seven times. On the seventh time, he is to throw into the river what is in his mouth (R. Caplice, "Namburbi Texts in the British Museum, I," *Or* 34 [1965] 121: 15′–18′). Caplice perceives (based on the admittedly questionable interpretation that KA.DU = *ipṭerū* "redemption price") that the silver is a ransom to the river for carrying off the evil. Perhaps there is a dual meaning here in the silver representing an offering to the river and being symbolic of the evil. The same mixing of motifs occurs in the rite the Philistines performed to rid themselves of the evil the ark caused. They make golden hemorrhoids and mice and send them with the ark back to the Israelites (1 Sam 6:3, 4, 5, 8, etc.). The golden objects are an offering to the angry God (an *ʾāšām* in Israelite terms) and also symbolically concretize the evils and their disposal.

Bathing in the river (e.g., *TuL*, 39: 16) can be viewed in the context of impurity disposal in the river. The patient by bathing releases the evils from his body which are then taken away by the river to the place of evil. Compare the statement from the "*Lipšur* Litanies": "may it be

river.[75] In addition to the river, other bodies of water, such as a well, may serve as places of disposal.[76]

An incantation addressed to the river frequently accompanies disposal in the river.[77] The form[78] of the incantation usually consists of an invocation of the river by means of an enumeration of its endowments

---

stripped off with the water of his body and the washwater of his hands; let the river carry it down to its bottom (*ana šapliša*)" (Reiner, "*Lipšur* Litanies," 138–39: 101–02).

[75]*UET* 6, 410 vs. 15–20; rs. 7–8 (= O. Gurney, "A Tablet of Incantations against Slander," *Iraq* 22 [1960] 222–26, cited in *CAD* M/1, 142a). Disposal or banishment by boat is also seen in the case of the *lamaštu* demon. In an incantation addressed to the demon, we read: "I have made for you a boat with sails; I will have you embark on it. I will have four dogs, two white, two black, embark with you. I will send you across the Ulaja river, the sea, to the midst of Tiamat" [*e-p*]*u-šak-ki* GIŠ.MÁ.GUR8 *šaḫ-ḫu-tu ú-še-el-li-ki ina* Š[À] [*ú*]-*še-el-li it-ti-ki* 4 *kalbê* 2 *piṣūti* 2 *ṣa*[*mūti u-še-*]*ib-bir-ki* ^íd^*ú-la-a-a tâmta*(-*ta*) *qi*[*r*-*biš tiāmat*] (D. W. Myhrman, "Die Labartu-Texte: Babylonische Beschwörungsformeln nebst Zauberverfahren gegen die Dämonin Labartu," *ZA* 16 [1902] 170–03: 44–46; cf. *CAD* M/1, 142). The banishment of the *lamaštu* demon is visually represented in plaques wherein the demon is seen on a boat riding on top of an ass (cf. Myhrman, "Labartu-Texte," 164–67 iv 3–11, where a model of an ass and the demon are made, provisioned, and eventually disposed of in the *ṣēru*). See *ANEP*, pls. 658, 857, and the descriptions; Saggs, *Greatness*, pl. 54b and pp. 303–04.

On boat disposal, see the Hittite Samuha ritual, rs. 48–49, where a model boat is loaded with "curses" and sent away in a ditch leading to the river.

[76]Cf. *TuL* 98: 15 where fingernails mixed with clay may be thrown into a well. Also Gurney, "Tablet of Incantations," 222: 19 where a boat filled with clay tongues may be thrown into a well (*burtu*).

[77]Caplice, "Namburbi Texts, III," 290: 27′–34′; "Namburbi Texts, I," 130 vs. 2′–9′; Shurpu ix 70–87 (cf. ix 58–69). On incantations addressed to rivers, see the listings in W. G. Kunstmann, *Die babylonische Gebetsbeschwörung* (LSS, n.s. 1/2; Leipzig; J. C. Hinrichs, 1932) 99 and W. Mayer, *Untersuchungen zur Formensprache der babylonischen "Gebetsbeschwörungen"* (StPM; Rome: Biblical Institute Press, 1976) 401–02.

[78]On the form and type of various incantations, see Kunstmann, *Gebetsbeschwörung*; A. Falkenstein, *Die Haupttypen der sumerischen Beschwörung* (LSS, n.s. 1/1; Leipzig: J. C. Hinrichs, 1931); Lambert, "DINGIR.ŠÀ.DIB.BA"; Mayer, *Untersuchungen*.

and strengths, followed by a statement of the patient's sore state with a request that the river help avert or do away with the evil.[79] An excellent example of this is found in the namburbi ritual cited in Chapter One (section 1.5.5). Just before a model dog representing and carrying the evil is thrown into the river, an incantation to the river requesting its help in removing the evil is recited three times. The last lines (15–16) carry the following request:

> Car[ry] that dog to the depths. Do n[ot re]lease it! Take it down to your depths. Remov[e] the evi[l] of the dog from my body! Give me happiness and health!

In another example, the river is besought to

> remove that evil! May your banks not release it! Bring it down to your *apsû!* Withdraw that evil! Give (the patient) a happy life![80]

Rivers and other bodies of water are an accessible aspect of the larger cosmological water system connected with the *apsû*. By discarding evils in them, one returns the evils to the *apsû,* their source.[81]

On land, the *ṣēru* "steppe, open country" and related areas are places of disposal. We recall the example from Shurpu (cited in Chapter One, section 1.5.4) in which wiping material is taken to the steppe and placed at the base of an *ašāgu*-bush.[82] Other places like the *ṣēru* serve as

---

[79]Other gods are enlisted to help the patient by incantation, e.g., Shamash (Caplice, "Namburbi Texts, I," 117 rs. 7´–22´; G. Meier, "Ein akkadisches Heilungsritual aus Boğazköy," *ZA* 45 [1939] 204–07 iii 27–iv 14), Ea and Marduk (Caplice, "Namburbi Texts, II," 14-15 vs. 15–rs. 5). See the extensive list in Mayer, *Untersuchungen*, 389–90.

[80]Caplice, "Namburbi Texts, I," 127: 10–12. On the translation, cf. *CAD* Ṣ, 66b.

[81]T. Jacobsen, *Toward the Image of Tammuz and Other Essays on Mesopotamian History and Culture* (Cambridge: Harvard University, 1970) 360–62, n. 21; *CAD* A/2, 194a. Cf. A. M. Rodriguez, "Substitution in the Hebrew Cultus and in Cultic-Related Texts" (PhD diss., Andrews University, 1980) 49–50.

[82]Other examples of disposal in the *ṣēru* are: plants which are masticated by the *āšipu* are taken there (Caplice, "Namburbi Texts, II," 34: 14-16); thread representing curse is discarded there (Shurpu v–vi 164/165). Paralleling disposal in the steppe is the stipulation that officiators participating in the cleansing of Nabu's cella must stay in the steppe (see chap. 1, section 1.5.1, lines 360–63). Figurines of the

dumping grounds. Breads in a wiping rite may be thrown in the *na-mi-e na-*[*du-ti*] "uninhabited open country."[83] Sweepings from a house may be thrown in the *ugāru* "open land."[84]

As in Hittite rituals, evils may be disposed of in the enemy country. In one example, the king is shaved and his hair is put in a vessel and then left at the enemy's border:

> He (i.e., the king) shall kneel. He submits to shaving. You put the hair of his body in a *laḫannu-šaḫarratu* vessel and leave it at the border of the enemy.[85]

---

lamaštu demon and the ass are taken out to the steppe (Myhrman, "Labartu-Texte," 164–67 iv 3–11).

[83]*KAR* 72: 4–5 (= Ebeling, "Namburbi [Part 4]," 182). Cf. *saḫaršubbâ lišalbissuma lištappudu namê* "may (the god) cover him with skin disease so that he must roam the desert" (BM 113927: 27, cited in *CAD* N/1, 251a).

[84]*KAR* 72: 6–7 (= Ebeling, "Namburbi [Part 4]," 182). *AHw* (1402) defines *ugāru* as "Feldflur, Ackerland." *Ugāru* can have a meaning close to *namû*, see *CAD* N/1, 251b (as "a place with no house or dwelling" *ašar bītu u šubtu la bašû*).

Other places may refer to where evils are disposed. In Maqlu iv 23, the patient complains *ana* EDIN *ki-di u na-me-e tap-qí-da-in-ni* "you (the sorceresses) have delivered me over to the steppe, open country, and plain." In another ritual, a figure of an ass (and the patient?) are taken to the *kīdu* area (Meier, "Heilungsritual," 202 ii 11; cf. 204 iii 20). But since *kīdu* can refer to the idea of "outside" as well as "outlying area, open country," it is most likely that here the model is just taken outside the house with no intent to refer to a remote place of disposal.

The *mudabiru* (or *madbaru*, see *CAD* M/1, 11–12), "steppe, desert" is found in a rite in *TuL* 74: 11. The context in which the term is used shows that it refers to the place of ritual performance, but not a place of disposal (see chap. 1, n. 132).

[85]*RAcc* 7:24–25 (cf. *ANET*, 339–40; also translated in *CAD* G, 18a). Cf. the statement in an incantation: "may it (the evil) blow to a foreign country like a wind" LIL.GIN$_7$ KI.KÚR.ŠÈ ḪÉ.GÍD.GÍD.DÈ (Caplice, "Namburbi Texts, III," 296: 8). B. Landsberger (*The Date Palm and its By-Products According to Cuneiform Sources* [*AfO* Beiheft 17; Graz: Ernst Weidner, 1967] 32–33, n. 103) interprets an inscription from Tell Halaf (in *AfO* Beiheft, 6, 13–14, #5, lines 12–14) as referring to a disposal of impurity in enemy land: *takpirtu bīt nakarkāni liškunū* "let them place the dirt wherever your enemy be!" More recently, however, *CAD* N/1, 159, leaves the word *nakarkānu* undefined.

More close to home, evils may be disposed of in the streets (*sūqu*) or plazas (*rebītu*). In the *assakī marṣūti* segment (cited in Chapter One, section 1.5.3), a goat, bread, and dough, used in a wiping rite, are scattered in the street.[86] In another rite, waters which carry away evil are poured in the plaza.[87] These places of disposal, though different from the preceding in that they are not removed from the population, are not particularly exceptional or odd since everyday refuse was thrown into the streets.[88] And though these places were close to home, they still are symbolic of the larger conceptual system of disposal in the nether world. An *utukkī lemnūti* text (cited in Chapter One, section 1.5.2) shows this. The skin of a *mašhultuppû*-goat is taken from the patient and thrown into the plaza. Expressions surrounding the disposal of the skin demonstrate the underworld connection: "whatever evil, [arise, go out] to the place of Erishkigal" and "let all evil return to the earth." Here "earth" is to be understood as the underworld.[89] Nevertheless, disposal in

---

Other texts indicate a connection of evil with the enemy's land. Sorceresses that cause a patient evil are designated as Gutians, Elamites, and citizens of Hanigalbat (Maqlu iii 78; iv 105–107). The *lamaštu* demon is designated as a foreigner (Myhrman, "Labartu-Texte," 178: 13–14, as a Sutean; 190 rs. 3, as an Elamite).

[86]Cf. *CT* 17.1: 5: *tak-pir-ta-šú a-na su-uq ir-bit-ti* [ ] "its wiping material in the street crossing [ ]."

[87]*Ana ri-bi-ti tu-bu-uk-ma* with an added statement *ma-ru-uš-tu šá e-mu-qí i-na-aš-ša-ru ri-bi-tu lit-bal* "the pain which lessened (his) strength, let the *rebītu* carry" (*CT* 17.32: 11, 13 = *DES* 2. 109). In another case, some object is attached to a man's head, left for a day, cut off at night, and thrown into the *rebītu* (*CT* 17.26: 75). Related perhaps to disposal in the *sūqu* and *rebītu* is taking impure materials to the KÁ "gate, door": *tak-pi-rat* É *ana* KÁ [*tutte*]*ru-ub-šá* "you shall take the wiping-material to the door" (Gurney, "Prophylactic Figures," 58: 60–61); *kīma tak-pi-ra-a-ti tuq-te-it-tu-u ana* KÁ *tu-še-ṣa* "when the wiping-rites are finished, you send (them) out to the door" (*BBR* #26 ii 3; cf. i 19–20).

[88]G. Contenau (*Everyday Life*, 33–34) says: "the household rubbish was thrown into the streets, where what was not eaten by dogs and scavenging animals was burnt dry by the sun and trodden underfoot." In connection with this statement we do find a ritual where a man is ritually wiped from head to foot with bread. The bread is then given to a dog to eat: NINDA *šú-a-tam a-na* UR.GI$_7$ *ta-na-*[*ad-din*] (*KAR* 114 rs. 8–9 = Ebeling, *Tagewerk*, 10: 18-21). See also "Ishtar's Descent to the Nether World," *ANET*, 108 rs. 24-25; *CAD* Ḫ, 7, under *ḫabannatû*.

[89]See chap. 1, n. 146.

the street could be dangerous for those in the community. In the "*Lipšur* Litanies," a patient requests release from a number of impure influences:

> If when I was walking in the street a cursed man touched me; if when I was crossing the *rebītu* I trampled in dirty washwater which had not drained away; . . .[90]

Thus the Mesopotamians did not always free themselves from the impurities that their rites removed.[91]

Some rites dispose of impurity by burying it or letting it soak into the earth. Ashes from the burned paraphernalia of a substitute king are buried.[92] In another ritual, a model of a tormenting ghost is made and buried, and an incantation is addressed to the ghost: "go away from the body of so and so; depart!"[93] Material used for wiping a patient may be buried.[94] *Lamaštu* figurines representing that demon's evil may be

---

[90]Reiner, "*Lipšur* Litanies," 142: 41′–43′. This type of contamination is found elsewhere: (4) *ri-bi-tú ina ba-ʾ-i-šú* (5) . . . *su-ú-qa su-la-a ina a-la-ki-šú* . . . (7) *ri-im-ka tab-ka ik-bu-us-ma* . . . (9) *ina me-e la i-ša-ru-ti še-ip-šú iš-ta-ka-an* "when he went through the plaza, when he walked through the street (and) way, he trampled in poured out washwater, he placed his foot in undrained (?) water" (*CT* 17.41: 4–9 = *DES* 1. 136; cf. also *CT* 17.38: 11–16 = *DES* 1. 138, cited in Reiner, "*Lipšur* Litanies," 148).

[91]Other examples of dirty water with detrimental effects are: "she washed me with her dirty water (to cause) my death" (*BRM* 4, 18: 4, cited in *CAD* M/2, 143b; cf. J. Laessøe, *Studies on the Assyrian Ritual and Series* bīt rimki [Copenhagen: Ejnar Munksgaard, 1955] 13 and n. 9); "they washed me with dirty water" *rim-k[i lu-]ʾu-ti u-ra-me-ku-in-ni* (Maqlu i 105; cited in *CAD* L, 258a; see here for other examples).

[92]W. G. Lambert, "A Part of the Ritual for the Substitute King," *AfO* 18 (1957) 110 vs. 1–8.

[93]Castellino, "Rituals," 258: 11–13 (= *TuL* 134: 11–13). Cf. also Castellino, "Rituals," 260: 24; 268: 15. In one text (*CT* 17.1: 7 = *DES* 2. 2) a *pūḫu* is to be disposed of in a *šatpu* "pit" (*AHw*, 1200, "Ausschachtung, Mulde"; E. Reiner [*Šurpu: A Collection of Sumerian and Akkadian Incantations* (*AfO* Beiheft; Osnabruck: Biblio, 1970) at iii 92] translates "pit") of the land.

[94](9) ÉN *an-ni-ta ina tak-pir-ti* ^{uzu}ÚR ŠITA$_5$ NÍG.SILAG.GÁ *šu-a-tum* (10) *ina* ḪABRUDA! *šá* ^{d}UTU.ŠÚ.A GAR-*an-ma ina* IM IN.BUBBU KÁ-*šú* BAD (*tepeḫḫi*) *ina* ^{na4}KIŠIB ŠUBA *u* NA$_4$.GÌN.NU (*šadāni*!) (11) KÁ-*šú tu-bar-ram* "this incantation you recite over the wiping material of his loins.

buried at a corner of a wall.[95] Water used to ritually wash may be discarded on the ground, so that "the earth (i.e., the underworld) may take the impurity away."[96] The water will soak into the ground and thereby enter the nether world which is conceived of as being not far from the ground's surface.[97]

Another form of disposal is burning. An excellent example is found in Shurpu:

> [An in]cantation-priest wipes (him) with ZÍD.MAD.GÁ-flour and throws it in the fire. (You recite) the incantation (entitled) "May Anu and Antu stand; may they avert sickne[ss]." You sprinkle [wa]ter on the patient. You take in your hands an onion, dates, matting, some wool, goat's hair, and red wool. You set it over the patient. You recite the incantation (entitled) "An evil curse like a *gallû*-demon." You wipe him (with the foregoing materials). . . . The incantation priest places (these things) in the patient's hand. He [p]eels the [onion] and throws (it) in the fire. He [s]trips off [the dates] and throws (them) into the fire. [He unrav]els the matting and does likewise. He undoes the wool and does likewise. [He undo]es [the goat's hair] and does likewise. He undoes the red wool and does likewise.[98]

You place dough in a hole toward the west. You stop up its opening with clay and chaff. You seal its opening with a seal of *šubû*-stone and hematite" (*CT* 23.1: 9–11; cf. *CAD* B, 102b). The wiping rite occurs in line 4. An outdated edition of this text is R. C. Thompson, "An Incantation against Rheumatism," *Proceedings of the Society of Biblical Archaeology* 30 (1908) 67–69.

[95]See n. 132 in chap. 1.

[96]Shurpu viii 89–90.

[97]See H. Tawil, "ʿAzazel The Prince of the Steepe [*sic*]: A Comparative Study," *ZAW* 92 (1980) 48–51.

[98]Shurpu i 11–21. The motif of unraveling or peeling away evil is found in Reiner, "*Lipšur* Litanies," 136: 79–80; 140: 12′–14′. These kinds of rites are more fully seen, together with their *Kultmittelbeschwörungen* in Shurpu tablet v–vi. "Curse" (*māmītu*) is to be peeled off like an onion, stripped off like dates, plucked apart like a tuft of wool, etc. See *CT* 4.5: 15–16 (noted in Reiner, *Šurpu*, 57) for onion peeling. Compare the Hittite Samuha ritual rs. 36–41, cited in chap. 1,

Finally, we may refer to ritual expressions of the hope that evils be removed far away from the patient. In Chapter Two (section 2.2) we saw examples from Mesopotamia where birds were sent away thereby effecting a removal of evil. The dispatch of a bird was used figuratively in incantations. A patient would hope that his sin or other evil be carried to heaven by a bird, or down to the depths of the sea by a fish.[99]

There are other incantations, found usually in namburbi rituals, which express the wish that the impurity be removed as far as possible from the patient. For example:

> May the evil of the *induḫallatu* lizard which fel[l] on m[e] and (the evil) of the *ṣurārû* lizard which I saw not approach me! May it not draw near! May it not com[e near]! May it not appear to me! May it cross the river! May it go over the mountain! May it be 3,600 miles distant! May it be released from my body! Like smoke may it ris[e to the heavens! Like an uprooted tamarisk let it not [return] to its place![100]

To conclude and summarize, Mesopotamian religion shows an interest in separating demonic impurities from the human sphere. The

---

section 1.3.7, where an onion is peeled in analogy of the removal of impurity.

Other examples of burning are: various figurines are burned on a *nappaṭu*-oven, then the oven is quenched and thrown into the river (*TuL* 118–19: 5–7); the paraphernalia of the substitute king is burned then buried (Lambert, "Part of the Ritual," 110: 1–8); images of sorcerers are burned (Maqlu ii 16, 146–47; iv 9–11, 105–116). Cf. Mayer, *Untersuchungen*, 163, on burning of figurines.

[99]See chap. 2.

[100]Caplice, "Namburbi Texts, I," 116: 5-9. Other examples: Caplice, "Namburbi Texts, I," 117: 22′–26′; "Namburbi Texts, II," 17: 13′–16′; 25: 10′–12′; 28: 11′–13′; 35 rs. 3′; "Namburbi Texts, III," 273: 11′–13′; 275: 22′–24′; 285: 7′–9′; rs. 6′–9′; 295–96 rs. 5–8; "Namburbi Texts, IV," 134: 12-15; Namburbi Texts, V," 162: 2′–4′; *OECT* 6, 24–27 vs. 11–13; *TuL* 51: 1–5. (bottom of the page); Lambert, "DINGIR.ŠÀ. DIB.BA," 274: 19–20; Reiner, "*Lipšur* Litanies," 136–39: 98–100. Note especially the incantation in Reiner, "*Lipšur* Litanies," 140–43: 7′–37′. All sorts of distance motifs are found here: "may my sin, like a drifting cloud, rain down into another field," "may my sin, like meteoric(?) iron, never return to its home," "may my sin like fresh water, never return to its place," etc. (Reiner's translations).

demons live where man does not—in the nether world and in related uninhabited places like the wilderness. When the demonic mingles with the human due to a person's sin or witchcraft, the person suffers, and rites are necessary to disentangle the two spheres and return evil to its origin. In such rites, we find incantations with statements directed at demons to make them return to their source. Furthermore, the disposal of impure materials resulting from the rituals is usually carried out in places that correspond to or are connected with the haunts of demons, such as the steppe, wilderness, river, enemy land, or the ground. All this shows that in Mesopotamia, disposal of evils was considered to be disposal in the nether world. Paralleling disposal in remote demonic locales are incantations expressing the hope that the evil will be removed a great distance from the patient. Burning of impure materials, too, shows the desire to remove the effect of such impurities from those affected. However, there is one anomaly in this picture: the disposal of impurity in the streets and plazas which are within the area of human habitation. To be sure, from the Mesopotamian ritual point of view, this was understood as disposal in the nether world. And indeed, the street posed no real problem as a disposal place since other refuse was dumped there. Nevertheless, such homebound defilement could maleficially affect persons. Thus an irresoluble tension must have existed between the ideal and actual practice in some Mesopotamian rituals of disposal.

9.4.2 Hittite Texts

In contrast to Mesopotamian rituals, evils disposed of in Hittite rituals are generally nondemonic.[101] Evidence of this nondemonic nature of evils is the preponderance of rituals that employ methods of purification centering solely on the removal of evil to the virtual exclusion of rites containing incantations exorcising demonic

---

[101]For this view, see O. Gurney, "The Hittite Ritual of Tunnawi," *JRAS* (1941) 58–59; *Some Aspects of Hittite Religion* (Oxford: Oxford University for the British Academy, 1977) 46–47; H. G. Güterbock, "Hittite Religion," *Forgotten Religions, Including Some Living Primitive Religions* (ed. V. T. A. Ferm; New York: Philosophical Library, 1949) 98; J. C. Moyer, "The Concept of Ritual Purity Among the Hittites," (PhD diss., Brandeis University, 1969) 140–41; H. M. Kümmel, "Die Religion der Hethiter," *Theologie und Religionswissenschaft* (ed. U. Mann;

personalities.[102] The evils removed in these rites, such as *papratar* "uncleanness," *alwanzatar* "sorcery," *ḫurtai-* "curse," *lingai-* "oath," *ešḫar* "blood, murder," *idalu- lala-* "evil tongue," *pangauwaš lala-* "the tongue of the many," *waštul-* "sin," *aštayaratar* "sin," and *idalu- inan* "evil sickness," to mention only a few, are nonvital, impersonal affections.[103] They are removed almost mechanically by using ritual detergents, objects of transfer, analogy, etc.,[104] and are generally given no attention as being personalities of any sort.

There are some exceptions to the foregoing picture of the nondemonic nature of evils, but these are few or restricted to certain types of evils. We recall from our study of Hittite parallels to the biblical scapegoat that a major evil was plague caused by an angry deity. The demonic nature of plagues is revealed in the Ashella ritual (cited in Chapter One, section 1.4.2, lines 19–23) where a plague is described as a god attacking human flesh. Of course, one may argue that since the etiology of plagues is, according to the Hittite description, a god (DINGIR), demonic evil strictly speaking is not found here.[105] Nevertheless, if demonic evil be defined as an unfavorable condition caused, exacerbated, or attended by malevolent supernatural beings as opposed to nondemonic evil where such beings are not present, then Hittite plagues must be considered demonic.

Other demonic beings that cause evil appear in Hittite sources. The ghosts of the dead are malevolent, especially the ones of persons who have been murdered. Rites are performed to appease them and to remove their "evil tongue."[106] In a ritual for healing, minor deities which are

---

Darmstadt: Wissenschaftliche Buchgesellschaft, 1973) 83–84; G. Furlani, "Il peccato nella religione degli Hittiti," *GSAI* 3 (1935) 136; D. H. Engelhard, "Hittite Magical Practices: An Analysis" (PhD diss., Brandeis University, 1970) 76.

[102]Cf. Gurney, *Aspects*, 46–47.

[103]On evils, see Engelhard, "Magical Practices," 61–62; Moyer, "The Concept of Ritual Purity," 38–40.

[104]See the motifs discussed in chap. 1, section 1.3.

[105]V. Haas, (*Hethitische Berggötter und hurritische Steindämonen* [Mainz: Philipp von Zabern, 1982] 173) translated DINGIR in the Ashella ritual as "Dämon." R. Stefanini (private communication) does not view angry gods as demons.

[106]G. F. del Monte, "Il terrore dei morti," *AION* 33 [n.s. 23] (1973) 373–85; A Ünal, "Einige Gedanken über das Totenopfer bei den

personified as sicknesses and hence demonic in nature are removed from a patient: "I have set aside Agalmati for you; I have repelled Annamiluli from your head; I have extinguished the fire in your head."[107] In the myth of the weather god at Lihzina, the *tarpi-* and *šipa-*, both evil-causing demons, are put in copper cauldrons in the sea so that they will henceforth be innocuous.[108] "Oath" is personified and called to partake of offerings of entreaty in another purification ritual.[109]

To recapitulate, evils in Hittite religion are generally nondemonic; demonic evils are infrequent.[110] As observed at the beginning of this section, this contrasts with the general demonic nature of evils in Mesopotamian religion. But though the evils disposed of in the two cultures are different, Hittite religion like Mesopotamian religion connects the disposal of evil with the underworld.[111]

A well known example showing that the place of evil is in the nether world is found in the Telepinu myth.[112] In the ritual section of the myth, Telepinu is called back from his place of hiding. His "wrath, anger, sin, and rage" are wished on their way to the underworld:

Hethitern," *Anadolu* 19 (1975–76) 177. Cf. the "terror of the dead" as an evil in Tunnawi iii 10.

[107]*KUB* 24.14 i 18–21. Cf. V. Haas, "Ein hethitisches Beschwörungsmotiv aus Kizzuwatna: seine Herkunft und Wanderung," *Or* 40 (1971) 411. The fuller ritual is transcribed and translated by Engelhard, "Magical Practices," 63–66.

[108]H. Hoffner, "Hittite *Tarpiš* and Hebrew *Terāphîm*," *JNES* 27 (1968) 65–66; "The Hittites and Hurrians," *Peoples of Old Testament Times* (ed. D. J. Wiseman; Oxford: Clarendon, 1973) 217, 227, n. 12; "An English-Hittite Glossary," *RHA* 25/80 (1967) 34 (under "demon"); and see below.

[109]House Purification iv 9–14.

[110]This topic needs to be investigated in detail.

[111]A. Goetze, *Kulturgeschichte Kleinasiens* (2d ed.; München: C. H. Beck, 1957) 159.

[112]On the placement of impurity in pots seen in the following examples, see Gurney, *Aspects*, 53; V. Haas, "Die Unterwelts- und Jenseitsvorstellungen im hethitischen Kleinasien," *Or* 45 (1976) 199–200; Hoffner, "Hittite *Tarpiš*," 65–66; "Second Millennium Antecedents to the Hebrew *ʾÔB*," *JBL* 86 (1967) 399; "Hittites and Hurrians," 217–18; M. Vieyra, "Ciel et enfers hittites," *RA* 59 (1965) 130; "Le sorcier hittite," *Le monde du sorcier* (SOr 7; Paris: Editions du Seuil, 1966) 114–15.

> Let it (i.e., the god's anger, etc.) go on the path of the Sun God of the underworld. The porter has opened the seven doors; he has drawn back the seven bolts. Below, in the Dark Earth, there stands a copper kettle, their [sic] cover is lead; their [sic] bolt is iron. Whatever goes in cannot come back out. In (it), it is destroyed. Let it seize Telepinu's wrath, anger, sin, and rage! Let it not come back![113]

The disposal of the anger and wrath of divinities is described in similar terms in the myths and rituals for other "disappearing" gods.[114]

The myth of the weather god at Lihzina contains an interesting variation of the foregoing picture of kettles of evil in the underworld, locating them in the sea:

> In the sea li[e] copper kettles. Their cover is lead. Therein he (i.e., the sun god) put [evil(?)[115]], he put the *tarpi*-demon, he put [ ], he put bloodshed, [he pu]t *ḫapanzi*-, he put sorrow,[116] he put tears, he put [ ], he put the *šipa*-demon,[117] [he put f]og, he put *ḫardi*-, [he] put sickness.[118]

In a ritual for the purification of a house, chthonic deities are called upon to take impurities to the underworld and fix them there:

---

[113]E. Laroche, "Textes mythologiques hittites en transcription," *RHA* 23 (1965) 97: 14–19; partially translated by Hoffner, "Hittite *Tarpiš*," 65, n. 33.

[114]"The Disappearance of the Weather God" (*CTH* 325), cf. Laroche, "Textes mythologiques," 118: 6–8; H. Otten and C. Ruster, "Textanschlüsse von Boğazköy-Tafeln (21–30)," *ZA* 63 (1973) 87; "Disappearance of DMAḪ" (*CTH* 334), cf. Laroche, "Textes mythologiques," 139: 5–9; Hoffner, "Hittite *Tarpiš*," 65, n. 34.

[115]This follows Hoffner, "Hittite *Tarpiš*," 65.

[116]Following Hoffner, "Hittite *Tarpiš*," 65, n. 30.

[117]Hoffner now rejects his suggestion of reading *lumpan* ("Hittite *Tarpiš*," n. 31) in favor of reading *ši-pa-an* ("The Hittites and Hurrians," 227, n. 12).

[118]*CTH* 331, cf. Laroche "Textes mythologiques," 130: 9–15; Hoffner, "Hittite *Tarpiš*," 65. These pots in the underworld have been compared to the Greek myth of Pandora's jar or box containing evils. See Hoffner, "Hittite *Tarpiš*," 66; "Second Millennium Antecedents," 399; Haas, "Die Unterwelts- und Jenseitsvorstellungen," 199–200.

> Anunnake gods, I have called you in regard to this matter. Decide the judgment of this house! Whatever evil bloodguilt is in it, take it and give it to the god of blood! Let him carry [it] down to the Dark Earth and there let him fix it![119]

Later on the officiator says:

> Memesarti of heaven and earth, Moon God, Ishhara, Oath, gods of curse and plague—whatever god who is hungry or thirsty—come! Eat! Drink! Give a[id] to me! Purify from house and city the evil, uncleanness, bloodguilt, oath, sin, curse! It has been bound at its feet and hands. Let the Dark Earth take it in![120]

One last incantation in this ritual is conceptually pregnant:

> As the ram mounts the ewe and it becomes pregnant, (so) may this city and building become a ram! May it mount the Dark Earth in the open country! M[ay] the Dark Earth become pregnant with bloodguilt, uncleanness, (and) sin! As a pregnant woman and sheep give birth, so may this city and building give birth to evil (and) bloodguilt! May the Dark Earth take it in [from(?)] the city![121]

Disposal in the underworld is also achieved by burying evils. An example from the Malli ritual (cited in Chapter One, section 1.3.9) makes this clear. The Old Woman collects the impurities to be disposed of plus various offering foods and goes outside. There she digs a hole, places the impurity in it, covers it up, and then hammers it down with pegs. She accompanies this action with an incantation:[122]

---

[119]House Purification iii 6–12.

[120]iv 9–15.

[121]iv 30–36.

[122]Malli ii 21′–25′. For other examples, see Malli ii 26′–33′; iv 5–10; Mastigga ii 26–34, 44–54; iii 14–18; StBoT 8 i 35–ii 3; iii 8–13; Huwarlu ii 36–41 (and see H. Kronasser, "Das hethitische Ritual KBo IV 2," *Die Sprache* 8 [1962] 98); Anniwiyani ii 6–8; *KUB* 30.34 iv 19–29 (cited above, chap. 1, n. 112). See Goetze, *Kulturgeschichte*, 159; Gurney, *Aspects*, 53; Hoffner, "Second Millennium Antecedents," passim; M. Vieyra, "Les noms du 'mundus' en hittite en assyrien et la phythonesse d'Endor," *RHA* 19/69 (1961) 47–55; Engelhard, "Magical Practices," 30.

> Whoever has bewitched this (person), now, I have taken his bewitching back (and) I have placed it down in the earth. I have fixed it. Let bewitching (and) evil dreams be fixed! Let it not come back up! Let the Dark Earth keep it!

Apart from digging a hole in which impure materials are put, impure water may be simply poured out on the ground and allowed to soak into the ground. This represents disposal in the nether world:

> Afterward, the offerer holds up three shekels of silver. He pours water from a *nammatu*-vessel on the three shekels of silver, while he says: "Whoever has spoken evil before the god, as the Dark Earth has swallowed down this water, thus may the Earth swallow down that evil word! Let these words be pure and untouched(?)! [L]et the god and offerer be pure from that [wo]rd!"[123]

Cathartic materials may be disposed of in rivers. For example, in the Ṭunnawi ritual, black clothing which is taken off of the patient is thrown into the river.[124] Disposing of impurities in seas and rivers, like burying and pouring out water, is a way of putting the evils in the underworld. The connection of the waters with the underworld is seen in the text (cited above) which describes the location of kettles of impurity in the sea. In texts of related content, these kettles are located in the underworld proper.

In the Huwarlu rite, mud from a river bank is used as a purifying detergent. The accompanying incantation says:

> Whatever evil word the gods keep seeing in the house, it has not overcome the house and man. This mud from the river bank has overcome it. Let it carry it back to the river bank! Let the Dark Earth overcome it![125]

---

[123]Samuha rs. 61–66. Cf. V. Haas and G. Wilhelm, *Hurritische und luwische Riten aus Kizzuwatna* (AOATS 3; Kevalaer and Neukirchen: Butzon und Bercker, and Neukirchener, 1974) 41; Haas, "Berggötter,"178.

[124]Tunnawi iii 12–16. See also Samuha rs. 48–50; Amihatna i 42–47; iii 30–39; House Purification iv 37–41. Cf. Engelhard, "Magical Practices," 185–87.

[125]Huwarlu i 50–54. On the connection of the sea and underworld, see Haas, "Die Unterwelts- und Jenseitsvorstellungen," 200; Goetze, *Kulturgeschichte*, 159.

Aside from disposing of evils in the nether world, Hittite texts also express the concern to remove impurity from the human environment. This idea is starkly seen in the Hittite laws:

> If someone purifies a person, he shall carry the leftover ritual materials to an *ukturi*- (literally: to [the] *ukturis*, plural). If he carries it to someone's field or house, it is sorcery (and) a case for the king.[126]

This law indirectly says that impure materials remaining after a purification rite could not be discarded at just any place. Because they were considered potentially damaging to those who would be near them or come in contact with them, they must be disposed of properly, specifically in an *ukturi*-.

What an *ukturi*- is is not entirely clear. The word (often plural but when in this form it is construed by translators as a singular) is connected with the adjective *ukturi*- "constant, continuous, eternal." Some have thought that an *ukturi*- was so named because a fire for burning corpses burned there continuously.[127] But this must be rejected since fires of this type are extinguished so that the bones might be gathered up.[128]

Though the etymology does not immediately help in defining the character of an *ukturi*-, a few texts show clearly that it was used as a place for disposing of evils. In one text we read:

> Let him purify it! Let him puri[fy hi]s land! Let him bring it to an *ukturi*- (literally a plural)! At (on, in?) the *ukturi*- (literally a plural) lies a kettle of iron. Its lid is of lead. Let him cover it![129]

In another:

> Kamrusepa purifies her house and hearth. She purifies her land. She purifies cattle and sheep and the pig and

---

[126]Law § 44b (see J. Friedrich, *Die hethitischen Gesetze* [DMOA 7; Leiden: Brill, 1971] 130–31; *ANET*, 191).

[127]Friedrich, *HW*[1], 233; H. Otten, *Hethitische Totenrituale* (DAWBIO 37; Berlin: Akademie, 1958) 141.

[128]A. Archi, "Il culto del focolare presso gli Ittiti," *SMEA* 16 (1975) 87; cf. Death Ritual 66:1–5, 12.

[129]*KUB* 9.11+ i 20–25, cited in E. Laroche, "Études de vocabulaire IV," *RHA* 53 (1951) 67; H. Otten, "[Review of *IBoT* 3]," *OLZ* 50 (1955) 393; *Totenrituale*, 141.

> little dog of man(?). She puts the impurity upon her head and goes to an *ukturi-* (literally a plural). In the *ukturi-* (literally a plural) everything is set (down).[130]

It is not certain whether the often found plural form of the word is evidence of the existence of multiple *ukturis.* One text, however, that deals with the cremation of corpses at an *ukturi-*[131] gives some evidence apart from that of the plural form of the word which suggests that there were several *ukturis.* The relevant passage reads: "At which *ukturi-* (literally plural) the dead burns, around that *ukturi-* (plural) they set down twelve loaves of bread."[132] The relative adjective construction here has a restrictive, not simply a descriptive, sense. It can be taken two ways. It may indicate that there were several *ukturi-* places, some for burning the dead and others for other purposes. Or it may indicate that there were several *ukturi-* places for burning the dead, only one or a few of which were used at any one time.

We can draw the following conclusions about an *ukturi-*: There are several *ukturi-* places. These are places for disposing of evil such as impure materials from purification rites and corpses. The impurities may be merely dumped there, burned, or placed in iron containers with lead lids. The implication from the law, cited above, is that *ukturis* are located apart from human habitation so that human fields or houses will not be harmed.[133]

---

[130]Bo 89 i 2–6, cited in Otten, *Totenrituale*, 141. Stefanini (private communication) has speculated on the basis of this mythological passage that *ukturi-* may have originally referred to the underworld meaning something like "the Eternal Place" and was used in a transferred sense of disposal places. This interesting idea requires further investigation.

[131]On cremation, Otten's index in *Totenrituale*, under *ukturi-*, esp. 66: 1, 10, 20. Also K. Bittel, "Hethitische Bestattungsbräuche," *MDOG* 78 (1940) 12–28; H. Otten, "Ein Totenritual hethitischen Könige," *MDOG* 78 (1940) 3–11; "Bestattungssitten und Jenseitsvorstellungen nach den hethitischen Texten," *WVDOG* 71 (1958) 81–84; L. Christman-Franck, "Le rituel des funérailles royales hittites," *RHA* 29 (1971) 61-111; Ünal, "Einige Gedanken"; O. Gurney, *The Hittites* (2d ed.; Middlesex: Penguin, 1954) 164-69; *Aspects*, 59-63. On cremation in ancient Palestine and Syria, see P. Bieńkowski, "Some Remarks on the Practice of Cremation in the Levant," *Levant* 14 (1982) 80–89 (on Hittite practice, see pp. 83–84).

[132]Death Ritual 66: 10–11.

[133]I do not believe the evidence allows the translation "pyre" (cf. Vieyra, "Ciel," 130; "Sorcier," 103; *CHD* L, 72a). The *ukturi-* is used for

The enemy land is a common place for the disposal of evils, especially plagues. We have already seen this in the Pulisa (lines 20–21), Ashella (lines 26–27), and Uhhamuwa (lines 23, 32–33) rituals studied in Chapter One where bearers of impurity carry plague back to enemy lands. In another plague ritual the offerer requests the angry deity to return to the foreign land whence he came:

> [Behold, I have come] before you, O god, with a sheep. You, god, who caused the plague, [turn back]! Go to the enemy land![134]

The return of evils to enemy lands is also a common theme in plague prayers.[135] For example, in a prayer to Telepinu, Mursili says:

> [Drive] the evil fe[ver], plague, famine, and grasshoppers(?)[136] from the land of Hatti. The enemy countries which are rebelling and angry . . . (here the text describes sacrilege committed by foreign peoples against Telepinu and his sancta) . . . [give] to these [enemy countries] evil fever, [plague, famine,] and grasshoppers![137]

Besides the foreign land, mountain areas, open plains, and meadows serve as disposal places.[138] In the Ambazzi ritual, the impurity laden mouse was sent to such areas: "Let this mouse take it to the high

---

more than cremation of the dead. Likewise, since burning does not always occur there, I would hesitate to translate it "burning-place" (cf. Friedrich, *Gesetze*, 31). It goes without saying that Goetze's translation of *kuptarra ukturiyaš* as "remnants of offerings" (*ANET*, 191) is no longer acceptable.

[134]Plague Ritual ii 6–9. Cf. lines 14–17. See Ambazzi iv 30–33.

[135]Cf. Mursili's second plague prayer (*CTH* 378 II; edited and translated by A. Goetze, "Die Pestgebete des Muršiliš," *Kleinasiatische Forschungen* 1 [1929] 206, 2:3; 214, 9:7); *KUB* 24.3 (*CTH* 376; edited by O. Gurney, "Hittite Prayers of Mursili II," *AAA* 27 [1940] pp. 28–29 C ii 31–37; pp. 32–33 D ii 14–15); Furlani, "Peccato," 142–43.

[136]The word is *karša-* (NAM logographically). *HW*[1] (102) and Hoffner ("Glossary," 47) both translated the word as "grasshopper(s)" with question marks. Goetze (*ANET*, 397) has "misery," but questions this.

[137]*KUB* 24.1 iii 16–iv 8 (parallels 24.2 vs. 10–11; and 24.3 iii 9–11). A translation of this text by Goetze appears in *ANET*, 397.

[138]See Haas, *Berggötter*, 110; Engelhard, "Magical Practices," 189–98. Cf. House Purification ii 57; iv 31, 44; Huwarlu ii 24–55.

mountains, the deep valley (and) the distant ways."[139] In a birth ritual, a goat which was touched to nine different areas of a patient's body "will carry off to the high mountains [ ]; it will carry off to the grass of the [Sun God]dess [of the earth]."[140]

As in Mesopotamian texts, Hittite texts also express the desire to remove evil far away from the patient's locale. In an analogy used in the purification of a house, the officiator says:

> As the wind blows chaff and carries it over the sea, thus may it blow the bloodguilt (and) uncleanness of this house and carry it over the sea![141]

In a birth ritual, threads and other materials representing evils are removed from a woman and placed near bread modeled in the shape of heavenly bodies. G. Beckman suggests that this manipulation represents the deposit of evils in the sky where they would be innocuous.[142]

Apart from disposing of evils in far away places, other methods may be used to make impurities harmless, such as burning them. In a ritual for DMAḪ and D*Gulšeš*, threads representing evil are put in a fire with the following accompanying analogy: "As I have [bu]rned [these threads] and they [will not return, so] may the (evil) words of the sorcerer [be burned] up!"[143]

---

[139]39–40; cited above in chap. 1, section 1.4.4.

[140]*KBo* 17.61 rs. 18 ′–19 ′, following G. Beckman's restoration ("Hittite Birth Rituals" [PhD diss., Yale University, 1977] 56, 74; cf. H. Otten and V. Souček, *Ein althethitisches Ritual für das Königspaar* [StBoT 8; Wiesbaden: Otto Harrassowitz, 1969] 97, n. 2). This goat is not actually dispatched, but killed (see rs. 22 ′–24 ′). Beckman ("Birth Rituals," 73–74) is correct in saying that these phrases about carrying away the evil are only metaphorical.

[141]House Purification ii 52–56. Cf. H. Otten's note in "Eine Beschwörung der Unterirdischen aus Boğazköi," *ZA* 54 (1961) 152.

[142]*KUB* 9.22+ iii 6–15 (Beckman, "Birth Rituals," 112, text H; see his commentary on pp. 137–38). Beckman's interpretation is supported by the expression in certain Akkadian rituals that the evil be removed to the heaven (see chap. 2, herein).

[143]*KUB* 17.27 iii 4–6 (restoration following Goetze, *ANET*, 347). On burning evils, see the *lustratio* rite in chap. 1, n. 112, where a goat is burned. Cf. Mastigga ii 5–14, 15–20, 22–24, etc. See Goetze, *Kulturgeschichte*, 159; Engelhard, "Magical Practices," 129–135.

Impurities may be sealed in containers to make them nondetrimental. We recall that in one ritual (cited above) purification materials were placed in an iron kettle and covered with a lead lid at an *ukturi*-.[144] In a ritual for the royal couple, the king and queen spit into a vessel which is then capped with a lead cover.[145] In the Mastigga ritual, the water with which the patients wash their heads, hands, and eyes is put in a bull's horn and is sealed, never to be opened until the "former kings" return.[146] This sealing of the water now impure after washing is to be considered an act of disposal.[147]

To conclude this section, the Hittites, like the Mesopotamians, perceived that the proper place of evil was the underworld and therefore developed a mythology and employed disposal methods that reflected this idea. But the Hittite view contrasts with that of Mesopotamia by considering most evils to be of a nondemonic and impersonal nature. Moreover, we hear very little, if anything, in Hittite texts about evils escaping from the underworld to afflict man. This makes us wonder if the disposal of impurity in Anatolia was considered a return of evil to its place of origin.

Hatti also sought to dispose of evils in remote locales, such as seas, rivers, the enemy land, mountainous areas, the open country, and in *ukturis*. Whether all of these places were to be ultimately connected with the underworld, as in the case of seas and rivers, is not clear. Further study and new texts will perhaps answer this question. Nevertheless, disposal in these places, as well as expressions of removing the evil beyond the sea or rites symbolizing the removal of impurity to the sky, show that a main concern was to discard evils so that they would no longer be deleterious to the people of Hatti. This same concern is found in burning, burying, or sealing up cathartic materials.

---

[144]We also recall the mythological scene of pots in the underworld containing evils with lids on them; see the discussion, above.

[145]StBoT 8 iv 34–36; cf. Haas, "Jenseitsvorstellungen," 199, n. 17.

[146]Mastigga iv 21–31. Cf. L. Rost, "Ein hethitisches Ritual gegen Familienzwist," *MIO* 1 (1953) 376; Haas, "Jenseitsvorstellungen," 209; H. Hoffner, "Histories and Historians of the Ancient Near East: The Hittites," *Or* 49 (1980) 329–30; Vieyra, "Ciel," 129; Ünal, "Gedanken," 177; Goetze, *Kulturgeschichte*, 171.

[147]Haas, "Jenseitsvorstellungen," 209; Vieyra, "Ciel," 129.

9.5 COMPARISON OF THE NONBIBLICAL CONCEPTION OF THE PLACE OF IMPURITY WITH THAT OF THE PRIESTLY WRITINGS

The main similarity we discover between the biblical and nonbiblical rites is the desire to remove evil far from the one affected. But how the different cultures achieve this is quite distinct. The Mesopotamian and Hittite rituals employ numerous means to thus remove evils. They bury them, discard them in seas or rivers, seal them in containers, send them to or deposit them in foreign lands, drive them to the wilderness or mountains, recite incantations banishing them away to distant places or the nether world, or burn them. The Priestly rituals, in contrast, are quite limited in their means of disposing of impurity. We do not find any burial, except in the case of corpses.[148] Impurities are not cast into a body of water,[149] sealed in containers, nor sent to the enemy land.[150] There are no incantations to express the hope that impurity will be removed. We only find dispatching impurity laden animals to the uninhabited wilderness or disposing of impurities there, burning, pouring impure *ḥaṭṭāʾt* blood at the base of the altar, and breaking

---

[148]In Second Temple times, the bird used to supply blood for the *ṣāraʿat* rite was buried. See chap. 2, n. 4.

[149]Cf. Mic 7:18–19: "Who is a God like you, forgiving transgression and forgiving iniquity for the remnant of his inheritance? He does not retain his anger forever because he desires kindness. He will again have compassion on us; he will overcome our transgressions—you will cast all their sins into the depths of the sea." Certainly this imagery obtains from the general milieu of Near Eastern disposal rites. Later Judaism developed a rite which took its name, *tašlîk*, from this verse. Part of the rite consisted of shaking out one's pockets into a body of water, which, from a popular point of view, symbolizes the transfer of sins to fish in the sea (cf. "Tashlikh," *EncJud* 15 [1972] 829–30; J. Z. Lauterbach, *Rabbinic Essays* [Cincinnati: Hebrew Union College, 1951] 299–433; A. Y. Brawer, "Sending the Goat to Azazel and the Bird of the Leper—Symbolic *Tašlîk*," *Beth Mikra* 12/30 [1967] 33 [Hebrew]). Disposal of evil in a river might be seen in Naaman's purification from *ṣāraʿat* in the Jordan (2 Kgs 5:10, 14; see n. 74, above) and possibly in the rite in Deut 21:1–9 where the heifer is killed by a perpetually flowing wadi (*naḥal ʾêtān*). Supposedly, its blood will flow away in the stream leaving the land unpolluted (see D. P. Wright, "Deuteronomy 21:1–9 as a Rite of Elimination," *CBQ*, forthcoming).

pottery. This limitation of disposal to just a few methods can be attributed to the systematization of methods of purification by Priestly writers.

The Priestly system has also given the rites a common goal of purification, which is to protect the sanctuary's holiness and the community's purity. The nonbiblical rites, on the other hand, have no common goal. At times they seek to establish the well-being of the sanctuary as in the *akītu* festival, or of society as in the Hittite plague rituals. But most often they are oriented toward the personal well-being of a suffering patient, with no larger social or cultic orientation.

Another and perhaps the most important contrast is the lack of demonic and underworld mythology in the Priestly disposal rites. The evil removed by these rites is not caused by the agency of demons.[151] The impurity is impersonal. Furthermore, the Bible in none of its sources has developed or perpetuated the concept that impurity originates from or belongs in the nether world (see Chapter One). Nor is there any real evidence that the wilderness, where several impurities are placed, and the nether world have a conceptual connection or that demons are connected with the underworld. The only hint of a connection between impurities and demons is in the dispatch of the scapegoat to Azazel in the wilderness. But it is clear that the position and function of Azazel has been greatly downplayed in this ritual. Therefore, the apparent connection exhibited here between impurity and the demon should also be downplayed and not be taken as indicative of a belief that impurities

---

[150]Cf. Zech 5:5–11 where the prophet sees an ephah-size container approach with a lead lid. Inside is a woman who represents wickedness (*hārišʿā;* v 8). This woman is cast into the container and the lid is set on the top of it. Two winged women come—a variation of disposal by means of birds, see chap. 2 of this work—and carry the container away in the air to be enshrined in Shinar (i.e., Babylonia). This prophetic image appears to derive from Near Eastern (specifically Hittite or North Syrian?) methods of disposing of evils in sealed containers. Note that this is an example of disposing of evils in the foreign or enemy land. Another example of disposal in an enemy's land in the Bible is the Philistine rite returning the ark and plague in 1 Sam 5–6.

[151]Contra B. Levine, *In the Presence of the Lord* (SJLA 5; Leiden: Brill, 1974) 79–91 and Neusner, *Idea of Purity,* 9–12. See J. Milgrom, "Israel's Sanctuary: The Priestly 'Picture of Dorian Gray,'" *RB* 83 (1976), 390-99; "The Graduated *Ḥaṭṭāʾt* of Lev 5:1–13," *JAOS* (1983) 252.

are sent to demons or demonic places.[152] The lack or limitation of this mythological connection of the underworld and impurity disposal in the Priestly writings is in striking contrast to the frequent mention of it in Hittite and Mesopotamian rituals. The silence of the biblical text about this view in comparison to the nonbiblical rites must surely mean that the concept has been purposefully dropped and ignored by Priestly writers in reaction to pagan beliefs.

---

[152]See chap. 1, section 1.1.3.

10

Conclusions

The main goal of this study has been to determine the system of ideas expressed by the Priestly rituals of disposal in the Bible. This goal has been achieved by a detailed descriptive investigation of each of the instances of the disposal of nonhuman bearers of impurity (Chapters One through Seven), by an analysis of the examples of the restriction and exclusion of human impurities (Chapter Eight), and by examining the notion of the place of impurity in the Priestly writings (Chapter Nine). An investigation of Hittite and Mesopotamian rites for the disposal of evils and the conception of the place where impurities are to be discarded has also contributed to reaching the aims of this study.

Comparison of the nonbiblical data with that in the Priestly writings produces a number of major observations. Though in this comparison one specific literary tradition in ancient Israel (i.e., P) is being compared to several combined traditions in the neighboring societies, the results of the comparison are instructive nonetheless. One conclusion is that the methods of disposal in P are not as extensive or radical as those in the nonbiblical rites. In the nonbiblical rites, evils and impure materials are buried, cast into a body of water (rivers, seas, or springs), sealed in containers, sent to the enemy land, driven to wilderness or mountainous areas, or burned. In the Priestly rites we only find the dispatch of impurity laden animals to the wilderness, the deposit of impurities outside the habitation, burial (only in the case of corpses), burning, pouring *ḥaṭṭāʾt* blood at the base of the altar, and breaking pottery.

In addition to the extensive means of disposal, the nonbiblical rites by their very quantity appear to have been used frequently. These rites are also very complex, often being composed of a long series of minor acts of elimination and purification. In the Priestly legislation, we find only a handful of elimination rites, and when these are compounded with other methods of purification, the resulting series are relatively short and simple. The use of elimination rites as conceived of by the Priestly system was probably not as frequent as in the other cultures we have studied. If one considers that the scapegoat rite was to occur only once each year, that the sanctuary *ḥaṭṭāʾt* described at the beginning of Lev 4 would have been performed infrequently, and that *ṣāraʿat* was probably a rare affliction, then elimination rites having close similarities with foreign rites such as we find in Anatolia and Mesopotamia (i.e., the scapegoat, the burning of the sanctuary *ḥaṭṭāʾt*, and the dispatch of birds) would have been quantitatively limited.

Related to the limiting of the methods and use of disposal in the Priestly legislation is the limitation of the evils removed by such rites. In the nonbiblical cultures elimination rites are used to remove all sorts of evils (sickness, plague, sin, witchcraft, sorcery, etc.) while in the Priestly literature they are used only to remove ritual impurity, except for the case of the scapegoat which carries away transgressions. Notably, in purifying from *ṣāraʿat*, the object of purification is not the disease or a sin that might have caused it, but the residual ritual impurity remaining after a person with *ṣāraʿat* has recovered (see Chapter Two, section 2.4).

Another important conclusion of this study is that the Priestly literature does not conceive of the disposal of impurity as disposal in the nether world as do Hittite and Mesopotamian cultures. The Priestly view is determined by other concerns. Its system of disposal is defined in relation to the sanctuary and the sanctuary habitation. All impurity must be kept away from the sanctuary and its sancta. Impurities that are communicable to the profane sphere must be kept apart from pure people and things in the habitation in order to preserve a general status of purity there. These severe impurities are either excluded from or disposed of outside the habitation, or restricted inside it. Incorrigible impurities are also destroyed to preserve purity. Only purifiable noncommunicable impurities, which are short-lived, can exist unrestricted in the community (see Chapters Eight and Nine).

In contrast to the Priestly examples, the nonbiblical rites do not exhibit a thoroughgoing concern to keep sanctuaries pure and to keep people pure for cultic purposes. It is true that there are some rites whose goal is to purify a sanctuary or to purify people for cultic activities. But these form only a small percentage of the total number of such rites in these cultures. More often than not, these rites have individual and personal orientation, seeking to remove the evils that affect a person.

This limitation in the methods of disposal and in the evils associated with it, and the orientation of disposal rites to the sanctuary are the peculiar stamp of Priestly system on rituals that presumably existed in a form more similar to Hittite and Mesopotamian disposal rites at a period prior to incorporating them into Priestly legislation. We found evidence of the pre-Priestly existence of the scapegoat rite in the name Azazel which has persisted in the Priestly form of the rite (see Chapter One, section 1.6). We also have good reason to suppose that the bird rite for purification from *ṣāraʿat* impurity existed in a pre-Priestly form (see Chapter Two). Priestly legislation has adopted these rites but has changed them to give them an expression concordant with its conceptual system. We may also suppose that implicit in the adaptation of these rites is a polemic against pagan rites of a similar nature. The reinterpretation of certain aspects of these rites would serve to guard against adopting pagan practices and ideas.

Appendix 1

The Disposal of Idolatrous Impurities in the Non-Priestly texts of the Bible

Non-Priestly sections of the Bible contain examples of the disposal and destruction of idolatrous materials or imagery connected with this phenomenon. A review of these passages will add perspective to our study of impurity disposal in the Priestly literature.

IN THE BOOKS OF KINGS AND CHRONICLES

The books of Kings and Chronicles say that certain reforming kings—Asa, Hezekiah, Manasseh, and Josiah—had occasion to root up various idolatrous accessories from the temple and around Jerusalem and dispose of them in the Kidron Valley, east of the city.[1]

---

[1]It is not integral to this study to assess the historical accuracy of the various examples of the disposal of idolatrous materials adduced below. Even those examples attested only in Chronicles which are perhaps tendentious creations, such as the repentance of Manasseh and his destruction of idolatrous materials, still reflect how these items might be discarded. On the tendency toward reform and the historical accuracy of the reports of such acts, see F. L. Moriarty, "The Chronicler's Account of Hezekiah's Reform," *CBQ* 27 (1965) 399–406.

(a) 1 Kgs 15:13; 2 Chr 15:16. Among Asa's efforts to restrict idolatry in Judah was cutting down an image[2] that the royal lady, Maacha, had made, crushing it to dust, and burning it in the Kidron Valley.

(b) 2 Chr 29:5, 16. When Hezekiah became king, he opened up the temple and made preparations to resanctify it. He commanded the Levites to remove the impurity (*niddâ*,[3] v 5; *ṭumʾâ*, v 16). The priests entered the temple building and brought out the impurity to the temple court. The Levites then took the impurity outside to the Kidron.

It is not clear what specific impurity is intended by the terms *niddâ* and *ṭumʾâ*. From the context of chapters 28 and 29, it could be said that general accumulated debris in the temple, and not idolatrous materials, were the object of disposal.[4] According to 28:24 (cf. 2 Kgs 16:17–18), Ahaz closed the temple down and pursued idolatrous practices outside the temple area. Hezekiah's call for resanctification was to rectify the closure of the temple. He opened the doors (2 Chr 29:3) and ordered the purification and sanctification of the temple

> because our fathers committed sacrilege and did what was evil in the sight of the Lord our God and forsook him. They turned their faces from the Lord's dwelling place, they turned their backs. Moreover, they shut

---

[2]The exact meaning of *mipleṣet* is unclear. The root *plṣ* indicates shaking, as of an earthquake (Job 9:6) or from horror and terror (Isa 21:4; Ezek 7:18; Ps 55:6; Job 21:6). Thus a meaning like "terrifying image" is suggested (cf. J. A. Montgomery and H. S. Gehman, *A Critical and Exegetical Commentary on the Book of Kings* [ICC; New York: Charles Scribner's Sons, 1951] 275; J. Gray, *I and II Kings: A Commentary* [OTL, 2d ed.; Philadelphia: Westminster, 1970] 348; J. M. Myers, *II Chronicles* [AB 13; Garden City: Doubleday, 1965] 87, 89; W. F. Albright, *Archaeology and the Religion of Israel* [5th ed.; Baltimore: Johns Hopkins, 1968; reprint, Garden City: Doubleday, 1968] 153; Kimhi, Altschuler, Levi ben Gershom).

[3]*Niddâ* here is to be taken in a general sense as "impurity," as the parallel *ṭumʾâ* shows. Cf. Ezek 7:19, 20; Lam 1:17; Ezra 9:11. See J. Milgrom and D. P. Wright, "*Niddāh*," *TWAT* 5 (1984) 250–53.

[4]For this view, see E. L. Curtis and A. A. Madsen, *A Critical and Exegetical Commentary on the Books of Chronicles* (ICC; New York: Charles Scribner's Sons, 1910) 464; I. Benzinger, *Die Bücher der Chronik* (KHC; Tübingen: J. C. B. Mohr, 1901) 122.

> the doors of the porch, put out the lamps, did not burn incense, and did not offer burnt offerings in the sanctuary to the God of Israel (vv 6–7).

All of this appears to indicate that the impurity removed was dirt that had collected since the closure of the temple. Nonetheless, there is some reason to believe that idolatrous impurities are, in fact, to be included in the terms *niddâ* and *ṭumʾâ*.[5] Just before the Chronicler tells us that Ahaz closed the temple, we are informed that he began to sacrifice to Syria's gods (28:22–23). This datum concerning Ahaz's idolatry apparently comes from the Chronicler's interpretation of 2 Kgs 16:10–16. These verses tell about the new altar Ahaz erected in the temple court following the design of an altar in Damascus. Though the writer of the passage in Kings did not openly consider the new altar to be idolatrous, it was obviously such for the Chronicler.[6] The Chronicler does not say where Ahaz's Damascus inspired worship took place, but it is clear that it was in the temple court where the altar was. Such idolatrous practice would naturally be accompanied by idolatrous materials. These materials would consequently be an object of disposal in Hezekiah's reform in chapter 29. Further support for interpreting *niddâ* and *ṭumʾâ* as including idolatrous impurities comes from the other passages that we are considering in this chapter in which reforming kings dispose of idolatrous impurities outside the city. One would expect the impurities that Hezekiah discarded outside the city to be of a similar nature.[7]

(c) 2 Chr 30:14. Those gathered in Jerusalem to take part in the Passover sponsored by Hezekiah removed the altars that were in the city and threw them into the Kidron.

(d) 2 Chr 33:15. The Chronicler, who tells us the story of Manasseh's repentance, says that the converted king removed idols from the temple and altars that he had built on the temple mount and around

---

[5]Rashi; Kimhi; Altschuler; C. F. Keil and F. Delitzsch, *Biblical Commentary on the Old Testament* (25 vols.; Grand Rapids: Eerdmans, 1950–56) 7. 450; W. Rudolph, *Chronikbücher* (HAT 1/21; Tübingen: J. C. B. Mohr, 1955) 295.

[6]Cf. Myers, *II Chronicles*, 163–64.

[7]Rudolph (*Chronikbücher*, 195, n. 4) gives another reason for including idolatrous impurities. The term *niddâ* is much too strong to indicate only dust and filth. Idolatrous objects must therefore be included also. Similarly, the *NJPS* translation has "abhorrent things" for *niddâ*.

Jerusalem, and threw them outside the city.[8] Though the exact place of disposal is not mentioned, the writers may have intended it to be the Kidron as the other examples in this study show.

(e) 2 Kgs 23:4, 6, 12. The most vigorous and thoroughgoing reformer, Josiah, removed from the temple the objects made for Baal, Asherah, and astral divinities, and burned them in the fields of the Kidron (*šadmôt qidrôn*,[9] v 4). He took the Asherah image out of the temple to the Kidron and burned it, crushed it, and scattered the dust on the graves of the people (v 6). He also broke apart the roof altars that former apostate kings had made and the altars Manasseh had put in the two courts of the temple and hurriedly cast the pieces into the Kidron.

---

[8]This is a contradiction of 2 Kgs 23:12 which says that Josiah needed to remove Manasseh's altars which were in the temple courts.

[9]M. R. Lehmann ("A New Interpretation of the Term *Šdmwt*," *VT* 3 [1953] 361–71) followed by J. S. Croatto and J. A. Soggin ("Die Bedeutung von *Šdmwt* im Alten Testament," *ZAW* 74 [1962] 44–50; see also N. J. Tromp, *Primitive Conceptions of Death and the Nether World in the Old Testament* [BibOr 21; Rome: Pontifical Biblical Institute, 1969] 50–53) have suggested connecting Hebrew *šdmwt* with Ugaritic *šdmt* meaning "field of (the god) Mot." Though the Hebrew word may in some way be connected with the term (there are philological problems which make this difficult, see Croatto and Soggin, "Bedeutung," 49–50; Tromp, *Primitive Conceptions*, 52), it does not appear that understanding the original etymology explains the Hebrew and the passages in which it occurs. Lehmann has incorrectly assessed the contextual meanings of *šdmwt* in Hebrew in anticipation of his conclusion that *šdmwt* has a negative chthonic cultic and mythological significance in the Bible. Two of his initial assumptions (p. 361) need to be reviewed. He states that (1) the word "always carries a connotation of non-Jewish pagan cults and/or peoples" and (2) when it occurs "in the agricultural sense, it bears the character of aridity and barrenness." The first assumption is in fact not evident in the contexts of the passages he lists (Deut 32:32; 2 Kgs 23:4; Isa 16:8; Jer 31:39; Hab 3:17). Though *šdmwt* is used with geographical names (some those of foreign peoples) it in no way has a non-Jewish cult connotation. Lehmann has read his conclusion about *šdmwt* into this assumption. In regard to the second assumption, when *šdmwt* appears in the agricultural sense (and in reality, this is the only sense it has), it indicates lushness or fruitfulness, not aridity or barrenness. It is paralleled by *tĕʾēnâ* "fig," *maʿăśê zayit* "olive produce," *ṣōʾn* "flock," and *bāqār* "herd" (Hab 3:17). Three of the five passages in which *šdmwt* occurs have parallels relating to the vine crop (*gepen*; Deut 32:32; Isa 16:8; Hab

THE IMPURE CHARACTER OF IDOLATROUS MATERIALS

The impurities discarded by these kings consisted of idols and their appurtenances, except for the case of Hezekiah where general accumulated debris were included. The Priestly writings do not discuss idols in their system of impurity and thus it appears that such items were not actually impure in the levitical sense.[10] Nevertheless, since these items were bound up with the serious sin of idolatry which threatened the whole structure of Israelite religion, they were highly abhorred and, consequently, termed impure in non-Priestly writings.[11] For example, Jeremiah relates that the Israelites had polluted the temple by placing their idolatrous abominations in it (Jer 7:30; 32:34). Ezekiel echoes this in his writings (5:11; cf. Chapter Eight, above). The Chronicler says that the priestly officers and people similarly polluted the temple (2 Chr 36:14). Idols themselves defile those in contact with them in a

---

3:17). The contexts of the Hebrew word are sufficient to yield the meaning "plantations, gardens, vineyards" for *šdmwt*.

Two passages that concern us in this appendix locate *šdmwt* in and around the Kidron Valley (2 Kgs 23:4 and Jer 31:39 [in the latter written *šrmwt*, but read *šdmwt*]). Some have thought that plantation areas in the Kidron would be impossible since the valley is a ravine (cf. J. Gray, *Kings*, 730). However, it is possible that *šdmwt* in these passages refers to the garden areas of the Kidron south of the Gihon spring. Kings had gardens in this area (2 Kgs 25:4; Jer 39:4; 52:7; Neh 3:15; the Fountain Gate and King's Pool were at the southern tip of the City of David; the Gate between the Two Walls may be the same as the Fountain Gate; see *The Book of Jerusalem [Seper Yerušalayim]* [ed. M. Avi-Yonah, vol. 1; Jerusalem and Tel-Aviv: Bialik Institute and Dvir, 1956] map 9; G. A. Barrois, "Fountain Gate," *IDB* 2 [1962], 323a; see also the map in *IDB* 3, 533). See D. Ussishkin, "*Qidrôn*," *EM* 7 (1976) 33–35.

[10]In the Holiness Code, Molech worship pollutes the Tabernacle (Lev 20:3). It is the sin, however, that pollutes and not any particular idolatrous instrument. In Lev 18:24, 30, Israel is warned not to defile itself by various practices, including Molech worship (v 21). This defilement is of a religious and moral nature, not of a levitical nature which necessitates purification rituals. Idols and other things are proscribed in 19:4 and 26:1–2, but no impurity is attributed to them.

[11]Cf. J. Döller, *Die Reinheits- und Speisegesetze des Alten Testaments in religionsgeschichtlicher Beleuchtung* (ATAbh 7/2–3; Münster: Aschendorff, 1917) 1–5.

noncultic sense (Ezek 20:7, 18; 22:3–4; 23:7, 30; 36:18, 25; 37:23). Idolatrous worship in general contaminates those who take part in it (Jer 2:22–23; Ezek 20:30; Ps 106:39). On the day of the Lord's wrath, materials and ornaments used for idols will be considered unclean (Ezek 7:19–21). Israel will consider idols unclean and throw them away as one would ostracize a menstruous woman (Isa 30:22).[12]

Antipathy toward idols is also evident in Deuteronomy which demands the destruction of idolatrous materials since they are *ḥērem*. The Israelites are cautioned to destroy all foreign cult installations and images (Deut 7:5). If they do not, a person appropriating a cult object will fall under the category of *ḥērem* with the idol (vv 25–26). The transfer of *ḥērem* status is conceptually similar to pollution from impurities.[13] But it is more serious than any type of contamination from impurities. Implicit in this transfer of status to the one who takes possession of an idol is a death sentence. Just as Achan, who pilfered *ḥērem* from Jericho, was put to death with his family and animals (Josh 7), so must the person who takes an idol.[14] Moreover, in Deuteronomy idolatry is apostasy for which the remedy is death.[15]

---

[12]Cf. also Gen 35:2; Zech 13:2; Ezra 9:11.

[13]Though I call this a *transfer* of *ḥērem* status, I do not mean that it is an impurity. Leviticus describes *ḥērem* as an extreme form of dedication and calls things so dedicated "most holy" (27:28; see chap. 9 n. 5). Thus the transfer of *ḥērem* status should be viewed as a type of sancta contagion. For a valuable discussion of this question, see J. Milgrom, "Sancta Contagion and Altar/City Asylum," *VTSup* 32 (1981) 296, n. 51. M. Greenberg ("Some Postulates of Biblical Criminal Law," *Yehezkel Kaufmann Jubilee Volume* [ed. M. Haran; Jerusalem: Magnes, 1960] 23-24) says the infective character of *ḥērem* is "wholly analogous to the contagiousness of the state of impurity."

[14]In instruction preparatory to the attack on Jericho, Joshua warns the Israelites not to take any of the *ḥērem* lest the whole camp become *ḥērem* (Josh 6:18). Achan disobeyed and the camp fell under this status (7:12). It appears that by determining that Achan was at fault, the *ḥērem* status was narrowed down to him. By putting him to death, Israel was then free of the status. On the transfer of *ḥērem* status, see 1 Kgs 20:42, where Ahab is judged as one who must give his life for letting Ben-Hadad, a man put under *ḥērem* by God, go free.

[15]In Deut 13, apostate individuals are put to death. Of particular note is that if a whole city apostatizes, it becomes *ḥērem* and all its people, cattle, and spoil are destroyed (vv 13–19). Also in Deuteronomy, foreign

In the rabbinic system of impurities, the idol and its accompaniments have been adapted to the Priestly system of impurity. The idol and its appurtenances pollute like a *šereṣ* carcass or like a menstruant.[16] That it can pollute like a *šereṣ* carcass is derived from Deut 7:26 which says that Israelites are to abhor (*šiqqēṣ*) idols. Since *šereṣ* animals are termed *šeqeṣ* in the Bible (cf. Lev 7:21 and chap. 11, throughout), the idol carries a similar impurity.[17] That an idol can pollute like a menstruant is derived from Isa 30:22 which mentions throwing away idols as if they were a menstruous woman. Furthermore, according to the rabbinic system, an idolatrous temple can pollute persons and objects by overhang.[18] Foods and wine that are offerings for an idol also pollute as carrion (*nĕbēlâ*).[19] In view of the temple cleansing passages and the other passages dealing with the impurity of and aversion toward idols and idolatrous worship, the assimilation of idols into the scheme of Priestly impurity by the Rabbis was a very natural and reasonable development.[20]

THE PLACE OF DISPOSAL

All examples of the riddance of idolatrous impurities from Kings and Chronicles, except for 2 Chr 33:15, explicitly state that the disposal occurred in the Kidron Valley. Also of note are the locative phrases "outside" (2 Chr 29:16), "outside Jerusalem" (2 Kgs 23:4, 6), and "outside the city" (2 Chr 33:15). The mention of the Kidron as the disposal place and the locative phrases show that the concern was to

---

peoples in Israel's inhabited land are *ḥērem* and must be destroyed because of the threat of leading Israelites into apostasy (Deut 7; 20:15–18). To be compared is Exod 22:19 where those who worship other gods acquire *ḥērem* status. See M. Greenberg, "Herem," *EncJud* 8 (1971) 344–50.

[16]*M. Šabb.* 9:1; *ʿAbod. Zar.* 3:6; *t. Zabim* 5:6 (cf. 5:5); *b. Šabb.* 82b; Maimonides, *MTor*, Ṭohora, Šeʾar ʾAbot haṭṬumʾot 6:1–5.

[17]See chap. 8, n. 63.

[18]*M. ʿAbod. Zar.* 3:6; *t. Zabim* 5:7; Maimonides, *MTor*, Ṭohora, Šeʾar ʾAbot haṭṬumʾot 6:6.

[19]*B. Ḥul.* 13b, 129a; *ʿAbod. Zar.* 29b; *t. Zabim* 5:8; Maimonides, *MTor*, Ṭohora, Šeʾar ʾAbot haṭṬumʾot 6:7–8; cf. *m. ʿAbod. Zar.* 2:3; 5:1.

[20]For a discussion of idolatrous impurity in the rabbinic system, see E. Feldman, *Biblical and Post-Biblical Defilement and Mourning: Law as Theology* (New York: Ktav and Yeshiva University, 1977) 45–47; J. Neusner, *The Idea of Purity in Ancient Judaism* (SJLA 1; Leiden: Brill, 1973) 13–18 (in the apocryphal literature, see pp. 34–38).

remove the impurity from the city's boundaries. The Kidron was chosen since it was an accepted disposal site close to the temple. We have already encountered examples of the disposal of other impurities in the Kidron. It was used as a burial area (see Chapter Five, section 5.3) and in Second Temple times there was a conduit which brought sacrificial blood, among other things, to the valley (see Chapter Seven, section 7.3.2).

Another indication that the Kidron and other valley areas around Jerusalem were places of impurity and refuse is found in Jeremiah's prophecy of the holiness that these places would receive when Jerusalem is rebuilt and extended in its boundaries:

> And the entire valley of corpses and ashes,[21] and all the fields[22] to the Kidron Valley to the corner of the Horse Gate on the east, shall be holy to the Lord (Jer 31:39).

---

[21] *Kol-hāʿēmeq happĕgārîm wĕhaddešen*, despite the definite article with *ʿēmeq*, is in construct relationship. The uncomfortable article is due to *kol* which causes the article to automatically follow, though technically incorrect and unexpected (cf. Josh 8:11; 1 Kgs 14:24; Ezek 45:16; GKC § 127g). Thus the phrase *happĕgārîm wĕhaddešen* need not be considered a gloss (cf. the commentaries).

It is not clear what is meant by the "valley of *pĕgārîm* and *dešen*." *Dešen* could refer to ashes from the temple altar (cf. Lev 6:3–4.; 1 Kgs 13:3, 5) and thus part of the name of the valley could come from its being the place where the altar ashes were disposed of (the ash dump; Lev 1:16; 4:12; 6:4; see chap. 6 of this work; cf. Rashi; Kimhi; Altschuler; J. Bright, *Jeremiah: A New Translation with Introduction* [AB 21; Garden City: Doubleday, 1965] 283). From such a cultic context, *pĕgārîm* could refer to carcasses of sacrificial animals disposed of in the valley (cf. Exod 29:14; Lev 4:12, 21; 8:17; 9:11; 16:27; see chap. 6 herein). Support for *pgr* meaning "offering carcass" may be drawn from Gen 15:11 (cf. J. Ebach, "*Pgr* = (Toten–) Opfer? Ein Vorschlag zum Verständnis von Ez. 43:7. 9," *UF* 3 [1971] 368, n. 15). This interpretation is taken by D. Hoffmann (*The Book of Leviticus [Seper Wayyiqraʾ]* [2 vols.; Jerusalem: Mossad Harav Kook, 1953] 1. 159, n. 4) and B. Duhm (*Das Buch Jeremia* [KHC 11; Tübingen: J. C. B. Mohr, 1901] 260).

I, however, question this interpretation of *pĕgārîm* since in all other instances, including Gen 15:11, *pgr* has a pejorative connotation, referring to human or animal carcasses (see my remarks in chap. 5, section 5.5). It seems unlikely that a place connected with the legitimate

Though there are textual, semantic, and geographical difficulties, the expectation that the valley areas would be made holy shows that they were considered unclean in some way. This notion of uncleanness would arise in part from the valleys being places of disposal.

---

cult, even though it was a dump site, would have a negative appellation. Taking a cue from the negative aspect of *pgr*, *pĕgārîm* could refer to corpses, or in this context, graves (cf. B. Mazar, *The Excavations in the Old City of Jerusalem Near the Temple Mount: Preliminary Report of the Second and Third Seasons, 1969–1970* [Jerusalem: Israel Exploration Society, 1971] 34). Thus this part of the name would indicate a place for burial.

But to understand the name of the valley as referring to the place where corpses were buried and where sacrificial ashes were deposited is still questionable, mainly because of the geographical line drawn in vv 37–39. It starts at the Tower of Hananel, north of Jerusalem, and appears to run counter clockwise down the western border, through the Hinnom Valley, over to the Kidron and northward up to the Horse Gate. If so, then the "valley of *pĕgārîm* and *dešen*" would have to be the Hinnom Valley (cf. W. F. Birch, "Note on Jer 31:38–40," *Palestine Exploration Fund Quarterly Statement* [1882] 58–59; P. Haupt, "Hinnom and Kidron," *JBL* 38 [1919] 45; L. E. Elliott-Binns, *The Book of the Prophet Jeremiah, with Introduction and Notes* [London: Methuen, 1919] 241; F. Nötscher, *Das Buch Jeremias* [HSAT 7/2; Bonn: Peter Hanstein, 1934] 237; Bright, *Jeremiah*, 283; J. A. Thompson, *The Book of Jeremiah* [NICOT; Grand Rapids: Eerdmans, 1980] 583–85). (W. Rudolph, [*Jeremia* (HAT 1/12, 3d ed.; Tübingen: J. C. B. Mohr, 1968) 205–06] connects the valley with the Rephaim Valley.) It is difficult to imagine that the disposal of altar ashes took place in the Hinnom Valley when the Kidron was much closer and accessible to the temple, as the examples of the disposal of idolatrous impurities found in the temple show.

For me, the proper interpretation is to connect the terms "corpses and ashes" with the illicit Tofet cult so often criticized by Jeremiah (2:23; 7:31–34; 19:1–6; 32:35). Children were sacrificed in the Hinnom Valley and burned as burnt offerings (7:31; 19:5; cf. 32:35). Thus the valley gets its name from the corpses of the children and the ashes from burning them as offerings (cf. F. Giesebrecht, *Das Buch Jeremia* [HKAT 3/2.1; Göttingen: Vandenhoeck und Ruprecht, 1894] 173–74; Nötscher, *Jeremias*, 237; A. Weiser, *Das Buch des Propheten Jeremiah* [ATD 20-21, 2 vols.; Göttingen: Vandenhoeck und Ruprecht, 1952–55] 2. 297–98; W. Rudolph, *Jeremia*, 205–07).

[22]See n. 9, above.

OTHER METHODS OF DISPOSAL

Finally, it may be noted that besides dumping outside the city, idolatrous impurities were also disposed of by burning and burying. In the examples adduced above, Asa and Josiah employed burning as part of the disposal process. There are other descriptions or prescriptions concerning the burning of idols. Moses burned the golden calf that the Israelites had made (Exod 32:20; Deut 9:21). David burned Philistine idols that were abandoned in battle (1 Chr 14:12).[23] Jehu burned cult pillars from the temple of Baal (2 Kgs 10:26). Josiah, in addition to the reforms already described, burned an Asherah at Bethel (2 Kgs 23:15) and also the bones of idolatrous priests whose ashes he then scattered on pagan altars in order to desecrate them (1 Kgs 13:2; 2 Kgs 23:16, 20; 2 Chr 34:5). Micah declares that a harlot's money, connected with idolatry, is to be burned (Mic 1:7). Deuteronomy prescribes that idolatrous materials are to be burned (Deut 7:5, 25; 13:17).

A case of burying idols for disposal is probably to be found in Gen 35:4. Jacob, when he was about to go to Bethel and there build an altar and worship God, ordered his household and company to rid themselves of their idols, purify themselves, and change their clothes. He collected the group's idols and earrings[24] and hid (*wayyiṭmôn*) them under a terebinth tree near Shechem. The verb *ṭmn* used here does not simply mean "bury," but rather "hide, cover up, stash away." It is used of hiding things in the ground (*ʾereṣ*, Josh 7:21), dust (*ʿāpār*, Isa 2:10), a cleft of a rock (*nĕqîq hasselaʿ*, Jer 13:4), sand (*ḥôl*, Exod 2:12), or stalks of flax (*pištê hāʿēṣ*, Josh 2:6).[25] Since it does not strictly mean bury, there is a question whether Jacob's "hiding away" is to be understood as a means of disposal or whether it indicates some other activity. O. Keel has rather recently attempted to show that at the root of this story lies a custom of burying divine statues and cultic ornaments that have been

---

[23]In 2 Sam 5:21, David and his men merely carry the idols away. M. Greenberg ("Herem," 349) suggests that the change in Chronicles is due to Deuteronomy's law that idols are *ḥērem* and must be destroyed.

[24]These ornaments are not necessarily amulets (cf. M. Weinfeld, *The Book of Genesis [Seper Berešit]* [Tel-Aviv: S. L. Gordon, 1975] 208), nor are they necessarily inscribed with symbols of foreign gods (see the discussion by Keel, "Das Vergraben der 'Fremden Götter' in Genesis XXXV 4b," *VT* 23 [1973] 306–07, n. 4).

[25]See Keel, "Das Vergraben," 306–07.

damaged and are unusable, or which have become obsolete.[26] Though this may ultimately have something to do with the story, it is difficult to believe that the biblical text at any of its levels of redaction[27] considered this as a reverent laying aside of obsolescent idols.[28] As we have seen in this appendix, the Bible elsewhere heaps opprobrium on idolatry. It cannot tolerate it. The *hāsirû* formula (in v 2b) in particular suggests that Jacob's act is to be understood as disposal. This formula occurs in other passages which deal with covenant making or reaffirming covenantal obligations. A group of people collectively recognize the blessings and power of *Yhwh,* commit to serve him alone, and reject (*hēsîr*) other foreign deities (cf. Josh 24:23; Judg 10:16; 1 Sam 7:3). The story in Gen 35 in its present form thus perceives this burial of gods as a disposal. This disposal and accompanying purification and change of clothing are not mainly to secure God's protection as the group travels to Bethel (cf. v 5), but are in preparation for arriving at Bethel and building an altar there.[29]

---

[26]Keel, "Das Vergraben," especially 326, 332.

[27]Keel ("Das Vergraben," 329–32) views v 2b ("remove the foreign gods which are in your midst and purify and change your clothes") and v 5 ("When they began to travel, the terror of God was on the cities which were around them; they did not pursue after the people of Jacob") as later additions.

[28]Keel ("Das Vergraben," 332) admits that even with E (the original text before the additions noted in n. 27, above), "wahrscheinlich hat auch schon E das Vergraben als eine Abrenuntiation verstanden." That is, the E version does not view this as a respectful retirement of obsolete gods, but views it as a rejection of them in favor of *Yhwh.*

[29]I cannot agree with Keel ("Das Vergraben," 329) that this purification cannot be in preparation for the worship that will take place at Bethel because it is 50 kilometers away from Shechem. We know from Exod 19:10–11 that purification for very sacred occasions can begin several days in advance. So here in Gen 35 Jacob and his people prepare well before their arrival and worship at Bethel. Furthermore, Jacob's words in vv 2–3 connect the purification with the goal of going to Bethel to there build an altar. It remains a question, however, if the preparations are to be understood as preparations for a pilgrimage (cf. G. von Rad, *Genesis: A Commentary* [OTL, rev. ed.; Philadelphia: Westminster, 1972] 336–37; Weinfeld, *Genesis,* 208 on v 2; see Keel's discussion, "Das Vergraben," 313).

Interestingly, the Book of Jubilees continues and augments the tradition that Jacob is disposing of foreign gods:

> And they handed over the strange gods and what was on their ears and what was on their necks and the idols which Rachel stole from Laban, her father, and she gave everything to Jacob, and he burned it and crushed it and destroyed it and hid it under an oak which was in the Land of Shechem (31:2).[30]

Here, Jacob does not simply bury the gods, but burns and crushes them as Josiah and others did when they disposed of idolatrous impurities.[31]

---

[30]Translation by O. S. Wintermute, *The Old Testament Pseudepigrapha* (ed. J. H. Charlesworth, 2 vols.; Garden City: Doubleday, 1983–85) 2. 114.

[31]On Gen 35:1–5, see also Nielsen, "The Burial of the Foreign Gods," *ST* 8 (1954) 103–122.

Appendix 2

Akkadian *Kuppuru*

In this appendix we will ascertain the nature of the ritual action indicated by the Akkadian D stem verb *kuppuru* (from *kapāru* A; *CAD* K, 178–80), describe briefly the syntax in which it is used, and examine the meaning of the related nouns *takpertu* and *kupīrātu.*[1]

THE VERB *KUPPURU*

The verb *kuppuru* has the meaning "to wipe, rub; purify by wiping." The basic meaning "rub" is clearly attested in medical and omen texts: DIŠ *pa-ni-šú ú-kap-pir*... DIŠ ZAG *pa-ni-šú ú-kap-pir* "if he rubbed his face... if he rubbed the side of his face";[2] BE ZA ŠU(!).MEŠ-*šú uk-ta-na-pár* "if a man constantly rubs his hands."[3] This meaning is also borne out

[1]Other studies of *kapāru/kuppuru* include: B. Landsberger, *The Date Palm and its By-Products According to Cuneiform Sources* (*AfO* Beiheft 17; Graz: Ernst Weidner, 1967) 30–34; B. Levine, *In the Presence of the Lord* (SJLA 5; Leiden: Brill, 1974) 123–27; H. Zimmern, *Beiträge zur Kenntnis der babylonischen Religion* (Leipzig: J. C. Hinrichs, 1901) 92. See also the lexicons. The most recent and extensive study is B. Janowski *Sühne als Heilsgeschehen: Studien zur Sühnetheologie der Priesterschrift und der Wurzel* KPR *im Alten Orient und im Alten Testament* [WMANT 55; Neukirchen: Neukirchener, 1982] 29–60). I am leaving out of consideration here *kapāru* in the G- and N-stems, and all of *CAD*'s *kapāru* B ("1. to strip, clip, to trim down, 2. *kuppuru* [same m(ea)n(in)gs]"). Another noun derived from *kapāru* A is *kupartu* which *CAD* (K, 549b) defines as "purification" (cf. *CAD* A/2, 460b). This noun is rare (*CAD* lists only one example) and therefore it will not enter the discussion in this appendix.

[2]*CT* 28.29: 8.

[3]*KUB* 37.210: 8; cf. *CAD* K, 179a; *AfO* 18, 77: 10. For usage in medical texts, cf. Janowski, *Sühne*, 40–41.

in passages dealing with the cleaning or polishing (*kuppuru*) of ornaments[4] and especially by ritual and medical texts where various materials are rubbed or wiped on the patient in order to purge him of the evils and diseases he suffers (see below). The verb can also be partially defined by its near synonym *muššudu* "to rub."[5] This latter verb is used in medical texts of rubbing the face, like *kuppuru*. Both verbs can be used of wiping a patient from head to toe: *ištu eliš ana šapliš tumaššad*[6] and TA SAG.DU-*šú* EN GÌR.II-*šú tu-kap-*[*pár-šú*] "you wipe him from his head to his feet."[7] In one text the two verbs appear together: *li-i-ša ina* SU[8] *kup-pu-ru a-ka-lu ša* SU LÚ[9] *muš-šu-du* "to wipe dough from the body, to rub bread from the man's body."[10]

Some instances of *kuppuru*, however, appear to reveal an abstraction of the literal meaning yielding "purify, purge" without indication of actual wiping: *mātkunu ugārkunu ka-pi-ra* "purify your land and field";[11] LÚ.MAŠ.MAŠ *u* LÚ.GALA URU.BI *ú-kap-ru-ʾ* "the *mašmaššu* and the *kalû* purify that city."[12] It is difficult to conceive of an entire house being wiped, let alone a city. Thus the abstract meaning "purify" without reference to actual wiping might recommend itself. However, in another text where a city and house are objects of the verb, the rites surrounding it indicate that in some way an actual wiping rite was performed. The ritual concerns the evil portended by a moth seen in the city, house, or temple:

> 7-*ta-àm* NINDA.MEŠ KI GI.IÁ KI [ ] URU *u* É *tu-kap-par ina na-mi-e na-*[*du-ti*] *lu-u ana* ÍD ŠUB-*di*
>
> [you obtain?[13]] seven breads together with a reed torch, a place [ ] you wipe the city and house, you

---

[4]*CAD* K, 179a. Cf. Janowski, *Sühne*, 32–33.

[5]*CAD* M/1, 351–52.

[6]*AMT* 64.1: 18 (citation follows *CAD* M/1, 352a).

[7]*KAR* 114 rs. 8.

[8]The parallel Sumerian line reads SU.TA "from the body."

[9]The parallel Sumerian line has SU.LÚ.TA "from the man's body."

[10]*ASKT* 87: 65–66.

[11]*AfO* Beiheft 6, 13–14, #5: 7–9 (citation follows *CAD* K, 179b). Cf. Landsberger, *Date Palm*, 32–33, n. 103.

[12]*RAcc* 38 rs. 12. The form *ú-kap-ru-ʾ* is taken by F. Thureau-Dangin (*Rituels accadiens* [Paris: Ernest Levoux, 1921] 57, n. 99) and by *CAD* (K, 179b) as an example of *kuppuru*.

[13]Ebeling (see n. 15) restores here [*par-si tašakan*].

throw (it) in either the unin[habited] steppe[14] or in the river.[15]

The disposal of wiping material here indicates that a wiping rite was in fact performed on the city and house. A hint as to how such wiping rites were performed on these larger objects is contained in a passage describing the purification of a building. After cultic arrangements have been set up, "the corners (of?) the rooms (*bītāti*), the gateway wings, the court, the roof, the beams, and the windows(?)" are touched (*lapātu*) with bitumen, gypsum, oils, honey, holy water, seven censers, torches, etc.[16] Following this, the *kuppuru* rite occurs:

7 MÁŠ.ḪUL.DÚB.MEŠ 7 MÁŠ.GI.IZI.LA₅.MEŠ 7 UDU.TI.LA.MEŠ 7 ŠAḪ.TUR.MEŠ 7 ^urudu^NÍG.KALA.GA-*e* 7 SU.GUD.GAL.MEŠ TER(?) KA(?) LILIZ ZABAR TÚG SA₅ ^kuš^USÀN ^dug^SILÀ.GAZ.MEŠ ŠE.EŠTUB ŠE.MUŠ₅ ŠE.IN.NU.ḪA ŠE.GIG ZÍD.ÀM GÚ.GAL GÚ.TUR GÚ.NÍG.ḪAR.RA *zì-dub-dub-bi-e* É *tu-kap-par-ma*

(With) seven *mašḫultuppû*-goats, seven *mašgizillû*-goats, seven "sheep of life"(?), seven piglets, seven *nigkalagû*-drums, seven great bull hides, TER KA (?), a bronze kettledrum, red cloth, a whip, a *sil(a)gazû*-vessel, *arsuppu*-meal, *šegušu*-meal, *inninu*-barley, wheat, emmer, chick peas, lentils, *kiššanu*, and flour heaps you wipe the house.[17]

The actual performance of wiping here is underscored by the ensuing direction to "transport the wiping material of the house (*takpirāt bīti*) to the door."[18] It is possible that the wiping rite was to be performed like

---

[14]*AHw* (771, under *nawûm*, I) suggests "unbewohnt" for *nadūti*.

[15]*KAR* 72: 3–5 (= E. Ebeling, "Beiträge zur Kenntnis den Beschwörungsserie Namburbi [Part 4]," *RA* 48 [1954] 182).

[16]O. Gurney, "Babylonian Prophylactic Figures and their Rituals," *AAA* 22 (1935) 58–59: 49–52.

[17]Lines 53–60 (= *BBR* #41–42, lines 21–28).

[18]Lines 60–61. All of these materials were probably not used in actual wiping, such as the *nigkalagû*-drums. These are probably used as part of the larger rite, in which other of these items were actually used as wiping material.

the "touching" rite occurring earlier in the ritual by wiping various key locales such as the corners, beams, windows, etc., of the building. Whether this was the way buildings were wiped or not, these examples show that we should always look for an actual wiping act in rituals that use the verb *kuppuru.*

Turning to the syntax of *kuppuru,* we find different ways in which the verbal objects may appear. The verb can take two accusatives, one of the patient who is wiped and one of the material with which he is wiped: *u-ri-ṣa šá* ŠÀ-*šú ta-as-su-ḫu a-ka-la li-i-šá* LÚ *šú-a-tú kup-pir-ma* "wipe that man (with) the goat whose heart you removed, and (with) bread (and) dough";[19] NÍG.SILAG.GÁ . . . SU NA *tu-kap-par-ma* "you wipe the man's body (with) dough";[20] 7 NINDA.ḪÁD.DA 7-*šá tu-kap-pár-šu* "you wipe him (with) seven dry breads seven times."[21] The text in which a house is wiped with seven *mašḫultuppû*-goats, seven *mašgizillû*-goats, etc. (cited above), is an example of this syntax.

The verb can also take the direct object of patient alone, with the object of wiping material implied from the preceding clauses: NINDA NÍG.SILAG.GÁ SAG.GÁ.NA Ù.ME.NI.GAR : *šu-kun-ma* LÚ.U$_{17}$.LU PAP.ḪAL.LA DUMU DINGIR.RA.NA Ù.ME.TE.GUR.GUR : *kup-pir-ma* "place bread (and) dough at his head; wipe the restless man, son of his god, (with it)";[22] *ṣa-lam an-du-na-ni-šú bi-ni-ma* ÚR LÚ TU.RA.KE$_4$ GE$_6$.Ù.NA U.ME.NI.NÁ . . . *ina še-ri zu-mur-šú kup-pir-ma* "make his substitute figure, lay it in the lap of the sick man at night; in the morning, wipe his body (with it)";[23] *si-bit a-kal tap-pi-in-ni el-li li-qí-[ma]* . . . *ina si-par-ri šu-ku-uk-ma* . . . *a-me-lu* DUMU DI[NGIR-*šú*] *šá ma-mit iṣ-bat-tu-šú ku-up-pi-ir-ma* "take seven loaves of pure *tappinni* bread, thread (them) on a bronze skewer . . . wipe the man, son of [his go]d, whom the curse seized (with it)";[24] SUM.SAR ZÚ.LUM.MA ŠU.[SAR] [SÍG].AKÀ SÍG.ÙZ SÍG.SA$_5$ *i-<na>* SU.II-*ka* TI-*qí-ma* [UGU L]Ú.GIG *tú-ka-ni* . . . *tú-kap-p*[*ar-šu*] "an onion, dates, matting, a tuft of wool, goat hair, and red wool you take in your hands, place it

[19]*CT* 17.11: 84–85 (= *DES* 2. 34). Cf. *CAD* A/1, 239a.

[20]*KAR* 92: 10. Cf. *CAD* K, 179a.

[21]G. Meier, "Ein akkadisches Heilungsritual aus Boğazköy," *ZA* 45 (1939) 202 ii 20.

[22]*CT* 17.31: 38–40 (= *DES* 2. 108).

[23]*CT* 17.30: 33–36 (= *DES* 2. 100).

[24]Shurpu vii 55–59.

[over] the patient . . . then you wipe him (with it)";[25] MÁŠ-*zu* KUD-*ma* LUGAL *tu-kap-pár* "you slaughter a goat, then you wipe the king (with it)";[26] *ku-un-šu el-le-tú* . . . *ku-un-šu ib-ba-tú* . . . *ku-un-šu na-mir-tú* . . . [*a-me-lu*] *mar i-li-<šu> kup-pir-ma* "pure emmer . . . clean emmer . . . bright emmer . . . wipe [the man], son of his god, (with it)."[27]

Still another way of indicating the activity is to have the object wiped in the accusative (sometimes omitted) with the wiping material preceded by the preposition *ina* indicating instrument: *ina* NÍG. SILAG.GÁ ŠE.MUŠ$_5$ GÌR-*šú tu-kap-par* "you wipe his foot with dough and *šegušu* barley";[28] LÚ.IŠIB *ina* ZÍD.MAD.GÁ *ú-kap-par-ma* "the *āšipu* wipes (him) with *maṣḫatu* flour";[29] *ina pag-ri* UDU.NITÁ LÚ.MAŠ.MAŠ É *u-kap-par* "the *mašmaššu* wipes the temple with the carcass of the ram."[30]

---

[25]Shurpu i 13–16.

[26]*BBR* #26 ii 1.

[27]E. E. Knudsen, "An Incantation Tablet from Nimrud," *Iraq* 21 (1959) 55: 27–37. Later in this text the patient is wiped with dough (57–60 rs. 27–41).

[28]*CT* 23.1: 4.

[29]Shurpu i 11.

[30]*RAcc* 141: 354.

CAD K, 179b, restores *PBS* 1/1.15: 18 to read: [*šarra ina*(?) ÉN . . . ḪUL].GAL MU.UN.DU$_7$.DU$_7$ *tu-kap-par* "you purify the king by means of the conjuration 'butting evil.'" It is not clear if this restoration is correct in view of the literal meaning of *kuppuru*. Perhaps what really lies behind this broken text is the idea that while wiping the king, one is to recite this particular incantation. Compare Knudsen, "Incantation Tablet," 55–58 vs. 37–38: "wipe the man, son of his god; recite the incantation of Eridu."

There are other minor examples of *kuppuru* worth noting here: *a-ka-lu šá zu-mur-ka ú-kap-pi-ru* (*CT* 17.33: 18 = *DES* 2. 114); *a-me-lu ma-ri* DINGIR-*šú ku-up-pir-ma* (*CT* 17.15: 24 = *DES* 2. 58); KÁ-*šú u na-ḫi-ra-šú tu-kap-pár* (*AMT* 25.6 ii 12); *na-ḫi-ri-šú tu-kap-p*[*ar*] (*AMT* 28.3: 5); ŠU.GUR.GUR-*ma* (*TDP* 1. 70: 2; R. Labat renders this as *tukappar-šú-ma*, *Traité akkadien de diagnostics et pronostics médicaux* [2 vols.; Paris: Académie Internationale d'Histoire des Sciences, 1951]); ŠU.GUR-*šú-ma* (*TDP*, 1. 116 ii 2). See Janowski (*Sühne*, 29–60) for a few additional examples.

THE NOUNS *TAKPERTU* AND *KUPĪRĀTU*

The related noun *takpertu* signifies "wiping material" and "wiping rite." Such a distinction in meaning is perhaps more a phenomenon of English translation than an actual reflection of meaning in Akkadian. Akkadian appears to fuse the two aspects together in some instances. A good example is from the Bit Rimki ritual tablet.[31] After the king has been wiped with various items, the text states: *kīma tak-pi-ra-a-ti tuq-te-it-tu-u ana* KÁ *tu-še-ṣa.* In the first phrase (through *tuq-te-it-tu-u*), *takpirāti* may be translated "wiping rites." However, the second phrase has the object *takpirāti* implicitly from the previous clause and its translation should be: "you have (the wiping materials) taken out to the door." Thus the term seems to have two senses in the same passage: "when you have finished the wiping *rites*, you have (them [i.e., the wiping *materials*]) taken out to the door." The same ambiguity is seen in a text which prescribes: *tak-pi-ra-at* É.MEŠ DINGIR.MEŠ DÙ.A.BI ù É.TUR.NUN.NA É ^{d}30 *tu-kap-par* "you perform the wiping rituals of all the divine temples and Eturnuna, Sin's temple."[32] Only a few lines later it says: *zì-sur-ra-a tak-pi-rat* (*sic*) *ù ga-rak-ku ana* ÍD ŠUB-*di* "you throw the flour circle, the wiping material, and the brazier into the river."[33] Ambiguity also exists in the cases where certain animals are designated *ana takperti* "for wiping material" or "for a wiping rite."[34] As will be evidenced, the majority of cases exhibits the sense of "wiping material."

The meaning "wiping material" occurs in cases where *takpertu* is thrown away or removed from the ritual scene (cf. also the foregoing examples): *tak-pir-ta-šú a-na su-uq ir-bit-ti* Š[UB?-*di?*] "[you thr]ow its wiping material into the square";[35] *tak-pi-rat* É *a-na* KÁ [*tutte*]*ru-ub-šá* "you shall take the wiping material of the house to the door";[36] *tak-pír-tu* É *na-kar-ka-ni liš-ku-nu* "let them put the wiping material (in) the *nakarkāni*-house";[37] ÉN *an-ni-ta ina tak-pir-ti* ^{uzu}ÚR ŠITA₅ NÍG.SILAG.GÁ *šú-a-tum ina* ḪABRUDA šá ^{d}UTU.ŠÚ.A GAR-*an* "you recite this

[31]*BBR* #26 ii 3. Cf. i 19–20.
[32]*BRM* 4.6 rs. 32 (= *TuL* 94).
[33]Line 37.
[34]*AfO* 10, 36, #63: 7–13; *KAJ* 189: 10; 192: 26; 221: 6.
[35]*CT* 17.1: 5 (= *DES* 2. 2).
[36]Gurney, "Prophylactic Figures," 58: 60–61 = *BBR* #41–42: 28–29.
[37]*AfO* Beiheft, 6, 14, #5: 12–14. See chap. 9, n. 85.

incantation over the wiping material of (his) loins; you place that dough in a hole toward the west."[38]

The meaning of *tak-pi-ra-ti eb-bi-ti* LUGAL *tu-kap-pár* in the Bit Rimki ritual is initially unclear.[39] It may be understood as: "you perform the pure wiping rites for the king." However, the context of the most complete example[40] suggests that the concrete meaning "wiping material" is more correct. The king is first wiped with a goat,[41] after which (EGIR-*šú*) "you wipe the king (with) pure wiping materials." These wiping materials are then disposed of.

There are some contexts where the meaning "wiping rite" seems to be the only one possible. The noun is used as the object of the verb *epēšu* to mean "perform a wiping rite."[42] It is also used in the phrase *tak-pi-ir-ti* É *šalmu* "(when) the wiping rite of the house is completed."[43]

Another noun formed from the root *kpr* is *kupīrātu* "wiping material" (always plural).[44] It occurs infrequently and only refers to wiping material.[45] Like *takpertu*, it may be discarded: *ku-pi-ra-ti-šú ana* ÍD ŠU[B-*di*] "you throw his wiping material into the river."[46]

---

[38]*CT* 23.1: 9–10.

[39]*BBR* #26 i 18–19; cf. ii 2–3; v 35; #28: 4.

[40]*BBR* #26 ii 1. Other examples are too broken to be of help.

[41]Ln 1. Similar examples are fragmentary: *tak-pir-tú ib-bi-tu* (*TuL* 108: 65); [*takpirāti ebbēti*] LUGAL *tukappar* (4 R 17 rs. 33 = *OECT* 6, 49).

[42]Ebeling, "Namburbi [Part 4]," 182: 5; *KAR* 230 rs. 2. *Takpertu* also occurs with the verb *ḫâbu* "to purify, exorcise": *tak-pir-tum* KI.BI *tu-ḫa-ab* "you purify this place by takpertu" (*RAcc* 44: 13; Thureau-Dangin [*Rituels*, 57, n. 105] suggests that *takribtum* in *RAcc*, 38: 23–24, be read as *takpirtum* yielding *tak-pir-tum* É.DINGIR.BI *tu-ḫa-ab* "you purify this temple by *takpertu*").

[43]Ebeling, "Namburbi [Part 4]," 182: 8. On *takpertu*, Janowski (*Sühne*, 47) says: "Die *taprist*-Bildung *takpertu* kann sowohl Gegenstandsbezeichnung 'das (durch die *kuppuru*-Handlung) Abgewischte, Gereinigte → die Abwischung' als auch—und dies häufiger—Handlungsbegriff 'die (zur kultischen Reinigung unternommene) Abwischung → die/der Reinigung/s-ritus' sein." Janowski sees the same basic distinction as I do, but in my view the most frequent meaning of *takpertu* appears to be "wiping-material," not "wiping-rite."

[44]*CAD* K, 550a.

[45]Cf. Shurpu vii 61. Janowski (*Sühne*, 45) is correct in saying: "*kupīrātu* (pl. von *kupirtu*) 'Reinigungskehricht' bezieht sich . . . auf die Substanz, die nach dieser Reinigung zurückbleibt."

[46]*LKA* 142: 17.

The foregoing brief examination of the verb *kuppuru* and related nouns has shown that the ritual action they signify is a purification rite performed by wiping. The meaning of *kuppuru* and the nouns should therefore never be abstracted to mean simply "purify" and "purification rite." The overwhelming majority of cases shows that this wiping rite was eliminatory in purpose; wiping materials which have contracted the impurity are thrown away.[47]

---

[47]The most perplexing case of *kuppuru/takpertu*, and therefore not included in the main body of this study, occurs in the Neo-Babylonian laws (G. R. Driver and J. C. Miles, *The Babylonian Laws* [2 vols.; Oxford: Clarendon, 1952–55] 2. 338–39 ii 24–41). Landsberger's judgment (*Date Palm*, 33) that "the pertaining passages . . . yield no understanding, unless radically emended" is hardly an exaggeration. The passage runs (Landsberger's transcription with modifications from *CAD* K, 179b):

> *amīltum ša nēpešu lu takpirtum ina eqel amēli lu ina sūqi lu ina [eleppi] lu ina utūni lu ina mimma šumšu tukappiru iṣṣī ša ina libbi tukappiru bilatsu ištēn adi 3 ana bēl eqli tanaddin šumma ina elippi tukappiru ina utūni u mimma šumšu tukappiru miṭīti ša ina eqli taššakkanu ištēn <adi> 3 tanaddin.*

Driver and Miles understood *kuppuru* here as "to cut off, remove" and, hence, the law for them dealt with removing wood, etc., from a person's field, ship, furnace, etc. However, Landsberger and *CAD* have understood *kuppuru* here in the ritual sense. Such is no doubt correct in view of the nouns *nēpešu* and *takpertu*. Nevertheless, the passage is opaque. I tentatively translate:

> A woman who performed a ritual or wiping ritual in a man's field, in a street, in a [boat], in a kiln, or in whatever—the wood(?)/trees(?) which she ritually wiped (or: used as wiping material; so *CAD*) therein, its load/produce she shall give three-fold to the field's owner. If she ritually wiped in a boat (or if) she ritually wiped in a kiln or whatever, the loss which occurs in the field she shall give three-fold.

Some of the problems are: (1) The meaning of *iṣṣī* is unclear. I do not know of any examples where trees or wood are used for wiping nor as recipients of a wiping rite. (2) The meaning of *biltu* is unclear. Does it refer to a load of wood or a quantity of wood used for wiping, or does it refer to the produce of trees which the woman might have damaged by her rite? (3) The meaning of *ina libbi* is unclear. In the field? In the trees? In the field, trees, boat, kiln, etc.? (4) What does the preposition *ina* mean? "By means of" (cf. Landsberger, *Date Palm*, 33: "with the help of a ship," "or with a kiln")? Or does it mean "in?" (5) What is the connection of doing the ritual with/in a boat or kiln and the loss that occurs in a field? These questions are at present insoluble.

Bibliography

Abercrombie, J. R. "Palestinian Burial Practices from 1200 to 600 B. C. E." PhD diss., University of Pennsylvania, 1979.

Abrahams, I. "Tabernacle." *EncJud* 15 (1972) 679–87.

Aharoni, Y. "Arad." *EM* 6 (1971) 370–82 (Hebrew).

________. "Excavations at Ramat Raḥel." *BA* 24 (1961) 98–118.

Aharoni, Y. and Amiran, R. "Tel Arad." *RB* 72 (1965) 556–60.

Ahituv, S. "*ʿĂzāʾzēl.*" *EM* 6 (1971) 113–15 (Hebrew).

________. "Azazel." *EncJud* 3 (1972) 999–1002.

Albeck, H. *The Six Orders of the Mishnah (Šisa Sidre Mišna).* 6 vols. Jerusalem and Tel-Aviv: Bialik Institute and Dvir, 1957–59.

Albright, W. F. *Archaeology and the Religion of Israel.* 5th ed. Baltimore: Johns Hopkins, 1968. Reprint. Garden City: Doubleday, 1968.

________. "The Babylonian Temple-Tower and the Altar of Burnt-Offering." *JBL* 39 (1920) 137–42.

________. "The Discovery of an Aramaic Inscription Relating to King Uzziah." *BASOR* 44 (1931) 8–10.

________. "The North Canaanite Poems of *Alʾeyan Baʿal.*" *JPOS* 14 (1934) 101–40.

Alon, G. *Studies in the History of Israel in the Days of the Second Temple and in the Period of the Talmud and Mishnah (Meḥqarim beToledot Yiśraʾel Bime Bayit Šeni ubiTequpat hamMišna wehatTalmud)* 2 vols. Tel-Aviv: Hakkibutz Hameuchad, 1967.

Altschuler, D. Commentary (*Meṣudat Ṣiyyon* and *Meṣudat Dawid*) on the Prophets and Writings, in the *Miqra'ot Gedolot.*

Amiran, R. "Two Tombs in Jerusalem from the Period of the Kings of Judah." In *Judah and Jerusalem (Yehuda wiYrušalayim)*, 65–72 and 8 pls. Jerusalem: Israel Exploration Society, 1957 (Hebrew).

Amiran, R.; Beck, P.; and Zevulun, U. *Ancient Pottery of the Holy Land from its Beginnings in the Neolithic Period to the Iron Age.* New Brunswick: Rutgers University, 1970.

Andersen, F. and Freedman, D. N. *Hosea, A New Translation with Introduction and Commentary.* AB 24. Garden City: Doubleday, 1980.

André, G. "*Ḥêq.*" *TWAT* 2 (1977) 912–15 (= *TDOT* 4 [1980] 356–58).

Archi, A. "Il culto del focolare presso gli Ittiti." *SMEA* 16 (1975) 77–87.

Arzi, P. "*Lîlît.*" *EM* 4 (1962) 498–99 (Hebrew).

Ashbel, D. "The Goat Sent to Azazel in the Wilderness (Lev 16:8, 10, 22)." *Beth Mikra* 27/3 (1966) 89–102 (Hebrew).

Atidiyah, M. "The Goat for Azazel." *Beth Mikra* 6/11–12 (1961) 80 (Hebrew).

Avigad, N. "The Epitaph of a Royal Steward from Siloam Village." *IEJ* 3 (1953) 137–52.

_________. "Excavations in the Jewish Quarter of the Old City of Jerusalem, 1970 (Second Preliminary Report)." *IEJ* 20 (1970) 129–40.

_________. *Monuments of the Kidron Valley (Maṣṣebot Qedumot beNaḥal Qidron).* Jerusalem: Bialik Institute, 1954.

_________. "The Second Tomb-Inscription of the Royal Steward." *IEJ* 5 (1955) 163–66.

Avi-Yonah, M. "The Newly Found Wall of Jerusalem and Its Topographical Significance." *IEJ* 21 (1971)168–69.

_________, ed. *The Book of Jerusalem (Seper Yerušalayim).* Vol. 1. Jerusalem and Tel-Aviv: Bialik Institute and Dvir, 1956.

Balkan, K., ed. *Ankara Arkeoloji Müzesinde bulunan Boğazköy Tabletleri.* İstanbul: Millî Eğitim Basımevi, 1948

Barkai, G. "On the Location of the Tombs of the Latter Kings of the Davidic Dynasty." In *Between Hermon and Sinai (Ben Ḥermon leSinay)*, ed. M. Broshi, 75–92. Jerusalem: Yedidi, 1977 (Hebrew).

Barkai, G. and Kloner, A. "Burial Caves North of the Damascus Gate." *IEJ* 26 (1976) 55–57.

Barkai, G.; Mazar, A.; and Kloner, A. "The Northern Burial Area of Jerusalem in the Days of the First Temple." *Qadmoniot* 8 (1975) 71–76 (Hebrew).

Barrois, G. A. "Tombs of the Kings." *IDB* 4 (1962) 668–69.

Barton, G. A. "The Origin of the Names of Angels and Demons in the Extra-Canonical Apocalyptic Literature to 100 A. D." *JBL* 31 (1912) 156–67.

Basham, A. L. *The Wonder That Was India.* London: Sigwick and Jackson, 1956. Reprint. New York: Grove, 1959.

Baumgarten, J. M. "The Pharisaic-Sadducean Controversies about Purity and the Qumran Texts." *JJS* 31 (1980) 157–70.

Baumgartner, W.; Koehler, L. H.; Hartmann, B.; and Kutscher, E. Y. *Hebräisches und aramäisches Lexikon zum Alten Testament.* 3d ed. 3 vols. Leiden: Brill, 1967–83.

Bayliss, M. "The Cult of Dead Kin in Assyria and Babylonia." *Iraq* 35 (1973) 115–25.

Beckman, G. M. "Hittite Birth Rituals." PhD diss., Yale University, 1977. [Now revised in book form, *Hittite Birth Rituals.* StBoT 29. 2d ed. Wiesbaden: Otto Harrassowitz, 1983.]

__________. *Hittite Birth Rituals: An Introduction.* SANE 1/4. Malibu: Undena, 1978.

Beer, G. "Der biblische Hades." In *Theologische Abhandlungen, Eine Festgabe zum 17. Mai 1902 für Heinrich Julius Holtzmann*, ed. W. Nowack, P. Lobstein, F. Spitta and E. Lucias, 3–29. Tübingen: J. C. B. Mohr, 1902.

Benzinger, I. *Die Bücher der Chronik.* KHC 20. Tübingen: J. C. B. Mohr, 1901.

Berman, H. "A Hittite Ritual for the Newborn." *JAOS* 92 (1972) 466–68.

Bertholet, A. *Leviticus.* KHC 3. Tübingen: J. C. B. Mohr, 1901.

_________. "Zu den babylonischen und israelitischen Unterweltsvorstellungen." In *Oriental Studies Published in Commemoration of the 40th Anniversary (1883–1892) of Paul Haupt as the Director of the Oriental Seminary of the Johns Hopkins University*, ed. C. Alder and A. Ember, 9–18. Baltimore: Johns Hopkins, 1926.

Bieńkowski, P. A. "Some Remarks on the Practice of Cremation in the Levant." *Levant* 14 (1982) 80–89.

Birch, W. F. "Note on Jer 31:38–40." *Palestine Exploration Fund Quarterly Statement* (1882) 58–59.

Bittel, K. "Hethitische Bestattungsbräuche." *MDOG* 78 (1940) 12–28.

Black, J. A. "The New Year Ceremonies in Ancient Babylon: 'Taking Bel by the Hand' and a Cultic Picnic." *Religion* 11 (1981) 39–59.

Blenkinsopp, J. "The Structure of P." *CBQ* 38 (1976) 275–92.

Bock, K. E. "The Comparative Method of Anthropology." *CSSH* 8 (1965–66) 269–80.

Böcher, O. "Dämonen: I. Religionsgeschichtlich." *TRE* 8 (1981) 270–74.

Boehm. "Lustratio." *Paulys Real-Encyclopädie der classischen Altertumswissenschaft* 13 (1926) 2029–39.

Bossert, H. T. "Untersuchung hieroglyphenhethitischer Wörter." *MIO* 2 (1954) 266–88.

Boyd, B. "Beer-Sheba." *IDBSup* (1976) 93–95.

Bozkurt, H.; Çiğ, M.; and Güterbock, J. G., eds. *İstanbul Arkeoloji Müzelerinde bulunan Boğazköy Tabletlerinden Seçme Metinler.* 3 vols. İstanbul: Maarif Matbaası, 1944–54.

Brawer, A. Y. "Sending the Goat to Azazel and the Bird of the Leper—Symbolic *Tašlîk*." *Beth Mikra* 12/30 (1967) 32–33 (Hebrew).

Bright, J. *Jeremiah, A New Translation with Introduction and Commentary.* AB 21. Garden City: Doubleday, 1965.

Brock, N. van. "Substitution rituelle." *RHA* 65 (1959) 117–46.

Broshi, M. "The Expansion of Jerusalem in the Reigns of Hezekiah and Manasseh." *IEJ* 24 (1974) 21–26.

________. "La population de l'ancienne Jerusalem." *RB* 82 (1975) 5–14. [A Hebrew version is found in *Between Hermon and Sinai (Ben Ḥermon leSinay)*, ed. M. Broshi, 65–74. Jerusalem: Yedidi, 1977.]

Brown, F.; Driver, S. R.; and Briggs, C. A. *A Hebrew and English Lexicon of the Old Testament.* Corrected ed. Oxford: Clarendon, 1953.

Browne, S. G. *Leprosy in the Bible.* 2d ed. Rushden: S. L. Hunt, 1974.

Budge, E. A. W., ed. *Hittite Texts in the Cuneiform Character in the British Museum.* London: Trustees of the British Museum, 1920.

Bühler, G. *The Laws of Manu.* SBE 25. Oxford: Clarendon, 1886.

________. *The Sacred Laws of the Aryas: Part I.* SBE 2. Oxford: Clarendon, 1879.

________. *The Sacred Laws of the Aryas: Part II.* SBE 14. Oxford: Clarendon, 1882.

Burkert, W. *Structure and History in Greek Mythology and Ritual.* Berkeley: University of California, 1979.

Cagni, L. *L'epopea di Erra.* Rome: Istituto di Studi del Vicino Oriente, Università di Roma, 1969.

________. *The Poem of Erra.* SANE 1/3. Malibu: Undena, 1977.

Caland, W. *Vaikhanasasmārtasūtram.* Bibliotheca Indica 251. Calcutta: Asiatic Society of Bengal, 1929.

Caplice, R. *The Akkadian Namburbi Texts: An Introduction.* SANE 1/1. Malibu: Undena, 1974.

________. "Namburbi Texts in the British Museum, I-V." *Or* 34 (1965) 105–31; 36 (1967) 1–38, 273–98; 39 (1970) 111–51; 40 (1971) 133–83.

Carruba, O. *Das Beschwörungsritual für die Göttin Wišurijanza.* StBoT 2. Wiesbaden: Otto Harrassowitz, 1966.

Cassuto, U. (M. D.). "*Bêt haḤopsît.*" *EM* 2 (1954) 75–76 (Hebrew).

________. *The Goddess Anath: Canaanite Epics of the Patriarchal Age.* Jerusalem: Magnes, 1971.

Castellino, G. "Rituals and Prayers Against 'Appearing Ghosts.'" *Or* 24 (1955) 240–74.

Cazelles, H. "Pureté et impureté: Ancien Testament." *DBSup* 9 (1979) 491–508.

Charlesworth, J. H., ed. *The Old Testament Pseudepigrapha.* 2 vols. Garden City: Doubleday, 1983–85.

Christ, H. *Blutvergiessen im Alten Testament: der gewaltsame Tod des Menschen untersucht am hebräischen Wort* Dām. Basel: Friedrich Reinhardt Kommission, 1977.

Christman-Franck, L. "Le rituel des funérailles royales Hittites." RHA 29 (1971) 61–111.

Clay, A. T. *Epics, Hymns, Omens, and Other Texts.* BRM 4. New Haven: Yale University, 1923.

Cochrane, R. G. and Davey, T. F. *Leprosy in Theory and Practice.* 2d ed. Bristol: John Wright and Sons, 1964.

Cohn, R. L. "Form and Perspective in 2 Kings V." *VT* 33 (1983) 171–84.

Conrad, L. I. "The Biblical Tradition for the Plague of the Philistines." *JAOS* 104 (1984) 281–87.

Contenau, G. *Everyday Life in Babylon and Assyria.* London: E. Arnold, 1959. Reprint. New York: W. W. Norton, 1966.

Cooke, G. A. *A Critical and Exegetical Commentary on the Book of Ezekiel.* ICC. Edinburgh: T. and T. Clark, 1936.

Cortese, E. "Le ricerche sulla concezione 'sacerdotale' circa puro-impuro nell'ultimo decennio." *RivB* 27 (1979) 339–57.

Croatto, J. S. and Soggin, J. A. "Die Bedeutung von *Šdmwt* im Alten Testament." *ZAW* 74 (1962) 44–50.

Cross, F. M. "The Priestly Tabernacle." In the *Biblical Archaeologist Reader, 1*, ed. G. E. Wright and D. N. Freedman, 201–28. Missoula: Scholars, 1975.

Curtis, E. L. and Madsen, A. A. *A Critical and Exegetical Commentary on the Books of Chronicles.* ICC. New York: Charles Scribner's Sons, 1910.

Danby, H. *The Mishnah.* Oxford: Oxford University, 1933.

Davies, Douglas. "An Interpretation of Sacrifice in Leviticus." *ZAW* 89 (1976) 387–99.

Davies, D. and Kloner, A. "A Burial Cave from the End of the First Temple Period on the Slope of Mt. Zion." *Qadmoniot* 11 (1978) 16–19 (Hebrew).

Davies, G. H. "Tabernacle." *IDB* 4 (1962) 498–506.

Deimel, P. A. *Šumerisches Lexikon.* 4 vols. Rome: Pontifical Biblical Institute, 1928–33.

Delcor, M. "Le mythe de la chute des anges." *RHR* 190 (1976) 3–53.

Dietrich, M.; Loretz, O.; and Sanmartin, J. "*Pgr* im Ugaritischen: zur ugaritischen Lexicographie IX." *UF* 5 (1973) 289–91.

Dillmann, A. *Die Bücher Exodus und Leviticus.* 3d ed. Leipzig: S. Hirzel, 1897.

Dinari, Y. "Customs Regarding the Menstruant: Their Sources and Development." *Tarbiz* 49 (1980) 302-24 (Hebrew).

Dion, P.-E. "Deutéronome 21, 1–9: Miroir du développement légal et religieux d'Israël." *SR* 11 (1982) 13–22.

Döller, J. *Die Reinheits- und Speisegesetze des Alten Testaments in religionsgeschichtlicher Beleuchtung.* ATAbh 7/2–3. Münster: Aschendorff, 1917.

Dols, M. W. "The Leper in Medieval Islamic Society." *Speculum* 58 (1983) 891–916.

________. "Leprosy in Medieval Arabic Medicine." *JHMAS* 36 (1979) 314–33.

Donner, H. and Röllig, W. *Kanaäische und aramäische Inschriften.* 3d ed. 3 vols. Wiesbaden: Otto Harrassowitz, 1971–76.

Douglas, M. *Purity and Danger: An Analysis of the Concepts of Pollution and Taboo.* London: Routledge and Kegan Paul, 1966.

Driver, G. R. "Three Technical Terms in the Pentateuch." *JSS* 1 (1956) 97–105.

Driver, G. R. and Miles, J. C. *The Babylonian Laws.* 2 vols. Oxford: Clarendon, 1952–55.

Driver, S. R. *A Critical and Exegetical Commentary on Deuteronomy.* ICC. 3d ed. Edinburgh: T. and T. Clark, [1901].

________. *An Introduction to the Literature of the Old Testament.* [6th ed.] Edinburgh: T. and T. Clark, 1897. Reprints. New York: Meridian, 1956. Gloucester: Peter Smith, 1972.

Driver, S. R. and White, H. A. *The Book of Leviticus.* New York: Dodd, Mead, and Co., 1898.

Duhm, B. *Das Buch Jeremia.* KHC 11. Tübingen: J. C. B. Mohr, 1901.

Duhm, H. *Die bösen Geister im Alten Testament.* Tübingen: J. C. B. Mohr, 1904.

Ebach, J. "*Pgr* = (Toten-)Opfer? Ein Vorschlag zum Verständnis von Ez. 43, 7.9." *UF* 3 (1971) 365–68.

Ebeling, E. *Aus dem Tagewerk eines assyrischen Zauberpriesters.* *MAOG* 5/3. Leipzig: Otto Harrassowitz, 1931.

________. "Beiträge zur Kenntnis den Beschwörungsserie Namburbi [Parts 1–9]." *RA* 48 (1954) 1–15, 76–88, 130–41, 178–91; 49 (1955) 32–42, 137–48, 178–92; 50 (1956) 22–33, 86–94.

________, ed. *Keilschrifttexte aus Assur juristischen Inhalts.* *WVDOG* 50. Leipzig: J. C. Hinrichs, 1927.

________, ed. *Keilschrifttexte aus Assur religiösen Inhalts.* *WVDOG* 28, 34. 2 vols. Leipzig: J. C. Hinrichs, 1919, 1923.

________. *Tod und Leben nach der Vorstellung der Babylonier.* Berlin: Walter de Gruyter, 1931.

Ebeling, E.; Kocher, F.; and Rost, L., eds. *Literärische Keilschrifttexte aus Assur.* Berlin: Akademie, 1953.

Eggan, F. "Social Anthropology and the Method of Controlled Comparison." *AA* 56 (1954) 743–63.

Eggeling, J. *Śatapatha Brâhmana.* SBE 12, 26, 41, 43, 44. Oxford: Clarendon, 1882–1900.

Ehrlich, A. B. *The Bible According to its Plain Meaning (Miqra' kiPešuṭo).* 3 vols. Berlin, 1899–1901. Reprint. New York: Ktav, 1969.

________. *Randglossen zur hebräischen Bibel.* 7 vols. Leipzig: J. C. Hinrichs, 1908–14.

Eichrodt, W. *Ezekiel: A Commentary.* OTL. Philadelphia: Westminster, 1970.

Eissfeldt, O. *The Old Testament: An Introduction.* New York: Harper and Row, 1965.

Eitrem, S. "A Purificatory Rite and Some Allied *Rites de Passage.*" *SO* 25 (1947) 36–53.

Elhorst, H. J. "Eine verkannte Zauberhandlung (Dtn 21 1–9)." *ZAW* 39 (1921) 58–67.

Elliger, K. "Die grossen Tempelsakristeien im Verfassungsentwurf des Ezechiel (42, 1ff.)." In *Geschichte und Altes Testament,* ed. W. F. Albright, 79–103. BHT 16. Tübingen: J. C. B. Mohr, 1953.

________. *Leviticus.* HAT 1/4. Tübingen: J. C. B. Mohr, 1966.

Elliott-Binns, L. E. *The Book of the Prophet Jeremiah, with Introduction and Notes.* London: Methuen, 1919.

Ember, M. "Taxonomy in Comparative Studies." In *A Handbook of Method in Cultural Anthropology,* ed. R. Naroll and R. Cohen, 697–706. New York: Columbia University, 1973.

Encyclopaedia Judaica. "Purity and Impurity, Ritual." *EncJud* 13 (1972) 1405–14.

________. "Tashlikh." *EncJud* 15 (1972) 829–30.

Engelhard, D. H. "Hittite Magical Practices: An Analysis." PhD diss., Brandeis University, 1970.

Enṣiqlopedya Talmudit. "*Diššûn hamMĕnôrâ.*" *ET* 8 (1957) 1–3.

________. "*Diššûn Mizbēaḥ haḤiṣôn.*" *ET* 8 (1957) 3–12.

________. "*Diššûn Mizbēaḥ hapPĕnîmî.*" *ET* 8 (1957) 12–18.

Epstein, Y. N. "On the Inscription of Uzziah." *Tarbiz* 2 (1931) 293–94 (Hebrew).

Evans-Pritchard, E. E. *The Comparative Method in Social Anthropology.* London: Athlone, 1963.

Falkenstein, A. *Die Haupttypen der sumerischen Beschwörung.* LSS n.s. 1/1. Leipzig: J. C. Hinrichs, 1931.

Feigin, S. "The Meaning of Ariel." *JBL* 39 (1920) 131–37.

Feinberg, C. L. "The Scapegoat of Leviticus Sixteen." *BSac* 115 (1958) 320–33.

Feldman, E. *Biblical and Post-Biblical Defilement and Mourning: Law as Theology.* New York: Ktav and Yeshiva University, 1977.

Finkelstein, L. *The Pharisees: The Sociological Background of Their Faith.* 3d ed. 2 vols. Philadelphia: Jewish Publication Society of America, 1962.

Firth, R. *Symbols: Public and Private.* Ithaca: Cornell University, 1973.

Fishbane, M. *Biblical Interpretation in Ancient Israel.* Oxford: Clarendon, 1985.

Fohrer, G. and Galling, K. *Ezechiel.* HAT 13. Tübingen: J. C. B. Mohr, 1955.

Forbes, R. J. *Studies in Ancient Technology.* Vol. 1. Leiden: Brill, 1955.

Forrer, E. *Die Boghazköi-Texte in Umschrift.* *WVDOG* 41, 42. Leipzig: J. C. Hinrichs, 1922, 1926.

Frank, C. *Lamastu, Pazuzu und andere Dämonen, ein Beitrag zur babyl.-assyr. Dämonologie.* *MAOG* 14/2. Leipzig: Otto Harrassowitz, 1941.

Frankfort, H. *The Problem of Similarity in Ancient Near Eastern Religions.* Oxford: Clarendon, 1951.

Frazer, J. G. *The Golden Bough: A Study in Magic and Religion; Part IV, The Scapegoat.* 3d. ed. London: Macmillan, 1913.

________. *The New Golden Bough: A New Abridgement of the Classic Work by Sir James George Frazer.* Ed. T. H. Gaster. New York: S. G. Phillips, 1959. Reprint. New York: New American Library, 1959.

Friedrich, J. "Aus dem hethitischen Schrifttum." *Der Alte Orient* 25 (1925) 1–32.

________. *Die hethitischen Gesetze.* DMOA 7. Leiden: Brill, 1971.

________. *Hethitisches Wörterbuch: kurzgefasste kritische Sammlung der Deutungen hethitischer Wörter.* Indogermanische Bibliothek. Heidelberg: Carl Winter, 1952.

________. *Hethitisches Wörterbuch: kurzgefasste kritische Sammlung der Deutungen hethitischer Wörter.* Indogermanische Bibliothek. Ergänzungshefte 1–3. Heidelberg: Carl Winter, 1957–66.

________. "Reinheitsvorschriften für den hethitischen König." *MAOG* 4 (1928–29) 46–58.

________. "Zu AO 25, 2 (Aus dem hethitischen Schrifttum, 2. Heft)." *ZA* 3 (1927) 177–204.

Friedrich, J. and Kammenhuber, A. *Hethitisches Wörterbuch.* 2d ed. Vol. 1. Heidelberg: Carl Winter, 1975–84.

Frymer-Kensky, T. "Pollution, Purification, and Purgation in Biblical Israel." In *The Word of the Lord Shall Go Forth: Essays in Honor of David Noel Freedman in Celebration of his Sixtieth Birthday*, ed. C. Meyers and M. O'Connor, 399–414. ASOR Special Volume Series 1. Philadelphia and Winona Lake: ASOR and Eisenbrauns, 1983.

Furlani, G. "Il peccato nella religione degli Hittiti." *GSAI* 3 (1935) 129–47.

________. *La religione degli Hittiti.* Storia delle religioni 13. Bologna: N. Zanichelli, 1936.

Gadegaard, N. "On the So-Called Burnt Offering Altar in the Old Testament." *PEQ* 110 (1978) 35–45.

Galling, K. "Altar." *IDB* 1 (1962) 96–100.

Gaster, T. H. "Azazel." *IDB* 1 (1962) 325–26.

________. "The Canaanite Epic of Keret." *JQR* 37 (1946–47) 285–93.

________. "Dead, Abode of the." *IDB* 1 (1962) 787–88.

________. "Demon, Demonology." *IDB* 1 (1962) 817–24.

________. *The Holy and the Profane: Evolution of Jewish Folkways.* New York: W. Sloan, 1955.

________. *Thespis: Ritual, Myth, and Drama in the Ancient Near East.* Garden City: Doubleday, 1961. Reprint. New York: W. W. Norton, 1977.

Gebhard, V. "Hethitische Sündenböcke." *ARW* 29 (1931) 243.

Gesenius, W. *Gesenius' Hebrew Grammar.* Ed. E. Kautzsch. Tr. A. Cowley. Corrected 2d ed. Oxford: Clarendon, 1946.

Geyer, J. B. "Mice and Rites in I Samuel V–VI." *VT* 31 (1981) 293–304.

Giesebrecht, F. *Das Buch Jeremia.* HKAT 3/2.1. Göttingen: Vandenhoeck and Ruprecht, 1894.

Görg, M. "'Ausschlag' an Häusern: zu einem problematischen Lexem in Lev 14, 37." *BN* 14 (1981) 20–25.

________. "*Gzr.*" *TWAT* 2 (1973) 1001–4 (= *TDOT* 2 [1975] 459–61).

________. "*Piggul* und *pilaegaeš* - Experimente zur Etymologie." *BN* 10 (1979) 7–11.

Goetze, A. *Kulturgeschichte Kleinasiens.* 2d ed. München: C. H. Beck, 1957.

________. "Die Pestgebete des Muršiliš." *Kleinasiatische Forschungen* 1 (1929) 162–251.

________. "[Review of *KBo* 9]." *JCS* 14 (1960) 115–16.

________, ed. *Verstreute Boghazköi-Texte.* Marburg: A. Goetze, 1930.

Goetze, A. and Pedersen, H. *Muršilis Sprachlähmung.* KDVS 21/1. Copenhagen: Levin and Munksgaard, 1934.

Goetze, A. and Sturtevant, E. H. *The Hittite Ritual of Tunnawi.* AOS 14. New Haven: American Oriental Society, 1938.

Goldschmidt, W. *Comparative Functionalism: An Essay in Anthropological Theory.* Berkeley: University of California, 1966.

Gonda, J. *Vedic Ritual: The Non-Solemn Rites.* HdO 2.4/1. Leiden: Brill, 1980.

Gordon, C. H. *Ugaritic Textbook: Grammar, Texts in Transliteration, Cuneiform Selections, Glossary, Indices.* Rome: Pontifical Biblical Institute, 1965.

Gramberg, K. P. C. A. "Leprosy and the Bible." *TGM* 11 (1959) 127–39.

Gray, G. B. *A Critical and Exegetical Commentary on Numbers.* ICC. Edinburgh: T. and T. Clark, 1903.

Gray, J. "Feudalism in Ugarit and Early Israel." *ZAW* 64 (1952) 49–55.

_________. *I and II Kings: A Commentary.* OTL. 2d ed. Philadelphia: Westminster, 1970.

_________. *Legacy of Canaan: The Ras Shamra Texts and Their Relevance to the Old Testament.* VTSup 5. Leiden: Brill, 1957.

Greenberg, M. "Crimes and Punishment." *IDB* 1 (1962) 733–44.

_________. "The Design and Themes of Ezekiel's Program of Restoration." *Interpretation* 38 (1984) 181–208.

_________. "Herem." *EncJud* 8 (1971) 344–50.

_________. "Some Postulates of Biblical Criminal Law." In the *Yehezkel Kaufmann Jubilee Volume,* ed. M. Haran, 5–28. Jerusalem: Magnes, 1960.

Grelot, P. "*Ḥofšī* (Ps. LXXXVIII 6)." *VT* 14 (1964) 256–63.

Groot, J. de. *Die Altäre des salomonischen Tempelhofes: eine archäologische Untersuchung.* Stuttgart: Kohlhammer, 1924.

Güterbock, H. G. "Hittite Religion." In *Forgotten Religions, Including Some Living Primitive Religions*, ed. V. T. A. Ferm, 83–109. New York: Philosophical Library, 1949.

Güterbock, H. G. and Hoffner, H. A. *The Hittite Dictionary of the Oriental Institute of the University of Chicago.* Vol. 3, fascicles 1–2 to date. Chicago: Oriental Institute of the University of Chicago, 1980.

Gurewicz, S. B. "Some Examples of Modern Hebrew Exegesis of the Old Testament." *Australian Biblical Reviews* 11 (1963) 15–23.

Gurney, O. R. "Babylonian Prophylactic Figures and their Rituals." *AAA* 22 (1935) 31–96 and pls. xi–xiv.

_________. "Hittite Prayers of Mursili II." *AAA* 27 (1940) 2–163.

_________. "The Hittite Ritual of Tunnawi [Review of A. Goetze and E. H. Sturtevant, *The Hittite Ritual of Tunnawi*]." *JRAS* (1941) 56–61.

_________. *The Hittites.* 2d ed. Middlesex: Penguin, 1954.

_________. *Some Aspects of Hittite Religion.* Oxford: Oxford University for the British Academy, 1977.

_________. "A Tablet of Incantations against Slander." *Iraq* 22 (1960) 221–27.

Guttmann, A. "Jerusalem in Tannaitic Law." *HUCA* 40–41 (1969–70) 251–75.

Haas, V. *Hethitische Berggötter und hurritische Steindämonen.* Mainz: Philipp von Zabern, 1982.

_________. "Ein hethitisches Beschwörungsmotiv aus Kizzuwatna: seine Herkunft und Wanderung." *Or* 40 (1971) 410–30.

_________. *Der Kult von Nerik: Ein Beitrag zur hethitischen Religionsgeschichte.* StPD 4. Rome: Pontifical Biblical Institute, 1970.

_________. *Magie und Mythen im Reich der Hethitier: I. Vegetationskulte und Pflanzenmagie.* Hamburg: Merlin, [1977].

_________. "Die Unterwelts- und Jenseitsvorstellungen im hethitischen Kleinasien." *Or* 45 (1976) 197–212.

Haas, V. and Thiel, H. J. *Die Beschwörungsrituale der Allaituraḫ(ḫ)i und verwandte Texte.* AOAT 31. Kevelaer and Neukirchen: Butzon und Bercker, and Neukirchener, 1978.

Haas, V. and Wilhelm, G. *Hurritische und luwische Riten aus Kizzuwatna.* AOATS 3. Kevelaer and Neukirchen: Butzon und Bercker, and Neukirchener, 1974.

Haldar, A. *The Notion of the Desert in Sumero-Accadian and West-Semitic Religions.* UUA 3. Uppsala and Leipzig: A. B. Lundequistska and Otto Harrassowitz, 1950.

Hallo, W. W. "New Moons and Sabbaths: a Case Study in the Contrastive Approach." *HUCA* 48 (1977) 1–18.

Hammel, E. A. "The Comparative Method in Anthropological Perspective." *CSSH* 22 (1980) 145–55.

Hanson, P. L. "Rebellion in Heaven, Azazel, and Euhemeristic Heroes in 1 Enoch 6–11." *JBL* 96 (1977) 195–233.

Haran, M. "*Mizbēaḥ.*" *EM* 4 (1962) 763–80 (Hebrew).

________. *Temples and Temple Service in Ancient Israel: an Inquiry into the Character of the Cult Phenomena and the Historical Setting of the Priestly School.* Oxford: Clarendon, 1978.

________. "Zeḇaḥ Hayyamîm." *VT* 19 (1969) 11–22.

Harrison, J. *Prolegomena to the Study of Greek Religion.* 2d ed. Cambridge: Cambridge University, 1908. Reprint. London: Merlin, 1962.

Harrison, R. K. "Leprosy." *IDB* 3 (1962) 111–13.

Haupt, P. *Akkadische und sumerische Keilschrifttexte.* Assyriologische Bibliothek 1. Leipzig: J. C. Hinrichs, 1881–82.

________. "Hinnom and Kidron." *JBL* 38 (1919) 45–48.

Heinisch, P. *Das Buch Ezechiel.* HSAT 8. Bonn: Peter Hanstein, 1923.

Henninger, J. "Pureté et impureté: l'histoire de religions." *DBSup* 9 (1979) 399–430.

Hertzberg, H. W. *I and II Samuel: A Commentary.* OTL. Philadelphia: Westminster, 1964.

Herzog, Z.; Aharoni, M.; Rainey, A. F.; and Moshkovitz, S. "The Israelite Fortress at Arad." *BASOR* 254 (1984) 1–34.

Hillers, D. "Demons, Demonology." *EncJud* 5 (1971) 1521–26.

Hoenig, S. B. "The New Qumran Pesher on Azazel." *JQR* 56 (1965–66) 248–53.

Hoffmann, D. Z. *The Book of Leviticus (Seper Wayyiqra*ʾ*)*. 2 vols. Jerusalem: Mossad Harav Kook, [1953].

Hoffner, H. A. "An English-Hittite Glossary." *RHA* 25/80 (1967) 7–99.

_________. "Histories and Historians of the Ancient Near East: The Hittites." *Or* 49 (1980) 283–332.

_________. "Hittite *Tarpiš* and Hebrew *Terāphîm*." *JNES* 27 (1968) 61–68.

_________. "The Hittites and Hurrians." In *Peoples of Old Testament Times*, ed. D. J. Wiseman, 197–228. Oxford: Clarendon, 1973.

_________. "Incest, Sodomy, and Bestiality in the Ancient Near East." In *Orient and Occident: Essays Presented to Cyrus H. Gordon on the Occasion of his Sixty-fifth Birthday*, ed. H. Hoffner, 81–90. AOAT 22. Kevelaer and Neukirchen: Butzon und Bercker, and Neukirchener, 1973.

_________. "Second Millennium Antecedents to the Hebrew *ʾÔḆ*." *JBL* 86 (1967) 385–401.

_________. "Symbols for Masculinity and Femininity: Their Use in Ancient Near Eastern Sympathetic Magic Rituals." *JBL* 85 (1966) 326–34.

Hollis, F. J. *The Archaeology of Herod's Temple*. London: J. M. Dent, 1934.

Hooke, S. H. "The Theory and Practice of Substitution." *VT* 2 (1952) 2–17.

Horovitz, H. S., ed. *The Sifre on Numbers and Sifre Zutta (Sipre ʿal Seper Bammidbar weSipre Zutta*ʾ*)*. Leipzig: Gustav Fock, 1917. Reprint. Jerusalem: Wahrmann, 1966.

Hulse, E. V. "The Nature of Biblical 'Leprosy' and the Use of Alternative Medical Terms in Modern Translations of the Bible." *PEQ* 107 (1975) 87–105.

Ibn Ezra, Abraham. Commentary on the Torah, found in the *Miqraʾot Gedolot.*

Jacobsen, T. *Toward the Image of Tammuz and Other Essays on Mesopotamian History and Culture.* Cambridge: Harvard University, 1970.

________. *Treasures of Darkness: A History of Mesopotamian Religion.* New Haven: Yale University, 1976.

Jakob-Rost, L. *Das Ritual der Malli aus Arzawa gegen Behexung (KUB XXIV 9+).* THeth 2. Heidelberg: Carl Winter, 1972.

Janowski, B. *Sühne als Heilsgeschehen: Studien zur Sühnetheologie der Priesterschrift und der Wurzel* KPR *im Alten Orient und im Alten Testament.* WMANT 55. Neukirchen: Neukirchener, 1982.

Jha, G. *Manu-Smṛti.* Vol. 3. Calcutta: University of Calcutta, 1929.

Jolly, J. *The Institutes of Vishnu.* SBE 7. Oxford: Clarendon, 1880.

Joüon, P. P. *Grammaire de l'Hebreu biblique.* 2d ed. Rome: Institut Biblique Pontifical, 1947.

Kaiser, O. *Isaiah 13–39: A Commentary.* OTL. Philadelphia: Westminster, 1974.

Kammenhuber, A. "Hethitisch *innarauu̯atar,* (LÚ)KALA-*tar* und Verwandtes." *MSS* 3 (1958) 27–44.

Kane, P. V. *History of Dharmasastra (Ancient and Mediaeval Religious and Civil Law).* 2d ed. Vol. 4. Poona: Bhandarkar Oriental Research Institute, 1973.

Kaufmann, Y. *The History of Israelite Belief: From Ancient Times Until the End of the Second Temple (Toledot haʾEmuna hay-Yiśreʾelit Mime Qedem ʿad Sop Bayit Šeni).* 4 vols. Jerusalem and Tel Aviv: Bialik Institute and Dvir, 1937–56.

________. *The Religion of Israel from Its Beginnings to the Babylonian Exile.* Chicago: University of Chicago, 1960. Reprint. New York: Schocken, 1972.

Keel, O. "Das Vergraben der 'Fremden Götter' in Genesis XXXV 4b." *VT* 23 (1973) 305–36.

Keil, C. F. and Delitzsch, F. *Biblical Commentary on the Old Testament.* 25 vols. Grand Rapids: Eerdmans, 1950–56.

Kelso, J. *The Ceramic Vocabulary of the Old Testament. BASOR* Supp. Studies, 5–6. New Haven: ASOR, 1948.

________. "Pottery." *IDB* 3 (1962) 846–53.

Kimhi, D. (Radaq). Commentary on the Prophets, found in the *Miqraʾot Gedolot.*

Kinnier-Wilson, J. V. "An Introduction to Babylonian Psychiatry." In *Studies in Honor of Benno Landsberger on his Seventy-fifth Birthday, April 21, 1965,* 289–98. AS 16. Chicago: Oriental Institute of the University of Chicago, 1965.

Knudsen, E. E. "An Incantation Tablet from Nimrud." *Iraq* 21 (1959) 54–61 and pls. xvi–xix.

Köbben, A. J. F. "Comparativists and Non-Comparativists in Anthropology." In *A Handbook of Method in Cultural Anthropology,* ed. R. Naroll and R. Cohen, 581–96. New York: Columbia University, 1973.

Koehler, L. and Baumgartner, W. *Lexicon in Veteris Testamenti Libros.* [2d ed.] Leiden: Brill, 1958.

Kraemer, J. L. "*Š^{e}qa^{ʿa}rūrōt:* A Proposed Solution for an Unexplained Hapax." *JNES* 25 (1966) 125–29.

Kramer, S. N. *Mythologies of the Ancient World.* Garden City: Doubleday, 1961.

Krauss, S. "Moriah-Ariel: II, 5. The Sepulchres of the Davidic Dynasty." *PEQ* (1947) 102–11.

Kronasser, H. "Fünf hethitische Rituale." *Die Sprache* 7 (1961) 140–67.

________. "Das hethitische Ritual KBo IV 2." *Die Sprache* 8 (1962) 89–107.

________. "Nachträge und Berichtigungen zu 7/1961, 140–167." *Die Sprache* 8 (1962) 108–13.

________. *Die Umsiedlung der Schwarzen Gottheit: Das hethitische Ritual KUB XXIX 4 (des Ulippi).* OAWS 241/3. Graz: Herman Böhlaus, 1963.

Kümmel, H. M. "Ersatzkönig und Sündenbock." *ZAW* 80 (1968) 289–318.

________. *Ersatzrituale für den hethitischen König.* StBoT 3. Wiesbaden: Otto Harrassowitz, 1967.

________. "Die Religion der Hethiter." In *Theologie und Religionswissenschaft,* ed. U. Mann, 65–85. Darmstadt: Wissenschaftliche Buchgesellschaft, 1973.

Kunstmann, W. G. *Die Babylonische Gebetsbeschwörung.* LSS n.s. 1/2. Leipzig: J. C. Hinrichs, 1932.

Kutsch, E. "Sündenbock." *RGG* 6 (1962) 506–07.

Labat, R. *Traité akkadien de diagnostics et pronostics médicaux.* 2 vols. Paris: Académie Internationale d'Histoire des Sciences, 1951.

Laessøe, J. *Studies on the Assyrian Ritual and Series* bît rimki. Copenhagen: Ejnar Munksgaard, 1955.

Lambert, W. G. *Babylonian Wisdom Literature.* Oxford: Clarendon, 1960.

________. "DINGIR.ŠÀ.DIB.BA Incantations." *JNES* 33 (1974) 267–322.

________. "A Part of the Ritual for the Substitute King." *AfO* 18 (1957) 109–12.

Landersdorfer, S. "Keilinschriftliche Parallelen zum biblischen Sündenbock (Lv 16)." *BZ* 19 (1931) 20–28.

________. *Studien zum biblischen Versöhnungstag.* Münster: Aschendorff, 1924.

Landsberger, B. *The Date Palm and its By-Products According to Cuneiform Sources. AfO* Beiheft 17. Graz: Ernst Weidner, 1967.

Langdon, S. H. *Babylonian Penitential Psalms.* OECT 6. Paris: Geuthner, 1927

________. "The Scapegoat in Babylonian Religion." *ExpTim* 24 (1912–13) 9–13.

Laroche, E. *Catalogue des textes hittites.* Paris: Éditions Klincksieck, 1971.

________. "Études de vocabulaire IV." *RHA* 53 (1951) 61–71.

________. "Textes mythologiques hittites en transcription." *RHA* 23/77 (1965) 61–178.

Lattey, C. "Vicarious Solidarity in the Old Testament." *VT* 1 (1951) 267–74.

Lauterbach, J. Z. *Rabbinic Essays.* Cincinnati: Hebrew Union College, 1951.

Leach, E. R. "The Comparative Method in Anthropology." *International Encyclopedia of the Social Sciences* 1 (1968) 339–45.

Lebrun, R. *Hymnes et prières hittites.* Louvain-la-Neuve: Centre d'Histoire de Religions, 1980.

________. "Les rituels d'Ammihatna, Tulbi et Mati contre une impureté = *CTH* 472." *Hethitica* 3 (1979) 139–64.

________. *Samuha foyer religieux de l'empire hittite.* Louvain-la-Neuve: Université Catholique de Louvain, Institut Orientaliste, 1976.

Lehmann, M. R. "A New Interpretation of the Term *Šdmwt.*" *VT* 3 (1953) 361–71.

Lendrum, F. C. "The Name 'Leprosy.'" *AJTMH* 1 (1952) 999–1008.

Lesêtre, H. "Lèpre." *DB* 4 (1908) 175–87.

Levi ben Gershom (Ralbag). Commentary on the Former Prophets, found in the *Miqraʾot Gedolot.*

Levine, B. *In the Presence of the Lord.* SJLA 5. Leiden: Brill, 1974.

________. "*Kippûrîm.*" *Eretz Israel* 9 (1969) 88–95 (Hebrew).

________. "*Piggûl.*" *EM* 6 (1971) 435–36 (Hebrew).

________. "The Temple Scroll: Aspects of its Historical Provenance and Literary Character." *BASOR* 232 (1978) 5–23.

Licht, J. S. "*Qeber, Qĕbûrâ.*" *EM* 7 (1976) 3–5 (Hebrew).

Löhr, M. *Das Ritual von Lev. 16 (Untersuchungen zum Hexateuchproblem III).* SKGG 2/1. Berlin: Deutsche Verlagsgesellschaft für Politik und Geschichte, 1925.

Loewenstamm, S. "*ʿEglâ ʿĂrûpâ.*" *EM* 6 (1971) 77–79 (Hebrew).

_________. "*Qeteb, Qoteb.*" *EM* 7 (1976) 109–10 (Hebrew).

_________. "*Šĕʾôl.*" *EM* 7 (1976) 454–57 (Hebrew).

_________. "*Šēdîm.*" *EM* 7 (1976) 524–25 (Hebrew).

Loffreda, S. "The Late Chronology of Some Rock-Cut Tombs of the Selwan Necropolis, Jerusalem." *Liber Annuus* 23 (1973) 7–36.

_________. "Typological Sequence of Iron Age Rock-Cut Tombs in Palestine." *Liber Annuus* 18 (1968) 244–87.

Lohfink, N. "*Ḥōpšî.*" *TWAT* 3 (1982) 123–28.

Loretz, O. "Ugaritisch-hebräisch *ḪB/PṮ, BT ḪPṮT-ḤPŠJ BJT HḤPŠJ/WT.*" *UF* 8 (1976) 129–31.

_________. "Die hebräischen Termini *ḤPŠJ* 'Freigelassen, Freigelassener' und *ḤPŠH* 'Freilassung.'" *UF* 9 (1977) 163–67.

Louf, A. "Caper emissarius ut typus Redemptoris apud Patres." *VD* 38 (1960) 262–77.

Macalister, R. A. S. *The Excavation of Gezer, 1902–1905 and 1907–1909.* 3 vols. London: For the Committee of the Palestine Exploration Fund by J. Murray, 1912.

Maimonides. *The Code of Maimonides: Book Eight: The Book of Temple Service.* Tr. M. Lewittes. New Haven: Yale University, 1957.

_________. *The Code of Maimonides: Book Nine: The Book of Offerings.* Tr. H. Danby. New Haven: Yale University, 1950.

_________. *The Code of Maimonides: Book Ten: The Book of Cleanness.* Tr. H. Danby. New Haven: Yale University, 1954.

_________. *Mišne Tora* (published in various editions).

_________. *More Nebukim* (published in various editions).

Mair, L. *An Introduction to Social Anthropology.* 2d ed. New York: Oxford University, 1972.

Masson, O. "A propos d'un rituel hittite pour la lustration d'une armée: Le rite de purification par le passage entre les deux parties d'une victime." *RHR* 137 (1950) 5–25.

May, H. G. "Ephod and Ariel." *AJSL* 56 (1939) 44–69.

Mayer, W. *Untersuchungen zur Formensprache der babylonischen "Gebetsbeschwörungen."* StPM 5. Rome: Biblical Institute Press, 1976.

Mazar, A. "Iron Age Burial Caves North of the Damascus Gate, Jerusalem." *IEJ* 26 (1976) 1–8.

Mazar, B. *The Excavations in the Old City of Jerusalem Near the Temple Mount: Preliminary Report of the Second and Third Seasons, 1969–70.* Jerusalem: Israel Exploration Society. [Originally in Hebrew in *Eretz Israel* 10 (1971) 1–34.]

________. "Excavations Near the Temple Mount." *Qadmoniot* 5 (1972) 74–90 (Hebrew).

McCarter, P. K. *I Samuel: A New Translation with Introduction, Notes and Commentary.* AB 8. Garden City: Doubleday, 1980.

Meier, G. "Ein Akkadisches Heilungsritual aus Boğazköy." *ZA* 45 (1939) 195–215.

________. *Die assyrische Beschwörungssammlung Maqlu.* AfO Beiheft 2. Berlin: Ernst F. Weidner, 1937.

Meissner, B. *Babylonien und Assyrien.* 2 vols. Heidelberg: Carl Winter, 1925.

Merton, R. K. *Social Theory and Social Structure.* Enlarged ed. New York: Free, 1968.

Michman, J. "Leprosy." *EncJud* 11 (1972) 33–36.

Milgrom, J. "The Alleged 'Demythologization and Secularization' in Deuteronomy." *IEJ* 23 (1973) 156–61.

________. "Altar." *EncJud* 2 (1972) 760–67.

________. "Atonement, Day of." *IDBSup* (1976) 82–83.

________. "Atonement in the OT." *IDBSup* (1976) 78–82.

_________. "The Book of Leviticus." In *The Interpreter's One Volume Commentary on the Bible*, ed. C. M. Laymon, 68–84. New York: Abingdon, 1971.

_________. *Cult and Conscience: The Asham and the Priestly Doctrine of Repentance.* SJLA 18. Leiden: Brill, 1976.

_________. "The Cultic *Šggh* and its Influence in Psalms and Job." *JQR* 58 (1967) 115–25.

_________. "Day of Atonement." *EncJud* 5 (1972) 1384–87.

_________. "ʿEglah ʿArufah." *EncJud* 6 (1971) 475–77.

_________. "First-born." *IDBSup* (1976) 337–38.

_________. "First-fruits." *IDBSup* (1976) 336–37.

_________. "The Function of the *Ḥaṭṭāʾt* Sacrifice." *Tarbiz* 40 (1970) 1–8 (Hebrew).

_________. "The Graduated *Ḥaṭṭāʾt* of Lev 5:1–13." *JAOS* 103 (1983) 249–54.

_________. "The *Ḥaṭṭāʾt* Offering and the Temple Cult in Jeremiah's Time." In *Studies in the Book of Jeremiah (ʿIyyunim beSeper Yirmeyahu)*, ed. B. Z. Luria, vol. 2, 123–45. Jerusalem: Miśrad habBiṭṭaḥon wehaḤebra hayYehudit haʿOlamit latTanak, 1973 (Hebrew).

_________. "Israel's Sanctuary: The Priestly 'Picture of Dorian Gray.'" *RB* 83 (1976) 390–99.

_________. "*Kipper ʿal/bĕʿad.*" *Leshonenu* 35 (1971) 16–17 (Hebrew).

_________. "Magic, Monotheism and the Sin of Moses." In *The Quest for the Kingdom of God: Studies in Honor of George E. Mendenhall*, ed. H. B. Huffmon, F. A. Spina and A. R. W. Green, 251–65. Winona Lake: Eisenbrauns, 1983.

_________. "*Mĕzûzâ.*" *TWAT* 3 (1984) 801–04.

_________. "The Paradox of the Red Cow (Num. XIX)." *VT* 31 (1981) 62–72. [A Hebrew version appears in *Beth Mikra* 89–90 (1982) 155–63.]

_________. "'Sabbath' and 'Temple City' in the Temple Scroll." *BASOR* 232 (1978) 25–27.

________. "Sacrifice and Sacrifices: the Sacrificial Prescriptions in Detail." *EM* 7 (1976) 233–51 (Hebrew).

________. "Sacrifices and Offerings, OT." *IDBSup* (1976) 763–71.

________. "Sancta Contagion and Altar/City Asylum." *VTSup* 32 (1981) 278–310.

________. "Sanctification." *IDBSup* (1976) 782–84.

________. "Sin Offering or Purification Offering?" *VT* 21 (1971) 237–39.

________. "The *Šôq hatTĕrûmâ*." *Tarbiz* 42 (1973–74) 1–14 (Hebrew). [An English tr. is found in *Studies in Cultic Theology and Terminology*, 159-70.]

________. *Studies in Cultic Theology and Terminology*. SJLA 36. Leiden: Brill, 1983.

________. *Studies in Levitical Terminology, I: The Encroacher and the Levite; the Term* ʿAbodah. UCPNES 14. Berkeley: University of California, 1970.

________. "Studies in the Temple Scroll." *JBL* 97 (1978) 501–23.

________. "The Temple Scroll." *BA* 41 (1978) 105–20.

________. "Two Kinds of *Ḥaṭṭāʾt*." *VT* 26 (1976) 333–37.

Milgrom, J. and Wright, D. P. "*Nāzāh*." *TWAT* 5 (1985) 322–25.

________. "*Niddāh*." *TWAT* 5 (1984) 250–53.

Monte, G. F. del. "Il terrore dei morti." *AION* 33 [= n.s. 23] (1973) 373–85.

Montgomery, J. A. "Soul Gods." *HTR* 34 (1941) 321–22.

Montgomery, J. A. and Gehman, H. S. *A Critical and Exegetical Commentary on the Book of Kings*. ICC. New York: Charles Scribner's Sons, 1951.

Morgenstern, J. "Amos Studies II: The Sin of Uzziah." *HUCA* 12–13 (1937–38) 1–20.

Moriarty, F. L. "The Chronicler's Account of Hezekiah's Reform." *CBQ* 27 (1965) 399–406.

Moyer, J. C. "The Concept of Ritual Purity Among the Hittites." PhD diss., Brandeis University, 1969.

________. "Hittite and Israelite Cultic Practices: A Selected Comparison." In *Scripture in Context II: More Essays on the Comparative Method*, ed. W. Hallo, J. C. Moyer and L. G. Perdue, 19–38. Winona Lake: Eisenbrauns, 1983.

Myers, J. M. *I Chronicles.* AB 12. Garden City: Doubleday, 1965.

________. *II Chronicles.* AB 13. Garden City: Doubleday, 1965.

Myhrman, D. W. "Die Labartu-Texte: Babylonische Beschwörungsformeln nebst Zauberverfahren gegen die Dämonin Labartu." *ZA* 16 (1902) 141–200.

Neiman, D. "*Pgr:* A Canaanite Cult-Object in the Old Testament." *JBL* 67 (1948) 55–60.

Neu, E. *Althethitische Ritualtexte in Umschrift.* StBoT 25. Wiesbaden: Otto Harrassowitz, 1970.

________. *Ein althethitisches Gewitterritual.* StBoT 12. Wiesbaden: Otto Harrassowitz, 1970.

Neufeld, E. "Hygiene Conditions in Ancient Israel (Iron Age)." *BA* 34 (1971) 42–66.

Neusner, J. *The Idea of Purity in Ancient Judaism.* SJLA 1. Leiden: Brill, 1973.

________. *Kelim Chapters One through Eleven.* SJLA 6, HMLP 1. Leiden: Brill, 1974.

________. *Kelim Chapters Twelve through Thirty.* SJLA 6, HMLP 2. Leiden: Brill, 1974.

________. *The Mishnaic System of Uncleanness.* SJLA 6, HMLP 22. Leiden: Brill, 1977.

________. *Negaim, Mishnah-Tosefta.* SJLA 6, HMLP 6. Leiden: Brill, 1975.

________. *Niddah Commentary.* SJLA 6, HMLP 15. Leiden: Brill, 1976.

________. *Parah Commentary.* SJLA 6, HMLP 9. Leiden: Brill, 1976.

_________. "The Scriptural Origins of Mishnah's Conception of *Maddaf*-Uncleanness: An Exercise in Analogical-Contrastive Exegesis." In *Method and Meaning in Ancient Judaism, Second Series*, ed. J. Neusner, 187–96. Chico: Scholars, 1981.

_________. *The Tosefta: Neziqin—The Order of Damages.* New York: Ktav, 1981.

_________. *Zabim.* SJLA 6, HMLP 18. Leiden: Brill, 1977.

Nickelsburg, G. W. E. "Apocalyptic and Myth in 1 Enoch 6–11." *JBL* 96 (1977) 383–405.

Nielsen, E. "The Burial of the Foreign Gods." *ST* 8 (1954) 103–22.

Nötscher, F. *Das Buch Jeremias.* HSAT 7/2. Bonn: Peter Hanstein, 1934.

North, C. R. "Ariel." *IDB* 1 (1962) 218.

Noth, M. *Leviticus: A Commentary.* OTL. Rev. ed. Philadelphia: Westminster, 1977.

_________. *Numbers: A Commentary.* OTL. Philadelphia: Westminster, 1968.

Nougayrol. J. "Einführende Bemerkungen zur babylonischen Religion." In *Theologie und Religionswissenschaft*, ed. U. Mann, 28–46. Darmstadt: Wissenschaftliche Buchgesellschaft, 1973.

Oettinger, N. *Die militärischen Eide der Hethiter.* StBoT 22. Wiesbaden: Otto Harrassowitz, 1976.

Oldenberg, H. *The Grihya-Sutras, Part II.* SBE 30. Oxford: Clarendon, 1892.

Oppenheim, A. L., *et al. The Assyrian Dictionary of the Oriental Institute of the University of Chicago.* 15 vols. to date. Chicago and Gluckstadt: Oriental Institute of Chicago and J. J. Augustin, 1956–.

Oppenheim, A. L. and Reiner, E. *Ancient Mesopotamia: Portrait of a Dead Civilization.* Rev. ed. Chicago: University of Chicago, 1977.

Otten, H. "Eine Beschwörung der Unterirdischen aus Boğazköy." *ZA* 54 (1961) 114–57.

________. "Bestattungssitten und Jenseitsvorstellungen nach den hethitischen Texten." *WVDOG* 71 (1958) 81–84.

________. *Hethitische Totenrituale.* DAWBIO 37. Berlin: Akademie, 1958.

________. *Ein hethitisches Festritual (KBo XIX 128).* StBoT 13. Wiesbaden: Otto Harrassowitz, 1971.

________. "Ein Reinigungsritual im Hethitischen: GIŠ*ḫatalkišna-*." *AfO* 16 (1952–53) 69–71.

________. "[Review of *IBoT* 3]." *OLZ* 50 (1955) 389–94.

________. "Das Ritual der Alli aus Arzawa." *ZA* 63 (1973) 76–82.

________. "Ein Totenritual hethitischen Könige." *MDOG* 78 (1940) 3–11.

________. "Die Uberlieferungen des Telipinu-Mythus." *MVAG* 46 (1942) 1–77.

Otten, H. and Rüster, C. "Textanschlüsse von Boğazköy-Tafeln (21–30)." *ZA* 63 (1973) 83–91.

Otten, H. and Souček, V. *Ein althethitisches Ritual für das Königspaar.* StBoT 8. Wiesbaden: Otto Harrassowitz, 1969.

Ouellette, J. "Temple of Solomon." *IDBSup* (1976) 872–74.

Pallis, S. A. *The Babylonian Akîtu Festival.* KDVS 12/1. Copenhagen: Bianco Lunos, 1926.

Parker, R. *Miasma: Pollution and Purification in Early Greek Religion.* Oxford: Clarendon, 1983.

Paschen, W. *Rein und Unrien: Untersuchung zur biblischen Wortgeschichte.* SANT 24. München: Kösel, 1970.

Patai, R. "The ʿEgla ʿArufa or the Expiation of the Polluted Land." *JQR* 30 (1939) 59–69.

________. *The Hebrew Goddess.* New York: Ktav, 1967. Reprint. New York: Avon Books, 1978.

Paul, S. M. "Cuneiform Light on Jer 9, 20." *Bib* 49 (1968) 373–76.

Pedersen, J. *Israel: Its Life and Culture I–II.* London: Oxford University, 1926.

Peter, R. "L'imposition des mains dans l'Ancien Testament." *VT* 27 (1977) 48–55.

Pilch, J. J. "Biblical Leprosy and Body Symbolism." *BTB* 11 (1981) 108–13.

Pinches, T. G. *A Selection from the Miscellaneous Inscriptions of Assyria.* The Cuneiform Inscriptions of Western Asia 4. London: Trustees of the British Museum, 1981.

Prince, J. D. "Le bouc emissaire chez les Babyloniens." *JA* (1903) 133–56.

Pritchard, J. B. *The Ancient Near East in Pictures Relating to the Old Testament.* 2d ed. Princeton: Princeton University, 1969.

________. *Ancient Near Eastern Texts Relating to the Old Testament.* 3d ed. Princeton: Princeton University, 1969.

Rabbinowitz, L. "Leprosy: In the Second Temple and Talmud; in the Aggadah." *EncJud* 11 (1972) 37–39.

Rad. G. von. *Genesis: A Commentary.* OTL. Rev. ed. Philadelphia: Westminster, 1972.

Radcliffe-Brown, A. R. "The Comparative Method in Social Anthropology." *JRAI* 81 (1951) 15–22.

Rahmani, L. Y. "Ancient Jerusalem's Funerary Customs and Tombs: [Parts One through Four]." *BA* 44 (1981) 171–77, 229–35; 45 (1982) 43–53, 109–19.

Ramban (Nachmanides). Commentary on the Torah, found in the *Miqra'ot Gedolot.*

Rashi. Commentary on the Torah, found in the *Miqra'ot Gedolot.*

Reed, W. L. "Burial," *IDB* 1 (1962) 474–76.

________. "Tombs." *IDB* 4 (1962) 663–68.

Reiner, E. "*Lipšur* Litanies." *JNES* 15 (1956) 129–49.

________. "La magie babylonienne." In *Le Monde du Sorcier*, 67–98. SOr 7. Paris: Éditions du Seuil, 1966.

________. *Šurpu: A Collection of Sumerian and Akkadian Incantations. AfO* Beiheft 11. Osnabruck: Biblio, 1970.

Rendtorff, R. *The Old Testament: An Introduction.* Philadelphia: Fortress, 1986.

Renger, J. "Untersuchungen zum Priestertum in der altbabylonischen Zeit [1. und 2. Teile]." *ZA* 58 (1967) 110–88; 59 (1969) 104–230.

Riemschneider, K. K. "Hethitisch 'gelb/grün.'" *MIO* 5 (1957) 141–47.

Ringgren, H. "Israel's Place Among the Religions of the Ancient Near East." *VTSup* 23 (1972) 1–8.

________. "Remarks on the Method of Comparative Mythology." In *Near Eastern Studies in Honor of William Foxwell Albright,* ed. H. Goedicke, 407–11. Baltimore: Johns Hopkins, 1971.

Rodriquez, A. M. "Substitution in the Hebrew Cultus and in Cultic-Related Texts." PhD diss., Andrews University, 1980.

Rogerson, J. W. *Anthropology and the Old Testament.* Oxford: Basil Blackwell, 1978.

Roifer, A. "The ʿEgla ʿArupa." *Tarbiz* 31 (1961) 119–43 (Hebrew).

Rosenkranz, B. "Ein neues hethitisches Ritual für ^{D}LAMA ^{KUŠ}*kuršaš*." *Or* 33 (1964) 238–56.

Rost, L. "Ein hethitisches Ritual gegen Familienzwist." *MIO* 1 (1953) 345–79.

Rowley, H. H. *Worship in Ancient Israel: Its Form and Meaning.* London: SPCK, 1967.

Rudolph, W. *Chronikbücher.* HAT 1/21. Tübingen: J. C. B. Mohr 1955.

________. *Jeremia.* HAT 1/12. 3d ed. Tübingen: J. C. B. Mohr, 1968.

________. "Ussias 'Haus der Freiheit.'" *ZAW* 89 (1977) 418.

Rummel, S. "Using Ancient Near Eastern Parallels in Old Testament Study." *BARev* 3/3 (1977) 3–11.

Rylaarsdam, J. C. "Atonement, Day of." *IDB* 1 (1962) 313–16.

Sabourin, L. "Le bouc émissaire, figure du Christ?" *Sciences Ecclesiastiques* 11 (1959) 45–79.

Saggs, H. W. F. *The Greatness that was Babylon: A Sketch of the Ancient Civilization of the Tigris-Euphrates Valley.* New York: Hawthorn, 1962.

Safrai, S. "The Worship of God in the Second Temple." In *The Book of Jerusalem (Seper Yerušalayim)*, ed. M. Avi-Yonah, vol. 1, 369–91. Jerusalem and Tel-Aviv: Bialik Institute and Dvir, 1956 (Hebrew).

Salonen, A. "Die Öfen der alten Mesopotamier." *Bagh. Mitt.* 3 (1964) 100–24.

Sandmel, S. "Parallelomania." *JBL* 81 (1962) 1–13.

Sarna, N. M. *Understanding Genesis.* New York: Jewish Theological Seminary of America, 1966. Reprint. New York: Schocken, 1970.

Sayce, A. H. "The Scapegoat Among the Hittites." *ExpTim* 31 (1919) 283–84.

Schapera, I. "Some Comments on Comparative Method in Social Anthropology." *AA* 55 (1953) 353–62.

Schwartz, B. "A Hittite Ritual Text." *Or* 16 (1947) 23–55.

Segal, M. H. "The Religion of Israel Before Sinai." *JQR* 53 (1962–63) 226–56.

Segert, S. "Die Sprache der moabitischen Königsinschrift." *ArOr* 29 (1961) 197–267.

Sellin, E. and Fohrer, G. *Introduction to the Old Testament.* Nashville: Abingdon, 1968.

Seux, M.-J. "Pur et impur en Mésopotamie." *DBSup* 9 (1979) 452–59.

Shatran, E. "*Qeber, Qĕbûrâ.*" *EM* 7 (1976) 5–24 (Hebrew).

Simons, J. *Jerusalem in the Old Testament: Researches and Theories.* Leiden: Brill, 1952.

Singer, M. B. "Summary of Comments and Discussion." *AA* 55 (1953) 362–66.

Skinner, J. *The Book of Ezekiel.* ExBib. New York: A. C. Armstrong, 1895.

Smit, E. J. "Death- and Burial Formulas in Kings and Chronicles Relating to the Kings of Judah." *OTWSuid-Afrika* 9 (1966) 173–77.

Smith, J. Z. *Imagining Religion: From Babylon to Jonestown.* Chicago: University of Chicago, 1982.

________. *Map is Not Territory: Studies in the History of Religion.* Leiden: Brill, 1978.

Smith, W. R. *The Religion of the Semites: The Fundamental Institutions.* [2d ed.] London: A. and C. Black, 1894. Reprint. New York: Schocken, 1972.

Snaith, N. H. *Leviticus and Numbers.* London: Thomas Nelson, 1967.

________. "The Meaning of *Śĕʿîrîm.*" *VT* 25 (1975) 115–118.

Soden, W. von. *Akkadisches Handwörterbuch.* 3 vols. Wiesbaden: Otto Harrassowitz, 1965–81.

Sommer, F. and Ehelolf, H. *Das hethitische Ritual des Papanikri von Komana.* Bogazköi-Studien 10. Leipzig: J. C. Hinrichs, 1924.

Souček, V. "Ein neues hethitische Ritual gegen die Pest." *MIO* 9 (1963) 164–74.

Speiser, E. A. *Genesis: Introduction, Translation and Notes.* AB 1. Garden City: Doubleday, 1964.

Sturrock, J., ed. *Structuralism and Since: From Levi-Strauss to Derrida.* Oxford: Oxford University, 1979.

Sturtevant, E. H. and Bechtel, G. *A Hittite Chrestomathy.* WDWLS. Philadelphia: Linguistic Society of America, University of Pennsylvania, 1935.

Sukenik, E. L. "The Funerary Tablet of Uzziah." *PEQ* 64 (1932) 106–07.

________. "Funerary Tablet of Uzziah, King of Judah." *PEQ* 63 (1931) 217–21.

________. "The Inscription of Uzziah, King of Judah." *Tarbiz* 2 (1931) 288–92 (Hebrew).

Szabó, G. *Ein hethitisches Entsühnungsritual für das Königspaar Tutḫaliḭa und Nikalmati.* THeth 1. Heidelberg: Carl Winter, 1971.

Talmon, S. "The 'Comparative Method' in Biblical Interpretation—Principles and Problems." *VTSup* 29 (1978) 320–56.

________. "On the Emendation of Biblical Texts on the Basis of Ugaritic Parallels." *Eretz Israel* 14 (1978) 117–24 (Hebrew).

________. "The 'Navel of the Earth' and the Comparative Method." In *Scripture in History and Theology, J. Coert Rylaarsdam Jubilee Volume*, eds. A. L. Merrill and T. W. Overholt, 243–68. Pittsburgh: Pickwick, 1977.

Tas, J. "On Leprosy in the Bible." In *Actes du VIIe Congrés International d'Histoire des Sciences*, ed. F. S. Bodenheimer, 583–87. Paris: Academie Internationale d'Histoire des Sciences and Hermann, 1953.

________. "*Ṣāraʿat*." *EM* 6 (1971) 774–78 (Hebrew).

Tatje, T. A. "Problem of Concept Definition for Comparative Studies." In *A Handbook of Method in Cultural Anthropology*, ed. R. Naroll and R. Cohen, 689–96. New York: Columbia University, 1973.

Tawil, H. "ʿAzazel The Prince of the Steepe [*sic*]: A Comparative Study." *ZAW* 92 (1980) 43–59.

Thompson, J. A. *The Book of Jeremiah*. NICOT. Grand Rapids: Eerdmans, 1980.

Thompson, R. C., ed. *Assyrian Medical Texts*. London: Oxford University, 1923.

________. *The Devils and Evil Spirits of Babylonia*. 2 vols. London: Luzac, 1903–04.

________. "An Incantation Against Rheumatism." *Proceedings of the Society of Biblical Archaeology* 30 (1908) 63–69, 145–52, 245–51.

Thureau-Dangin, F. "Un Acte de Donation de Marduk-Zâkir Šumi." *RA* 16 (1919) 117–56.

________. *Rituels accadiens*. Paris: Ernest Levoux, 1921.

Tromp, N. J. *Primitive Conceptions of Death and the Nether World in the Old Testament*. BibOr 21. Rome: Pontifical Biblical Institute, 1969.

Turner, V. "Sacrifice as a Quintessential Process: Prophylaxis or Abandonment." *HR* 16 (1977) 189–215.

Tur-Sinai, N. H. "ʾAriʾel." *Leshonenu* 14 (1946) 1–6 (Hebrew).

________. "*ʾĂriʾēl.*" *EM* 1 (1954) 558–60 (Hebrew).

Ünal, A. "Einige Gedanken über das Totenopfer bei den Hethitern." *Anadolu* 19 (1975–76) 175–83.

Ussishkin, D. "A Monolithic Tomb Recently Discovered in Silwan Village." *Qadmoniot* 3 (1970) 25–27 (Hebrew).

________. "The Necropolis from the Time of the Kingdom of Judah at Silwan, Jerusalem." *BA* 33 (1970) 34–46.

________. "On the Shorter Inscription from the 'Tomb of the Royal Steward.'" *BASOR* 196 (1969) 16–22.

________. "*Qidrôn.*" *EM* 7 (1976) 33–35 (Hebrew).

________. "The Rock Called Peristereon." *IEJ* 24 (1974) 70–72.

Vaux, R. de. *Ancient Israel.* London: Darton, Longman, and Todd, 1961. Reprint. 2 vols. New York: McGraw-Hill, 1965.

________. *Studies in Old Testament Sacrifice.* Cardiff: University of Wales, 1964.

Vieyra, M. "Ciel et enfers hittites." *RA* 59 (1965) 127–30.

________. "Les noms du 'mundus' en hittite et en assyrien et la phythonesse d'Endor." *RHA* 19/69 (1961) 47–55.

________. "Rites de purification hittites." *RHR* 119 (1939) 121–53.

________. "Le sorcier hittite." In *Le monde du sorcier*, 99–125. SOr 7. Paris: Éditions du Seuil, 1966.

Vincent, L. H. "L'autel des holocaustes et le caractere du Temple d'Ézéchiel." *Analecta Bollandiana* 67 (1940) 7–20.

Vincent, P. L.-H. and Steve, P. A. M. *Jerusalem de l'Ancien Testament.* Paris: J. Gabalda, 1954.

Virolleaud, C. "La lutte de Mot, fils des dieux et d'Aleïn, fils de Baal." *Syria* 12 (1931) 195–224.

Vriezen, T. C. "The Term *Hizza*: Lustration and Consecration." *OTS* 7 (1950) 201–35.

Wanke, G. "Dämonen: II Altes Testament." *TRE* 8 (1981) 275–77.

Weill, R. *La Cité de David, compte rendu des fouilles executées à Jerusalem, sur le site de la ville primitive, campagne de 1913–14.* Paris: P. Geuthner, 1920.

Weinfeld, M. *The Book of Genesis (Seper Berešit).* Tel-Aviv: S. L. Gordon, 1975.

________. "Social and Cultic Institutions in the Priestly Source Against Their Ancient Near Eastern Background." In *Proceedings of the Eighth World Congress of Jewish Studies: Panel Sessions—Bible Studies and Hebrew Language*, 95–129. Jerusalem: World Union of Jewish Studies, 1983.

________. "The Teaching of Julius Welhausen: A New Estimation After a Century Since the Appearance of his Book *Prolegomena to the History of Ancient Israel.*" *Shenaton* 4 (1980) 62–93 (Hebrew).

Weiser, A. *Das Buch des Propheten Jeremiah.* ATD 20–21. 2 vols. Göttingen: Vandenhoeck and Ruprecht, 1952–55.

________. *The Psalms: A Commentary.* OTL. Philadelphia: Westminster, 1962.

Weiss, I. H., ed. *The Sifra: The Book Torat Kohanim (Sipra᾽ debe Rab: hu᾽ Seper Torat Kohanim).* Wien: Yaʿqob hakKohen Schlassberg, 1862.

Wenham, G. J. *The Book of Leviticus.* NICOT. Grand Rapids: W. B. Eerdmans, 1979.

Willemaers, N. "Contribution iconographique à l'histoire du rituel hittite: II. Confrontation avec les textes (1)." *Hethitica* 2 (1977) 53–78.

Wold, D. J. "The *Kareth* Penalty in P: Rationale and Cases." In *Society of Biblical Literature 1979 Seminar Papers*, vol. 1, 1–45. Missoula: Scholars, 1979.

________. "The Meaning of the Biblical Penalty *Kareth.*" PhD diss., University of California, Berkeley, 1978.

Wright, D. P. "Azazel." *ABD*, forthcoming.

________. "Deuteronomy 21:1–9 as a Rite of Elimination." *CBQ*, forthcoming.

________. "The Gesture of Hand Placement in the Hebrew Bible and in Hittite Literature." *JAOS* 106 (1986) 433-46.

________. "Purification From Corpse-Contamination in Num. XXXI 19–24." *VT* 35 (1985) 213–23.

________. "Red Heifer." *ABD*, forthcoming.

Wright, D. P. and Jones, R. N. "Leprosy." *ABD*, forthcoming.

________. "Discharge." *ABD*, forthcoming.

Wright, D. P. and Milgrom, J. "*Sāmak*." *TWAT* 5 (1986) 880–88.

Yadin, Y. "The First Temple." In *The Book of Jerusalem (Seper Yerušalayim)*, ed. M. Avi-Yonah, vol. 1, 176–90. Jerusalem and Tel-Aviv: Bialik Institute and Dvir, 1956 (Hebrew).

________. "Temple: First Temple: Structure." *EncJud* 15 (1972) 946–52.

________. *The Temple Scroll (Megillat hamMiqdaš)*. 3 vols. Jerusalem: Israel Exploration Society, 1977.

Yeivin, S. "The Sepulchres of the Kings of the House of David." *JNES* 7 (1948) 30–45.

Zatelli, I. *Il campo lessicale degli aggettivi di puritá in Ebraico biblico.* QS 7. Firenze: Istituto di Linguistica e di Lingue Orientali, Università di Firenze, 1978.

Zevit, Z. "The *ʿEglâ* Ritual of Deuteronomy 21:1–9." *JBL* 95 (1976) 377–90.

Zimmerli, W. *Ezechiel.* BKAT 13/1, 2. 2 vols. Neukirchen: Neukirchener, 1969.

Zimmern, H. *Beiträge zur Kenntnis der babylonischen Religion.* Leipzig: J. C. Hinrichs, 1901.

Zuntz, L. "Un texto ittita di scongiuri." *ARIVSLA* 96/2 (1936–37) 477–546.

Subject Index

Ablution, see Washing
Adytum, definition, 16
Aggrandizement of ritual materials, 59
Akītu festival, 62–65, 72, 273
Akkadian texts, see Mesopotamian texts
Altar, 70, 147–59; see Offerings; Sacrifices
Analogy, 39–41, 45, 56, 72, 78, 262, 265, 270
Anger, 33, 50, 83, 84, 263, 264; see Demon(s)
Animal, impurities, 94–95, 105, 178, 185–86, 216, 222, 225, 227, 245, 246; large land animals, 205–06; *šereṣ*, 94–95, 98, 170, 185–86, 198, 200–06, 213, 214, 285; see Dog; Pig
Annulment, 42–43, 72
Anointing, 63; see Oil
Anthropology, 3, 6
Appeasement, 38–39, 45, 47, 48, 49, 50, 51, 53, 54, 56, 57, 62, 73, 74; see Sacrifice
Arad, 158
ʾĀšām, 139, 148, 232, 233, 234, 253
Ash dump, 134, 144, 145, 243
Ashes, as detergent, 109, 169; see Red Cow; Water of purgation
Atonement, Day of, 15–31, 64–65, 76, 78–80, 130, 218, 233; performance of the rite, 16–17
Azazel, 16–17, 49, 50, 53–54, 58, 69, 72–74, 273–74, 277; see also Hebrew Word Index under *ʿăzāʾzēl*
Bathing, see Washing; Water
Biblical studies, 5–6
Binding and loosing, see Thread manipulation; Unraveling
Bird; Hittite bird rites, 33, 82–83; Mesopotamian bird rites, 80–81, 249, 260; see *Ṣāraʿat*, bird rites
Birth, see Sexual impurity, parturient
Birth ritual, 106
Blessing, 39, 40, 69, 82, 83; see Invigoration
Blood, as an impurity, 108, 109, 227, 233, 245, 272, 275, 286; for purification, 16–21, 36, 76–77, 78–79, 129–31, 147–59; see *Ṣāraʿat*, bird rites,
Bloody deed ("blood" as an evil), 40, 42, 52, 82, 84, 262, 265,

270
Borderline prescription, 111–12
Bread, 68, 70, 294
Bread of Presence, 232
Breath, 210
Burial, 44, 61, 69, 82, 156–57, 258–59, 265–66, 272, 275, 288–90, 297; archaeological evidence for corpse burial, 120–22, 128; corpses, 115–128
Burning, disposal, 87, 90–91, 129, 132, 134–35, 139–140, 143, 144–46, 249, 259, 268–69, 270, 272, 275, 288, 290; execution, 116; extinguishing rite, 40; see Fire
Carrying versus touching, 185–86
Cat, 108
Cedar Wood, 77
Censer, 63, 67, 70, 253
Clay, 36
Colors, as representing afflictions, 36, 41
Combing, 34
Communicability, see Impurity
Comparative method, 5–9; contrastive comparison, 8–9, 31–32, 49–50, 53–55, 57, 58, 60, 64–65, 66–67, 68, 69, 72–74, 83–86, 93, 232, 247, 272–74; historical reconstruction, 8, 73–74; interpretive comparison, 6–8, 22, 25, 28, 93, 151–53
Concession, 132
Concretizing, 41–42, 48, 52, 56, 66–67, 72, 84
Contact, rites, 34, 61–62, 66, 67–68, 83; types of contacts with impurities, 180–219; see Carrying; Transfer
Containers, with impurity, 263–64, 267, 271, 272; see Nether world
Contrastive comparison, see Comparative method
Corpses 268; contamination, 9, 96–98, 107, 109, 115–128, 165, 166, 167, 168, 169–172, 173, 178, 179, 196–200, 207–08, 222, 224, 225, 226, 227, 241–42, 245; see Burial; Cremation
Court of sanctuary, 237–38, 241, 242
Cow dung, 109
Cremation, 267–68
Curse, 40, 43, 68, 69, 84, 98, 254, 259, 262, 263
Death, as an evil, 36, 37, 38, 56
Decoration, 46, 47, 48, 51, 53, 56
Deformities, bodily, 165–66, 178
Demon(s), 21–25, 61, 62, 63, 65–67, 73, 84; angry god, 47, 51, 56, 57, 73, 262; connection with impurity, 248–50, 261–63, 273–74; figures of speech, 25; in the wilderness, 27–29; pejorative terminology, 23–24; see Azazel; Impurity
Detergents, 34–36, 41
Disease, see Sickness
Disposal, 43; in Nether world, 25–30; terminology, 1; see Nether world
Distancing evil, 85–86; expressions of, 260, 270; see Wilderness
Divination of evil, 48
Dog, 43–44, 59, 69–72, 84, 104–06, 108, 201, 202, 205,

255, 257, 268
Dough, 68, 292, 294, 295, 297
Drum, 293; see Sound
Earth, as a purifying agent, 109
Earthenware, 76, 93–113, 130, 184, 196, 198, 205, 207, 210, 216, 226, 246, 272–73, 275
Earwax, 108
Eating, as disposal, 132–34; place of eating sacrifices, 144, 232–242; prohibition, 167, 186, 200–04; sacrifices, 164, 165, 166, 185
Economic concessions, 93, 112–13
Enemy land, 45–46, 49–50, 51, 52–53, 56, 256–57, 261, 269, 272, 273, 275
Entreaty, 38–39, 45, 58, 66, 72
Evils, 50, 73, 84, 276; see Blood; Curse; Impurity; Plague; Sicknesses; Word
Evil word, see Word
Exclusion, 164–228, 232, 245–47, 275
Excrement, 108, 109
Execution, 116–17
Exegesis: descriptive historical, 2; inner biblical, 22, 201–04
Expiation, 147; see Atonement; *Ḥaṭṭāʾt*
Extinguishing, see Burning
Famine, 269
Fat, as an impurity, 108
Fertility, 40
Figurine, 33, 41–42, 43–44, 61, 70–72, 82, 252, 253, 255–56, 258, 260, 294
Fire, 33, 36, 63, 67, 108, 109, 110, 111, 170, 208, 263; see Burning
First born, 235, 242
First ripe/processed produce, 235, 238
Fish, 61, 81, 249, 252, 260
Fixing evil, 35, 264–65, 265–66; see Prevention
Flour; 253; as detergent, 36, 259, 293, 295; flour circle, 61, 68, 296
Foreign land, see Enemy Land
Frequency of elimination rites, 73
Fright (an evil), 82, 84
Fungus, 88, 90
Gezer, 159
Glückwunschformel, 45
Goat, 61–62, 65–66, 67–68, 83, 257, 270, 293, 294, 297; see Azazel; *Ḥaṭṭāʾt;* Scapegoat
God: custodian of evil, 58; evil or angry, see Anger; Demon(s); Theology
Gradations, 17, 20, 153–54, 185–86, 232, 235–36, 243–47
Greece, 122, 134
Handlaying, 17, 51, 54–55
Ḥaṭṭāʾt, 9, 16–21, 65, 78, 95–96, 129–46, 147–59, 217–18, 219, 222, 225, 227, 232, 233, 234, 242, 243, 245, 246, 272, 275, 276
Healing, 84
Heart, animal, 67
Heqdēš, 236, 238
Ḥērem, 235, 238, 284–85; see Hebrew Word Index, *ḥērem*
Hermeneutics, 3, 31–32; see Exegesis
Historical reconstruction, see Comparative method
Hittite texts, 31–60, 82–83, 261–71; purification motifs, 31–45

Holiness, 86, 89, 124–25, 163–67, 171, 223, 227–28, 273, 276, 286; see Holiness; Place, holy; Profanation; Sanctification
Holy: foods, 220; materials, disposal of, 134, 143–44; see Holiness; Holy Sphere; Place
Holy sphere, 163–67
Hyssop, 77
Idols, idolatry, 5, 23, 123, 124, 156, 279–290
Impurity: character of, 186; classes of impurity in P, 98, 276; communicable and non-communicable, 163–64, 179–228; cultic versus moral, 85, 283–84; degrees of impurity in Indian texts, 108–110; demonic, 248–52, 261–63, 271, 273–74; Hittite, 43, 84; Mesopotamian, 64–65; not a sin in Bible, 19; place of, 49–50, 231–274; relation to sin, 17–21, 85, 173–77; sacrificial, 129–31 (see *Ḥaṭṭāʾt*); sexual, 19; see Animal impurities; Corpse Contamination; Evils; Pollution; *Ṣāraʿat;* Sexual impurity
Incantation, 59, 64, 68, 70, 71, 81, 250, 253, 254–55, 295; in P, 60
Incense, 64
Indian texts, 105, 107–110
Intercourse, 223; see Sexual impurity
Interpretive comparison, see Comparative method
Intoxicants, as impurities, 108, 109
Invigoration, 45, 56–57, 83; see Blessing
Kidron, 116, 120, 126, 127, 155–56, 279, 280, 281, 282, 285–87
Kings of Judah and Israel, 118–27
Laundering, 182–83, 185–86, 211 (and 181–219, passim); see Washing,
Laver, 156–57
Leniency in P, 112–13
Leprosy, see *Ṣāraʿat*
Lustratio, 52, 59
Maddāp uncleanness, 185
Mediation, 82
Menstruation, see Sexual impurity
Mesopotamian Texts, 60–72, 80–81, 248–261
Methodology, see Comparative method
Milluʾîm, 135–38, 140, 233, 234
Minḥâ, 139, 140, 232, 234, 238
Molech, 19
Mot, 22
Mountain area, see Wilderness
Mouse, 57, 269
Nail clippings, 108
Namburbi, 61, 69–72, 81, 84
Nazirite, 237, 239–40
Nether world, 1, 25–30, 73, 232, 272, 273, 276; in Bible, 25–30, 67; in Hittite texts, 44, 52, 263–71; in Mesopotamian texts, 66, 250–61; see Disposal
Newness of ritual materials, 98–99
Oath, 40, 41, 43, 262, 263, 265
Offering(s), 22–23, 123; appeasement, 24; Hittite, 38–39, 44, 53, 54–55, 105;

Mesopotamian, 62, 70, 253; see Appeasement; Sacrifice
Oil, 70, 178; see Anointing
ʿŌlâ, 139, 144, 147–48, 157, 158, 232, 234
Omen, 37, 38, 71–72
Onion, 294; analogy, 43, 259
Open country, see Wilderness
Outside habitation, 115, 116, 128, 134, 155, 285–86; see Exclusion; Kidron; Wilderness,
Overhang, pollution by, 98, 196–99, 207, 208–09, 213; see Pollution, aerial
P, see Priestly corpus
Parturient, see Sexual impurity
Passing through gates or between parts of animals, 34–35
Passing objects along side of, 63, 67; see Waving
Passover, 166; see *Pesaḥ*
Perspiration, 108
Pesaḥ, 135–138, 145, 235, 242
Phlegm, 108, 109
Pig, 59, 104–06, 201, 267, 293
Place: holy, 163–67, 231, 232–35; impure, 88, 134, 231, 243; pure, 134, 231, 233, 235–43; relationship of holy, pure, and impure places, 243–47
Plague, 45–50, 50–55, 73, 262, 265, 269, 276
Plants (as detergent), 36
Plaza, 61, 66, 257–58, 296; see Street
Pollution: aerial, 19; perpetual, 220; of sanctuary, 19, 239; see Impurity; Overhang
Prayer, 38, 47, 82
Prevention, 43–44, 53, 55, 72; see Fixing evil
Priestly corpus, 4, 179–80
Priests, 165, 215, 218, 219
Profanation, 140–43, 145, 149
Profane sphere, 163–64, 167–68
Purification: graded, 16–17; motifs, Hittite, 31–45
Pus, 109
Quarantine, 88, 90, 210–12
Ram, 64–65
Ramat Rahel, 176
Red Cow, 131, 135, 169, 185, 215, 216–17, 221, 222, 225, 227, 243, 245
Restriction while impure, 163–228, 232, 245–47, 275
River, disposal in; see Water, disposal in bodies of
Sacrifices, 112, 159, 237–42; disposal of, 129–46; historical development, 135–38; holy and most holy, 232, 235–36; see Offering(s); see *ʾĀšām; Ḥaṭṭāʾt; Heqdēš; Ḥērem; Milluʾîm; Minḥâ;* Offerings; *ʿŌlâ, Pesaḥ; Šĕlāmîm;* Tithe; *Tôdâ*
Sacrificial impurity, 96
Sacrilege, 174
Salt (as detergent), 36
Sanctification, 36, 48, 83, 96, 147, 241; desanctification, 155, 157; see Holiness; Profanation
Sanctuary: purification of in Bible 16–21, 276; purification of in Hittite sources, 36, 43; purification of in Mesopotamian sources, 62–65; purity of, 86
Ṣāraʿat, 75–86, 115–16, 164, 165, 168, 169, 172, 173–77, 178, 276; bird rites, 19, 75–

86, 214–15, 222, 225, 227, 245, 272, 277; fabrics with, 87, 90–91, 215, 222, 225, 227; human with *ṣāraʿat*, 76–77, 98, 208–210, 220, 222, 224, 226, 233, 234, 245; infected house, 76, 112, 186, 206–208, 209, 222, 245; materials infected with, 87–91, 112, 225, 227, 244; person purifying from, 212–13, 222, 224, 227; person suspected of, 210–12, 222, 224, 227; see Hebrew Word Index under *ṣāraʿat*
Scapegoat 10, 15–74, 130, 214, 215, 217–18, 219, 222, 225, 227, 245, 276; the English term, 15, 21–22; see Azazel and the Hebrew Word Index under *ʿăzāʾzēl*
Scarlet material, 77
Scouring, 109
Šĕlāmîm, 135–38, 140–43, 147–48, 164, 165, 167, 232, 235, 236, 237, 238, 239, 242
Sexual impotence, 35
Sexual impurity, 95, 115, 164, 165; genital flows in general, 169, 172, 178, 179; intercourse with a menstruant or *zābâ*, 191, 195, 220, 224, 226, 245; menstruant, menstruation, 172, 178, 179, 181, 187, 188, 189–92, 193, 194, 195, 220, 223–24, 226, 245, 284, 285; parturient, 166–67, 172, 178, 179, 195, 220, 222, 224, 226, 245; semen, 108, 109, 171, 172, 178, 179, 183, 196, 198, 227, 245; *zāb*, 95, 98, 168, 169, 172–73, 181–89, 191, 193, 194, 198, 209–10, 213, 220, 222, 223, 224, 226, 245; *zābâ*, 172–73, 185, 187, 188, 193–95, 209, 220, 222, 223, 224, 226, 245
Shrine, definition, 16
Shutting up, see Quarantine
Sickness, 38, 52, 57, 66, 67, 69, 73, 81, 82, 84, 85, 248, 249, 250, 256, 262, 269, 276
Sin, 85, 174, 276; in Hittite texts, 36, 40, 262, 263, 265; in Mesopotamian texts, 81, 84, 248–49; see Impurity
Sorcery, 41–42, 43, 69, 73, 249, 262, 266, 276
Sound, in exorcisms, 63; see Drum
Spitting, 34, 59, 61, 68, 69, 183, 189, 271
Sprinkling, 63, 76–77, 170, 259; see Water
Street, 68, 257–58, 261; see Plaza
Substitute, substitution, 6, 24, 37–38, 41, 45, 47–49, 51, 53, 54, 56, 62, 64, 66, 70–72, 73, 294
Symbols, 3, 32, 47
Tašlîk, 272
Tears, 108, 109
Tension (an evil), 57, 58
Theology, Priestly, 21–25, 49, 72–74, 80, 83–86, 147–48, 232, 246–247, 272–74, 275–77
Thread manipulation, 41–42, 43, 45, 47, 50, 52, 56, 253, 255, 259
Tithe, 236, 238, 242
Tôdâ, 135–38, 141, 235

Torch, see Fire
Tongue, see Word
Transfer, 32–34, 37, 41, 47, 52, 54, 56, 57–58, 59–60, 69, 72, 78, 262; see Contact rites
Treaty, 41
Unraveling, 259–60; see Onion; Thread manipulation
Urine, 108, 109
Uzziah inscription, 125
Waiting until evening and ablution, 220–22
War camp, 171–72, 173, 179, 222
Washing, 36, 61, 84, 90, 109, 111, 156–57, 170, 178, 181–219, 253–54; see Laundering; Waiting until evening; Water
Water, 36; disposal in bodies of, 64, 71, 252–55, 260, 264, 266, 272, 275, 293, 296, 297; impure, 258; pouring out, 83; see Sprinkling
Water of purgation, 98, 170, 186, 196–97, 215–16, 222, 225, 227
Waving rite, Hittite, 33–34, 58, 59, 82–83; see Passing objects along side
Wilderness, 26, 29–30, 52, 59, 61–62, 64, 68, 69, 76–77, 78; 85–86, 87–91, 255–56, 261, 267–68, 269–71, 275, 293; demons, 27–29, 250, 251, 252
Wine, 36, 40, 178
Wiping, Akkadian *kuppuru*, 64, 67–68, 133, 258, 259, 291–99
Witchcraft, 73
Word: evil, 36, 43, 66, 84, 262, 266; magical, 58

Text Reference Index

Hebrew Bible 345
Ancient Versions 358
Apocryphal and Intertestamental Texts 359
Temple Scroll 359
New Testament 360
Josephus and Philo 360
Rabbinic Texts 361
Hittite Texts 364
Akkadian Texts 370
Ugaritic Texts 375
Indian Texts 375

Hebrew Bible

Genesis
7:2–3 205
7:8–9 205
15:11 123, 124, 286
15:17 30
21:14–16 29
27:3 94
31:35 189
35 289
35:1–5 290
35:2 284, 289
35:2–3 289
35:4 288
35:5 289
38:24 91
38:24–25 116

Exodus
2:12 288
4:6–7 208
12:1–14 235
12:4 137
12:10 96, 136, 137
12:11 138
13:12–13 235
13:13 144
15:22 29
16:16–18 137
16:19 137
16:20 137
16:24 137
19:10–11 196, 289
19:10–15 167, 179

19:14–15 196
22:19 285
22:28–29 235
22:30 205
23:18 136
23:19 235
27:1–8 157
27:3 134
28:42 181
29:11 234
29:12 130, 147
29:14 132, 134, 243, 286
29:16 148
29:19–20 154
29:20 148
29:22–28 232
29:26–28 235
29:31 233, 234
29:31–32 234
29:31–34 232
29:33 233
29:34 96, 136, 139, 142
29:36 130
29:42 234
30:10 17, 130
30:19 156
30:19–21 156
32:20 288
34:19 235
34:20 144
34:25 136
34:26 235
38:1–7 157
40:30–32 156
40:31 156

Leviticus
1 112, 232
1:3 234
1:4 17, 148
1:5 148
1:7 148
1:11 148
1:15 148
1:16 134, 286
2:3 232
2:12 235
3 232
3:2 17, 148, 234
3:8 17, 148
3:13 17, 148
4 20, 219
4:1 19
4:1–5:13 19
4:2–12 132
4:4 17, 234
4:5–7 16, 20
4:6 130
4:7 130, 147
4:8 21, 22
4:10 21
4:11 64
4:11–12 134, 243
4:12 286
4:13–21 132
4:16 20
4:16–18 16, 20
4:17 130
4:18 130, 147
4:21 20, 134, 243, 286
4:22–35 132
4:24 17
4:25 19, 130, 147
4:26 21
4:29 17
4:30 19, 130, 147
4:33 17
4:34 19, 130, 147
5:1–13 112
5:2 19, 200, 204, 205
5:5–13 246
5:9 130, 147
5:13 19
6:3 134, 181

6:3–4 143, 286
6:4 134, 243, 286
6:9 232, 233, 234
6:9–10 232
6:10 139
6:11 139
6:16 232
6:18 232
6:18–22 132
6:19 232, 233, 234
6:20 96, 131, 132, 149, 219, 233
6:20–21 219
6:21 132, 184, 208, 216, 219, 232
6:23 132, 134, 232, 243
7 232
7:2 148
7:6 232, 233
7:6–7 139
7:7 139
7:9–10 232
7:11 96
7:14 148
7:15 96, 136, 235
7:16–18 235
7:17 136
7:17–18 96
7:18 141, 142, 143
7:19 140, 164
7:19–21 164, 239
7:20 164, 165
7:20–21 145, 238, 239
7:21 164, 165, 200, 204, 205, 285
7:32–34 235
8:15 130, 147
8:17 132, 134, 243, 286
8:19 148
8:22–24 154
8:24 148
8:25–29 232
8:31 234
8:31–32 232
8:32 96, 136, 139
8:35 138
9:4 236
9:8–11 132
9:9 130, 147
9:11 134, 243, 286
9:12 148
9:14–20 236
9:18 148
10:4–5 115, 196
10:12 232, 233, 234
10:12–13 236
10:12–14 233
10:13 232
10:14 167, 236, 237
10:14–15 235
10:16 139
10:16–18 132
10:17 132, 232, 233, 234, 235
10:17–18 133
10:18 132, 235
11 105, 187, 201, 204, 285
11:2–3 203
11:2–8 202, 205
11:2–23 201, 202, 203
11:4 97
11:4–8 201, 202, 203
11:5 97
11:6 97
11:7 97
11:8 97
11:9–12 203
11:9–23 201, 202
11:10–12 200
11:13–19 203
11:20–23 203
11:24 203, 206
11:24–25 185, 204

11:24–26 205
11:24–28 202, 203
11:24–38 201, 203
11:24–40 201, 202, 203
11:25 206
11:26 97, 206
11:27 97, 206
11:27–28 185, 204, 205
11:28 97, 206
11:29–38 200, 201, 202, 203
11:31 185, 204
11:31–35 205
11:32 94, 170, 184, 185, 208, 216
11:32–33 94, 111
11:32–35 94, 95
11:33 95, 205
11:34 205
11:35 94, 97
11:36 185, 204
11:36–38 205
11:37 205
11:38 97
11:39 206
11:39–40 186, 201, 204, 205
11:40 185, 206
11:41–42 200
11:41–45 200, 201, 203, 206
11:43–44 203
11:44 200
12 172, 195
12:2 166, 189, 195, 222
12:4 166, 167, 222, 223, 238
12:4–5 195
12:5 166, 189, 195, 222
12:6 234
12:6–8 112, 166, 223
13 177, 208
13–14 75, 177
13:2–8 211
13:4 174, 210, 211
13:5 174, 210, 211
13:6 211, 212
13:11 97, 174
13:13 159
13:15 97
13:18–23 211
13:21 174, 210, 211
13:23 211, 212
13:24–28 211
13:26 174, 210, 211
13:28 211, 212
13:29–37 211
13:31 174, 210
13:32 211
13:32–33 211
13:33 174, 210
13:34 210, 211, 212
13:36 97
13:37 174
13:44 97
13:45 210
13:46 97, 173
13:47–59 90, 109, 112, 215
13:50 174, 215
13:51 97
13:51–52 215
13:52 90
13:54 174, 215
13:54–58 77
13:55 90, 97, 215
13:56 90
13:56–57 91
13:56–58 90, 91
13:57 90, 215
13:58 90, 91
14 177, 206, 208
14:1–32 178
14:2–4 76
14:2–7 76, 214

14:2–32 209
14:3 173, 174
14:5 76, 95, 98
14:6–7 76
14:7 76, 78, 214
14:8 169, 173, 212, 213, 221, 224
14:8–9 191
14:8–10 212
14:9 151, 213
14:10–11 112
14:11 234
14:13 233, 234
14:14 154
14:17 154
14:20 213
14:21–22 112
14:23 234
14:25 154
14:28 154
14:33–53 206
14:34 168
14:34–45 88
14:34–53 87
14:36 89, 98, 112, 206, 207
14:37 206
14:37–38 76
14:37–53 76, 89
14:38 174
14:39–42 77
14:40 89, 134, 243
14:41 89, 134, 243
14:43–45 77, 206
14:44 89, 97
14:45 89, 134, 243
14:46 174, 207
14:46–47 77, 88, 89, 98, 186, 207, 211
14:47 207
14:48 77, 174
14:48–53 76, 77, 88,89, 206, 209, 214
14:49 77
14:50 95, 98
14:50–51 77
14:52 78
14:52–53 77
14:53 78, 214
15:2 97, 181, 183
15:2–15 169, 172, 173, 181
15:4 97, 184
15:5 184, 185, 187, 188, 191
15:5–6 188, 189, 191, 193
15:6 184, 187, 188, 191
15:7 181, 183, 184, 213
15:8 183
15:9 97, 184
15:9–10 184, 187, 188, 189, 191, 193, 195
15:10 184, 185, 187, 188, 191
15:11 183, 184, 213, 221
15:12 84, 95, 111, 184, 191, 208, 216
15:13 183, 185, 191, 193
15:13–15 193
15:14 234
15:16 179, 181, 183, 196
15:16–18 196
15:17 184, 196
15:18 179, 196
15:19 172, 181, 183, 189
15:19–24 189, 222
15:20 97, 191
15:20–22 195
15:21–22 187, 188, 189, 191, 192, 193
15:21–23 191
15:23 192
15:24 191, 192
15:25 97, 193

15:25–26 189
15:25–30 169, 172, 173, 193
15:26 193
15:26–27 195
15:27 187, 188, 189
15:28 193
15:28–30 185, 193
15:29 234
15:31 19
15:32 196
15:33 189, 193
16 15, 20, 22, 25, 30, 49, 54
16:3 79
16:5 79
16:7 234
16:8 16, 17, 21, 22
16:8–10 217
16:10 17, 21, 69
16:11–19 79
16:14 16, 130
16:15 16, 130
16:15–19 79
16:16 16, 17, 18, 130
16:18–19 17, 130
16:19 18
16:20 17, 96
16:20–22 79, 217
16:21 17, 18, 20, 95, 96, 216
16:22 17, 18, 30
16:24 218, 233
16:26 19, 21, 29, 65, 130, 169, 217, 221
16:27 64, 132, 134, 243, 286
16:27–28 130, 219
16:28 65, 169, 217, 221
17 23, 24
17:3–9 24
17:4 234
17:5 28, 234
17:6 148
17:7 22, 23, 28
17:9 234
17:13 159
17:15 185
17:15–16 204, 205, 206, 221, 246
17:17 23
18:19 189
18:21 24, 283
18:24 283
18:30 283
19:4 24, 283
19:5–8 235
19:6 96, 136
19:7 141, 142
19:8 142
19:13 137
19:17 233
19:21 234
20:2–5 24
20:3 19, 283
20:14 91
20:18 189
21 242
21:1–4 167, 196
21:9 91
21:10–12 167, 196
21:16–23 165
21:22 165
22:3 165
22:4 165, 198, 208
22:4–5 198
22:4–6 165, 181, 198
22:4–7 196
22:5 204
22:5–6 200
22:6 185
22:6–7 164, 165, 221, 198
22:8 205
22:10–16 236

22:29–30 235
22:30 96, 136
23:10 235
23:19 232
24:4 198
24:9 232, 233
24:14 17, 116
24:23 116
26:1 24
26:1–2 283
26:30 124
27:27 144
27:28 235, 284
27:29 144
27:30 236
27:30–31 236
27:30–33 236
27:32 236
27:32–33 236

Numbers
1:3 171
2 171
2:4 171
4:13 134
5 171
5:1–4 168, 169, 171, 172
5:2–3 172, 173, 178, 181, 196, 208, 245, 246
5:2–4 172
5:3 172
5:17 95, 98
5:23 98, 208
6 239, 240
6:5 143, 167
6:6–12 167, 196
6:9 143, 167
6:9–12 143
6:10 234
6:10–11 242
6:11 143, 167
6:13 234
6:14 237
6:14–20 240
6:17 237
6:18 143, 237
6:19 143
6:19–20 237
9:6–13 166
9:6–14 196
9:12 96, 136
10 171
10:9 171
10:14 171
10:35–36 171
12:10–15 85, 208
12:12 175, 178
12:14–15 174
14:29 124
14:32 124
14:33 124
15:20–21 235
15:35–36 116
18:10 234, 235
18:11 165, 235, 236
18:11–19 236
18:12 235
18:13 165, 235, 236
18:14 235
18:15 144
18:15–18 235
18:17 148
18:19 236
18:25–29 236
18:25–32 236
18:27 236
18:30 236
18:31 236
18:32 236
19 80, 168, 171, 173, 196, 221, 242
19:2 170
19:2–8 169
19:2–10 216

19:3 135
19:7 131, 169, 185, 215, 216, 221
19:8 131, 185, 216
19:9 131, 135, 197, 216, 217, 243
19:9–10 169
19:10 131, 171, 185, 216
19:11 196
19:11–22 215
19:12 170, 197
19:13 19, 170, 197, 246
19:14 97, 196
19:14–15 170, 198
19:14–16 97
19:15 96, 97, 98, 198, 208
19:15–18 109
19:16 97, 196, 199
19:17 98
19:18 97, 170, 196
19:18–19 170, 197, 198
19:19 170, 185, 191, 197, 221
19:20 19, 170, 197, 246
19:21 98, 131, 171, 186, 197, 216, 217
19:22 197, 198
20:1 117
21:5 29
27:18 17
27:23 17
31 171, 172
31:13 169
31:13–24 196
31:19 170, 197
31:19–24 96, 107, 111, 169, 170
31:20 170, 198
31:21 170
31:21–23 198
31:23 94, 170, 197, 198
31:24 169, 170, 171, 185, 191, 197, 221
35:16 94
35:18 94
35:22 94

Deuteronomy
4:28 23
7 285
7:5 284, 288
7:25 288
7:25–26 284
7:26 285
8:15 27, 29
9:21 288
10:6 117
12:6–7 235, 236, 242
12:11–12 235, 236, 242
12:15 166
12:16 148, 159
12:17–18 236, 242
12:21–22 235
12:22 166
12:24 148, 159
12:27 148
13 284
13:13–19 284
13:17 288
14:3–21 205
14:22–23 236, 242
14:26 242
14:28–29 236
15:20 235, 242
15:22 166
15:23 148, 159
16:4 136
16:5–7 235
16:7 242
16:11 242
17:5 117, 174
18:4 235
20:15–18 285
21:1–9 5, 272

21:19 117
21:21 117
22:5 94
22:21 117
22:24 117, 174
23:10–15 171, 172, 196
23:11–12 179
23:12 169, 221
23:13 178
23:15 171
24:8 208
26:2 235
26:10 235
26:12 236
26:14 166
27:7 242
28:36 23
28:64 23
29:16 23
32:17 23
32:32 282

Joshua
2:6 288
6:17–19 235
6:18 284
7 284
7:12 284
7:21 288
7:24–25 117
7:25 91
8:11 286
8:29 174
20:4 174
24:23 289
24:30 117
24:33 116

Judges
2:9 117
9:35 174
9:44 174
10:2 117
10:5 117
10:16 289
12:7 117
12:10 117
12:12 117
12:15 117
13:4 167, 205
13:5 167
13:7 167, 205
13:14 167
16:31 116
18:11 94
18:16–17 94

1 Samuel
1 240
1:4 237, 240
1:7–9 237, 240
1:18–19 237, 240
2 240
2:13–17 237, 240
5–6 5, 273
6:3 253
6:4 253
6:5 253
6:8 253
6:10–16 53
7:3 289
9:12–25 237, 240
9:22 240, 241
16:5 166
17:46 124
20:26 166, 196
21:4–7 171, 196
25:1 117
28:3 117

2 Samuel
2:32 117
3:29 85, 173, 181, 208
5:21 288

11:4 189
11:11 196
12:31 30
17:29 29
21:9 117
21:14 117
23:31 22

1 Kings
2:10 118
2:34 117
3:25 30
3:26 30
7:33 151
11:43 118
13:2 288
13:3 286
13:5 286
14:24 286
14:31 118
15:8 118
15:13 280
15:24 118
16:6 117
16:28 117
18:30–35 158
20:42 284
21:13 117
22:35 151
22:37 117
22:51 118

2 Kings
2:20 98
5 85, 177, 208
5:1–2 177
5:3 174
5:6 174, 177
5:7 174
5:9 177
5:10 84, 272
5:11 174
5:13–14 84
5:14 272
5:27 85
6:4 30
7:3–4 174
7:3–10 208
8:24 118
9:28 118
10:8 174
10:26 288
10:35 117
12:22 118
13:9 117
13:15–17 55
13:20–21 116
14:16 117
14:20 118
15:5 85, 174, 208
15:7 118, 119
15:38 118
16:10–16 281
16:13 148, 155
16:15 148, 155
16:17–18 280
16:20 118
19:18 23
19:35 124
20:21 119
21:18 119
21:26 119
23:4 282, 283, 285
23:6 116, 120, 282, 285
23:12 282
23:15 288
23:16 116, 288
23:20 288
23:30 119
25:4 283

Isaiah
2:8 23
2:10 288

2:20 23
9:19 30
13 28
13:3 196
13:21–22 27, 29
14:19 124
16:8 282, 283
21:4 280
22:15–16 116
22:16 116
30:22 23, 189, 223, 284, 285
34 28
34:3 124
34:4 28
34:11 27
34:11–15 29
34:13 27
34:14–15 27
35:1 29
35:6 29
35:7 29
37:19 23
37:36 124
40:19–20 23
41:18 29
43:19 29
43:19–20 29
44:9–20 23
46:6–7 23
48:5 23
53:8 30
61:10 94
65:4 142, 196
66:17 205
66:24 124

Jeremiah
2:6 26, 27
2:22–23 284
2:23 287
2:24 29
2:31 26, 27
7:30 293
7:31 287
7:31–34 287
9:9 29
9:20 29
10:1–15 23
12:10 29
13:1 94
13:4 288
17:6 29
19:1–6 287
19:5 287
22:6 29
23:10 29
31:37–39 287
31:39 (40) 123, 124, 282, 283, 286
32:14 95
32:34 283
32:35 287
33:5 124
35:2 241
35:4 241
39:4 283
41:9 124
50:39 28, 29
51:17–18 23
51:43 29
52:7 283

Ezekiel
1:18 151
4:12 142
4:12–13 205
4:14 142
5:11 283
6:5 124
7:18 280
7:19 280
7:19–20 189
7:19–21 284

7:20 280
10:12 151
13:4 29
16:17 94
16:24 151
16:26 181
16:31 151
16:39 151
18:6 189
20:7 284
20:18 284
20:30 284
20:32 23
22:3–4 284
22:10 189
23:7 284
23:20 181
23:30 284
24:17 210
24:22 210
27:26 94
36:17 189
36:18 284
36:25 284
37:11 30
37:23 284
39:11–16 196
40:17–18 241
42:1–14 233
42:13 233
42:14 241
42:16–20 241
43 124, 153
43:7–9 122, 124, 196
43:13 151, 152
43:13–17 149
43:14 150, 151, 152
43:15 149, 150
43:16 149
43:16–17 152
43:17 150, 151, 152, 153
43:18 148, 154, 154
43:20 130, 150, 153, 154
43:21 135
43:22 130
43:23 130
44:1 135
44:7 135, 181
44:9 135, 181
44:11 135
44:19 241
44:25–27 167, 196
44:26–27 167
44:27 242
44:30 235, 235
45:16 286
45:18 130
45:19 130, 150, 153, 154
46:1–3 241
46:19–20 233
46:20 241
46:21 241
46:21–22 241
46:23–24 241
46:24 241
47:3 94
47:4 94

Hosea
2:5 29
8:6 23
13:2 23
13:14 28–29

Joel
1:19 29
2:22 29

Amos
6:5 94
8:3 124

Micah
1:7 288

3:7 210
7:18–19 272
7:19 5

Nahum
3:3 124

Habakkuk
2:18–19 23
3:17 30, 282, 283

Zephaniah
2:12–14 29
2:14 28

Haggai
2:13 196

Zechariah
5:5–11 5, 86, 273
5:8 273
13:1 197
13:2 284

Malachi
1:3 28, 29

Psalms
55:6 280
63:2 27
65:13 29
78:52 29
88:6 30, 175, 176
102:7 29
106:36 23
106:37 23
106:38 23
106:39 284
107:4 29
107:33 29
107:35 29
107:40 27
115:4–7 23
129:3 151
135:15–17 23
136:13 30
143:6 27

Job
3:19 175
6:18 27
9:6 280
12:24–25 27
13:12 151
15:26 151
16:22 30
21:6 280
22:28 30
24:5 29
38:26 29
39:5–6 29

Canticles
8:6 22

Lamentations
1:17 280
3:54 30
4:3 29

Esther
2:1 30

Daniel
7:6 151

Ezra
9:11 280, 284

Nehemiah
3:15 283
3:31 135
10:37 235
10:38 235

10:38–39 236
12:44 235, 236
13:5 236
13:12 236

1 Chronicles
5:9 29
14:12 288
15:16 94

2 Chronicles
4:6 156
4:9 150
6:13 150
9:31 118
11:15 23
12:16 118
13:23 118
15:16 280
16:14 118
20:24 124
21:1 118
21:20 119
23:19 167
24:16 118
24:25 119
25:28 118
26:16–21 208
26:20–21 85
26:21 30, 174, 177
26:23 119
27:9 118
28–29 280
28:22–23 281
28:24 280
28:27 119
29 281
29:3 280
29:5 280
29:6–7 280–81
29:16 280, 285
29:22 148, 155
30:14 281
30:16 148, 155
31:5 235
31:6 236
32:33 119
33:15 281, 285
33:20 119
34:5 288
35:11 148, 155
35:24 119
36:14 283

Ancient Versions

Greek

Leviticus
15:9 184
15:23 192
15:24 192
15:27 187, 195

Ezekiel
43:15 150

Targum Onqelos

Leviticus
5:2 200
14:37 88

Numbers
6:18 143

Targum Pseudo-Jonathan

Leviticus
14:8–10 213

Numbers
6:18 143
19:17 98

Syriac

Leviticus
5:2 200

Apocryphal and Intertestamental Texts

Baruch
4:35 28

1 Enoch
8:1 22
9:6 22
10:4–8 22
13:1 22
54:5–6 22
55:4 22
69:2 22

Jubilees
31:2 290
31:10 242
32:15 242
49:16–21 242

Tobit
8:3 28

Temple Scroll

16:10–14 135
17:8–9 242
21:3 242
22:11–14 242
22:13–14 242
31:10–33:7 156
32:12–15 156
32:15 157

40–46	242	46:17–18	178
43	242	47:5–6	178
45:7–10	178	47:6	178
45:11–12	178	47:7–18	178
45:12–13	166	48:10–14	178
45:12–14	178	48:11–14	127
45:13	166	48:14–17	178
45:17–46:1	178	51:2–5	204
46:1–4	178	52:9	242
46:13–16	178	52:13–21	242
46:16–18	178	52:16	242

New Testament

Matthew
12:43 28

Luke
11:24 28

Acts
7:58 117

Hebrews
13:12 117

Revelation
18:2 28

Philo and Josephus

Josephus

Antiquities
3.11.3 § 261 224
3.9.3–4 §§ 230–35 139
18.2.3 §§ 36–38 126

Wars
5.5.6 § 227 224

Philo

De Specialibus Legibus
1.40 §§ 220–23 140

Rabbinic Texts

Mishnah

Šabbat
9:1 285

Pesaḥim
3:8 145, 240
7:8 145, 240
7:9 240

Šeqalim
8:6 145
8:7 145

Yoma
3:10 156
4:2 24
4:4 156
5:6 155
6:5–6 24
6:6 24, 218
6:7 132, 218

Megilla
1:7 174, 211
1:11 240

Nazir
6:8 143

Soṭa
2:2 99

Baba Batra
2:9 126

Makkot
3:2 145
3:3 240

ʿAboda Zara
2:3 285
3:6 285
5:1 285

Zebaḥim
5:1–2 148, 155
5:3 139, 155
5:5 232
5:6 240
5:6–8 240
6.1 139
8:4 145
8:5 145
8:7 156
8:8 156
8:9 156
8:11 156
11:7 96
12:5 145
12:6 132, 218
13:2 145

Menaḥot
6:1 232
6:2 232

Temura
7:4 76, 143
7:6 156

Keritot
6:1 145, 156

Meʿila
3:3 155

Tamid
5:5 156

Middot
2:5 143, 237
3:2 155
3:3 145

Kelim
1:1 204, 213
1:2 216
1:3 191
1:4 209
1:5 211, 222
1:7 126
1:8 169, 222, 240
2:1 94, 95
2:3 95
3:1–8 95
9:5 99
10:1 208
15:1 94
15:2–4 94
16:1–4 94
17:1–3 94
20:1 94
27:1 94
30:1 94

ʾOholot
1:2–3 200
5:6 208
16–18 126

Negaʿim
8:8 209, 211
12:5 112
12:7 77
13:1 77
13:4 207
13:7 209
13:8 215
13:9–10 186
13:11 209
13:12 207
14:1 76, 99
14:2 213

Para
5:5 98
8:7 220

Ṭoharot
1:9 220
1:2 286
2:6 220

Nidda
7:4 127, 223

Zabim
2:4 186
5:1 186
5:6 185, 189, 191, 209, 213
5:6–10 186
5:6–12 222
5:8 185
5:10 185, 213
5:11 191

Tosefta

Megilla
1:12 211

Baba Batra
1:7 127
1:11 125, 126, 127, 156

Zebaḥim
5:12 145
6:9 155
6:16 232
7:6 145
8:16–24 156
10:11 96
11:18 145

Temura
4:16 145, 156

Negaʿim
6:2 126
8:6 213

7:4 207
7:6 215
7:11 209
7:12 208
7:13 207

Nidda
6:15 127, 224

Zabim
5:2–5 186
5:3 209
5:5 285
5:6 285
5:7 285
5:8 285

Babylonian Talmud

Šabbat
82b 285

Pesaḥim
67a 169

Yoma
37a 156
67b 218

Megilla
8b 174, 211

Yebamot
103b 215

Nedarim
64b 175

Soṭa
15b 99

Baba Qamma
2a, b 222

Sanhedrin
47a 175

ʿAboda Zara
29b 285

Zebaḥim
21a 156
104b 145

Ḥullin
13b 285
129a 285

Nidda
9a 216
32b–33a 185
33a 191

Jerusalem Talmud

ʿErubin
5:3 (22d) 126

Yoma
3:8 (41a) 156

Nazir
9:3 (57d) 126

Soṭa
2:2 [17d] 99

Other Texts

Sipra
Meṣoraʾ Par 2:11 213
Meṣoraʾ 5:4–6 186
Meṣoraʾ, Zabim 4:1 184, 185
Meṣoraʾ, Zabim 4:2 184, 185

Meṣora', Zabim Par 4:9 189
Meṣora', Zabim Par 4:15 193

SipreNumbers
10 (Horovitz 16: 6) 99
127 (Horovitz 164-65) 200
128 (Horovitz 165–66) 98
158 (Horovitz 214:10–14) 200

'Abot de-Rabbi Natan
A 35:2 126
B 39 126

Semaḥot
14 126

Hittite Texts

ABoT
25 iii 24–25 103

Allaiturahhi
94–96 iv 9′–15′ 36
136: 41′–42′ 33
138 ii 13–18 36
210: 61′–64′ 33
210: 64′–65′ 33

Ambazzi
i 19 57
i 34–44 57
ii 2 39
ii 2–5 57
ii 2–8 40
ii 7–8 40
ii 15–20 42
ii 15–23 58
ii 20 57
ii 25–28 40
ii 29 57
ii 34–37 58
ii 34–42 24, 57
ii 37–39 54, 58
ii 39–40 58, 266
ii 41 58
ii 41–45 39
iii 25 57
iii 33 57
iii 38–47 57, 58
iv 10 57
iv 28–32 44
iv 30–33 269

Amihatna
i 30–31 40
i 35–38 40
i 42–47 266
i 48 33
ii 2–3 33
iii 9–12 40
iii 17–24 40
iii 30–39 266
iii 40 33
iv 20–21 33

Anniwiyani
i 10–25 42
i 16–21 34
i 27 83
i 36–39 35
ii 6–8 265
ii 9–18 35
ii 27–33 39
iii 42–44 40
iv 1–5 40

Ashella
(i) 1–32 50–51
(i) 2 51
(i) 4–6 51
(i) 7–10 53
(i) 8–10 52
(i) 12–14 39, 53
(i) 15 51, 52
(i) 16–17 53
(i) 18–23 53, 54
(i) 19–23 262
(i) 19–23 39, 53
(i) 20–21 47, 59
(i) 25 53
(i) 25–26 52
(i) 26 52
(i) 26–27 269
(i) 27 53
(i) 28–31 53
(i) 32 53

Ayatarsa
i 6–8 39
i 36 33

Birth Ritual
C vs. 9 33
H ii 4–8 44
H ii 12–14 33
H iii 6–15 270
164 vs. 24–26 106
168 rs. 28–30 107
168 rs. 28 101

Bo
89 i 2–6 268
2072 ii 33–34 100
4951+ rs. 17 100
6342 x+8 100

BoTU
ii 24 100

Building Ritual
iv 9–12 40
iv 13–16 40
iv 17–21 40
iv 22–25 40

Death Ritual
18 vs. 16–18 33
20 ii 3 100
22 iv 3 100
32 vs. 19 100
32 vs. 29 100
46 iv 26 100, 103
66: 1 268
66: 1–5 267
66: 10 268
66: 10–11 268
66: 12 267
66: 20 268
72 ii 3 100
74 ii 14 100
74 ii 22 100
76 iii 32 100
76 iii 39 100, 103
82 i 8′ 100

Evocatio
i 19 106

Gassuliyawiya Prayer
vs. (i) 10–14 47
ii 18–26 39

Goetze, A., "Die Pestgebete des Muršiliš"
206, 2:3 269
214, 9:7 269

Gurney, O., "Hittite Prayers of Mursili II"
28–29 C ii 31–37 269
32–33 D ii 14–15 269

Haas, V., "Ein hethitisches Beschwörungsmotiv aus Kizzuwatna"
413: 35–37

House Purification
i 24–27 40
i 28–34 40
i 39–ii 7 39
ii 52–56 270
ii 57 269
iii 1–12 44
iii 6–12 265
iv 9–14 263
iv 9–15 265
iv 30–36 265
iv 31 269
iv 37–41 266
iv 44 269

Huwarlu
i 7–18 40
i 14 59
i 19–21 34
i 23–26 44
i 27–32 42
i 33–37 42
i 39–47 36
i 44–46 39
i 44–47 36
i 48–52 36
i 48–54 36
i 50–54 266
i 55–60 36, 40
i 62–70 33, 59
ii 5–9 33
ii 5–14 58–59
ii 6 59
ii 7 59
ii 8–13 59, 60
ii 9–10 47
ii 10 59
ii 12 59
ii 13–23 44
ii 24–55 269
ii 28 59
ii 30–31 59
ii 36–41 265

Instructions to Temple Officials
i 15–20 36
iii 60–65 36
iii 70–75 36

KBo
2.4 ii 7 100
2.4 ii 8 100
2.4 ii 9 100
2.4 ii 33 100
9.119 iv 11–12 33
9.126 103
12.96 i 21 102
15.2 rs. 21 100
15.2 rs. 27 100
15.9 ii 21 100
15.9 iv 13 100
17.61 rs. 18′–19′ 270
17.61 rs. 22′–24′ 270
17.65+ vs. 11 100
17.65 vs. 24–26 106
17.65+ vs. 24 100
17.65+ rs. 28–29 103
17.65+ rs. 28 100
17.68 100

KUB
2.13 i 43 100
2.13 i 46 100
5.7 vs. 34 106
6.45+ ii 34–36 82
7.33 vs. 15 100
9.11+ i 20–25 267
9.22+ iii 6–15 270
11.9 iv 23 100
12.26 ii 1–10 34

12.44 iii 2–9 44
13.3 ii 29–iii 2 41
13.4 iii 59–60 105
13.4 iii 64 100, 101
13.4 iii 64–68 105
13.4 iv 28 104
15.34+ 38
15.34 ii 25–27 40
17.10 iii 8–12 33
17.27 ii 1–5 36
17.27 ii 20–25 39
17.27 ii 25 102
17.27 ii 25–37 102
17.27 ii 28–41 43
17.27 ii 36 102
17.27 iii 4–6 270
21.27 iv 26–46 82
24.1 iii 16–iv 8 269
24.14 i 18–21 263
24.2 vs. 10–11 269
24.3 269
24.3 iii 9–11 269
29.8 ii 8–11 55
30.10 vs. 2–5 82
30.33 iv 5–9 83
30.33 iv 9 84
30.34 iv 9–14 83
30.34 iv 19–29 52, 265
30.35 iv 2–4 83
41.1 iii 3 100, 104
41.11 i 12 83

Laroche, E., "Textes mythologiques hittites en transcription"
97:14–19 264
118: 6–8 264
130: 9–15 264
139: 5–9 264

Laws (Hittite)
11 104
12 104
44b 267
74 104
187–88 105
199–200 105

Malli
i 31–36 42
i 31–ii 16 41
i 37–40 42
ii 16′–25′ 44
ii 21′–25′ 265
ii 26′–33′ 265
ii 26′–33′ 39, 44
ii 34′ 39
ii 34′–39′ 44
ii 39′ 39
ii 44′–54′ 34, 33
ii 63′ 100, 104
iii 2′–4′ 34
iii 33′–34′ 36
iii 36′–37′ 34
iv 5–10 265
iv 14–29 39

Mastigga
passim 33
i 2–4 133
i 31′–35′ 40
ii 5–14 270
ii 15–20 270
ii 21–22 36
ii 22–24 270
ii 26–34 34, 265
ii 35–43 34
ii 44–54 40, 265
ii 55–iii 6 40
iii 14–18 265
iii 14–16 59
iii 14–19 34
iii 20 36
iii 32–33 104
iii 35 104
iii 38–42 133

iii 38–43 39
iii 44–48 39
iii 49 100
iii 49–53 39
iii 54–iv 8 40
iv 6–7 36
iv 7 41
iv 12–13 104
iv 17–20 36
iv 21–25 36

Mastigga (parallel version; cf. *ANET*, 351)
i 8–10 133–34
ii 47–53 133

Mursilis Sprachlähmung
vs. 9–11 48
vs. 11–12 55
vs. 15–16 55
rs. 36–37 55

Papanikri
i 4 103
i 25–26 36
i 39–47 39
i 45 103
ii 31 106
ii 38 100
ii 55–iii 1′ 33
iv 9–10 33
iv 40 103

Paskuwatti
i 18–29 35

Plague Ritual
i 31–33 39
ii 3–17 39
ii 6–9 269
ii 14–17 269

Pulisa
i 1–43 45–47
i 4 48
i 7 47
i 10–11 47
i 11–12 48
i 13–14 47
i 16 47, 48
i 16–17 47, 59
i 16–21 39
i 18 47
i 19–20 48
i 20–21 49, 269
i 22 48
i 22–41 48
i 23 47
i 24 48
i 25–26 48
i 27–31 48
i 33 48
i 35–36 59
i 35–37 48
i 37–38 49
i 40–41 48
i 42–43 49

Samuha
rs./ii 36–41 259
rs./ii 36–37 40
rs./ii 36–41 43
rs./ii 38–39 40
rs./ii 42–47 43
rs./ii 48–49 254
rs./ii 48–50 266
rs./ii 58–61 40
rs./ii 61–66 266

Soldiers Oath
in general 41

StBot 2
vs. 7 36
vs. 22–25 39

StBoT 3
8 vs. 7′–11′ 37
8 vs. 13′–16′ 37
10 vs. 20′–24′ 38
10 vs. 26′–27′ 36
10 vs. 30′ 36
151 iv 51–56 36

StBoT 8
i 3′–6′ 34
i 11′ 84
i 12′ 84
i 14′–17′ 34, 36
i 35–ii 3 265
i 36′ 34
ii 4–12 39
ii 11 84
ii 30–iii 9 33
ii 41–45 34
ii 44–iii 13 33, 82
ii 45–46 82
ii 51 82
iii 1–2 82
iii 3 82
iii 6–7 82
iii 8 82
iii 8–13 265
iii 10–13 82
iii 10–16 39
iii 11 84
iii 12 84
iii 19 84
iii 20 84
iv 2 84
iv 5 84
iv 5–10 39
iv 14–22 42
iv 14–34 34
iv 34 34
iv 34–36 271
iv 36–37 83

StBoT 22
iii 36–38 102

Telepinu
ii 5–9 39
ii 15–18 40
ii 19–21 40
ii 23–25 40

Tunnawi
i 20 100, 102
i 20–21 103
i 57 33
i 60–62 33
i 60–64 59
i 63–64 33
ii 4–5 33
ii 8–9 33
ii 12–16 266
ii 18–20 40
ii 21 36
ii 28–40 42
ii 46–49 41
ii 52–53 33
ii 52–54 33
ii 53 102
ii 61 36
ii 62–iv 5 34
iii 10 263
iii 17–20 59
iii 35–42 35
iii 43–45 40
iii 46–53 35
iv 7–13 40
iv 15–23 40
iv 24–28 39
iv 29–37 39

Tuthaliya and Nikalmati
i 22–28 39
i 29–37 39
ii 5–7 40
ii 12–16 40

ii 17–21 39
ii 22–29 39
ii 30–35 39
ii 36–40 39
ii 41–44 39
iii 28′–39′ 39
iii 51′–52′ 40

Uhhamuwa
ii 17 56
ii 17–19 56
ii 17–33 55–56
ii 19–20 57
ii 20–21 56
ii 21–22 56
ii 23 56, 269
(ii) 24–31 39
ii 25–26 59
ii 25–27 56
ii 26 56
ii 27–31 56
ii 32–33 56, 269
ii 38–39 57
ii 54–57 39
iii 1–5 39

Ulippi
iii 19–20 33
iii 65–66 33
iv 38–40 36

VAT
6212 100

VBoT
3 iii 9–16 44
24 i 27 83

Akkadian Texts

AfO
10, 36, #63: 7–13 296
18, 77: 10 291

AfO Beiheft
6, 13–14, #5: 7–9 292
6, 14, #5: 12–14 256, 296

Akītu (See p. 62, n. 133)
342 63
345–47 62
346–63 63–64
348 63
350 63
351 63
354 64
356 63
359–60 252
359 64
360–63 64, 255
364–68 65
369–70 65

AMT
25.6 ii 12 285
28.3: 5 295
64.1: 18 292

ASKT
87: 65–66 292

Assakī Marṣūti, See *CT* 17.10–11

BBR
#26 i 18–19 297

#26 i 19–20 257, 296
#26 ii 1 295, 297
#26 ii 3 257, 296
#26 v 35 297
#28: 4 297
#41–42: 21–28 293
#41–42: 28–29 296

BRM 4
6 rs. 32 296
6 rs. 37 296
18: 4 258

BWL
40: 51 251
40: 52 250
40: 53 250
40: 54 251
40: 55 250
52: 5 251, 252
52: 6 251
52: 7 252
52: 8 252
52: 9 250
215 iii 5–16 106

Cagni, L., *L'epopea di Erra*
i 185 251

Caplice, R., "Namburbi Texts in the British Museum"
I, 117 rs. 7′–22′ 255
I, 117: 22′–26′ 260
I, 121: 15′–18′ 253
I, 127: 10–12 255
I, 130 vs. 2′–9′ 254
II, 1–8 vs. 10–11 71
II, 1–8 vs. 10–rs. 21 69–71
II, 1–8 vs. 12 72
II, 1–8 vs. 14–17 72
II, 1–8 vs. 17–22 72
II, 1–8 vs. 23 72
II, 1–8 vs. 24–33 72
II, 1–8 vs. 29–30 72
II, 1–8 vs. 36 72
II, 1–8 vs. 36–rs. 3 72
II, 1–8 rs. 4–5 72
II, 1–8 rs. 6–14 72
II, 1–8 rs. 8 72
II, 1–8 rs. 10–11 72
II, 1–8: rs. 15–16 255
II, 1–8 rs. 15–18 72
II, 1–8 rs. 19–20 72
II, 14–15 vs. 15–rs. 5 255
II, 15 rs. 11 252
II, 17: 13′–16′ 260
II, 25: 10′–12′ 260
II, 28: 11′–13′ 260
II, 34: 14–16 255
II, 34–38 rs. 6′ 81
II, 35 rs. 3′ 260
III, 273: 11′–13′ 260
III, 273–78 vs. 11′ 81
III, 273–78 rs. 28′–29′ 81
III, 275: 22′–24′ 260
III, 285 rs. 6′–9′ 260
III, 285: 7′–9′ 260
III, 289: 22′ 253
III, 290: 26′–27′ 253
III, 290: 27′ 253
III, 290: 27′–34′ 254
III, 290: 28′ 253
III, 295–96 rs. 5–8 260
III, 296: 8 256
IV, 134: 12–15 260
V, 133:6 252
V, 135: 15′ 252
V, 136: 3 252
V, 140: 4′ 81
V, 162: 2′–4′ 260
V, 163 61
V, 168: 2′–5′ 253
V, 168:4′ 252
V, 169 vs. 8′ 250
V, 169 vs. 9′ 252

Castellino, G., "Rituals and Prayers Against 'Appearing Ghosts'"
246: 13 251
258: 11–13 258
260: 24 258
268: 15 258

CT
4.5: 15–16 259
12: 3 251
16.1: 25 251
16.1: 29 251
16.1: 30/31 249
16.1: 37 251
16.9 ii 15–25 249
16.12: 13 250
16.12: 25 249
16.12: 30–35 249
16.14 iv 15 249
16.14 iv 25–30 249
16.14: 40–45 249
16.15 v 48 249
16.19: 1–15 249
16.19: 30–34 249
16.2: 40–45 249
16.21: 144 249
16.21: 145–53 249
16.29: 57 252
16.29: 95 252
16.29: 99 251
16.32: 157 251
16.37: 15 251
16.44: 103 251
16.44: 105 251
17.1: 5 257, 296
17.1: 7 258
17.8 vii 13–22 252
17.10–11: 68–89 63, 67–68
17.10–11: 77–80 68
17.10–11: 82–85 68
17.10–11: 86 63, 68
17.10–11: 87 68
17.11: 84–85 294
17.12: 5 250
17.13: 18 250
17.15: 24 295
17.19: 2 251
17.19–20: 36–51 67
17.22: 140–44 81
17.22: 157–58 250
17.25: 2 251
17.26: 73–79 67
17.26: 75 257
17.30: 33–36 294
17.31: 38–40 294
17.32: 1–20 61
17.32: 11 257
17.32: 13 257
17.33: 18 295
17.38: 11–16 258
17.41: 2 250
17.41: 4–9 258
23.1: 4 295
23.1: 9–10 297
23.1: 9–11 258–59
28.29: 8 291

Driver, G. R. and Miles, J. C., *The Babylonian Laws*
2. 338–39 ii 24–41 298

Ebeling, E., *Aus dem Tagewerk eines assyrischen Zauberpriesters*
10: 18–21 257

Ebeling, E., "Beiträge zur Kenntnis den Beschwörungsserie Namburbi"
4, 182: 5 297
4, 182: 8 297

4 R
17 rs. 33 297

18, 6:4–5 251
59, 2 rs. 12–16 81

Gurney, O., "Babylonian Prophylactic Figures and Their Rituals"
58–59: 49–52 293
58–59: 53–60 293
58–59: 60–61257, 293, 296
86: 137 251
86:131 252
86–89: 115–16 66
86–89: 115–37 65–66
86–89: 117–18 66
86–89: 119–23 67
86–89: 124–25 67
86–89: 126–31 66
86–89: 130–31 67
86–89: 132–33 66
86–89: 132–35 66
86–89: 136–37 66, 67

Gurney, O., "A Tablet of Incantations Against Slander"
222:19 254

Ishtar's Descent to the Nether World, *ANET* 108
rs. 24–25 257

KAJ
189: 10 296
192: 26 296
221:6 296

KAR
33 vs. 1 62
33 rs. 7 62
33 rs. 10 62
62 rs. 34–35 252
72: 3–5 293
72: 4–5 256
72: 5 253
72: 6–7 252, 256
92: 10 294
114 rs. 8 292
114 rs. 8–9 257
230 rs. 2 297

Knudsen, E., "An Incantation Tablet from Nimrud"
55: 27–37 295
55–58 vs. 37–38 295
56:44–47 249
56:55 249
57:23 249
57–60 rs. 27–41 133
57–60 rs. 38–41 81

KUB
37.210: 8 291

Lambert, W., "DINGIR.ŠÀ.DIB.BA Incantations"
274: 19–20 260

Lambert, W., "A Part of the Ritual for the Substitute King"
110 vs. 1–8 258, 260

LKA
142: 17 253, 297
154 rs. 12–13 251

Maqlu
i 105 258
i 135–43 249
ii 16 260
ii 31–69 248
ii 125–34 103
ii 146–47 260
iii 78 257
iv 9–11 260
iv 23 256
iv 25 69

iv 105–07 257
iv 105–16 260

Meier, G. "Ein Akkadisches Heilungsritual aus Boğazköy"
202 ii 11 256
202 ii 20 294
204–07 iii 27–iv 14 255
204 iii 20 256

Myhrman, D. W., "Die Labartu-Texte"
160: 23–27 61
164–67 iv 3–11 254
164–66 iv 3–11 61
170–03: 44–46 254
178: 13–14 257
190 rs. 3 257
192: 20–25 61
194: 34–38 61

Namburbis, See Caplice

OECT 6
24–47 vs. 11–13 260
25 rs. 7–11 81
40–41, 72–73 248
49 297

PBS
1/1.15: 18 295

RAcc
7: 24–25 256
38 rs. 12 292
38: 23–24 297
44:13 297
141: 354 295

Reiner, E., "*Lipšur* Litanies"
136–39: 98–100 260
136: 81–95 248
136: 79–80 259
138–39: 101–02 254
140–43: 7′–37′ 260
140: 12′–14′ 259
140: 22′ 81, 249
142: 37′ 81, 249
142: 41′–43′ 258

Shurpu
i 11 295
i 11–21 259
i 13–16 295
ii 248
iii 92 258
iv 45–55 248
iv 79 250
v-vi 259
v-vi 1–22 248
v-vi 164/165 255
vii 1–20 249
vii 1–36 248
vii 2 250
vii 19/20 248, 249
vii 37 67
vii 37–50 67
vii 51 67
vii 53 67
vii 53–70 24, 68–69
vii 55–59 294
vii 58–59 69
vii 60–61 69
vii 64 255
vii 67–68 69
vii 67–70 69
vii 69–70 69
vii 71–85 69
viii 89–90 259
ix 58–69 254
ix 70–87 254

TDP
1. 70: 2 295
1. 116 ii 2 295

TuL
39: 16 253
51: 1–5 260
56: 27 253
68 vs. 13–14 67
73–76 See *KAR* 33
74: 11 256
94: 30 253
94:31 253
94 rs. 32 296
94 rs. 37 253, 296
98: 15 254
98: 15–16 253
108: 65 297
118–19: 5–7 260
119: 10 253
134: 11–13 258

UET 6
410 vs. 15–20 254
410 rs. 7–8 254

Utukkī Lemnūti, See Gurney

Ugaritic Texts

UT 51.viii 7 175
UT 67.v.15 175

Indian Texts

Ap-Dh
I 5 17:9–10 109
I 5 17:10 111
I 5 17:11 110
I 5 17:12 110

Baud-Dh
I 5 8:32 109, 110
I 5 8:33 110
I 5 8:35 110
I 5 8:48 109
I 5 8:49 109
I 6 13:26–27 110
I 6 13:26–28 108
I 6 13:28 108
I 6 13:32 109
I 6 14:1–2 110

Gaut-Dh
1:29 110, 111
1:31 110
1:34 109

GG
III 2 60 109

Manu
V 111 110
V 112 109, 110
V 114 110
V 123 109, 111
V 126 109

SB
12 5 2:14 109

Vai-G
3:16 109
10:3 110, 111
3:51 110
3:58–59 109
3:59 111

Vas-Dh
3:48 109
3:49 110, 111
3:49–50 110

Vis
23:1–5 108
23:6 109

Word Index

Hebrew

ʾăbaddôn, 26
ʾōḥîm, 27–28
ʾiyyîm, 27–28
ʾammâ (ʾammat hammayim), 155
ʾsp, 174
ʾereṣ, 26
ʾereṣ gĕzērâ, 30
ʾāšām, see Subject Index, *ʾĀšām*
bôr, 26
bêt haḥopšît, 174–77
bêt hakkiyôr, 156
bêt yhwh, 177
bikkûrîm, 235
bāśār, 181–82
gab, 151, 152, 153
gĕbûl, 152, 153, 154
gzr, *gĕzērâ*, 30
deber, 26, 28–29
dûmâ, 26
dayyôt, 27–28
hāʾăriʾēl, 149, 152, 153
harʾēl, 149, 152, 153
hizzâ, 148
heqdēš, see Subject Index, *Heqdēš*
hqṭyr, 129
zāb, see Subject Index, Sexual impurity
zāraq, 148, 154
ḥṭʾ; *ḥiṭṭēʾ*, 130; *hitḥaṭṭāʾ*, 170
ḥaṭṭāʾt, see Subject Index, *Ḥaṭṭāʾt*
ḥêq (hāʾāreṣ), 151–54, 158
ḥupšâ, 176
ḥopšî, 175–76
ḥuqqat hattôrâ, 170
ḥōreb, 26
ḥorbâ, 26
ḥērem, 144; see Subject Index, *Ḥērem*
ḥōšek, 26
ṭmʿ, 26; *yiṭmāʾ*, 198, 205; *ṭāmēʾ hûʾ*, 89, 97; *ṭumʾâ*, 280, 281
ṭmn, 288
yāṣaq, 147
yĕšîmôn, 26
kĕlî, 94–95, 96, 98
kipper, 130
kārēt, 145, 164, 167, 246
lîlît, 26–28
midbār, 26, 29–30
midrās, 95
māwet, 26
mê niddâ, see the Subject Index, Water of purgation
milluʾîm, see Subject Index, *Milluʾîm*
minḥâ, see Subject Index, *Minḥâ*
musgār, 210
mipleṣet, 280
mipqād, 135
māṣâ, 147, 148
mĕqôm haqqōdēš, 232–35
māqôm ṭāhôr, 235–36

māqôm ṭāmēʾ, 243
māqôm qādôš, 232–35
mašḥît, 26
niddâ, 197, 280, 281
naḥălê bĕlîyaʿal, *26*
nzh, 148
nātan, 148
sgr, *hisgîr*, 174; see *musgār*
swr, *hāsîrû*, 289
ʿăzāʾzēl, 21–25; and see the Subject Index, Azazel, Scapegoat
ʿăzārâ, 149, 150, 152, 153, 154
ʿōlâ, see the Subject Index, *ʿŌlâ*
ʿāpār, 26
ʿărābâ, 26
piggûl, 140–43
pgr, *peger*, 123–24, 286–87
plṣ, 280
pesaḥ, see the Subject Index, *Pesaḥ*
pĕśāʿîm, 20
petaḥ ʾōhel môʿēd, 234
petaḥ haššāʿar, 174
ṣĕḥîḥâ, 26
ṣiyyâ, 26
ṣiyyîm, 27–28
ṣalmāwet, 26
ṣimāʾôn, 26
ṣāraʿat, 2, 75–86, 87–91; and see the Subject Index under *Ṣāraʿat*
qāʾat, 27–28
qeber, 26
qdš, 166
qeṭeb, 26
qōṭeb, 28–29
qṭr, 129
qippôd, 27–28
qippôz, 27–28
rēʾšît, 235
rāmâ, 151
rpʾ, 174
rešep, 26
śādê, 26
śāṭān, 26
śāʿîr, *śĕʿîrîm*, 22–23, 27–28
śrp, 129
śĕrāpîm, 26
šĕʾôl, 26
šēdîm, 26
šdmwt, 282–83
šaḥat, 26
šĕlāmîm, see the Subject Index, *Šĕlāmîm*
šāpak, 147, 148, 159
šĕqaʿărûrōt, 88
šqṣ, 202, 285; *šeqeṣ*, 200, 285
šereṣ, 200; see Subject Index, Animal impurities
tôdâ, see the Subject Index, *Tôdâ*
tannîm, 27–28

Akkadian

aburriṣanu, 248
aḫḫāzu, 66, 248
alluḫappu, 248
alû, 66, 248
apsû, 61, 81, 250, 255
arallû, 250
ardat lilî, 248
arnu, 81, 84
arurtu, 248
asakku, 81, 248
ašāgu, 69
ašru parsu, 30
ašru, 248
ašû, 248
barīrītu, 248
bennu, 248
bibītu, 248
dimītu, 248
diʾu, 84, 248
erṣitu, 250
eṭimmu, 66, 248
gallû, 66, 248
gizillû, 63
gulūlu, 248
ḫaʾattu, 248
ḫâbu, 297
ḫāʾitu, 248
ḫallulaja, 248
ḫimṭu, 248

ḫupšu, 175
ilu limnu, 248
imḫullu, 248
irat irṣitim, 151
irat kigalli, 151
išid šamê, 251
kapāru, 291;
kuppuru, 67, 133, 291–99; see Subject Indexunder Wiping
kattillu, 248
kibbu, 248
kīdu, 256
kilili, 248
kinūnu, 248
kiskilīlu, 248
kišittu, 248
kūbu, 248
kupīrātu, 253, 291, 296, 297
labaṣu, 66, 248
lamaštu, 61, 66, 248, 254, 258
liʾbu, 248
lilissu, 63
lilītu, 28, 248
lilû, 28, 248
māmītu, 81, 84, 248
mašḫultuppû, 65–66
mašmaššu, 62–63, 292
miqtu, 248
mudabiru, 61–62, 256
madbaru, 256
mukīl rēs lemutti, 248
mûtu, 248
namtaru, 81, 84, 248
namû, 256
nignakku, 63
qāt ili, 248
rābiṣu, 66, 248
rebītu, see Subject Index under Plaza
sibitti, 248
sibtu, 248
ṣēru, 85, 251, 255–56
šaggašu, 248
šešgallu, 65
šiptu, 248
šubūʾu, 63
šūlu, 248
šuruppû, 248
takpertu, 291, 296–98
ugāru, 85, 256
ūmu, 248
utukku, 66, 248
zaqīqu, 248

Sumerian

GI.IZI.LÁ, 63
Ì.GIŠ.ERIN, 63
NÍG.KALA.GA.URUDU, 63
NÍG.NA, 63

Hittite

alanza(n)-, 35
alwanzatar, 262
aštayaratar, 262
ep-, šer, 33
ešḫar, 84, 262
ḫattalkišna-, 35
ḫatuga-, 84
ḫurtai-, 262
irma-, 84
idalu-, 84
idalu- inan, 262
idalu- lala-, 262
kallar uttar, 59
karap-, 106
karša-, 269
kartimmiyatt-, 84
lala-, 84
lingai-, 262
nakušši-, 133
pangauwaš lala-, 262
papratar, 84, 262
šawar, 84
šipa-, 263

tarpi-, 263
ukturi-, 44, 267–69, 271
waḫnu-, 33
warnu-, 33, 107
waštul, 262

Hittite Akkado- and Sumerograms

GIR4, 99–107
PUḪIŠU, 47–48

Arabic

ḫbṯ, 176
ʿḏr, *150*
qaʿara, 88

Aramaic

māʿn dĕpĕḥar, 98
paḥătān, 88

Ugaritic

btḫpṯt, 175–76
pgr, 123–24

www.ingramcontent.com/pod-product-compliance
Lightning Source LLC
Chambersburg PA
CBHW021758220426
43662CB00006B/110
9781555400576